Balancing Democracy

CW01095227

CONTENTS

CONTRIBUTORS

Roland Axtmann is Senior Lecturer in Politics and International Relations at the University of Aberdeen.

Benjamin Barber is Whitman Professor of Political Science and Director of the Walt Whitman Center for the Culture and Politics of Democracy at Rutgers University, New Jersey.

Alastair Davidson is a member of the Institute for Advanced Studies, Princeton and Professor of Citizenship Studies, Swinburne University of Technology, Melbourne.

Jeroen Doomernik is a senior research fellow at the Institute for Migration and Ethnic Studies at the University of Amsterdam.

Michael Dyer is Lecturer in Politics at the University of Aberdeen.

Barry Hindess is Professor of Political Science at the Australian National University, Canberra.

Paul Hirst is Professor of Social Theory in the Department of Politics and Sociology at Birkbeck College, University of London.

Mary Kaldor is Professor and Principal Research Fellow and Programme Director in the Centre for the Study of Global Governance at the London School of Economics.

Zdenek Kavan is Lecturer in International Relations in the School of European Studies, University of Sussex.

Peter Leslie is Professor of Political Science at Queen's University, Kingston, Ontario.

Subrata Kumar Mitra is Professor of Politics, University of Nottingham.

Martin J. Murray is Professor of Sociology at the State University of New York, Binghamton.

Julie Smith is Fellow of Robinson College, Cambridge and Teaching Fellow in European Studies at the Centre of International Studies, Cambridge University. She also serves as Head of the European Programme at the Royal Institute of International Affairs, London.

Derek Urwin is Professor of Politics and International Relations at the University of Aberdeen.

Klaus von Beyme is Emeritus Professor of Political Science at the University of Heidelberg.

Thembisa Waetjen is Adjunct Professor in the Department of Sociology, University of Oregon.

PREFACE

This book addresses one of the classical concerns of comparative politics: the formation and maintenance of stable democracies. How have political scientists analysed democracy? What are the ideas and ideals that are contained in the concept of 'democracy'? How are notions of sovereignty, territoriality, nation, multiculturalism, representation, rights of individuals, of groups and of communities implicated in our understanding of 'democracy'? What institutional manifestations have these ideas, ideals and theoretical constructs in the 'real' world? How will 'democracy' and democratic institutions develop or change as the new millennium gets underway? The chapters provide, not crystal ball gazing, but an attempt at detecting socio-political trends, highlighting chances for further democratization and dangers for democratic stability.

In the first introductory chapter, Roland Axtmann provides a basic definition of 'liberal democracy' and asserts that democratic rule by the sovereign people has been understood to be exercised in the sovereign, territorially consolidated nation state. This assumption also informed the scientific analysis of modern democracy and unites the three dominant analytical approaches in political sociology: pluralism, elitism and Marxism. In the second introductory chapter, Axtmann then discusses why the idea, and ideal, of sovereignty, with its related notions of unity and hierarchy, that conceptually grounds democracy in the European nation state, has come under attack.

In his chapter, Derek Urwin shows that democracy is essentially a socio-territorial concept, inextricably linked to the two distinct elements of territorial organization, those of state and nation. Urwin traces the dynamics of territorial politics as a result of political attempts to accommodate ethnonational communities and identities and the ensuing fracturing of a unitary notion of 'nation'. In the following chapter, Jeroen Doomernik and Roland Axtmann discuss immigration and its effects on a unitary notion of the 'people'. They argue that, in our global age, immigration is here to stay and that, as a matter of fact, the liberal democratic state is prone to accept unsolicited immigration. The liberal democratic state must therefore face up to the challenge of redefining the notion of citizenship in the light of this fact: the institutionalization, not of a 'postnational citizenship', but of a 'multicultural citizenship' will be the task in the near future. Following on from this discussion, Barry Hindess argues that 'representative democracy' is not best suited for allowing for a 'politics of difference'. Once we have left behind notions of 'uniformity', that inform our traditional understanding of 'democracy', the institutional solution for multiculturalism and heterogeneity lies in 'associational pluralism'.

Michael Dyer's chapter on political-constitutional reform in the United Kingdom opens the discussion of democracy and democratic politics in particular states. He sketches the Westminster model and its three key institutions of parliamentary sovereignty, the 'first-past-the-post' electoral system, and strong executive rule. He then discusses how this model is currently being modified as a result mainly of political pressures for devolved government in the Celtic 'fringe'. Peter Leslie's chapter analyses the present strains on Canadian unity. In Canada, Westminster-style cabinet government was married to a federal division of powers. An explanation of Canada's present troubles, so Leslie claims, is to be sought in a combination of social forces, institutional design and geographical position: no discussion of regional and ethnic conflict, nor of federal–provincial and interprovincial relations, can afford to neglect one of the dominant facts of Canadian history, namely the continental context – and now the global context as well. Leslie shows how Canada actively searches for political solutions to the manifold challenges its democratic system faces. As Alastair Davidson discusses in his chapter, Australia, on the other hand, has a closed political system, incapable of political-constitutional reform and of broadening its democracy to accommodate demands for political plurality and difference. The indigenous people and the new ethnic minorities must turn outwards to the international community and pursue strategies of transnational political mobilization in order to gain support for their demands, whereas both 'conservative' and 'progressive' political forces remain wedded to an outdated communitarian national position. India, yet another former British colony, has succeeded in developing and sustaining democratic institutions. Subrata Mitra asks, in his contribution, how a poor society with no democratic tradition of its own could achieve this. Concentrating on political parties and elections, Mitra analyses how these institutions affect the existence of a public sphere in India.

The following three chapters analyse more recent cases of democratization. Thembisa Waetjen and Martin Murray trace the transition to democracy in South Africa and analyse the political and social cleavages that continue to challenge the consolidation of democracy in post-apartheid South Africa. Klaus von Beyme provides a detailed account of institution-building and constitutional change in Russia in the late stages of Gorbachev's rule and after by placing political development firmly within the context of the struggle of competing political forces. In the end, von Beyme arrives at a sceptical assessment of the future of democracy in Russia. Mary Kaldor and Zdenek Kavan consider the role of civil society both in the collapse of state socialism in Central and Eastern Europe and in the current phase of the consolidation of the post-Communist regime. They, too, sound a sombre note regarding the future of democracy. They notice the prevalence of political apathy and the concern with issues of economic wellbeing and law and order, rather than with democracy and civic engagement, among the majority of the population. The combination of neo-liberalism and nationalist populism, as well as the weakness of the rule of law, has created, according to Kaldor and Kavan, a 'new dark post-totalitarian phenomenon'.

The final three chapters address issues of democratic rule 'beyond the nation state'. Paul Hirst reasserts his view that current 'economic globalization' is not a new phenomenon and that similar processes could be discerned in the nineteenth century. He sees a political space for extended international governance and the institutionalization of 'global' regulatory mechanisms. However, he is adamant that it is democratic practices within (above all) the Western liberal-capitalist nation states, rather than the (utopian) institutions of a cosmopolitan democracy, that make the institutions of international governance both possible and legitimate. Julie Smith discusses one specific democratic institution 'beyond the nation state', the European Parliament. She considers the nature and functions of the European Parliament, its role in the democratic functioning of the European Union (EU) and asks how far it can help overcome the perceived democratic deficit of the EU. Her assessment is that, given institutional and constitutional reforms, the European Parliament could lead to a democratically legitimate Europe. The book ends with a chapter by Benjamin Barber. He reflects upon the future of political participation and citizen engagement in an 'age of globalization'. In a world in which privatization of state functions and rampant commercialization of ever more aspects of social life sap the energy for political engagement, will new telecommunications technologies offer new opportunities for 'strong', participatory democracy? Barber is sceptical. Citizenship and a robust, effective civil society are under threat today. What it takes to 'make democracy possible', is the courage of individuals to engage in politics. Barber reminds us that democracy may have many 'structural' prerequisites (as Axtmann discusses in the first chapter), but it fundamentally depends on individuals who experience the need collectively to determine their own 'fate' and who have the political will to organize politically to achieve this objective.

It is a pleasure to express my gratitude to the contributors to this volume who not only wrote splendid chapters but also responded with good grace to my editorial suggestions (and my occasional reminder that we had an agreed deadline with the publishers). They were asked to write their pieces with a student readership in mind. This meant keeping 'technical' jargon as well as endnotes to a bare minimum. Yet, I am sure the reader will find that the chapters do not only inform, but also bristle with stimulating ideas and insights, challenging the reader to draw up his or her own 'balance sheet' of democracy and democratic rule.

A special word of thanks is due to Julie Smith and Michael Dyer. They agreed to take over the chapters from colleagues who had to withdraw for health reasons, when this project was already in its final stages. Thanks also to Caroline Wintersgill, our commissioning editor, for keeping faith in this project by agreeing to several 'last' deadlines for submission of the script.

Roland Axtmann
Aberdeen, February 2000

CHAPTER 1

INTRODUCTION I: BALANCING DEMOCRACY IN POLITICAL SCIENCE

Roland Axtmann

In this introductory chapter, I set out to provide a basic definition of 'liberal democracy', concentrating on the ideas of sovereignty, the nation state, citizenship and representation. Democratic rule by the sovereign people, so I assert, is exercised in the sovereign, territorially consolidated nation state. I then move on to a consideration of how comparative politics and political sociology, as two subfields of political science, have set about analysing modern democracy. I suggest that three general approaches can be usefully distinguished: pluralism, elitism and Marxism, and I show how each of these approaches leads to a different understanding of modern democratic politics. In the final section, I present arguments from within each of these approaches regarding the transitions to democracy and the prerequisites of democracy. This chapter, then, sets the scene for, and complements, other chapters in this book that discuss the problem of developing and consolidating democratic structures and institutions in a wide variety of cases.

SOVEREIGNTY, THE NATION STATE AND DEMOCRACY

In 'pre-modern' Europe, political authority was shared between a wide variety of secular and religious institutions and individuals – between kings, princes and the nobility, bishops, abbots and the papacy, guilds and cities, agrarian landlords and 'bourgeois' merchants and artisans. The modern state project aimed at replacing these overlapping and often contentious jurisdictions through the institutions of a centralized state. This endeavour was legitimized by the theory of state sovereignty. This theory claimed the supremacy of the government of any state over the people, resources, and, ultimately, over all other authorities within the territory it controlled. 'State sovereignty' meant that final authority within the political community lay with the state whose will legally, and rightfully, commanded without being commanded by others, and whose will was thus 'absolute' because it was not accountable to anyone but itself (Anderson, 1996; Axtmann, 1996).

A 'sovereign' right to ultimate authority and control does not imply an ability to exercise it and the history of state formation can be analysed as the protracted efforts of rulers and their staff to translate 'juridical' sovereignty into 'empirical' sovereignty. On the one hand, the sovereignty of the state presupposed the eradication of internal contenders for supremacy. On the other hand, the 'idea' of sovereignty was premised on the notion of 'unity'. In Thomas Hobbes's classical formulation, without a common power man remains in a 'state of nature' in which his life is 'solitary, poore, nasty, brutish, and short' and men are nothing but a 'confusion of a disunited Multitude' (Hobbes, 1991/1651, pp. 89, 122). 'Sovereignty' means the reduction of all individual wills 'unto one Will', thus establishing 'a reall Unitie of them all, in one and the same Person', and 'the Multitude so united in one Person, is called a Common-Wealth, in latine CIVITAS' (p. 120). The sovereign, thus established, 'is the publique Soule, giving Life and Motion to the Common-Wealth' (p. 230). The sovereign is the 'very able Architect' who designs 'one firme and lasting edifice' by abolishing diversity and irregularities or by explicitly sanctioning them (p. 221). For example, '[w]here there be divers Provinces, within the Dominion of a Common-Wealth, and in those Provinces diversity of Lawes ... |they| are now Lawes, not by vertue of the Praescription of time, but by the Constitutions of their present Soveraigns' (p. 186). As far as individuals are concerned, they must be forced into uniformity:

> [T]here is in mens aptnesse to Society, a diversity of nature, rising from their diversity of Affections; not unlike to that we see in stones brought together for a building of an Aedifice. For as that stone which by the asperity, and irregularity of Figure, takes more room from others, that it selfe fills; and for the hardnesse, cannot be easily made plain, and thereby hindereth the building, is by the builders cast away as unprofitable, and troublesome: so also, a man that by asperity of Nature, will strive to retain those things which to himself are superfluous, and to others necessary; and for the stubbornness of his Passions, cannot be corrected, is to be left, or cast out of Society, as cumbersome thereunto. (p. 106)

'Governing' by the 'sovereign' thus aimed to take on the form of the artful combination of space, people and resources in territorialized containments, and the policing, monitoring and disciplining of the population within these spaces became the foundation, and the manifestation, of state sovereignty. As a result of historical developments that spanned several centuries, the modern territorial state came into existence as a differentiated ensemble of governmental institutions, offices and personnel that exercises the power of authoritative political rule making within a continuous territory that has a clear, internationally recognized boundary. It thus possesses 'internal' sovereignty that is typically backed up by organized forces of violence and that grounds the state's 'external' sovereignty vis-à-vis other states and its demands for non-interference in internal matters. Hence, 'sovereignty' has a spatial dimension in that it is premised on the occupation and possession of territory. This spatial dimension manifests itself most clearly in the drawing of territorial boundaries that separate the 'inside' from the 'outside'. This territorial exclusion is, in turn, the prerequisite for identifying the source of sovereignty within the bounded territory and for defining 'us' in contradistinction to 'them'.

During the first few decades after the French Revolution the notion of the 'nation' state came to stand for the idea that legitimate government could only be based upon the principle of national self-determination and that, at least ideally, state and nation ought to be identical with one another. In the imagery of the 'nation', the plurality and antagonisms of 'society' were moulded into a political entity. The nation became the 'unitary' body in which sovereignty resided. Yet, who or what was to constitute the nation? In the French tradition, the nation was constituted as a unity of individuals who willed to form a voluntary association between themselves and who, as citizens, enjoyed civil equality and equal political citizenship rights as 'of right'. French nationhood is thus state-centred and constituted by political unity. At the same time, the concept of the 'general will' and the notion of *la République une et indivisible* have imparted on this conceptualization of nationhood a strong sense of uniformity and universality that is adverse to all particularisms. As a logical consequence, and in the tradition of the absolutist state, the centralized post-revolutionary Jacobin state embarked on a policy of centralization, assimilation and the eradication of regional and other differences.

This assimilationist tendency is not unique to the French conceptualization of nation. It can also be found in that tradition that sees a nation, not as a bearer of universal political values, but as a predetermined community bound by blood and heredity. In this tradition, of which Germany has been a main representative, the nation is conceptualized as an organic cultural, linguistic, or racial community. Ethno-cultural commonalties form the basis for the integration of a collectivity of individuals into a nation. In this conceptualization of nationhood, membership in the nation, defined as a community of descent with common culture and language, is the presupposition of citizenship in the nation's state. Territorial boundaries are determined by considerations for ethnic homogeneity; citizenship rights are premised upon membership in the ethno-cultural group; the objective of the state is the welfare of the ethno-cultural community; and ethno-cultural conflicts, including those of a religious or linguistic kind, are politically more sensitive and more important than those linked to socio-economic cleavages or gender issues, for example (Brubaker, 1992; Kamenka, 1973; also Chapter 3 by Derek Unwin in this volume).

As a result of political struggles in the nineteenth and twentieth centuries, democracy came to be linked to the nation state through the institution of citizenship for members of the national community. The British sociologist, T.H. Marshall (1963, p. 74) distinguished three types of citizenship rights: civil, political, and social. According to Marshall, civil citizenship rights are instrumental in securing 'liberty of the person, freedom of speech, thought and faith, the right to own property and to conclude valid contracts and the right to justice'. These civil rights can be defended through the system of formal law courts. The state in which civil rights prevail is a constitutional state. The struggle over the establishment of civil rights was waged in the late eighteenth and in the first half of the nineteenth century between the privileged aristocracy and the rising bourgeoisie. The axis of this socio-political conflict was freedom versus privilege. The challengers to the established order were united by a common goal: the establishment of the constitutional state. But the liberal-bourgeois movements of the nineteenth century also mobilized against the established order for political citizenship rights: 'the right to participate in the exercise of political power, as a member of a body invested with political authority or as an elector of the members of such a body.' The state in which such political rights can be exercised is a constitutional parliamentary system. To the extent that the winning of rights of political participation was restricted to the bourgeoisie, the working class, too, became involved in this political struggle, not just against the old privileged class but against the newly enfranchised middle class as well. In the struggle of the working-class movements, however, the socio-political struggle, which had centred around the issue of freedom versus privilege, was complemented, and somewhat marginalized, by another type of conflict: the struggle of the working-class movement for social justice and economic security against private property, economic power and concomitant political power of aristocracy and bourgeoisie alike. The challengers to the established order demanded not only civil and political liberties; the labour movement now also demanded rights to resources. The struggle was over the establishment of social rights: 'the whole range from the right to a modicum of economic welfare and security to the right to share to the full in the social heritage and to live the life of a civilised being according to the standards prevailing in the society.' The constitutional state with its parliamentary system should become a democratic welfare state. This, at least, was the aim of the social democratic labour movement (Offe, 1985).

Liberalism, as a political philosophy and a political ideology, revolves around the key assumption of the inalienable liberty of the individual, its autonomy and self-determination. It stipulates that an individual must be free to decide for herself or himself what goals he or she wishes to pursue in life. It upholds the idea that each person is to have an equal opportunity to enjoy liberty, and that no person's liberty is more important or valuable than any other's. Liberalism aims to create a society in which conditions obtain that enable the individual to exercise her or his capacity of self-rule. In that respect its key concern is with curtailing the power of other individuals as well as of government to interfere with an individual's freedom. The democratic idea centres upon the assumption of the capacity of individuals as citizens to govern themselves, or, to put it differently, to determine for themselves their collective life. It is assumed, first, that every adult individual can be rightly considered to be, in principle, sufficiently well qualified to participate in the democratic process of governing the state to whose laws they are subjected. It is further assumed that 'among adults no persons are so definitely better qualified than others that they should be entrusted with the complete and final authority over the government of the state' (Dahl, 1998, pp. 75, 76, 78).

However, we should note that, as a matter of fact, in Western 'liberal' democracies, individuals must be members of the state, must be its 'nationals', in order to possess citizenship rights. In contrast to the conceptualization of popular sovereignty as the self-rule of nationals in their capacity as citizens, the 'radical' democratic principle stipulates that everyone who is permanently subjected to rule and domination in a legal order must have a part in the exercise of that sovereignty that ultimately legitimates that rule (Dahl, 1989, chap. 9). Citizenship status would therefore be distinct from nationality and would adhere to all permanent residents, who would be subject to the same qualifications as the 'nationals'. Such a disjuncture of citizenship and nationality is, however, alien to the political reality of 'liberal' democracy. The collective 'self' whose own determination modern political liberalism aims to ensure in the democratic process is the politically organized nation. A systemic linkage between democracy and nation state is therefore presupposed. Democratic rule by the sovereign people is exercised by citizens in the sovereign, territorially consolidated nation state. It is assumed that only in a sovereign state can the people's will command without being commanded by others. Hence 'state sovereignty' and 'popular sovereignty' are inextricably intertwined in 'liberal' democracy.

'Liberal' democracy is premised upon an acceptance of this dual notion of self-determination: the capacity of the individual to govern herself or himself, and the capacity of individuals as citizens to govern themselves as a political community. 'Liberal' democracy further assumes that in large territorial states the political self-rule of autonomous and competent individuals in their capacity as citizens cannot be exercised in the form of a 'direct democracy'. 'Direct democracy', which had obtained in classical Greece and Rome from around 500 BC, had as its key feature the direct and immediate participation of the citizens in the deliberation and decisions on public matters in the citizens' assembly. The classical Greek notion of democracy was premised on the assumption that, in order for democratic rule to uphold the common good of the political community, the citizen body had to be highly homogeneous as high levels of economic inequality, of religious, cultural or racial diversity would tend to produce political conflict and disagreements over the common good. A shared sense of the common good was seen to require a citizen body that was harmonious in its interests. Homogeneity and uniformity of interests and opinions were the prerequisites of democracy; democracy was not seen as that institutional arrangement that would create harmony out of diversity but as the 'rule of the many' sharing a common understanding of the common weal. It was argued that heterogeneity of interests and opinions could only be avoided in a small city state. Only in the polis could citizens acquire the knowledge of their city and their fellow citizens by direct observation, experience or discussion that would allow them to gain an understanding of the common good. Furthermore, it was only in the polis that citizens could assemble in public, decide directly on the laws and policies, and participate actively in the administration of the city. Hence, the direct and active participation of the citizens in law making, law execution, and law adjudication was seen as the core element of democracy. The idea that citizens could be 'represented' by other people was quite alien to classical democratic thinking. Only through this direct and active participation in public matters for the common good, could human beings realize their 'nature' and be good, 'virtuous' citizens (Dahl, 1989).

'Liberal' democracy, on the other hand, assumes that in geographically expansive territorial states with a numerically large population and pronounced social, economic, political and cultural heterogeneities, such 'direct democracy' must be replaced by a representative democracy: modern democracy is representative democracy in that political rule is exercised by officials whose power derives from their election by the citizens and whose power is constrained by their accountability to the citizens as voters. Modern democracy is therefore a system of self-rule in which the principle of representation obtains and where representation is grounded in the institution of election on the basis of universal adult suffrage: political decision-makers are chosen in frequent and fairly conducted competitive elections. Electoral competition, in turn, presupposes the institutionalization of a number of other principles. Associational autonomy allows for the formation of organized political groups such as political parties or interest groups. This is only possible in a political community that upholds civil liberties and, in particular, the freedom of expression, of movement and of association as well as the free access to sources of information that are not controlled by political power holders (Dahl, 1998, pp. 84–99).

ENGAGING WITH DEMOCRACY IN POLITICAL SCIENCE

Themes and Topics

David Held (1996, pp. 335–6) has concisely pointed out that, in the debate on democracy, it has been assumed that 'the state has control over its own fate, subject only to compromises it must make and limits imposed upon it by actors, agencies and forces operating within its territorial boundaries, and by the agents and representatives of other governments and states'. In political science, this assumption manifested itself in the supposition that the 'nation' state was the container of 'national' society; that politics, social structures and social processes were, so to speak, territorially 'caged' within the frontiers of the state. This supposition put the relationship between 'state' sovereignty and 'popular' sovereignty, between 'state' and 'society', at the centre of comparative politics and political sociology; at the centre of international relations were the interactions between 'sovereign' states, their respective 'foreign policies' and the formation and transformation of the 'interstate system'.

The analysis of democratic politics inside the 'cage' of the territorial state concentrated on a relatively small number of well-defined major topics. Taking 'state' sovereignty as the starting point, there arises, first, the question of the institutional arrangement of political functions in modern polities. Does the state have a federal or unitary structure? Which powers accrue to the centre and which to the regions or subnational governments? Is it a parliamentary or presidential system? If it is presidential, how powerful is the presidency in relation to the legislature? More generally, which modi are in operation to determine the relationship between the legislature, the executive and the judicature? Is it a majoritarian democracy in which the will of the majority dominates – circumscribed by the constitutional protection of the minority? Or is it a 'consociational' democracy in which policies are determined on the basis of negotiation and compromise between groupings in society each of which enjoys constitutionally entrenched rights of participation and representation as well as the power of veto? How does the prevailing institutional order affect the policy capacities of the state, as well as the political, economic and cultural inclusiveness of the political system and its legitimacy? Second, the formation of the modern state was accompanied by the rise of professional politicians and political entrepreneurs. This rise led to concerns regarding the recruitment of political decision-making elites; their social composition; and the kind of internal 'leadership' structure that pertains within the elites. Furthermore, in modern polities, 'state' sovereignty is enacted through state bureaucracies. A concern with 'public administration' translates into questions about bureaucratic decision-making, bureaucratic policy formulation and policy implementation. At issue is the formation of society through state activity, or, to put it differently, the 'etatization of society'.

To the extent that the state becomes an important force that determines to a large extent the life chances of individuals, it becomes imperative for state subjects to turn themselves into citizens and aim to influence and control the state and the government. Hence, taking 'popular' sovereignty as a starting point in political science, the 'socialization of the state' becomes the focus of analysis. It is in the form of political participation by the people that 'popular' sovereignty is enacted. Citizenship rights, as already stated above, are the prerequisites for participation as well as, historically, its outcome. With regard to political participation, there have been three main areas of research in political science. First, interest in the patterns and institutions of representation and interest mediation led to the analysis of parliamentary assemblies, electoral systems, voting behaviour, political parties, interest groups and political movements. Second, recognition of the conflict-ridden nature of modern society led to the analysis of modern society's cleavage structure and investigations into the institutionalization of conflict. Though often seen as of major importance, the class cleavage as a result of the socio-economic structure of capitalism has traditionally been considered – at least outside Marxist political analysis – as only one amongst several cleavages. Socio-political conflicts along the agrarian-industrial-environmental cleavage; the national-ethnic-racial cleavage; the religious cleavage; the centre-periphery cleavage; the gender cleavage or the materialist-postmaterialist cleavage have been identified and their institutionalization in country-specific party systems has been analysed. Third, whereas, after the introduction of the universal franchise, political equality of the citizens had become the – often constitutionally enshrined

– principle of modern democracy, the unequal distribution of resources such as money, knowledge, time or organizational skills amongst different groups in society – be they based on class, gender, race or ethnicity – resulted in an unequal distribution of chances for political participation. The ideal of universal participation has therefore been contrasted with the reality of group-differentiated participation. Moreover, at issue is here also the fair and equitable representation of individuals, groups and communities in the political arena. Many of these topics are addressed in contributions to this volume, in particular in the chapters on Russia, India, Australia and South Africa.

The recognition of societal cleavages leads 'naturally' to the question about the stability and order in conflict-ridden society. There are the affective ties and feelings of obligations towards the community that are stimulated by nationalism and patriotism. There is the 'dull compulsion of everyday life', of which Karl Marx spoke. And Émile Durkheim, the French sociologist, emphasized the solidarity and high level of societal reciprocity that he saw as the result of the division of labour in general, and interdependent specialization in modern society in particular. However, the main concern in political science has been with two other mechanisms: coercion and consensus, respectively.

Classically, one line of inquiry could run back to Niccolò Machiavelli, Thomas Hobbes or Max Weber and emphasize the importance of constraint and coercion exerted by the state to enforce obedience in the 'well-ordered' political community. But classically, too, emphasis could be put on the importance of the existence of a fundamental value consensus in society. Aristotle had spoken of the importance of 'political friendliness' and the sense of 'partnership' and 'restraint' for the 'good life' in the Greek *polis*. Edmund Burke spoke in the eighteenth century of the 'cake of custom', which would affect the peaceable workings of political institutions. The Frenchman Alexis de Tocqueville recommended 'self-interest rightly understood' and admonished citizens to 'temperance, moderation and self command' as virtues without which no peaceable community was possible – sentiments endorsed by the Englishman Walter Bagehot in the late nineteenth century who recommended 'animated moderation'. In many ways, the research into 'political culture' and the cultural underpinnings of democracy, which was given an enormous boost with the publication of Gabriel Almond's and Sidney Verba's study on *The Civic Culture* in 1963, can be seen to stand in this 'classical' tradition. Democracy and political stability in democratic states, so it has been claimed, are premised on a value consensus on political procedures, the range of policy alternatives and the legitimate scope of politics as well as on the right balance between

active and passive citizens and between obedience and informed critique
as a result of successful political socialization (Held, 1996, pp. 208–11,
218). In recent years, this line of argument has been extended in the
debate on 'social capital' and 'social trust'. Arguably, both political
participation in the form of collective action and a commitment to the
rules of the democratic game depend upon social trust, the core component of 'social capital'. For Robert Putnam, 'social capital' refers to
features of social organization, such as core values and norms and
networks, that facilitate social co-ordination and co-operation for mutual
benefit. As Uslaner (1999, p. 122) asserts:

> Both social capital and connectedness are important for what they
> produce. Communities with strong positive values (including trust in
> others) and ties that bind people to one another will have more
> powerful norms of generalized reciprocity and cooperation. Trust as a
> moral resource leads us to look beyond our own kind. It means that
> we downplay bad experiences and cooperate when we are not sure
> that others will oblige.

Following Putnam, analysts have paid particular attention to voluntary and non-governmental associations, where, so it is argued, that
mutual trust can be built up, a 'civic culture' of tolerant and active
engagement with other individuals can form and 'social capital' in the
form of 'friendliness' and the ability to co-operate can be accumulated:
active involvement in secondary associations is seen as the source of both
social capital and of its generalization beyond the confines of the association that results in trust of 'strangers' outside the group (on 'social
capital' and 'trust' see Coleman, 1988; Putnam, 1993; Putnam, 1995a and
1995b; Fukuyama, 1995; Rich, 1999; Warren (ed.), 1999). Translated into a
more 'political' language, 'trust in government', for example, is seen as
the result of 'generalized' interpersonal trust. However, there is much
debate on whether this is an adequate conceptualization of 'political'
trust in democratic societies. Jean Cohen, for example, insists on the
importance of institutions:

> If one knows one can expect impartiality from a judge, care and
> concern from a doctor, protection from police, concern for the
> common good from legislators, and so on, then one can develop
> confidence (instead of cynicism) that shared norms and cultural
> values will orient the action of powerful actors. But confidence of this
> sort also presupposes public spaces in which the validity of such
> norms and the fairness of procedures can be challenged, revised, and
> redeemed, or reinforced through critique. Democracy goes with trust
> and civic initiative or engagement to the degree to which institutions

(political or otherwise) exist that are receptive to the influence and/or input of collective actors in an appropriate way. (Cohen, 1999, pp. 222–3; see also Offe, 1999; Warren, 1999. At stake is a conceptualization of 'civil society' that is more than the cosmos of 'secondary associations' between 'the family' and 'the state'; see Cohen and Arato, 1992; Axtmann, 1996, chap. 2; Shils, 1997; see also the contribution by Kaldor and Kavan to this volume.)

These have been some of the key subject matters through which political science, and the subfields of comparative politics and political sociology, in particular, have endeavoured to understand and explain democratic politics in modern society. To simplify further, political scientists have arguably used three distinctive approaches to analyse these topics: pluralism, elitism and Marxism.

Approaches: Pluralism, Elitism, Marxism

Behaviouralism versus institutionalism

After the Second World War, American political science came to dominate political science, and American political science, in turn, became dominated by behaviouralism. In the behavioural transformation of the social sciences in the 1950s and 1960s, the analysis of political (as well as social and economic) institutions, and thus also of the state, was downgraded. The theoretical tenets of behaviouralism are quickly stated. First, at the centre of analytical attention is the actual human being; hence, political behaviouralists study 'the political process by looking at the relation of it to the motivations, personalities, or feelings of the participants as individual human beings' (Easton, 1953, p. 205). Second, collective behaviour is seen to be an emergent effect of the behaviour of individuals and their interactions and transactions and it is argued that 'institutions can and must be analyzed in terms of the behaviour of their molecular units, the individuals' (Eulau, 1966, p. 15). Third, (political) behaviour, in turn, is seen to be dependent on, and caused by, social and psychological factors. Fourth, the aim of behaviouralism is not the mere description of political processes but their explanation and prognosis on the basis of law-like statements in which political and social regularities are posited; empirical generalizations that hold good for many cases rather than descriptive statements of individual facts are to be formulated. Fifth, these theoretical and explanatory statements are to be verified (or falsified) by confronting them with observable behaviour (Ricci, 1984, chap. 5; Seidelman, 1985, chap. 5; Gunnell, 1986, chap. 1).

Behaviouralists argued firmly against the reification of social and political institutions by denying that they could be analysed as entities set apart from the individuals whose behaviour formed and sustained them. When such a position was developed in the 1950s, in the American intellectual context this meant a decisive break with the academic traditions in political science. Until the end of the First World War, the analysis of the formal structure of government and of the constitutional-legal relationships between state agencies and political institutions had been at the centre of American political science. However, since the late nineteenth century, this 'legal' institutionalism was increasingly challenged by a 'realist' institutionalism that, in the tradition of Walter Bagehot's analysis of the *English Constitution*, aimed at the analysis of the 'living reality' of institutional interconnections that was thought to lie behind their constitutional arrangements. The inquiry into the actual, rather than legal, interrelationships between governmental agencies, political parties, political associations and interest groups became the analytical focus in studies such as Woodrow Wilson's *Congressional Government* or James Bryce's *The American Commonwealth*. But both 'legal' and 'realist' institutionalism considered the institution to be the empirical-analytical subject matter as well as the theoretical reference point of political science; the individual political actor remained outside the analytical interest of political scientists.

A political scientist who could be claimed by the behaviouralists in the 1950s as one of the early critics of either form of institutionalism was Arthur F. Bentley (Crick, 1959, chap. 7). He argued in 1908 that, operating behind the formal legal-institutional disguises of society and the state, group interaction constituted the reality of political life. Bentley's criticism of institutionalism, which was based on his group theory, could be seen by behaviouralists as a precursor of their tenets for at least three reasons. First, he argued that there is no group without its interests and the bearers of these interests are individuals: 'What we actually find in this world, what we can observe and study, is interested men, nothing more and nothing less. That is our raw material and it is our business to keep our eyes fastened to it' (Bentley, 1908, p. 212). Second, instead of analysing political (and social) life in terms of institutions, he proposed to analyse it in terms of activity; thus the programmatic title of his book *The Process of Government*. It is this anti-institutionalism and the concomitant emphasis on (group) activity that led him to posit that '[t]he "state" is like the "social whole": we are not interested in it as such, but exclusively in the processes within it' (Bentley, 1908, p. 263). Third, Bentley claimed that concentrating on political processes and overt activity would lay the foundation 'upon which a coherent system of measurement [of political life, RA] can be built up' (Bentley, 1908, p. 202). Political life thus becomes accessible to scientific treatment: 'Measure conquers chaos' (Bentley, 1908, p. 200).

The conceptualization of political life as a continuous flow of activities was one of the hallmarks of behaviouralism. It led David Easton to a definition of 'politics' as that particular type of social activity which constitutes the 'authoritative allocation of values for a society' (Easton, 1953, p. 134). In the political process, valued and scarce objects are allocated for the whole society through enforceable and sanctioned commands that are considered as binding by the people to whom they are intended to apply or who are affected by them (Easton, 1953, pp. 131–4). This particular kind of activity, 'the authoritative allocation of values for a society', is, so Easton claimed, the subject matter of political science. According to Easton, this activity may express itself through a variety of institutions; it is not the exclusive domain of the state. The state is a political institution peculiar to certain historical conditions: there were periods in history when states did not exist, and the same may perhaps be true in the unknown future – but, nevertheless, there was, and will be, a need for the authoritative allocation of values. The state is thus only one of the historical configurations of social interactions and institutions through which allocative decisions are made that are considered binding by most members of society most of the time (Easton, 1953, p. 113). A general theory of politics that addressed itself to the permanent and enduring problem of the authoritative allocation of values could therefore not be based on the concept of the 'state' because it referred to a historically unique and distinct mechanism of allocation. Easton thus proposed to replace the concept of the 'state' with that of the 'political system' as the most comprehensive orienting concept for political research. This 'political system' was conceived of as a sort of 'black box' into which inputs from its social environment in the form of generalized support and (group) specific demands flow. These inputs are converted through a variety of political institutions and processes into outputs in the form of binding policy decisions which, in turn, may – through feedback loops – influence the social environment and thus, eventually, the political system itself (Easton, 1965).

The state was thus jettisoned as an analytical concept and central theoretical concern in the endeavour to formulate a general theory of politics which defined a particular type of timeless and ubiquitous activity ('the authoritative allocation of values for a society') as its proper subject matter. Furthermore, the model of the political system also expressed the idea that, through inputs, demands generated in the social environment of the political system were transmitted into the political system as a challenge to be converted into binding policy decisions. At least analytically, it was a theory that discussed politics from the vantage point of 'society'. Some of these views were shared by the new sub-discipline of political sociology which was institutionalized in the late 1950s. It aimed to analyse the 'social bases of politics', as the subtitle of the major text of political sociology at that time, Seymour Martin Lipset's *Political Man* (1959/1960), made clear. Political behaviour was seen as determined by the position of political man (and woman) within the system of social and economic inequality. In order to understand politics, it was necessary to analyse the social structure and, in particular, its specific form of stratification. How do the three main paradigms within political sociology – pluralism, elitism and Marxism – analyse modern democratic politics?

Pluralism

For American pluralist theorists in the 1950s and 1960s, modern demo-cratic society was characterized by a diffusion of political power amongst a wide variety of social groups as well as the dispersal of political decision centres. They conceded that there are many inequalities in society and that not all social groups have equal access to equal influence resources. But it was also argued that '[v]irtually no one, and certainly no group of more than a few individuals, is entirely lacking in some influence resources' (Dahl, 1961, p. 228). There exists a rough power equilibrium between the most important social groups such as capital and labour, and this system of countervailing power is bolstered by the fact that economic power is separated from political power: economic power does not translate necessarily (or even typically) into political power or vice versa.

In modern society, power is not cumulative; power is dispersed among numerous social groups that are spread throughout society. These social groups represent diverse and competitive interests. Hence, they are in conflict with each other over the power to influence, or determine, policy outcomes. The state is the arena in which these contending social groups aim to achieve their policy objectives; in effect, governments are seen to react to the purposive exercise of power by social groups, and policies are the result of an 'endless process of bargaining' (Dahl). The democratic character of pluralist politics is seen to be ensured through mainly two mechanisms. First, pluralist society is populated by a plethora of minor-ities each of which pursues its idiosyncratic interests by mobilizing power resources at its disposal. In a sense, democracy is not rule by the majority, but government by minorities. For Robert Dahl, the main issue in democratic theory and practice is not the 'tyranny of the majority'. Rather, 'the more relevant question is the extent to which various minorities in a society will frustrate the ambitions of one another with the passive acquiescence or indifference of a majority of adults or voters' (Dahl, 1956, p. 133). Second, cross-cutting allegiances both stabilize the political order and contribute to its democratic character:

> If most individuals in the society identify with more than one group, then there is some positive probability that any majority contains individuals who identify for certain purposes with the threatened minority. Members of the threatened minority who strongly prefer their alternative will make their feelings known to those members of the tentative majority who also, at some psychological level, identify with the minority. Some of these sympathizers will shift their support away from the majority alternative and the majority will crumble. (Dahl, 1956, pp. 104–5)

In the course of verifying (or, rather, falsifying) the pluralist assumptions since the 1960s, most pluralists came to accept that 'the liberal state plays a critically important role in aggregating, balancing, and reconciling conflicting demands; it is continuously active as a broker and mediator, working out and facilitating the acceptance of policy compromises on the part of competing groups' (Nordlinger, 1981, p. 152). Individual government departments were conceived as just another kind of interest group. These departments might even participate in building structures of 'corporate pluralism' granting privileged access to decision-making processes to some distinct outside pressure group(s) and thereby limiting the role of other groups and parliament in policy making. This view had by now considerably moved away from conceiving of the state as simply an arena in which social groups competed and whose policies were determined by the societal parallelogram of demands and resources.

Furthermore, neo-pluralists recognized that business interests occupy a position of special importance compared to other social interests when it comes to influencing public policies. Well-organized, financially well-endowed groups with primary interests in narrow bands of public policy tend to become the dominant social groups in capitalist democracies: '[T]he state enfranchises the "most interested and best organized" business, labor, agricultural, trade, and professional associations as the exclusive representatives of particular societal interests ... public officials are "beholden" to and often are the "captives" of, the specialized demand groups within their narrow constituencies' (Nordlinger, 1981, p. 44–5). In effect, neo-pluralists accepted that the capacity of governments to act in ways that interest groups may desire is constrained. The main constraints are imposed by the requirements of private capitalist accumulation. Large private corporations have the discretionary power to withhold resources necessary for economic growth. Governments are likely to lose legitimacy if economic prosperity is not sustained. It is therefore in their own interest to accommodate those interests that can cause depression, inflation, or unemployment (Lindblom, 1977). While the neo-pluralists thus emphasized the actual hierarchy of power in modern capitalist society, at the same time they showed that the pluralist brokerage state is, in effect, only 'relatively' autonomous.

Elitism

Elite theorists, too, have become increasingly concerned with analysing the state. Classical elite theory had seen society divided into a creative, self-conscious elite group that ruled over a mass of passive, manipulable and unorganized individuals. For Vilfredo Pareto, elite power derived from particular psychological qualities of individuals that made them fit for leadership roles. For Gaetano Mosca and Robert Michels, on the other hand, elite power stemmed from superior organization and the possession of functional skills by certain members of society. In their insistence on the passivity of the mass, elite theorists distanced themselves from pluralists for whom individuals organize in a multiplicity of groups and parties in order to act on their interests. In their insistence that elite power is not necessarily based on economic power, elite theorists took issue with the economic reductionism of crude Marxism.

Many elite theorists have analysed modern society as made up of networks of organizations. Each of these bureaucratic organizations is commanded by elites who attempt to manage resources and extend their domain of control. They follow Max Weber in ascribing to the bureaucratic form of administrative organization a maximum of efficiency and technical superiority. It is on the basis of this efficiency and superiority that bureaucratic organization becomes the dominant type of organization because complex societies are dependent on it for the satisfaction of the needs of their members.

But it is not only the concern with bureaucratic organization that these 'managerialist' elite theorists take from Weber. They agree that any conceptualization of the 'state' must refer to the state as that political organization whose administrative staff successfully upholds the claim to the monopoly of the legitimate use of physical force in the enforcement of its order (Weber, 1968, p. 54). The state's centrality in modern organized society and its autonomy rests ultimately upon its monopoly of the legitimate use of coercion within the territory over which it claims sovereignty. This unique access to the instruments of coercion makes the economic elites dependent upon the state. In this perspective, then, states are conceived of as compulsory associations claiming control over territories and the people within them: 'The modern state is a compulsory association which organizes domination' (Weber, in Gerth and Mills, 1967, p. 82). To sustain domination and protect state power (against internal as well as external challengers), they attempt to extract and mobilize resources from society. The core of any state is thus administrative, legal, extractive, and coercive organizations.

According to Weber, modern society was dominated by bureaucratic administration. Only the great 'charismatic' leader would be capable of reining in bureaucratic rule. It was in parliament that the leader would prove his worth and show his mettle. Once selected in this arena, the leader would seek electoral approval from the masses. But once elected, the leader would not rule as the executor of the will of the electorate, but rule exclusively by virtue of his own personal responsibility and by virtue of personal authority that derived formally from the consensus of the 'ruled' (Weber, 1994, pp. 209–33, 316–52). For Weber, then, the principle of free leadership selection was the essence of democracy. This 'elitist' understanding of democracy was given another coherent statement by Joseph Schumpeter in 1942 in his book *Capitalism, Socialism, and Democracy*. For Schumpter, democracy was not 'government by the people', but 'government approved by the people'; democracy was the rule of the politician:

> [T]he role of the people is to produce a government, or else an intermediate body which in turn will produce a national executive or government. And we define: the democratic method is that institutional arrangement for arriving at political decisions in which individuals acquire the power to decide by means of a competitive struggle for the people's vote. (Schumpeter, 1976/1942, p. 269)

Democracy is thus an arrangement for the establishment of political leadership. The citizens' role in a democracy is limited to the act of voting. Furthermore, once politicians have been elected, the voters should withdraw from politics. However, '[t]hey must not withdraw confidence too easily between elections and they must understand that, once they have elected an individual, political action is his business and not theirs' (Schumpeter, 1976/1942, p. 295). It is within this Weberian and Schumpeterian tradition that contemporary democratic elitism considers elite competition for electoral support as a key element of a democratic system. In elections, the passive and disorganized mass of voters becomes the arbiter of the political conflict. Elections enable the masses to remove from power an elite group that is unresponsive to their wishes. Furthermore, the multiplicity of sectional elites, their relative autonomy from each other on the basis of their respective control of resources, and the relative autonomy of some other elites from the elites of the state and government restrict elite power (Etzioni-Halevy, 1993).

Marxism

Finally, Marxist theory, too, has embarked on a voyage of intellectual discovery which led to a sustained theorizing of the 'state' granting, eventually, 'relative' autonomy to the capitalist state. In the *Communist Manifesto* of 1848, Marx and Engels had argued that 'the executive of the modern state is but a committee for managing the common affairs of the whole bourgeoisie' (Marx, in Tucker, 1978, p. 475). The state was thus seen as the political instrument wielded by the economically dominant class to sustain its class rule. Though the state may well act on behalf of the ruling class, this did not necessarily mean that it worked at its behest. Marx went beyond this instrumentalist position in the *Eighteenth Brumaire* where he analysed the 'exceptional' historical situation in mid-nineteenth-century France where the class struggle was 'frozen' by an inability of any one class to exhibit its power over the state. In this situation of a precarious power equilibrium of the antagonistic classes, the state (bureaucracy) may gain autonomy from class control. But since the Bonapartist state did not change the capitalist relations of production, 'in the last instance', it remained dependent on the bourgeoisie for capital accumulation to secure tax revenues for its own consumption and military expansion.

More recent Marxist theories of the capitalist state took their cue from Marx's analysis of the Bonapartist state. Their central tenet has been that the state is compelled to fulfil certain 'functions' in capitalist societies that objectively serve the common, long-term interests of the capitalist class. It has been argued that the nature of the state and its activities can be deduced from the changing systemic requirements of capitalism as a mode of production rather than from the composition of state and government personnel and the attempts by capitalists to influence its operation and policies. The containment of class struggle as well as the creation of legal and monetary frameworks for market capitalism, investment in infrastructure and welfare, or provision for the reproduction of the labour force have been analysed as functional contributions of the state to the reproduction of the capitalist mode of production in the long term. In order to fulfil these functions the state had to be 'relatively' autonomous. But functionalist Marxists remain aware of the fact that the capitalist state depends on the investment decisions of the large capitalist interests because it is excluded from the organization of capitalist pro-duction and the allocation of private capital. Both for the achievement of its policy goals and the maintenance of its revenues the state has to depend on economic growth generated within the capitalist economy. The state thus has to operate in such a way that the long-term needs of capital are met.

Since, for Marx, modern society was class society, 'all struggles within the State, the struggle between democracy, aristocracy, and monarchy, the struggle for the franchise, etc., etc., are merely the illusory forms in which the real struggles of the different classes are fought out among one another' (Marx, in Tucker, 1978, pp. 160–1). In this sense, then, as Marx and Engels remarked in the *Communist Manifesto*, '[p]olitical power, properly so called, is merely the organized power of one class for oppressing another'. Once the conditions for the existence of class antagonisms and of classes generally will have been swept away in a revolution, bourgeois society will be replaced by 'an association, in which the free development of each is the condition for the free develop-ment of all' (Marx, in Tucker, 1978, pp. 490–1). In such an association, there is no need, nor any material ground, for political power: commu-nism means the end of politics. The transition from a society in which 'liberal', bourgeois democracy is a chimera and sham because it leaves the property relations untouched, indeed, is built upon these property relations, to communist society in which politics has come to an end and in which there is no basis for democracy, is made through the establish-ment of the 'dictatorship of the proletariat'. Marx saw in the Paris Commune of 1871 a blueprint for an alternative model of democracy (Marx, in Tucker, 1978, pp. 629–42). All holders of political offices would be subject to frequent elections and act according to the instructions they receive from their constituencies under constant threat of being recalled. Only this mechanism, so Marx asserted, would ensure adequate repre-sentation of the people's views. To guard against the formation of an independent political class and against bureaucratization, there would only be a short tenure of office. Executive and legislative functions would be integrated. A people's militia would replace the army and police forces. At the centre of this arrangement was a network of directly elected committees:

The 'machinery' of the 'liberal' state would be replaced by the Commune structure. All aspects of 'government' would then ... be fully accountable to the majority: 'the general will' of the people would prevail. The smallest communities would administer their own affairs and elect delegates to larger administrative units (districts, towns) which would, in turn, elect candidates to still larger areas of administration (the national delegation). (Held, 1996, p. 145)

As Held observes, this model constituted 'a form of government which sought to combine local autonomy with a system of representatives who are in principle directly revocable delegates' (Held, 1996, p. 146, n. 8).

PREREQUISITES OF DEMOCRACY AND DEMOCRATIZATION

Democratization and 'Modern Dynamic Pluralist Society'

As I have just argued, at the centre of Marxist analysis of modern politics is the claim of a systemic link between capitalism and (bourgeois) democracy. Whereas in Marxism, the logic of capitalism is held to superimpose itself upon the logic of democracy, 'pluralism' takes a more ambivalent stance regarding the connection between democracy and the economic order. On the one hand, 'the inequalities in resources that market-capitalism churns out produces serious political inequalities among citizens' (Dahl, 1998, p. 178). On the other hand, it is also argued that there is a kind of 'elective affinity' between democracy and market-capitalism. Seymour Martin Lipset, the author of *Political Man*, famously argued in the late 1950s that '[t]he more well-to-do a nation, the greater the chances that it will sustain democracy' (Lipset, 1983, p. 31; see also for a recent statistical account Przeworski/Limongi, 1997). And he asserted that 'all the various aspects of economic development – industrialization, urbanization, wealth, and education – are so closely interrelated as to form one major factor which has the political correlate of democracy' (Lipset, 1983, p. 41). Robert Dahl has listed the interrelated characteristics of 'modern dynamic pluralist society' (MDP), as he calls it, that are congenial to the development and sustenance of democracy:

> a relatively high level of income and wealth per capita, long-run economic growth in per capita income and wealth, a high level of urbanization, a rapidly declining or relatively small agricultural population, great occupational diversity, extensive literacy, a comparatively large number of persons who have attended institutions of higher education, an economic order in which production is mainly carried on by relatively autonomous firms whose decisions are strongly oriented toward national and international markets, and relatively high levels of conventional indicators of well-being, such as physicians and hospital beds per thousand persons, life expectancy, infant mortality, percentage of

families with various consumer durables, and so on. (Dahl, 1989, p. 251)

Dahl is, of course, aware of the fact that there are cases where a democratic political system has been established prior to the formation of an MDP society, such as the United States or India. Furthermore, 'although democracy has existed only in countries with a market-capitalist economy, market-capitalism has existed in non-democratic countries' (Dahl, 1998, p. 170). But the often-adduced cases of South Korea and Taiwan show, so Dahl claims, that, 'in the long run', market-capitalism and economic growth may be downright unfavourable for non-democratic regimes. The key factor is that market-capitalism 'creates a large middling stratum of property owners who typically seek education, autonomy, personal freedom, property rights, the rule of law, and participation in government. The middle classes ... are the natural allies of democratic ideas and institutions' (Dahl, 1998, p. 168).

The cases of India and the USA show, then, that an MDP society is not strictly necessary for the development of democracy; the cases of South Korea and Taiwan show that an MDP society is not sufficient for democracy. Hence, Dahl, but also Lipset (1994) and others writing in their tradition, list further factors favourable to democracy. 'External' conditions must be favourable: 'Democratic institutions are less likely to develop in a country subject to intervention by another country hostile to democratic government in that country' (Dahl, 1998, p. 147). The influence of the Soviet Union in Eastern Europe after the Second World War may serve as an example. In addition to the formation of an MDP society, Dahl identifies three further 'internal' conditions that are favourable and essential for democracy. The means of violent coercion must be dispersed or neutralized, and the military and police forces must be under civilian control. A political culture and beliefs that support democratic ideas, values, and practices must prevail in society, and particularly among political activists. Finally, '[d]emocratic political institutions are more likely to develop and endure in a country that is culturally fairly homogeneous and less likely in a country with sharply differentiated and conflicting subcultures' (Dahl, 1998, pp. 149–50). I shall return to this question of democracy in culturally segmented societies, that has been discussed in recent years mainly in the context of 'multiculturalism', in the next chapter.

Democratization, Class and Capitalist Development

'No bourgeoisie, no democracy' has also been the result of Barrington Moore's classical study on *The Social Origins of Dictatorship and*

Democracy. However, at the centre of Moore's argument is an analysis of
class relations and political institutions. In his wide-ranging comparative
historical analyses, Moore sets out to explain the changes of the political
institutional order that accompanied the transition from agrarian to
industrial societies. The societies under investigation face the same
problem: the destruction of the traditional agrarian economy by commercialization – the production of agrarian goods for urban markets.
These societies, however, solve the task of 'taming' the agrarian sector in
different ways – by bourgeois revolutions in the cases of England
(1640–1660), France (1789–1815) and the United States of America
(1860–1865) that led, eventually, to the establishment of capitalist-
democratic regimes; by unsuccessful or abortive bourgeois revolutions
in the cases of Germany (1848) and Japan (1868) that led, eventually, to
fascist dictatorships; and by peasant revolutions as in the cases of Russia
(1917) and China (1927–1949) that led, eventually, to communism. Not all
societies, therefore, cover an essentially identical path during 'modernization'. Economic modernization ('commercialization' of agriculture)
leads to variations in political structures: how can these variations be
explained? Moore asserts that an explanation of these alternative devel-
opmental routes must focus on the class structure as well as on the set of
existing class coalitions in each society. Moore's hypothesis stipulates
that '[t]he ways in which the landed upper classes and the peasants
reacted to the challenge of commercial agriculture were decisive factors
in determining the political outcome' (Moore, 1966, p. XVII).

Moore concentrates on four major variables in order to account for
variations in political structure: the relationship of the landed upper
classes to the monarchy; the response of the landed upper classes to the
requirements of production for the market in its consequence for the
agrarian class structure; the relationship of the landed upper classes with
the urban elite; and the role of revolutionary violence. In the last instance,
the historically specific form of the integration of the agrarian and urban
economies is the decisive factor in Moore's explanatory model. The
greater the distance between the elites in the countryside and the cities,
the more likely the uncontrolled and unbalanced growth of state power
and the possibility of a crisis-ridden transition into the modern world
with either fascist or communist dictatorship. On the other hand, the
closer the contact and co-operation between these elites, the more likely
the development of a democratic political order. According to Moore, for
democracy to triumph, it is necessary for the monopolistic power of
arbitrary rulers to be broken. An alliance between aristocracy and bourgeoisie must check royal absolutism. However, this alliance must not be
so strong as to permit a common front against the urban and rural

working class because, ultimately, the bourgeoisie needs allies against the aristocracy that allow it to demand and institute democracy. In the case of the 'democratic' path to modernity, Moore thus highlights the importance of a plurality of class forces with the bourgeoisie in a dominant, yet not a monopolistic position. An important factor for this constellation to obtain was the use of revolutionary force in order to repress those rural interests that were opposed to commercialization. In the fascist route, on the other hand, landed interests retain the privileged political position in the state and their social dominance in society, whereas an economically strong bourgeoisie remains politically weak. Revolutionary violence is directed against the peasantry in order to protect the landed interests and against the urban working class in order to incorporate them into the authoritarian regime. Finally, in the communist route, a revolutionary elite, leading the peasantry and the working class, achieves state power because neither bourgeoisie nor the landed upper classes succeed with political or economic modernization. Revolutionary violence 'in the countryside' is directed, initially, against the agrarian ruling class; but state violence is then used against the 'reactionary' peasantry such as the Kulaks.

This line of inquiry has recently been followed by Rueschemeyer, Stephens and Stephens (1992) in a study that examines the relation between the transformations of society that came with capitalist economic development and the long-term chances of democratic forms of rule. The authors identify three main explanatory factors: the balance of power among different classes and class coalitions; the structure, strength and autonomy of the state apparatus and its interrelations with civil society; and the impact of transnational power relations on both the balance of class power and on state–society relations (1992, p. 5). They see the chances of democracy as fundamentally shaped by the balance of class power, and they therefore put forward two key assertions: first, 'capitalist development is associated with democracy because it transforms the class structure, strengthening the working and middle classes and weakening the landed upper class'; second, 'democracy was a result of the contradictions of capitalist development and … it could be consolidated only if the interests of the capitalist classes were not directly threatened by it' (pp. 7 and 10).

Consistent with Moore's argument, the authors show that the landed upper classes, which were dependent on labour-intensive and labour-repressive agrarian production, were the most consistently anti-democratic force (Rueschemeyer, Stephens and Stephens, 1992, pp. 7–10; 270–3; see Ertmann, 1998, for a critical evaluation of this thesis). The most consistently pro-democratic force, so they claim contrary to Moore, was the working class, particularly in those constellations in which it was insulated from the hegemony of the dominant class and where it was not mobilized by a charismatic but authoritarian leader or a hegemonic party linked to the state apparatus. The bourgeoisie, the capitalist class or 'big business', however, would generally only support the installation of constitutional and representative government, but would oppose the political inclusion of the lower classes. The political position of the middle class, which the authors define in the Latin American context as composed of 'urban professionals, state employees and employees in the private sector, artisans and craftsmen, and small entrepreneurs, some-times joined by small and medium farmers' (p. 185), is seen as ambivalent. Where the middle classes were confronted with intransigent dominant classes and had the option of allying with a sizeable working class, they embraced full democracy: 'However, if they started feeling threatened by popular pressures under a democratic regime, they turned to support the imposition of an authoritarian alternative' (p. 8). As the working class could nowhere push through democracy on its own but depended on finding allies, the position of the middle classes determined regime outcomes. Finally, the peasants and rural workers played a varied role in the development of democracy. Though they shared an interest in democracy with the urban working class, 'they acted much less frequently in support of it, in part, because they followed the lead of large landlords and in part because they had much greater difficulty organizing themselves' (pp. 272–3).

With regard to state structure, Rueschemeyer, Stephens and Stephens argue that, the more resources state elites control independently of socioeconomic classes and civil society groups and the more they con-stitute a hierarchically integrated and ideologically united state apparatus, the less likely it is that the subordinate classes of the popula-tion are strong enough to impose democratic rule on the system of domination (pp. 65–6). In this context, it is important to point out the authors' disagreement with positions such as Robert Dahl's. As we have noticed when discussing Dahl's notion of a 'modern dynamic pluralist society', democracy is seen to be facilitated by social mobilization and by the development of relatively autonomous groups that are arising in an ever more differentiated modern structure as a result of market-capitalism. For Rueschemeyer, Stephens and Stephens it is the shift in the power of conflicting class interests as the correlate of social mobilization and pluralization that is fundamentally important to democratization. They insist that the density of autonomous organizations in civil society – which they define as 'the totality of social institutions and associations, both formal and informal, that are not strictly production-related nor governmental or familial in character' (p. 49) – is important on three counts: 'as a way in which the empowerment of subordinate classes is realized, as a shield protecting these classes against the hegemonic influence of dominant classes, and . . . as a mode of balancing the power of state and civil society' (p. 49).

Finally, transnational power structures have highly contingent effects. For example, if economic dependency in the periphery of the world system manifests itself in economic growth being dependent upon agrarian exports, then the power of the 'anti-democratic' landed upper classes is consolidated. If industrialization is being attempted with imported capital-intensive technology, then the 'pro-democratic' working class is being kept small and weak. Geopolitical structures may both strengthen and weaken democracy. For example, there is a strong relation between warfare and democratization: modern mass-mobilization warfare involves the willing participation of the subordinate classes, both in the field and at home in the factories. This has typically led states to making concessions to the subordinate classes. However, whether these concessions can be retained after the end of the military conflict is by no means certain. There is also Dahl's argument about the interests of foreign powers in trying to promote or prevent democratization (Rueschemeyer, Stephens and Stephens, 1992, pp. 69–73). And as the geopolitical and geoeconomic restructuring of Central and Eastern Europe since 1989 demonstrates, the desire of former state socialist countries to join the European Union has not only resulted in determined efforts at democratization, but has made foreign economic support and the marketization of the economy dependent on the prior formation of a democratic polity: democracy preceded capitalism.

Democratization and Elite Transactions

Both Dahl's and Lipset's 'pluralist' concern with the prerequisites of democracy and Moore's and Rueschemeyer, Stephens and Stephens' class-based analysis of the relationship between capitalism, power and democracy share a fundamentally 'structuralist' approach: the importance of concrete political actors and the concrete choices they may make in historically specific situations are downplayed in their importance for regime change. However, it has been argued forcefully that such a neglect seriously hampers our understanding of regime transition. As Karl (1990) has put it, 'Rather than engage in a futile search for new preconditions, it is important to clarify how the mode of regime transition (itself conditioned by the breakdown of authoritarian rule) sets the context within which strategic interactions [between elite groups, RA] can take place because these interactions, in turn, help to determine whether political democracy will emerge and survive'. In the process of democratization, individual and collective actors must 'translate' economic and social forces into democratic political institutions. Political action is therefore a pivotal factor of democratization. How do 'democrats' manage to achieve democracy without being killed by those political forces of the 'old regime' who have the control over weapons and other means of physical coercion? How can they achieve democracy without being starved to death by those economic actors who control the productive resources? Strategic political action is indispensable for their survival. There is, finally, then, the 'elitist' approach to democratization to be considered.

To situate the analytical concern with elite interactions, we may turn to Alfred Stepan's (1986) discussion of ten alternative paths from authoritarian, non-democratic regimes to political democracy. In the first three paths, warfare and conquest play integral parts in redemocratization. First, redemocratization takes place 'when a functioning democracy that has been conquered in war restores democracy after the conqueror is defeated by external force' (p. 66). Denmark, the Netherlands, Norway and Belgium after the end of their occupation by Nazi Germany are the obvious cases. Second, redemocratization after external liberation may entail deep, constitutional democratic reformulation. France and the foundation of the Fourth Republic after the Second World War or Greece after the 1944–49 Civil War are, despite different outcomes, the main examples for this path. Third, as the cases of Germany and Japan after their defeat in 1945 demonstrate, democratization may result from the defeat of an authoritarian regime by democratic powers who then install a working political democracy by dismantling the military and the institutions of the authoritarian state apparatus.

International war and external intervention may thus lead to democratization. Yet, the termination of authoritarian regimes and the move towards redemocratization can also be initiated by the elites of the authoritarian regime themselves. Again, Stepan distinguishes three paths in those transitions in which authoritarian powers make the move towards democracy. First, as in the case of Spain after the death of Franco in 1975, redemocratization may be initiated by the civilian or civilianized political leadership; or, second, as in Brazil in 1974, individual leaders of the military government may be the prime mover for regime termination; and, finally, the 'military-as-institution' may want to return to democracy in order to protect its fundamental corporate interests. Greece in 1973 and Portugal in 1974 are prime examples for this path. In both cases, external threats – the risky intervention in Cyprus in the case of

Greece, and the colonial wars in the case of Portugal – played a central role in the extrications of the military-as-institution.

Finally, rather than the transition to democracy being initiated by regime forces, the termination of the authoritarian regime may be caused by oppositional forces. First, in 'society-led regime termination', 'a transformation could be brought about by diffuse protests by grassroots organizations, massive but uncoordinated general strikes, and by general withdrawal of support for the government' (Stepan, 1986, p. 78). The student uprising in Greece in 1973 or the general strike in Peru in 1977 make these two cases approximations of this type of regime transition. More recently, the German Democratic Republic and Czechoslovakia in the autumn of 1989, when the state socialist societies in Central and Eastern Europe collapsed, may serve as examples. Second, a grand oppositional pact may be constructed that brings together reform-minded members of the regime and members of oppositional groupings. Columbia and Venezuela in 1958, Spain after the Monclao Pact of 1977 are Stepan's examples, and we may add Poland and Hungary in 1989 as further examples of a transition to democracy through transaction. Third, democratization may be the result of an organized violent revolt co-ordinated by democratic reformist parties, as happened in Costa Rica in 1948 where a social democratic 'national liberation movement' defeated the regime, or in Bolivia in 1952 where the National Revolutionary Movement (MNR) seized power. Finally, as the cases of Russia, China, Vietnam or Cuba show, there may be Marxist-led revolutionary wars that lead to regime change; however, as these cases also demonstrate, the transitions did not lead to either 'liberal' or 'democratic' regimes.

While taking any of these paths depends on strategic choices made by individual and collective actors, strategic elite interactions are of singular importance in three of them. In the transition in which redemocratization has been initiated by the civilian or civilianized political leadership, the military-as-institution remains a force of significant power: 'Thus the civilian leadership is most likely to persist in its democratizing initiative (and not to encounter a military reaction) if the democratic opposition tacitly collaborates with the government in creating a peaceful framework for the transition' (Stepan, 1986, p. 73). As the case of Spain after Franco shows, the co-operation between the government and oppositional forces in the transition decreased the chances of a military reaction. Redemocratization as a result of the extrication of the military from the political arena also depends on the creation of a political and legal framework, agreed upon by the power holders and the opposition, since a re-entry of the military can only be prevented if its corporate interests

are secured and its officers are not prosecuted for earlier crimes and
wrongdoings. The case of the former Chilean dictator, General Pinochet,
should be seen in this light, for example.

Yet the path that leads towards redemocratization as a result of a party
pact is, manifestly, the prime case for the importance of strategic elite
interactions and elite settlements. Typically, in this case, several groupings of political actors can be discerned, depending on, firstly, whether
they are committed to maintaining authoritarian rule, or to political
reform, or, finally, to a complete 'rupture' with the regime, and, secondly, with which degree of intensity they are prepared to fight for
achieving their preference. Within the elite of the authoritarian regime,
'hardliners', who would be prepared to confront any opposition head on
and, if necessary, by coercive means, may be confronted by 'softliners',
who would be prepared to negotiate with the opposition about political
liberalization or even a move towards democracy. Within the opposition,
'opportunistic' former supporters of the regime who may not have a
serious commitment to democratization but would hope to secure their
position or gain something from it, will form one grouping. 'Radicals'
within the opposition will demand major political and economic
changes, and are not prepared to compromise with the old regime and
opt, if necessary, for revolutionary violent 'rupture'. Finally, the 'moderates' will be in favour of democratization yet consider it imperative to
respect the position of the traditional political, military and economic
elites (Colomer, 1991; Potter, 1997, p. 15).

As comparative evidence from Latin America or from Eastern Europe
(in particular, from Poland and Hungary) suggests, for a negotiated
transition to succeed, the regime 'hardliners' and the opposition 'radicals' should be neutralized by the 'softliners' and 'moderates'
respectively or else be persuaded to follow a reformist course. Much
depends on the agreement on the question as to 'who shall govern in the
interim between the decision to liquidate an authoritarian regime and the
moment in which a government can be formed that would be based on a
free democratic election' (Linz, 1990, p. 151). At stake, obviously, is the
key question about the control of political resources in the transition
period and the changes to regime structure and in the society prior to
elections. Juan Linz asserts that there are three factors that have an
impact on these transactions and the solution to the fundamental issue of
establishing basic rules of the political process. There is the relative
balance of power among the negotiating parties; but much depends also
on the level of trust in the fairness of those participating in the institutionalization of democracy. There is also the 'pressure from below' that
propels the negotiations onwards and constitutes one of their constrain-

ing conditions. However, Linz hastens to put the importance of 'the people' into perspective:

> It should never be forgotten that in transitions, average men and women, students, and workers are demonstrating in the streets, taking risks in organizing illegal groups, distributing propaganda, and in a few cases, such as in Romania and Nicaragua, assaulting the seats of power ... However, a leaderless and disorganized people filling the squares and demanding a change of regime may be unable to negotiate a transfer or sharing of power, or processes to achieve such a goal, and may be pushed to intransigent positions, and, thus, their efforts will end if not in revolutions, then in repression. (Linz, 1990, p. 152)

Hence, for Linz (and Stepan, too) the emergence of 'structured opposition' in favour of democratization is a necessary condition for bringing about democracy.

In this chapter, I have suggested that, since in 'liberal' democracy it is assumed that only in a sovereign state can the people's will command without being commanded by others, 'state sovereignty' and 'popular sovereignty' are considered to be inextricably intertwined. This assumption also provided arguably the analytical framework for mainstream political science. We must now move to a critical consideration of this assumption. This will be the task of the following chapter.

FURTHER READING

Robert Dahl's *On Democracy* (1998) is a masterly and admirably succinct overview of the origins and ideals of democracy and of the actualities and potentialities of democratic rule. It should be read in conjunction with David Held's *Models of Democracy* (1996), which combines an introduction to the history of democratic thought with a discussion of what democracy means today. A valuable introduction to *The Concepts and Theories of Modern Democracy* (1993) is provided by Anthony Birch. Birch, in turn, may be usefully complemented by Arend Lijphart's *Patterns of Democracy*, in which he analyses and compares 'government forms and performance in thirty-six countries'. In its discussion of 'concepts' rather than 'thinkers', it nicely complements Held's book. Roland Axtmann's *Liberal Democracy into the Twenty-first Century: Globalization, Integration and the Nation-State* addresses questions of sovereignty, state, nation and democracy from both a theoretical and a 'comparative politics' perspective. The textbook on *Democratization* (1997), edited by David Potter *et al.*, traces the story of democratization in the modern world. Rueschemeyer, Stephens and Stephens in their *Capitalist Development and Democracy* (1992) provide a critical review of the academic literature on democratization as well as developing an original and sophisticated explanation of the rise of democracy.

BIBLIOGRAPHY

Anderson, James (1996) The Shifting Stage of Politics: New Medieval and Post-modern Territorialities, *Environment and Planning (Society and Space)* 14, 133–53.

Axtmann, Roland (1996) *Liberal Democracy into the Twenty-first Century: Globalization, Integration and the Nation-State*. Manchester: Manchester University Press.

Bentley, Arthur F. (1908) *The Process of Government: A Study of Social Pressures*. Evanston, IL: The Principia Press of Illinois.

Birch, Anthony H. (1993) *The Concepts and Theories of Modern Democracy*. London: Routledge.

Brubaker, W. Rogers (1992) *Citizenship and Nationhood in France and Germany*. Cambridge, MA: Harvard University Press.

Cohen, Jean (1999) Trust, Voluntary Association and Workable Democracy: The Contemporary American Discourse of Civil Society. In M. Warren (ed.), *Democracy and Trust*. Cambridge: Cambridge University Press, pp. 208–48.

Cohen, Jean and Arato, Andrew (1992) *Civil Society and Political Theory*. Cambridge, MA: MIT Press.

Coleman, James (1988) Social Capital in the Creation of Human Capital, *American Journal of Sociology* 94, 95–120.

Colomer, Josep M. (1991) Transitions by Agreement: Modeling the Spanish Way, *American Political Science Review* 85, 1283–1302.

Crick, Bernard (1959) *The American Science of Politics: Its Origins and Conditions*. London: Routledge & Kegan Paul.

Dahl, Robert A. (1956) *A Preface to Democratic Theory*. Chicago: University of Chicago Press.

Dahl, Robert A. (1961) *Who Governs? Democracy and Power in an American City*. New Haven and London: Yale University Press.

Dahl, Robert A. (1989) *Democracy and Its Critics*. New Haven and London: Yale University Press.

Dahl, Robert A. (1998) *On Democracy*. New Haven and London: Yale University Press.

Easton, David (1953) *The Political System: An Inquiry into the State of Political Science*. New York: Alfred A. Knopf.

Easton, David (1965) *A Systems Analysis of Political Life*. New York: Wiley.

Ertmann, Thomas (1998) Democracy and Dictatorship in Interwar Western Europe Revisited, *World Politics* 50, 475–505.

Etzioni-Halevy, Eva (1993) *The Elite Connection: Problems and Potential of Western Democracy*. Cambridge: Polity Press.

Eulau, Heinz (1966) *The Behavioral Persuasion in Politics*. New York: Random House (fourth edition).

Fukuyama, Francis (1995) *Trust: The Social Virtues and the Creation of Prosperity*. New York: Free Press.

Gerth, H.H. and Mills, C. Wright (eds) (1967) *From Max Weber: Essays in Sociology*. London: Routledge & Kegan Paul.

Gunnell, John G. (1986) *Between Philosophy and Politics: The Alienation of Political Theory*. Amherst: University of Massachusetts Press.

Held, David (1996) *Models of Democracy*. Cambridge: Polity Press (second edition).

Hobbes, Thomas (1991/1651) *Leviathan*. Cambridge: Cambridge University Press.

Kamenka, Eugene (1973) Political Nationalism – the Evolution of the Idea. In E. Kamenka (ed.), *Nationalism: The Nature and Evolution of an Idea*. Canberra: National University Press, pp. 2–20.

Karl, Terry Lynn (1990) Dilemmas of Democratization in Latin America, *Comparative Politics* 23, 1–21.

Lijphart, Arend (1999) *Patterns of Democracy: Government Forms and Performance in Thirty-six countries*. New Haven, CN: Yale University Press.

Lindblom, Charles (1977) *Politics and Markets: The World's Political-Economic Systems*. New York: Basic Books.

Linz, Juan J. (1990) Transitions to Democracy, *Washington Quarterly*, Summer 1990, 143–64.

Lipset, Seymour M. (1983) *Political Man: The Social Bases of Politics*. London: Heinemann (second edition; first edition published in 1959/1960).

Lipset, Seymour M. (1994) The Social Requisites of Democracy Revisited, *American Sociological Review* 59, 1–22.

Marshall, T.H. (1963) Citizenship and Social Class, in *Sociology at the Crossroads*. London: Heinemann, pp. 67–127.

Moore, Barrington (1966) *Social Origins of Dictatorship and Democracy: Lord and Peasant in the Making of the Modern World*. Boston: Beacon Press.

Nordlinger, Eric A. (1981) *On the Autonomy of the Democratic State*. Cambridge, MA: Harvard University Press.

Offe, Claus (1985) Challenging the Boundaries of Institutional Politics: Social Movements since the 1960s. In C. Maier (ed.), *Changing Boundaries of the Political*. Cambridge: Cambridge University Press, pp. 63–105.

Offe, Claus (1999) How Can We Trust Our Fellow Citizens? In M. Warren (ed.), *Democracy and Trust*. Cambridge: Cambridge University Press, pp. 42–87.

Potter, David (1997) Explaining Democratization. In D. Potter, D. Goldblatt, M. Kiloh and P. Lewis (eds), *Democratization*. Cambridge: Polity Press, pp. 1–40.

Potter, D., Goldblatt, D., Kiloh, M. and Lewis, P. (eds) (1997) *Democratization*. Cambridge: Polity Press.

Przeworski, Adam and Limongi, Fernando (1997) Modernization: Theories and Facts, *World Politics* 49, 155–83.

Putnam, Robert D. (1993) *Making Democracy Work*. Princeton, NJ: Princeton University Press.

Putnam, Robert D. (1995a) Bowling Alone: America's Declining Social Capital, *Journal of Democracy* 6, 65–78.

Putnam, Robert D. (1995b) Tuning in, Tuning out? The Strange Disappearance of Social Capital in America, *PS: Political Science and Politics* 28, 664–83.

Ricci, David M. (1984) *The Tragedy of Political Science: Politics, Scholarship, and Democracy*. New Haven and London: Yale University Press.

Rich, Paul (1999) American Voluntarism, Social Capital and Political Culture, *Annals* (AAPSS) 565, 15–34.

Rueschemeyer, Dietrich, Stephens, Evelyne Huber Stephens and John D. Stephens (1992) *Capitalist Development and Democracy*. Cambridge: Polity Press.

Schumpeter, Joseph A. (1976/1942) *Capitalism, Socialism and Democracy*. London: Allen & Unwin.

Seidelman, Raymond (1985) *Disenchanted Realists: Political Science and the American Crisis, 1884–1984*. Albany: State University of New York Press.

Shils, Edward (1997) *The Virtue of Civility: Selected Essays on Liberalism, Tradition and Civil Society*. Indianapolis, IN: Liberty Fund.

Stepan, Alfred (1986) Paths towards Redemocratization: Theoretical and Comparative Considerations. In G. O'Donnell, P. Schmitter, L. Whitehead (eds), *Transitions from Authoritarian Rule*. Baltimore: Johns Hopkins University Press, volume 3, pp. 64–84.

Tucker, Robert C. (ed.) (1978) *The Marx–Engels Reader*. New York and London: Norton (second edition).

Uslaner, Eric M. (1999) Democracy and Social Capital. In M. Warren (ed.), *Democracy and Trust*. Cambridge: Cambridge University Press, pp. 121–50.

Warren, Mark E. (1999) Democratic Theory and Trust. In M. Warren (ed.), *Democracy and Trust*. Cambridge: Cambridge University Press, pp. 310–45.

Warren, Mark (ed.) (1999) *Democracy and Trust*. Cambridge: Cambridge University Press.

Weber, Max (1968) *Economy and Society*. Berkeley: University of California Press.

Weber, Max (1994) *Political Writings*. Edited by Peter Lassman and Ronald Speirs. Cambridge: Cambridge University Press.

CHAPTER 2

INTRODUCTION II: BETWEEN POLYCENTRICITY AND GLOBALIZATION
Democratic Governance in Europe

Roland Axtmann

As I have discussed in the previous chapter, the idea, and ideal, of sovereignty, with its related notions of unity and hierarchy, conceptually grounds democracy in the European nation state. Yet, as this idea(l) has come to be questioned, so the state and hierarchical 'governing' has come under attack. In this chapter, I shall discuss some of the salient political and social transformations that challenge us to reconconceptualize democracy.

POLYCENTRICITY, 'RISK SOCIETY' AND MULTICULTURALISM

Modern society is characterized by functional differentiation. Politics, economics, science, education, and religion, for example, have become differentiated in separate 'subsystems'. From a political perspective, institutional differentiation with considerable (and constitutionally protected) autonomy meant a diffusion of social power and, by the same token, a limitation to any attempts at centralizing power. Differentiation also allowed for a more 'efficient' realization of the respective goals of the 'subsystems': for example, knowledge could be more efficiently produced once science and religion had become differentiated, or the production of commodities and the satisfaction of needs could be more efficiently organized once politics and economics had become institutionalized as distinct structures of social action. Functional differentiation meant the diffusion of social power and limitations to the centralization of power – after all, this lies behind the differentiation of 'state' and 'civil society'. It also resulted in 'efficiency' gains and a historically unprecedented degree of societal dynamic (Willke, 1992; Beck, 1994). How can functionally autonomous subsystems be co-ordinated in such a way that negative costs cannot be externalized?

Some sort of co-ordination is already in place. Over the last couple of decades, policy networks have been established in Western societies, bringing together state actors and other subsystem actors in formal and informal systems of negotiation: 'The state becomes a collection of interorganizational networks made up of governmental and societal actors with no sovereign actor able to steer or regulate ... A key challenge for government is to enable these networks and to seek out new forms of co-operation' (Rhodes, 1996, p. 666; see also Knoke, 1990; Marin and Mayntz (eds), 1991; Scharpf, 1991; Knoke *et al.*, 1996). These network relations are characterized by the reciprocity and interdependence of its constituent units and by their mutual adjustment on the basis of bargaining and trust. 'Governance', as Rhodes (1996, p. 658) remarks, 'is about managing networks'. 'Liberal' democracy, however, is focused on hierarchy. It is a mechanism that is meant to allow to control and hold accountable through political participation state actors who 'legally command' in the name of the people. Modern society as functionally differentiated society cannot be co-ordinated hierarchically from a centre, the state, but has to rely on the integrative effects of networks. But these network structures raise questions of democratic accountability. With politics becoming 'flat', losing its hierarchical structure as the role of the state as the commanding regulator of 'society' evaporates – not into 'thin air' but into the multi-layered and intertwined networks – 'liberal' democracy has lost, as it were, its reference point. To sustain it, democracy may have to follow suit and move into 'society'.

The problem of 'co-ordination' is compounded by the rise of new policy issues. In the past, the welfare state provided some kind of protection from socially and industrially produced hazards and damages through voluntary or compulsory insurance schemes. Welfare state programmes covered the hazards and risks of industrial accident, illness (health), old age (pensions), unemployment and poverty (for example, family allowances). If the state did not provide protection from these hazards through 'national insurance contributions', then, at least in principle, private insurance could be purchased. While protection from these 'old' risks is still part of the 'services' that wide sections of the population expect the state to provide, the contemporary state is also confronted with a completely new set of tasks. The development of nuclear, chemical, genetic and military technologies has resulted in unprecedented ecological hazards and risks to the wellbeing and even survival of humankind. These new risks differ in many ways from the 'old' risks. First, they are limited neither in space nor in time. A nuclear catastrophe in Russia, for example, affects hill farmers in the Scottish Highlands, possibly for years to come. And mutations of the genetic code as a result of such a catastrophe may manifest themselves only in future generations. Second, they tend to be unaccountable. The destruction of the ozone layer cannot be traced to any one particular cause and any one particular (group of) person(s) that could be held legally accountable for it. There is thus no liability for damages. Third, they tend to be incalculable. In many cases, such as the building of nuclear reactors or genetic engineering, risks can only be tested and assessed after 'production'. Finally, they tend to be uncompensatable. No insurance scheme is available that would provide compensation for causing potentially global irreparable damage (Beck, 1992; Lash and Urry, 1994).

These developments result in the increase in risks and a decrease in protection from them because of their specific quality. At the same time, however, it is expected of the state that it pursue a policy of risk limitation, *vide* the increased importance of environmental policies. But the state can perform this task only under severe restrictions. As a welfare state, the state remains dependent on success in international economic competition as it provides the material resources needed for social policies. This success, however, is premised on the application of scientific innovations and new technologies. A policy that aimed at radically curtailing innovative but risk-producing research would therefore be unlikely to gain wide consensus. The second constraint results from the difficulty of knowing with any great degree of certainty what kind of risks a particular innovation will produce and therefore what the result of a particular policy will be. Genetic engineering, for example, may result in producing plants resistant to bacteriological decease, and thus help to solve hunger; but it may also result in the creation of a 'super race' through the selection of particular genes. These 'cognitive' problems are compounded by the fact that there is no consensus among the population regarding the moral validity of 'progress'. 'Cognitive' uncertainty is thus complemented by 'moral' uncertainty. Moreover, the new tasks assigned to the state are not open to mechanisms of 'command and obedience'. Though in some areas, such as the behaviour of individuals with regard to the environment, monetary inducements or penalties (fines/taxes) can be used to influence behaviour, with regard to many risks monetary penalties are useless (for example, HIV/AIDS). In these instances, the state has to rely on education and persuasion.

What may have to be created are fora of public deliberation about risks and risk prevention which are populated not just by experts, members of networks and the state who all claim to represent the 'demos', but also by the 'demos' itself. Both the question of the democratic control of power ensconced in networks and the challenges of new, cognitively and morally polyvalent policy issues would therefore require sustained efforts at creating a more participatory, 'strong' democracy (Benjamin Barber).

Yet, as many chapters in this volume amply demonstrate, even the definition of the 'demos' itself has become ever more problematic and has raised questions about political integration and political rule in general. In the last few decades, we could witness that in ever more countries national and ethnic communities with distinct languages, histories and traditions have demanded the recognition and support for their cultural identity. At stake in these struggles is the demand by these 'minorities' for group-differentiated rights, powers, status or immunities that go beyond the common rights of citizenship. These claims may encompass demands for territorial autonomy – ranging in its form from federalism to devolution to the status of 'autonomous' region in either symmetrical or asymmetrical arrangements; for self-government in certain key matters such as education, health or family law; for guaranteed representation in the political institutions of the larger society on the basis of quota systems favourable to the group and guaranteed veto powers over legislation and policies that centrally affect the respective minorities; and for group-specific legal exemptions. These demands are premised upon the belief that only by possessing and exercising these rights, powers, and immunities will it be possible for these communities to ensure the full and free development of their culture. A policy of assimilation, which aims to incorporate (or 'melt') the 'minority' into the dominant 'majority' culture, is therefore not an option (Kymlicka, 1995; Rex, 1998). Barry Hindess discusses many of the salient democratic issues raised by multiculturalism in his contribution to this book.

In his chapter for this book, Derek Urwin discusses some of the problems that arise from federalization as one form of the territorial management of ethnonational cleavages in plural societies. Peter Leslie's discussion of Canada provides more detailed information on one particularly interesting case of contested 'territorial politics' as does Michael Dyer's analysis of political-constitutional reform in the United Kingdom. As the case of Switzerland, which is highly fragmented in both religion and language, shows, for federalism to provide an adequate institutional solution to cultural cleavages, the units within the federal system must be sufficiently autonomous to accommodate the different communities and possess adequate powers to meet their cultural needs. These communities should be already separated along territorial lines and should therefore also be fairly homogeneous culturally, so that cultural cleavages within the 'unit' are relatively few. But for a federal system not to dissolve as a result of secessionist movements, 'the citizens must have a national identity and common goals and values sufficiently strong to sustain the federal union' (Dahl, 1998, p. 155). This appears to be the case in Switzerland, yet seems to be precarious, for example, in Belgium and even more so in Canada.

Power-sharing between 'cultural' communities in the form of a 'consociational' democracy can be a further way of meeting demands for cultural recognition. As Arend Lijphart (1977) has suggested, consociational democracy has the following features: grand coalition governments which incorporate the leaders of the political parties that represent the main segments of the culturally divided society; a 'proportional representation' (PR) electoral system that ensures each cultural community a share of seats in parliament that is roughly proportional to the relative size of its vote; proportional employment and expenditure rules that apply throughout the public sector; each community enjoys a high degree of autonomy in dealing with all those matters that are central to its cultural 'identity' or 'interests', backed up by constitutional vetoes for each cultural community. Manifestly, for a consociational democracy to be created, and to work successfully, very special conditions have to prevail. These include

> high tolerance for compromise; trustworthy leaders who can negotiate solutions to conflicts that gain the assent of their followers; a consensus on basic goals and values that is broad enough to make agreements attainable; a national identity that discourages demands for outright separation; and a commitment to democratic procedures that excludes violent or revolutionary means. (Dahl, 1998, p. 154)

The current attempt at conflict resolution in Northern Ireland is clearly along the lines of power sharing and consociationalism. Time will tell whether the conditions specified by Dahl will prevail and thus allow for this current effort to succeed.

Considering political demands for communal self-government, Bhikhu Parekh has suggested that cohesive communities, which have democratically accountable self-governing institutions and allow their members a right of exit

> have a vital role in giving their members a sense of rootedness, harnessing their moral energies for common purposes, and sustaining the spirit of cultural pluralism. Rather than seek to dismantle them in the name of abstractly and narrowly defined goals of social cohesion, integration and national unity, the state should acknowledge their cultural and political value and grant them such support as they need and ask for ... Conducting the affairs of a society as complex as ours is too important a task to be left to the state alone. It requires ... encouraging cohesive communities to run their affairs themselves

under the overall authority of the state is an important dimension of
that partnership. (Parekh, 1994, p. 107)

Such a 'partnership' raises the question of the very nature, authority, and
permanence of the multicultural state of which these various cultural
communities are part. Our prevailing assumptions of common citizenship, common identity, and social and political cohesion will be
questioned. The question will also have to be addressed how these
communities can co-ordinate their actions in areas of common concern or
common interest, for example, with regard to the environment, the
economy, or military security. The much more fragmented, decentralized institutional pattern emerging from this diversity would have to
allow for, first, democratic communal self-government; second, a public
debate on the matters communities have in common; third, protection of
legitimate powers to uphold autonomy; and, fourth, the political co-
ordination of the communities that keeps them part of one larger
community. Again, the net effect would appear to be a state that acts as
the co-ordinator of these political and cultural networks that are formed
by a plethora of 'cultural' communities. Given that many of these
communities have 'transnational' political, economic and cultural links
with their 'home country' and retain a sense of loyalty to, and possibly
derive even their identity from, their 'place of origin', the state will find
it difficult to facilitate or even steer their interactions within the state
territory (Cohen, 1997; some aspects of the problematic relationship
between transnational migrants, the democratic liberal state and citizenship are discussed by Doomernik and Axtmann in their contribution to
this volume).

GLOBALIZATION

The idea of 'polycentricity' and the issue of 'governance' are also of
central importance in the debate on 'globalization'.

We have seen in our discussion on sovereignty in the previous chapter
that, at least in Europe in the past, the state was considered to be the
'ultimate power' that could impose, and enforce, order within a territory.
Political rule in general, and the regulatory, steering and co-ordinating
capacities of the state in particular, has been territorially bounded in its
reach. The success of the nation state in the last 200 years or so as well as
its universality and legitimacy were premised on its claim to be able to
guarantee the economic wellbeing, the physical security and the cultural
identity of the people who constitute its citizens. However, ever more
societal interactions cross borders and become transnational. They

become therefore detached from a particular territory. For example, global capitalism and the global division of labour, the global prolifera-tion of nuclear weapons, the global reach of environmental and health risks, global tourism and mass migration, or global media and commu-nication networks now challenge the effectiveness of the organizational form of the nation state. The links between the citizens and the nation state are becoming ever more problematic. The citizens demand political representation, physical protection, economic security and cultural cer-tainty. But in a global system that is made up of states, regions, international and supranational organizations, non-governmental orga-nizations and transnational corporations, the nation state finds it increasingly difficult to accommodate these interests and mediate between its citizens and the rest of the world (Beetham, 1984; Horsman and Marshall, 1994; Axtmann and Grant, 2000).

Arguably, we are witnessing a steady replacement of the centralization and hierarchization of power within states and through states in the international system by the pluralization of power among political, economic, cultural and social actors, groups, and communities within states, between states, and across states. 'Sub-system autonomy' as a consequence of 'functional differentiation' – which is the force behind 'polycentricity' – is thus radicalized through the release of societal interactions from the 'cage' of the territorial state. We move into a 'plurilateral' world of diffused and decentralized power where there is a variety of different loci of power as well as crosscutting and intersecting power networks (Cerny, 1993; Luke, 1993; Castells, 1996, 1997, 1998).

In this world, states have also been losing the monopoly, which they had acquired over the last 200 years or so, of representing 'their' people in the 'international' arena, and their dominant position in this arena is increas-ingly challenged (Rosenau, 1997). International governmental organizations (IGOs) such as NATO, the UN, the International Labor Organization, the International Monetary Fund, the World Bank or the World Trade Organi-zation constitute distinctive collective political actors and thereby add to the complexity of the 'international' system that had formed around the power-political interests of states. However, as associations of states on the basis of multilateral treaties in accordance with international law these organiza-tions do not ultimately diminish the dominance of states in the 'international' system. Indeed, IGOs can usefully be understood as manifes-tations of the efforts by states to claw back some competencies regarding the control of societal interactions across borders by going 'international' and opting for 'international' co-operation.

But, as we are well aware, many more actors populate global politics, amongst them ever more prominently non-governmental organizations

(NGOs). It has been calculated that there are well over 15,000 recognizable NGOs that operate in three or more countries and draw their
finances in more than one country (Gordenker and Weiss, 1995, p. 357).
Moreover, an increasingly dense network structure that connects NGOs
globally has come to be established:

> New communication technologies are helping to foster the kinds of
> interaction and relationships that were once unthinkable except
> through expensive air travel. Scaling certain kinds of transnational
> efforts from neighbourhoods and regions to the global level and
> scaling down to involve grassroots organizations are no longer
> logistic possibilities, but may be treated as institutional imperatives.
> (Gordenker and Weiss, 1995, p. 365)

As a result, the number of 'international' non-governmental organizations (INGOs) has increased. There are transnational federations of
NGOs such as Save the Children, Amnesty International, Oxfam, *Médi-
cins sans Frontières*, or the International Federation of Red Cross and Red
Crescent Societies, all of which operate on a global scope and whose
chapters in individual countries have a high degree of autonomy. And
there are formal coalitions of NGOs that bring together organizations
with different objectives, such as the International Council of Voluntary
Agencies (ICVA) in Geneva, which was originally designed as an organizational structure for European NGOs, but now comprises primarily
those of the 'Third World'; or a network such as EarthAction, which is
one of the largest global NGO networks with over 700 member associations in about 125 countries. Further prominent examples of INGOs are
the Socialist International, the International Confederation of Free Trade
Unions, the International Olympic Committee, PEN or the World Council of Indigenous Peoples. If we add the 'business non-governmental
organizations' ('BINGOS') such as multi- and transnational corporations
to this list of non-governmental actors in the 'international' arena, a
complex network of 'global' actors emerges.

Let us put these developments into a broader context. We are witnessing a disaggregation of international political authority as a result of the
increase in the number of global political actors. This does not mean that,
of necessity, there are no effective political mechanisms through which
orderly and reliable responses could be made to global issues. Rather,
what we have seen forming over the last couple of decades is a structure
of 'global governance'. As the 'Commission on Global Governance'
observed in 1995:

[Governance] is the sum of the many ways individuals and institutions, public and private, manage their common affairs. It is a continuing process through which conflicting or diverse interests may be accommodated and co-operative action may be taken ... At the global level, governance has been viewed primarily as intergovernmental relationships, but it must now be understood as also involving non-governmental organizations (NGOs), citizens' movements, multinational corporations, and the global mass media of dramatically enlarged influence. (Commission on Global Governance, 1995; also: Rosenau, 1997, chap. 8)

For the authors of this report, 'global governance' does not mean 'global government'. Rather than opt for a hierarchical model that puts one agency – such as the state – at the apex of the political authority structure, the Commission envisages a political model in which a multiplicity of actors pursue collaborative solutions to common problems in the spirit of collective responsibility. 'Global governance' is meant to emphasize the need, and the desirability, of the collaboration of public and private actors starting from the local level and running right through to the global level. Hence, supporters of the idea of 'global governance' do not argue in favour of establishing a sovereign, centralized institution at the global level that could authoritatively impose order, if need be through coercive means. On the contrary, they start from the empirical observation of a multiplicity of actors at the global stage and the (alleged) incapacity of states as the traditional international actors to solve global problems. They then deduce from this fact the necessity of setting up decentralized and plural mechanisms of political co-operation and regulation.

We gain an insight into what is involved in 'global governance' if we look at one specific issue area. It is often maintained that the global economy cannot be politically regulated. However, this is by no means the case. The International Monetary Fund, the World Bank and the General Agreement on Tariffs and Trade (GATT)/World Trade Organization are major regulatory international governmental organizations. They have been instrumental in removing political control over economic processes and institutions through a policy of 'liberalization' and are still engaged in ensuring the continuation of this 'neo-liberal' policy (see Hirst and Thompson, 1996). Yet, these institutions could also provide the organizational structure for regulatory control of the world economy once the reign of the 'neo-liberal' ideology is challenged by political actors. And while 'liberalization' and 'deregulation' of economic and financial transactions were important public policy objectives in many liberal-capitalist countries in the 1980s and 1990s, the re-regulation

of activities of transnationally mobile private individuals who present
risks to the state has also gained increasing importance for the state. The
regulation and supervision of international banks may serve as an
example. For example, from 1975 onwards, the 'Basle Committee on
Banking Regulation and Supervisory Practices', an informal consultative
group under the auspices of the Bank for International Settlements at
Basle in Switzerland, has agreed on a number of 'concordats' for the
supervision of foreign banking establishments in order to improve the
capacity of states to control the risks inherent in international banking.
While these 'concordats' are not laws, and the agreements are non-
binding, they have nevertheless resulted in the harmonization of
municipal laws on banking regulations, namely the United States Foreign Bank Supervision Enhancement Act of 1991 and the European
Union's Directive on the Supervision of Credit Institutions on a Consolidated Basis of 1992. For Wiener (1999), this is but one example of an
observable trend towards the functional harmonization of municipal law
in a number of areas (such as money laundering or copyright infringe-
ments on the Internet) that attempts to mitigate national differences and
create functionally assimilated regulatory spaces that transcend state
borders (for an analysis of 'regulatory competition and re-regulation' in
the European Union, see Scharpf, 1998, chap. 3). The thrust of Wiener's
study is the claim that 'because of this functional similarity of municipal
law spilling over state borders, municipal law has become an aspect of
international governance' (Wiener, 1999, p. 10). It also means, according
to Wiener, that the state is not, of necessity, 'hollowed out' as a result of
economic and financial 'globalization', but must – and indeed does – find
new policy solutions to confront the challenges of transnationally mobile
civil society actors (Hirst's chapter in this volume can be usefully placed
within the context of this argument).

There is also a host of private regulatory systems. There are debt
security or rating agencies, which are private entities, that organize
information for suppliers and borrowers of capital. These agencies have
a vital function for the global economy in which there is a constant flow
of capital in search for profitable investment. These agencies rank or rate
the creditworthiness of debtors, assessing their liquidity and solvency
and hence the risks a lender takes when investing in bonds or securities
of issuers. This activity frequently involves the assessment of the creditworthiness of public issuers, for example national governments or
municipal governments, whose policies may very well be influenced by
the likely approval or disapproval by the rating agencies. Another
private regulatory mechanism is international commercial arbitration.
The global economy, as much as national economies, operates legally

through contractual arrangements for the sale of goods, joint ventures, construction projects, distributorships, and the like. The settlement of disputes over contracts has increasingly become the task of international commercial arbitration bodies. Rather than submit to the courts of the other party – which in a dispute over an international contract would involve litigation in a possibly 'alien' legal system – parties agree on conflict resolution through private bodies. There were about 120 arbitration centres by 1991, with another seven established by 1993. Among the centres established more recently were those of Bahrain, Singapore, Sydney, and Vietnam. Among the most important international institutions involved in commercial arbitration are the International Chamber of Commerce in Paris with members from some 100 countries and national committees in 60; the American Arbitration Association; and the London Court of International Commercial Arbitration. But there are also other, increasingly important, centres such as the Chinese International Economic and Trade Arbitration Commission. Two sets of figures may attest to the increasing importance of these agencies. The International Chamber of Commerce (ICC) received its first 3000 requests for arbitration between 1923, when it was founded, and July 1976. The next 3000 requests came in the next eleven years. In 1991, the ICC dealt with 333 cases; in 1992 with 337; and in 1993 with 352. The number of arbitrators has also risen dramatically – and this within a very brief period of time: there were about a thousand arbitrators by 1990, yet by 1992 this number had already doubled. Much of this arbitration is done by big multinational legal firms and with Anglo-American law dominant in international transactions, arbitration tends to privilege Anglo-American law firms and thus contributes to the globalization of Anglo-American law (see the discussion in Sassen, 1996; also Wiener, 1999, chap. 7).

Finally, the policy of economic regionalization is an attempt at governance, too (Ross, 1998). In recent years, we have noticed a trend towards an interpenetration of the advanced capitalist countries, and, in particular, the intensification of transfers among three economic macro-regions: North America, Europe, and the Asian Pacific. This spatial dimension of economic globalization is reinforced by political attempts to institutionalize regional economic co-operation all around the world. Examples of such economic regionalization abound: the North American Free Trade Agreement (NAFTA) between the United States, Canada and Mexico and the European Union (EU) are prominent examples. But one could also mention, for example, the Asian-Pacific Economic Co-operation (APEC), founded in 1989, the Association of South East Asian Nations (ASEAN) and the evolving regional security dialogue institutionalized in the ASEAN Regional Forum (ARF), or MERCOSUR (Southern Cone Common Market) that was established in 1991.

Amongst these economic regions and regional associations, Europe has developed a particularly high degree of regional cohesiveness with a complex governance structure now emerging within the European Union (EU). How best to categorize this emerging structure is a heatedly contested question (Schmitter, 1992; Caporaso, 1996; Marks *et al.*, 1996; Armstrong and Bulmer, 1998; Hix, 1998). Joseph Weiler provides a crisp summary (Weiler, 1999, pp. 272–8). Some analysts see states as the key players and governments (primarily the executive branch) as the principal actors and privileged power holders. The EU is the international arena in which governments interact and, in pursuit of their respective interests, negotiate and bargain with each other. Other analysts agree that states are privileged players, but perceive the community/EU to be more than simply an arena in which international diplomacy is conducted. But contrary to the view of the 'intergovernmentalists', these 'supranationalists' assign great importance to Community institutions such as the Commission, the Council, the European Parliament or the European Court of Justice: they, too, are important players in the European 'polity'. Finally, there are those analysts who take an 'infranational approach'. According to Weiler, 'infranationalism' is based 'on the realization that increasingly large sectors of Community norm creation are done at a meso-level of governance'. The actors involved tend to be, not governments or the Community institutions, but rather, 'both at Union and Member state levels, administrations, departments, private and public associations, and certain, mainly corporate, interest groups' (Weiler, 1999, pp. 98, 273; see Lord, 1998, for a succinct discussion of the effects of these structures and networks for democracy in the EU).

Weiler is surely right to suggest that governance in the EU is a mixture of intergovernmentalism, supranationalism and infranationalism. This 'messy' structure of political regulation, co-ordination and decision-making is likely to be further complicated by the trend towards 'differentiated integration', instigated by the 1992 Treaty on European Union and the Treaty of Amsterdam. These treaties envisage a division between a substantial common base on the one hand and a set of open partnerships in particular policy sectors on the other. The common base is defined to include the direct regulation of the single market through a co-ordinated set of policy measures. Beyond that common base, however, variation is organized sector by sector (Walker, 1998). The British and Danish opt outs in respect of the final stages of Economic and Monetary Union or the British opt out in respect of the Protocol on Social

Policy are examples of 'differentiated integration' as are the provisions of 'enhanced co-operation' between interested EU countries in justice and home affairs and common security and foreign policy. Neil Walker has argued that differentiated integration will mean that we may have to envisage 'a number of different "Europes", their breadth and depth dependent upon the integration arrangements specific to the policy field in question, and embedded in a complex network of relations with one another and with the various Member States' (Walker, 1998, p. 356). But politically organized 'Europe' transcends the EU. The Council of Europe, the Organization for Security and Co-operation in Europe and the 'Europe' constituted by the signatories of the European Convention on Human Rights, for example, add further political layers to the 'European' polity. And we should also take cognizance of the fragmentation of 'nation' states that manifests itself in 'regional' and 'ethno-national' movements, for example in Spain, Italy, Belgium or the United Kingdom. These 'subnational' entities have been demanding unmediated representation in 'Europe' – indeed, they aim to create a 'Europe of the regions' rather than a 'Europe of nation states' (never mind a 'supranational' Europe), and hence construct yet another 'Europe'.

In Europe, then, complex 'governance' structures are forming within the 'polycentric' 'nation' states. Furthermore, a region-wide complex 'governance' structure has emerged that, at the same time, is a constituent element in an emerging global governance structure (Axtmann, 1998). For example, in the recent 'banana war' we could detect the triangular 'governance' formation of USA, EU and WTO, but also the separate involvement of France and Great Britain as former colonial powers, and of the former colonies within the group of African, Caribbean and Pacific (ACP) countries as well as that of US multinationals such as Chiquita, Dole and Del Monte. We have heard of warnings issued by the British American Chamber of Commerce about the devastating effect of sanctions on both sides of the Atlantic; of a group of Scottish politicians representing the four main Scottish parties setting off to Washington to bring their concerns about sanctions against Scottish goods directly to leading US senators; and of calls by the Scottish National Party on expatriate members in the US to lobby Congress to get the decision on sanctions reversed (*Guardian*, 6 March 1999, p. 9).

DEMOCRACY BEYOND THE NATION STATE

The individuals, groups, and communities that partake in the creation of these supra- and transnational networks and who are affected by them, will be empowered and constrained in new ways. In the past 200 years or so, it has been the nation state that determined, by and large, their political 'liberty' and 'identity' and mediated the effects of the 'outside' world. In the plurilateral world, the idea of a *summa potestas* (highest authority) that resides in the state as that institutional arrangement empowered to make, and enforce, collectively binding decisions has lost, if not its appeal, then its justification. And so has the notion of the sovereignty of the people as a united, homogeneous body legitimating the sovereign power of 'its' state through a constitution that manifests the principle of *voluntas populi suprema lex* ('the will of the people be the highest law').

The problem that these developments pose for democracy can be summarized as follows. As a result of a high level of societal differentiation and the increasing transnationalization of a wide range of societal interactions, the effective political solution of ever more societal problems is being sought at a level above or outside the nation state. However, many transnational interactions, and the transnationalization of economic action in particular, have hurried ahead of the current possibilities for their political regulation. At the same time, the structures and mechanisms of international regulatory policy making – such as IGOs – are, in turn, more advanced than the institutions for their democratic control. This creates an extreme tension between the effectiveness of political problem solving at the 'international' level, on the one hand, and democratic legitimacy, which remains embedded in 'domestic' political institutional arrangements, on the other. This tension is aggravated by the repercussions of international policy making on domestic societies. Democratic politics at the nation state level is increasingly curtailed as a result of the binding force of international political agreements. While 'democracy beyond the nation state' remains weak, 'democracy within the nation state' is weakened as well.

This is for mainly two reasons. Firstly, extraterritorial 'global' forces both invade the political space of the nation state and, because of their extraterritoriality, are operating outside its controlling reach. They challenge the democratic polity both as space invaders and space evaders. Secondly, international policy agreements restrict the range of democratically contested domestic policy options. The formation of the human rights regime since 1948, codified in a number of 'covenants', may serve as an example. For better or worse, human rights qualify the notion of the rightful authority of the state: 'How a state treats its own citizens, and even what legal and constitutional arrangements it has, can thus no longer be regarded as a purely internal matter for the government concerned' (Beetham, 1998, pp. 61–2; also: Miller, 1994, chap. 7; Jacobson, 1996).

David Held, one of the foremost analysts of these developments, has claimed that 'globalization . . . raises an entirely novel set of political and normative dilemmas . . . namely, how to combine a system of territorially rooted democratic governance with the transnational and global organization of social and economic life' (Held *et al.*, 1999, p. 431). Held and his collaborators pinpoint the problem succinctly:

> National boundaries have traditionally demarcated the basis on which individuals are included and excluded from participation in decisions affecting their lives; but if many socio-economic processes, and the outcomes of decisions about them, stretch beyond national frontiers, then the implications of this are serious, not only for the categories of consent and legitimacy but for all the key ideas of democracy. At issue is the nature of a political community – how should the proper boundaries of a political community be drawn in a more regional and global order? In addition, questions can be raised about the meaning of representation (who should represent whom and on what basis?) and about the proper form and scope of political participation (who should participate and in what way?). As fundamental processes of governance escape the categories of the nation-state, the traditional national resolutions of the key questions of democratic theory and practice look increasingly threadbare. (Held *et al.*, 1999, 446–7)

According to Held, the challenge is to create and entrench democratic institutions at regional and global levels – complementing those at the nation-state level – which would enable the peoples of the world to express and deliberate upon their aims and objectives in a progressively more interconnected global order (Held, 1995a, chaps. 10–12; Held, 1996, pp. 353–60; Held, 1998, pp. 21–6; on 'global democracy' see also Falk, 1995; Linklater, 1996, 1998a, 1998b and 1999; Hutchings and Dannreuther, 1999; Höffe, 1999).

For Held, the concept of 'cosmopolitan democracy' refers to 'a model of political organization in which citizens, wherever they are located in the world, have a voice, input and political representation in international affairs, in parallel with and independently of their own governments' (Held, 1995b, p. 13). Held's model does not aim for a world government or a federal world state. He accepts that democracy must be institutionalized on many levels, ranging from the local/municipal to the subnational and national levels and through the regional level to the global level. Some of the institutional innovations are defined as long-term objectives, others as short-term objectives. The short-term objectives aim, for example, at the reform of the United Nations with a modification of the veto arrangement in the Security Council and a reconsideration of representation on it to allow for adequate regional accountability; the creation of regional parliaments (for example, in Latin America and Africa) as well as the enhancement of the role and power of such bodies where they already exist (as in the case of the EU); the creation of a new, international Human Rights Court; and the establishment of an effective, accountable military force. Within the UN context, Held proposes the establishment of an independent assembly of democratic peoples, directly elected by them and accountable to them, whose rule would have been agreed upon in an international constitutional convention involving states, IGOs, INGOs, citizen groups and social movements. This new assembly could become an authoritative centre for the examination of the most pressing global problems: 'health and disease, food supply and distribution, the debt burden of the "Third World", the instability of the hundreds of billions of dollars that circulate the globe daily, global warming, and the reduction of risks of nuclear and chemical warfare' (Held, 1995a, p. 274).

In this brief summary, I have only listed Held's short-term innovations which he considers to be necessary for moving towards democratic global governance. And although there are many more facets to Held's model of 'cosmopolitan democracy', it is nevertheless possible to indicate a few queries that will have to be addressed when this model is further developed. Held foresees that the new democratic political institutions would override states in clearly defined spheres of activity 'where those activities have demonstrable transnational and international consequences, require regional or global initiatives in the interests of effectiveness and depend on such initiatives for democratic legitimacy' (Held, 1998, p. 24). This is an exceedingly vague statement. In the 'age of globalization', which activities do *not* have demonstrable transnational and international consequences? Who, or which bodies, decide whether regional or global initiatives are warranted? Who enforces the appropriation of decision-making powers by regional or global bodies? As Held (1995a, p. 276) himself argues, states are reluctant to submit their disputes with other states to arbitration by a 'supreme authority': who then enforces the decisions taken by these bodies? How realistic is it to stipulate – as either a short-term or long-term objective – the formation of an 'effective' and 'accountable' international military force?

There is woefully little analysis of the 'prerequisites' of 'cosmopolitan democracy'. Philip Resnick (1998) has argued that prospects for global democracy are held back by uneven economic development, diverging political traditions, cultural and ethnic identities, and solidarities that are primarily local or national in character. To return to the theme of the connection between economic development and democracy, which I discussed in the previous chapter, issues of economic and social equality will have to be put back on to the agenda if we wish to create the conditions for global democracy. The extreme inequality of living conditions between North and South must be addressed. Resnick (1998, p. 131) is right to point out that 'the very parameters of global economic development further the concentration of wealth and power in the core countries'. International governmental organizations such as the International Monetary Fund, the World Bank or the World Trade Organization have played an important role in shaping national public policies and creating a political and legal institutional infrastructure for global capitalism. They have been very much under the control of the richest and most powerful countries and have been implicated in retaining structures of inequality. As René Dumont has observed:

> The growing gap between the rich and the poor countries is becoming more and more intolerable. If it continues unabated, we could by the middle of the next century have more than ten billion poor on our little planet, facing a billion rich. Such a situation would be politically untenable. (Quoted in Resnick, 1998, p. 132)

In this context, it is interesting to note that Held has increasingly downplayed the economic aspects in his model of 'cosmopolitan democracy'. In 1995 (1995a, pp. 279–80), Held listed under short-term objectives the 'foundation of a new co-ordinating economic agency at regional and global levels' and the 'introduction of strict limits to private ownership of key "public-shaping" institutions' such as the media. The long-term objectives included the 'establishment of the accountability of international and transnational economic agencies to parliaments and assemblies at regional and global levels' as well as a 'guaranteed basic income for all adults, irrespective of whether they are engaged in market or household activities'. If these objectives can be very broadly grouped under the heading of 'economic democracy and its prerequisites', no such objectives are listed in the summary table in Held's *Models of Democracy* (1996, pp. 358–9) nor in his recent chapter on 'Democracy and globalization' (1998, p. 25). In short, the connection between economic development and global democracy appears to be seriously undertheorized.

Furthermore, while a call for the establishment of regional parliaments appears to be unproblematic from within a democratic position, the European example shows that this is by no means the case (see Julie Smith's chapter on the European Parliament and democracy in this volume). First, political development in the past has shown that it is around the conflict and cleavage structure within the bounded territory of the nation state that intermediary institutions such as political parties, interest groups, voluntary associations, trade unions or the mass media have been organized. Citizens tend to avail themselves of the national intermediary institutions as the means of their political participation. To put it differently, the role of the citizen has been firmly institutionalized at the level of the nation state.

Even after 40 years of European integration, we still find that intermediary structures remain 'nationalized'. As yet, there is no European party system that would aggregate and articulate social and political interests on a Europe-wide level. So far, political parties are national actors that, at best, aim to translate interests of their *national* constituencies into the European political system. And while there has been an increase in lobbying by interest groups in Brussels since the Single European Act, it has been above all large business interests that have achieved a certain degree of Europeanization of their interests and begun to build up common transnational organizations. On the whole, the degree of 'Europeanization' of other than business interests has been low. Citizens still direct their interests, concerns and demands to their national, or subnational, government, not to 'Brussels'. This is part of the reason why a European public opinion has not yet formed. Under these circumstances, in which the intermediary structures necessary for interest and opinion formation as well as for the constitution of a genuine European 'public' are not in place, whom or what could a European Parliament possibly represent? Only if there is a genuine process of European-wide, transnational interest formation does it become necessary for reasons of democratic legitimacy to institute the European Parliament as that mechanism through which diverse interests have to be channelled, reconciled and acted upon.

Second, a key feature of parliamentary rule is policy making on the basis of decisions taken by a parliamentary majority. Yet the principle of majority rule does not suffice to generate legitimacy of the political system as a whole. The application of majority rule as a legitimating principle is premised on a sociopolitical and sociocultural context that is conducive to the defeated minority's acceptance of the majority decision. The existence of such a congenial context cannot be taken for granted. Democratic legitimacy as an effect of parliamentary majority rule has a number of preconditions (Scharpf, 1992). First, there must be no fundamental ethnic, linguistic, religious, ideological or economic cleavages in a society. Second, the political community must have developed a collective identity based on shared citizenship and political equality as well as shared normative orientations so that differences in specific policy areas will not be dramatized into fundamental differences over the institutional order of the political community. In national political systems it is the intermediary institutions that play a central part in the generation of a collective identity as well as in processing conflicts among interests and differences in cultural orientation in such a way that they can be integrated into the political system. It is the dynamics of the intermediary structure that hold open the promise for minorities possibly to turn their current minority position into a majority position at some point in the future. Neither of these two preconditions for the acceptance of parliamentary majority decisions as legitimate is as yet in place in Europe with its historical, cultural, linguistic, and political-institutional diversity and economic disparities. To expect that decisions by the European Parliament would meet with widespread acceptance under these circumstances would appear to be unwarranted, even foolhardy.

Third, there is, however, no denying the fact that its direct election has given the European Parliament a considerable degree of political legitimacy. The question is how best to build on this legitimacy under the condition of a lacking European intermediary structure. Any type of political union in Europe will bring together nation states that, for centuries, have had their own political, social and cultural histories and institutional order (Lepsius, 1992). The multinationality and multi-ethnicity of Europe are a fact that cannot be wished away. The post-Maastricht debates on the Union have shown that there is no widespread support for a European integration that would discard these histories, pry open these institutional orders and subdue them to transnational European organizations. The institutions of inter-governmentalism are the appropriate reflection of this reality. Indeed, the democratic legitimacy of European integration stems in large part from its intergovernmental decision-making process. After all, democratically elected and democratically accountable politicians determine European politics through negotiations in the Council of Ministers.

This creates two distinct sets of problems. First, there are two operative forms of legitimation to be found in the EU. The first type is mediated through the democratic structure of member states and underlies the institution of the Council of Ministers. The other form of legitimation is mediated through the European Parliament and its democratic mandate through direct elections by the citizens of the member states of the European Union. In a sense, the 'democratic deficit' can be reconceptualized, not as a lack of democracy, but as a concern, and debate, about how best to mediate these two forms of legitimacy. The second problem is inherent in the very logic of legitimacy on the basis of intergovernmentalism. For governments to be held accountable by their national parliaments for decisions taken in the Council, intergovernmental negotiations either have to be based on rules of unanimity or must provide for a right of veto for governments. Only on that basis can responsibility for policies be attributed to individual governments and can governments be held accountable by their parliament. The veto should be defended as a means, firstly, to protect the interests of the constituent national units within the European Union, thus, in effect, upholding 'minority rights' in a 'multinational' political community; and, secondly, to uphold parliamentary scrutiny over governments. From the point of view of democratic legitimacy and accountability, then, it can be argued that the principle of unanimity and the right of veto occupy a central place in the decision-making structure of the EU.

Finally, I have suggested above that governance in the EU is a mixture of intergovernmentalism, supranationalism and infranationalism. I further argued that this 'messy' structure of political regulation, co-ordination and decision making is likely to be further complicated by trends towards 'differentiated integration' within the European Union and a multiplicity of European IGOs outside the European Union. Why should we reasonably assume that the enhancement of the role and power of the European Parliament would allow citizens to exercise democratic control over the 'authoritative allocation of values' by the participants in these crosscutting and intersecting networks of power?

Taken together, these queries of some aspects of Held's model of 'cosmopolitan democracy' should not be understood as a critique of a normative commitment to 'democracy beyond the nation state' (see, however, Miller, 1995 and 1999 and Zolo, 1997 for a critique along those lines, and also the debate in Hutchings and Dannreuther, 1999; see also Hirst's critical comments on 'cosmopolitan democracy' in this volume). Rather they are an invitation to continue the equally important task of specifying the political, economic and cultural preconditions for democratization at the global level. Yet, Benjamin Barber reminds us in his contribution that there is an urgent need to enhance the opportunities for political participation and citizen engagement 'on the local level'. Arguably, such a 'strong democracy' is the prerequisite for a 'global democracy' whose institutions and procedures are not hijacked by the 'usual' elites.

FURTHER READING

Manuel Castell's masterful study on *The Information Age*, which has been published in three volumes in 1996, 1997 and 1998, is a good starting point for understanding the changes in the political, social and economic world as it is developing as we enter the new millennium. David Held and his collaborators also chart *Global Transformations* (1999) in politics, economics and culture, complementing Castell's analysis from within a particular perspective on 'globalization'. In *Along the Domestic-Foreign Frontier: Exploring Governance in a Turbulent World*, James Rosenau (1997) analyses from the vantage point of an analyst of international relations the enormous changes which are transforming world affairs. How these changes impact on our understanding of democracy and democratic institutions is discussed in David Held's book on *Democracy and the Global Order: From the Modern State to Cosmopolitan Governance* (1995) and in Roland Axtmann's *Liberal Democracy into the Twenty-first Century* (1996). The effects of multiculturalism on liberal democracy are discussed by Will Kymlicka in *Multicultural Citizenship* (1995). Bhikhu Parekh's *Rethinking Multiculturalism* is a brilliant discussion of cultural diversity and political theory. Christopher Lord succinctly discusses *Democracy in the European Union* (1998) and J.H.H. Weiler's *The Constitution of Europe* (1999) provides a sophisticated argument on democracy in the EU from the perspective of comparative law.

BIBLIOGRAPHY

Armstrong, Kenneth and Bulmer, Simon J. (1998) *The Governance of the Single European Market*. Manchester: Manchester University Press.

Axtmann, Roland (1996) *Liberal Democracy into the Twenty-first Century: Globalization, Integration and the Nation-State*. Manchester: Manchester University Press.

Axtmann, Roland (ed.) (1998) *Globalization and Europe: Theoretical and Empirical Investigations*. London: Pinter.

Axtmann, Roland and Grant, Robert (2000) Living in a Global World: Globalisation and the Future of Politics. In T.C. Salmon (ed.), *Issues in International Relations*. London: Routledge, pp. 25–54.

Beck, Ulrich (1992) *Risk Society: Towards a New Modernity*. London: Sage.

Beck, Ulrich (1994) The Reinvention of Politics: Towards a Theory of Reflexive Modernization. In U. Beck, A. Giddens and S. Lash (eds), *Reflexive Modernization: Tradition and Aesthetics in the Modern Social Order*. Cambridge: Polity Press, pp. 1–55.

Beetham, David (1984) The Future of the Nation-State. In G. McLennan, D. Held and S. Hall (eds), *The Idea of the Modern State*. Milton Keynes: Open University Press, pp. 208–22.

Beetham, David (1998) Human Rights as a Model for Cosmopolitan Democracy. In D. Archibugi, D. Held and M. Köhler (eds), *Re-imagining Political Community: Studies in Cosmopolitan Democracy*. Cambridge: Polity Press, pp. 58–71.

Caporaso, James A. (1996) The European Union and Forms of States: Westphalian, Regulatory or Post-modern? *Journal of Common Market Studies* 34, 29–52.

Castells, Manuel (1996, 1997, 1998) *The Information Age: Economy, Society and Culture. Volume 1: The Rise of the Network Society* (1996); *Volume 2: The Power of Identity* (1997); *Volume 3: End of Millennium* (1998). Oxford: Blackwell.

Cerny, Philip (1993) Plurilateralism: Structural Differentiation and Functional Conflict in the Post-Cold War World Order, *Millennium* 22, 27–51.

Cohen, Robin (1997) *Global Diasporas: An Introduction*. London: UCL Press.

Commission on Global Governance (1995) *Our Global Neighbourhood*. Oxford: Oxford University Press.

Dahl, Robert A. (1998) *On Democracy*. New Haven and London: Yale University Press.

Falk, Richard (1995) *On Humane Governance: Toward a New Global Politics*. Cambridge: Polity Press.

Gordenker, Leon and Weiss, Thomas G. (1995) Pluralising Global Governance: Analytical Approaches and Dimensions, *Third World Quarterly* 16, 357–87.

Held, David (1995a) *Democracy and the Global Order*. Cambridge: Cambridge University Press.

Held, David (1995b) Introduction. In D. Archibugi and D. Held (eds), *Cosmopolitan Democracy*. Cambridge: Polity Press.

Held, David (1996) *Models of Democracy*. Cambridge: Polity Press (second edition).

Held, David (1998) Democracy and Globalization. In D. Archibugi, D. Held and M. Köhler (eds), *Re-imagining Political Community: Studies in Cosmopolitan Democracy* Cambridge: Polity Press, pp. 11–27.

Held, David, Grew, Anthony, Goldblatt, David and Perraton, Jonathan (1999) *Global Transformations: Politics, Economics and Culture*. Cambridge: Polity Press.

Hirst, Paul and Thompson, Grahame (1996) *Globalization in Question*. Cambridge: Polity Press.

Hix, Simon (1998) The Study of the European Union: The 'New Governance' Agenda and Its Rivals, *Journal of European Public Policy* 5, 38–65.

Höffe, Otfried (1999) *Demokratie im Zeitalter der Globalisierung*. Munich: Beck Verlag.

Horsman, Mathew and Marshall, Andrew (1994) *After the Nation-State: Citizens, Tribalism and the New World Disorder*. London: HarperCollins.

Hutchings, Kimberly and Dannreuther, Roland (eds) (1999) *Cosmopolitan Citizenship*. Basingstoke: Macmillan.

Jacobson, David (1996) *Rights across Borders: Immigration and the Decline of Citizenship*. Baltimore and London: Johns Hopkins University Press.

Knoke, David (1990) Networks of Political Action: Towards Theory Construction, *Social Forces* 68, 1041–63.

Knoke, David *et al.* (1996) *Comparing Policy Networks: Labour Politics in the US, Germany, and Japan*. Cambridge: Cambridge University Press.

Kymlicka, Will (1995) *Multicultural Citizenship: A Liberal Theory of Minority Rights*. Oxford: Clarendon Press.

Lash, Scott and Urry, John (1994) *Economies of Signs and Spaces*. London: Sage.

Lepsius, M. Rainer (1992) Beyond the Nation-State: The Multinational State as the Model for the European Community, *Telos* 91, 57–76.

Lijphart, Arend (1977) *Democracy in Plural Societies: A Comparative Exploration*. New Haven and London: Yale University Press.

Linklater, Andrew (1996) Citizenship and Sovereignty in the Post-Westphalian State, *European Journal of International Relations* 2, 77–103.

Linklater, Andrew (1998a) Cosmopolitan Citizenship, *Citizenship Studies* 2, 23–41.

Linklater, Andrew (1998b) *The Transformation of Political Community*. Cambridge: Polity Press.

Linklater, Andrew (1999) The Evolving Spheres of International Justice, *International Affairs* 75, 473–82.

Lord, Christopher (1998) *Democracy in the European Union*. Sheffield: Sheffield University Press.

Luke, Tim W. (1993) Discourses of Disintegration, Texts of Transformations: Re-reading Realism in the New World Order, *Alternatives* 18, 229–58.

Marin, Bernd and Mayntz, Renate (eds) (1996) *Policy Networks: Empirical Evidence and Theoretical Considerations*. Frankfurt am Main: Campus.

Marks, Gary, Hoogte, Liesbet and Blank, Kermit (1996) European Integration from the 1980s: State-centric v. Multi-level Governance, *Journal of Common Market Studies* 34, 341–78.

Miller, David (1995) *On Nationality*. Oxford: Oxford University Press.

Miller, David (1999) Bounded Citizenship. In K. Hutchings and R. Dannreuther (eds), *Cosmopolitan Citizenship*. London: Macmillan, pp. 60–80.

Miller, Lynn H. (1994) *Global Order: Values and Power in International Politics*. Boulder: Westview Press (third edition).

Parekh, Bhiku (1994) Minority Rights, Majority Values. In D. Milliband (ed.), *Reinventing the Left*. Cambridge: Polity Press, pp. 101–9.

Parekh, Bhikhu (2000) *Rethinking Multiculturalism: Cultural Diversity and Political Theory*. Basingstoke: Macmillan.

Resnick, Philip (1998) Global Democracy: Ideals and Reality. In R. Axtmann (ed.), *Globalization and Europe*. London: Pinter, pp. 126–43.

Rex, John (1998) Transnational Migrant Communities and the Modern Nation State. In R. Axtmann (ed.), *Globalization and Europe*. London: Pinter, pp. 59–76.

Rhodes, R.A.W. (1996) The New Governance: Governing Without Government, *Political Studies* 44, 652–67.

Rosenau, James N. (1997) *Along the Domestic-Foreign Frontier: Exploring Governance in a Turbulent World*. Cambridge: Cambridge University Press.

Ross, George (1998) European Integration and Globalization. In R. Axtmann (ed.), *Globalization and Europe*. London: Pinter, pp. 164–83.

Sassen, Saskia (1996) *Losing Control? Sovereignty in an Age of Globalization*. New York: Columbia University Press.

Scharpf, Fritz (1991) Die Handlungsfähigkeit des modernen Staates am Ende des zwanzigsten Jahrhunderts, *Politische Vierteljahresschrift* 32, 621–34.

Scharpf, Fritz (1992) Europäisches Demokratiedefizit und deutscher Föderalismus, *Staatswissenschaften und Staatspraxis* 3, 293–306.

Scharpf, Fritz (1998) *Governing in Europe: Effective and Democratic?* Oxford: Oxford University Press.

Schmitter, Philipe C. (1992) Representation and the Future of the Euro-polity, *Staatswissenschaften und Staatspraxis* 3, 379–405.

Walker, Neil (1998) Sovereignty and Differentiated Integration in the European Union, *European Law Journal* 4, 355–88.

Weiler, J.H.H. (1999) *The Constitution of Europe*. Cambridge: Cambridge University Press.

Wiener, Jarrod (1999) *Globalization and the Harmonization of Law*. London and New York: Pinter.

Willke, Helmut (1992) *Ironie des Staates: Grundlinien einer Staatstheorie polyzentrischer Gesellschaft*. Frankfurt aM: Suhrkamp.

Zolo, Danilo (1997) *Cosmopolis: Prospects for World Government*. Cambridge: Polity Press.

CHAPTER 3

NATIONALISM, TERRITORIALITY AND DEMOCRACY

Derek Urwin

Debates about the meaning of democracy and what it entails have been legion. However, if there is a prevalent popular conception about the essence of democracy, it is – at the risk of some gross oversimplification – that it is something that cleaves to two basic principles. It is believed, first, to be rooted in the individual, relating to an absolute equity across individuals in terms of an array of rights, freedoms and liberties to which each is inherently entitled. From this perspective arises the second element of popular perception – that those who govern are selected by and are ultimately responsible to those whom they seek to govern.

This generalization, crude as it may be, may nevertheless suffice as a starting point for a survey of the territorial context within which both democracy and the individual exist. It is merely a truism to state that no one resides, as it were, in splendid isolation, monarch of all that is surveyed. Whatever else it may be, democracy is essentially a socio-territorial concept: without that context, rights and freedoms become meaningless. The emergence and establishment of democracy as a principle of political organization is, historically, inextricably related to the two dominant elements of territorial organization, those of state and nation.

STATE AND NATION AS CONTEXT

The establishment of the state as the foundation of international order is conventionally held to be a consequence of the Treaties of Westphalia in 1648. They helped foster 'a world view in which discrete, quasi-independent territorial units were seen as the primary building blocks for social and political life' (Murphy, 1996, p. 82). Two central principles characterized the evolving state system. They were, first, that a state had rigid geographical boundaries that defined the territorial reach of its legal and political authority; and second, that within these territorial confines the state and its government enjoyed sovereignty, an exclusive right to rule over all who lived within them. From at least the nineteenth century, control by a state over its territory intensified with the development of more effective infrastructures and mechanisms in law and administration. These processes were aided by a concomitant economic transformation that integrated local economies into a more readily recognizable state-wide system of production, distribution and exchange.

The territorial consolidation of the state was boosted further by the concurrent force of nationalism, which, in the wake of the American and French Revolutions, stimulated the merging together of a political nationalism with traditional and local ethnocultural identities into a broader sense of societal community. The idea of nation could buttress the territoriality and sovereignty of the state because it provided a powerful reason why rule by the state should be accepted by those it controlled. The state could be cast, as it were, as the epitome of the nation. During the nineteenth century, the distinction between the twin concepts of state and nation became increasingly blurred, eventually to marry in the concept of the culturally homogenized nation state. Not only, however, did state and nation to all intents and purposes become synonymous; the nation-state idea, based upon legitimacy, consensus and a bond of identity between individual and state defined in terms of citizenship, became widely accepted as the norm for and ultimate objective of territorial organization. It subsequently provided, in the twentieth century, a basis for demands for the collective right of putative nations to self-determination, to acquire a state of their own.

The accelerating processes of state consolidation and nation building provided a territorial referent for democratization. The notion of popular sovereignty paralleled that of state sovereignty, to the extent that democracy became 'the democracy of the nation-state' and its emergence 'associated with the development of the nation-state' (Huntington, 1991, p. 13). In essence, therefore, there seems to have been a widespread consensus on a symmetry between the nation state and the democratic community. At the extreme, a nation could be defined as being nothing more than 'an association of citizens' (Schwarzmantel, 1991, p. 207). Furthermore, this was an assumption that was embraced by almost all regimes, democratic or otherwise, which came to regard themselves as guardians of the nation-state ideal, the collectivity of which was a common and natural allegiance defined politically by the binding force of citizenship.

However, while differences of opinion over the meaning of nation are as numerous as those over democracy, one thing can be stated with some certainty. It is that nation, and the identity associated with it, cannot be defined solely, or even primarily, in terms of citizenship. This is not the place to venture into the complexities of what constitutes nationalism and its relationship to ethnicity. It may perhaps be sufficient to accept that all definitions, at the least, tend to concur on the centrality of an ascriptive identity embedded in a range of recognizable sociocultural stigmata, including shared symbols, myths and values. The resultant cultural and psychological sense of shared community is further reinforced by geographical attachments, for 'those who share a place share an identity' (Mackenzie, 1976, p. 130).

Nielsen (1985) has proposed that a nation state may be defined as a political entity where all members of a particular ethnocultural group are to be found in only one state where, furthermore, the group comprises the overwhelming bulk of the population. Applying this definition to the contemporary world, he identified a global total of only 31 nation states. Irrespective therefore of how national identity or other stigmata of ethnocultural diversity are defined, it would seem to be the case that 'real' nation states are the exception rather than the rule. Almost all states have been multicultural or multinational in the sense that they have contained within them more than one identity with both group and territory. It follows that there can be, within states, variable perceptions of the state held by groups possessing both a strong collective awareness that culturally they are fundamentally different from the other citizens of the state, and a powerful emotive attachment to a specific territory within the state.

By itself, such ethnocultural diversity need not constitute a problem for either democracy or the state. When, however, it becomes politicized – leading almost inevitably to demands for special treatment precisely because of cultural diversity and specific territorial location – it can become a severe dilemma for both. Until the latter half of the twentieth century, it was more conventional to accept that such a scenario was highly unlikely, if not implausible, since the universal egalitarianism inherent in democratization was believed to iron out these differences, absorbing ethnonational distinctiveness in the wider culture of a state-wide democratic and national community. At the extreme was the so-called French model of democratic citizenship where, it has been held, 'cultural assimilation is the price that must be paid . . . for integration into the political community' (Mitchell and Russell, 1996, p. 67). However, as Nielsen and others have pointed out, such cultural assimilation has rarely been total. In recent decades discontent among indigenous ethnonational minorities, generated by fears of cultural assimilation and discrimination and directed against the state, has become a visible political feature of contemporary democracies.

It follows from what has been said that there is a potential conflict between democratization and ethnocultural diversity. The former, in the phrases used by Taylor (1992), demands 'the politics of universalism', while the latter raises the spectre of 'the politics of difference'. More recent developments have heightened the potential impact of that disjunction, contributing to the rise or regeneration of minority ethnonationalism. Contemporary democracies have become more centralized. More extensive regulatory frameworks and the standardizing implications of the welfare state have contributed to a perception among such minorities of a more remote, more bureaucratic and more depersonalized state. Equally, political organizations have also followed the centralizing trend, becoming more state-oriented, more elitist and more dominated by a new breed of professional politicians. In seeking to spread their message, politicians prefer the television studio to the hustings. The advent and rapid spread of mass electronic communication has therefore provided political leaderships with a means of appealing directly and instantaneously to a state-wide and, as it were, almost undifferentiated electorate on a kind of face-to-face basis. In mid-nineteenth-century Britain it could be said that general elections had not yet become general (Hanham, 1959). By the late twentieth century, elections were becoming national rather than general, almost blandly homogenized with a strong quasi-plebiscitary quality. It is possible to see how in this process ethnonational minority groups might acquire a feeling of marginalization. A heightened perception that they were no longer able to live separate but parallel lives with some ability to have control over their own destiny was buttressed by feelings of being disadvantaged in some way vis-à-vis the remainder of the state's population.

Where such feelings of marginalization take root, one consequence has been the emergence of organizations seeking to mobilize ethnonational discontent politically and to argue for redress of the perceived grievances and inequalities. Such assertions of the politics of difference raise a unique challenge to state authority. They pose a potential threat to the territorial legitimacy and integrity of the state, since any manifestation of indigenous ethnonational politics invariably demands some kind of change or adjustment to the structure and nature of territorial management.

ETHNONATIONAL CONCERNS AND DESIRES

To a considerable extent, therefore, contemporary minority ethnonationalism is the outcome of a conjunction between, on the one hand, feelings of unease and dissatisfaction with the more centralist modern democratic state and, on the other, the continued presence of distinctive cultural and psychological loyalties, folk memories and footprints. In turn, the latter are inextricably related to a communal attachment to place, to the particular territory in which lives are lived, interests defined, and information received and interpreted. The basic issue facing ethnonational minorities in democratic states relates to the need to balance political rights and concerns about political participation with economic and cultural rights and concerns about the distribution of resources. In other words, the problem is, in one sense, not unique: it comes back to the nature of citizenship. However, from another angle, it is unique. The collectiveness of the community and its territorial connections enter into the equation to confuse the straightforward egalitarian individualism of democracy.

We can perhaps say that in a state that contains more than one ethnonational group, each with a distinctive sense of identity that has become politicized, there are two broad kinds of citizens' rights. The individual right to be able to develop and utilize fully one's own abilities and talents irrespective of cultural background or heritage exists per-force alongside the collective right of the ethnonational community to respect for its cultural heritage and customs. The latter right lies at the core of identity, and is the factor that, in modern times, has been placed at risk by centralizing trends. The resurgence of political ethnonationalism in contemporary democracies is a consequence of a heightened concern that the ability of individuals to live according to their abilities within their own territories and cultural communities has been significantly diminished. Arguments have been put more forcibly that limitations on individual options, real or perceived, have nevertheless obliged members of minority communities to sacrifice their culture for their career, or vice versa. What political ethnonationalism has demanded of the democratic state is the simultaneous right to both individual options and cultural roots.

While the rhetoric of some ethnonational political movements has targeted independence as the long-term or ultimate goal – the achievement of nation-state status – none has demonstrably received the backing of the overwhelming bulk of its perceived clientele. More typically, the latter have tended towards displaying and responding to a more generalized unease over the cultural and territorial status quo. Perhaps partly because of this more diffuse atmosphere, ethnonationalism in contemporary democracies, unlike its predecessors, has by and large demonstrated in practice a willingness to settle for adjustments to that status quo; it has not necessarily called into question the integrity of the state within the context of an all-or-nothing contest. In essence, the dominant theme has been a search for access to, or a redistribution of, power as a solution to real or perceived grievances that adversely affect the collective roots of the community or the options available to individuals within it.

Broadly speaking, the political demands made of the state have consisted of three elements. There may, first, be demands for redressing
what are seen in the minority community as inequalities in citizenship.
These demands may range from the restitution of formal equality to
rectify real or imagined disparities to, more typically, demands for some
kind of positive discrimination in terms of rights or policies that incorporate special treatment of the ethnonational group and/or the territory
that it calls home. There may also, second, be demands for cultural rights.
These can range from concessions of a purely symbolic nature linked to,
for example, language use or the public display and deployment of
various defining cultural stigmata, to the right to employ the latter in
public life and contexts anywhere within the state. Finally, and most
importantly for democracy and the state, there may be demands for an
institutional and political recognition of the collectivity of the community through a restructuring of the style and organization of territorial
management. Restructuring may be restricted to the community and its
territory, through, for example, the granting of some form of autonomy
or devolution. Alternatively, the state may seek to accommodate the
community's demands within a broader federalization of the national
territory. Either way, institutional change pushes positive discrimination
to a higher level of distinctiveness.

In short, ethnonational politics places demands upon states and governments on behalf of cultural communities and geographic territories
that tend not to be congruent with national populations or state boundaries. The politics of difference, not of universalism, is their prime
concern. Whatever the specific content of the demands, the essence of the
case is invariably that the community and the territory are held to merit
a special status or treatment different from and more beneficial than that
available to other areas of the state or elements of its population. The
territorial dimension of the demands carries further implications for
individual rights, since if the demands are conceded, the consequence
will entail adjustments to the way in which a state manages its territory.
Demands made on behalf of an ethnonational minority, as in Quebec or
Scotland, invariably require it to take control over its perceived territorial
home, a kind of promised land, and hence, more significantly, over all
who live there irrespective of political opinions, cultural identity, or
wishes. In this way, an ethnonational challenge merely underlines a
potential dissonance between the maintenance of state integrity, democratic equality, and full political legitimacy.

Any such challenge can therefore pose rather unique problems for
democratic governments which, as Laponce (1960, p. 43) pointed out
some time ago, 'have a natural tendency to integrate the societies they

govern'. In previous phases of the development of the democratic state, governmental responses tended to be based, even if rather inchoately, on the assumption that ethnonational unhappiness was a dying vestige of a bygone era, increasingly irrelevant in a nation state based upon an egalitarian citizenship. At best, therefore, ethnonational concerns could safely be ignored or tolerated as perhaps amusing and antiquated curiosities. Where their nuisance value increased in volume to a point where it might be seen as being potentially harmful to the integrating drive of the nation state, centralizing policies specifically intended to hasten the demise of ethnonational distinctiveness (for example, in education) could always be, and sometimes were, adopted.

A stance of indifference ultimately proved unsustainable in the second half of the twentieth century, which witnessed the growth and consolidation of more questioning and assertive electorates. Within this context, there appeared a new and more extensive wave of ethnonational concern and challenges to the centralizing nature of democratic politics. From Canada to Italy, from the United Kingdom to Spain, elites in long-established states were forced to confront the nation-state myth and reconsider their traditions and styles of territorial management. In pondering how to address such concerns, central elites have available to them a whole gamut of responses, ranging in extent from total acquiescence (implying a possible dismemberment of the state) to total resistance. The former has never been seriously or willingly considered in any modern democracy. The latter pole, by contrast, has had its attractions and admirers, and can be considered to be the first of three broad strategic options available to central governments.

THE CONTAINMENT OPTION

In that option, which can be loosely described as a strategy of containment and control, democratic elites seek to ensure the continued integrity of both state and society by eliminating or neutralizing the ethnonational challenge. Such an outcome may be achieved by one of two means. First, governments could attempt to ignore the problem, arguing for instance that the ethnonational community is already a full and equal partner in a democratic society and that therefore no further action is necessary or desirable. Alternatively, democratic governments can attempt to act more coercively. They can strive to centralize policy direction further, with the objective of speeding up the assimilation of minorities into the cultural mainstream. Or they may recognize that the cultural differences are not only real but also insurmountable. Where governments are persuaded of total incongruity, they may decide to offend the nation-state principle by constructing and maintaining a kind of ethnonational segregation or apartheid as the best means of sustaining societal integrity and stability. A government that went down that route could still perhaps argue that the solution has not offended the principles of democratic egalitarianism: the cultural communities would still be equal, even if separate.

While the containment option has certainly not been alien to the democratic experience, it has in more recent times been expressed prominently only in a few policy areas, most notably perhaps that of language planning and rights. However, to be successful, a control option must presuppose a relatively unsophisticated political system and a society that, *de facto*, is fundamentally structured along such vertical and geographical lines that, moreover, would tend to be highly impermeable. By contrast, modern democracies are more likely to be highly complex and complicated animals, where political agendas are multifaceted and pluralistic. At best, ethnonational concerns have to jostle for attention on that agenda in the face of intense competition from a host of other interests. In any case, modern democracies, in an information-rich and media-dominant environment, are too open and too pluralistic for elites to be able to develop or sustain this kind of directive repression or containment for any length of time. The more probable reaction to a policy of control, in fact, is an intensified resentment and backlash among the affected ethnonational community. The more British and Spanish governments, for example, sought to 'control' politics in Northern Ireland and the Basque country respectively, the more their efforts seemed to meet with open hostility. In short, the community has to be treated reasonably and not excluded from influence by openly discriminatory policies. This is perhaps best summed up in a study of Northern Ireland which concluded that 'majoritarian democracy only works well when key conditions are present: when the exclusion of the minority is temporary, and when the issues dividing the majority from the minority are not fundamental' (McGarry and O'Leary, 1990, p. 269).

The essential point here is that, because of its distinctive cultural and geographical overtones, politicized ethnonationalism tends always to be fundamental. The politics of identity and of difference can easily generate zero-sum competition, making it extremely difficult, at best, for governments to opt for containment and control even as a temporary expedient. The adoption of containment might appear to be superficially attractive as a device enabling the survival of territorial integrity, but it might carry the cost of a loss of full political legitimacy. Whether governments can then afford to ignore the negative impact in terms of democratic principles and practices is a risk that can, of course, be taken, but in practice governments in modern pluralist democracies have been obliged to accept the obverse. Policies of control directed against ethnonational political mobilization and organization, and which are both sufficiently rigorous and cost effective, can rarely be implemented successfully, simply because democratic structures and practices militate against any simultaneous attempt to preclude the associated ethnonational communities from any possibility of participating in and seeking a share of political influence and power.

Containment and control of ethnonational communities is not, therefore, a strategy that has a great deal of democratic appeal – only perhaps as a holding device or strategy of last resort. Democratic elites and governments have sought rather to go down the route of accommodation and compromise. How far down the road they are willing to go will vary from one context to another. On occasions government responses can be *ad hoc* in nature, merely seeking to address a highly specific complaint without acknowledging the existence of the broader context of general principles of ethnonational rights, roots and options. Traditionally, such *ad hoc* responses characterized British responses to complaints from the Celtic fringe. For example, Welsh linguistic and cultural demands were often met in specific areas (such as bilingual road signs) without any central admission of the general issue of distinctiveness within equity that lay behind the demands. It would, however, make some sense to focus more upon how democratic responses have sought to develop, and have reflected, a more systematic approach to ethnonational concerns.

REDISTRIBUTION AS AN OPTION

By the mid-twentieth century, as a consequence of disparities thrown up by continuing economic transformation, the impact of social democratic ideas, the economic crises of the inter-war years, and two world wars, the democratic principle of equality had expanded beyond political rights to incorporate socioeconomic rights. Democracies became welfare states. Within the welfare-state concept, the principle of redistribution became perhaps the major motor force seeking to ensure socioeconomic rights. The politics of redistribution were almost always discussed and evaluated in economic and monetary terms. When ethnonational concerns began more vigorously to press for inclusion on democratic political agendas, governments were easily persuaded, in wishing to respond positively to these concerns, that they could do so within the welfare-state context. The principle of redistribution was extended from the level of individuals and social classes to incorporate cultural communities and

culturally distinctive regions. One prominent feature of the late twentieth century was government efforts to 'buy' ethnonational peace
through the utilization of public largesse, using money to provide public
goods and benefits for cultural and territorial, as well as economic,
purposes.

The most typical format adopted can be summarized by the phrase
'regional economic policy'. By eschewing any public recognition of
words and phrases that could be obviously linked to issues of identity,
governments were stressing the pre-eminence of central authority and
the territorial integrity of the state. In practice, however, democratic
governments went down the regional economic policy route only when
they could be persuaded that such a strategy would be of considerable
benefit to the state economy as a whole. At the extreme, the new regional
units established in France in recent decades were specifically charged
with implementing a national economic modernization plan; the allay-
ment of regional concerns was not to be their business. The central thrust
of regional economic policy, perhaps even of distributive strategies as a
whole, tended to be national economic growth and development rather
than mollifying ethnonational discontent through decentralized politics.

If for no other reason, a strategy of regional redistribution therefore
proved impossible to sustain as a panacea for the alleviation or removal
of ethnonational unhappiness. But other facets of redistribution also
contributed to the same conclusion. All policies have an impact on all
regions; the nature of that impact is heavily influenced by the interaction
between a policy and the varying territorial contexts on the ground. That
makes it extremely difficult to distinguish what is specifically regional
about a regional policy. Furthermore, whereas a regional economic
policy might at one level be about the territorial redistribution of resources and benefits, at another it tends to represent and contribute towards
further centralization: it invariably involves an increase in bureaucratic
decision making at the expense of the existing democratic structures of
territorial representation. Policies of regional redistribution, in fact, run
the risk of generating the same negative consequences as policies of
containment, stoking further the fires of ethnonational indignation or
even providing conditions for its emergence in situations where political
discontent had previously been non-existent or dormant. Ethnonational
communities that had held that they were disadvantaged could see their
belief in territorial injustices being confirmed, whereas those that had
hitherto enjoyed economic advantages could be persuaded that resources and benefits generated within their own community and territory
could be diverted elsewhere by the state.

Above all, however, it is fallacious to believe that a liberal use of money and redistribution is a solution for all ethnonational complaints. In this, as in many other aspects of life, the cliché that money cannot buy everything has some validity. In the 1960s Belgian governments spent huge sums of money on policies intended to resolve the growing chasm between the linguistic communities of Flanders and Wallonia, but ultimately with no success. Economic concerns have never constituted the totality of ethnonational agitation, nor perhaps have they ever lain at the core of that agitation. Ultimately, economic complaints are a consequence of a much broader perception of cultural and territorial injustices contained within the existing state structures and policies. That broader conception demands, if democratic governments are serious in a willingness to be seen to be addressing issues arising out of the politics of difference, a political response. Sooner or later, therefore, contemporary democratic governments have been obliged to consider a political response, to move away from containment and/or redistribution towards evaluating the possibility and desirability of adopting strategies and measures that, in effect, amount to a form of positive discrimination in favour of specific ethnonational communities.

POSITIVE DISCRIMINATION AS AN OPTION

By and large, democratic governments have, at the end of the twentieth century, conceded the legitimacy of at least some aspects of ethnonational claims, and have sought to develop a political response that accepts that some communities and territories are different, and that therefore they merit special treatment. The net outcome has been the abandonment in practice, if not in theory, of the integrated and 'egalitarian' nation state. In recent decades the record of political forays by democracies into the restructuring of territorial management as a means of maintaining the imperatives of the state whilst simultaneously attempting to address the politics of difference is both extensive and informative. The particular formula adopted varies considerably in its details from state to state – even on occasions within an individual state – but we can identify two broad channels of action that are available to governments.

Whatever the policy details, accommodation of the politics of difference will oblige governments to consider either territorial or community concessions, or possibly some combination of the two. Territorial accommodation essentially involves a grant of power being ceded to one or more geographical regions – that is, some form of devolution. The degree of concession may range from the minimal to the ultimate step of full-scale and constitutional federalization. The latter route was the one

followed by Belgium between 1958 and 1994. Community accommodation, by contrast, only indirectly involves geographical devolution (even
though, in practice, the latter is almost always part of the outcome). It
might be more appropriate to define the community option as a kind of
consociational approach that applies some form of proportionality to
how access to power, decision making and other kinds of public goods is
distributed among distinctive or conflicting ethnonational groups. The
'proportional package' (*Proporzpaket*) of 1969/1972 introduced by Italy in
the Alto Adige (South Tyrol) as a structure to meet the complaints of the
region's warring German and Italian communities has often been offered
as the prototypic community approach. Furthermore, whether governments opt for a territorial or community strategy, the experience of
modern democracies suggests that they may also have to consider
whether to introduce a standard formula applicable to all communities
across the whole of the state's territory, or to offer special, and hence
preferential, treatment to only some communities or some regions. If the
latter is chosen, the prevailing structures and styles of democratic territorial management in the remainder of the state can be left untouched.

The decision by a democracy to go down either the territorial or
community route is influenced and circumscribed by a multitude of
factors. In any one situation the most important inhibiting conditions
include the historic relationship between the ethnonational community
and the centralizing processes of state building, the geographical environment of both the state and the community, and both the specific
institutional structure of the state itself and its traditions and conceptions
of how territory ought to be managed.

We do not have the space to offer any detailed review of exactly how
governments in different democracies have responded in terms of the
restraints within which they have to operate. We can note, however, that
the federal structure of Switzerland allowed for the resolution of the Jura
dispute by the creation of a new canton of the Jura. Equally, the country's
federalism permitted Canadian governments more flexibility in dealing
with the claims of Quebec nationalism. By contrast, the transition of
Belgium from a unitary to a federal state incorporated elements of a
community strategy, something deemed necessary to cope with the
bilingual nature of Brussels. Ultimately, the political (and territorial)
federalism of Flanders, Wallonia and Brussels was paralleled by a
cultural federalism based upon linguistic communities. Like Belgium,
the United Kingdom and Spain have had to face ethnonational pressures
on more than one front. Unlike Belgium, they eschewed a more systematic approach for one that allowed for differential strategies for different
regions and communities. After the failure to achieve Home Rule all

round in the 1880s, all British governments have accepted different solutions and options for Wales, Scotland and (Northern) Ireland, while with the constitution of 1978 Spain granted more autonomy to the Basque provinces and Catalonia than to other regions, including the equally distinctive but politically quiescent ethnonational region of Galicia.

Without pursuing the above cases in any more detail, we can nevertheless offer a broad summation of the recent democratic experience of accommodation in terms of two broad conclusions. First, even extensive concessions or the presence of existing frameworks, such as a federal structure, within which accommodation may more easily be achieved do not necessarily lead to the elimination of the politics of difference as an issue. In Belgium and Canada, ethnonational politics and demands have not disappeared because of the creation or extension of federalization. Second, territorial strategies appear to have been the alternative more readily favoured by governments. This latter conclusion ought not to be surprising. Because ethnonationalism almost invariably posits a symbiosis between community and region, and because political claims lodged before the state are usually premised on the existence of such a symbiosis, a territorial response intuitively tends to be seen as the more logical.

There are, however, several issues that need to be addressed if democratic governments decide to pursue the territorial option. Two are particularly important. The first is that any concessions to ethnonational aspirations, no matter how minimal or cosmetic they may seem or are intended to be, may have an exactly opposite effect. A concession may introduce a ratchet effect into the equation, raising community expectations to an even higher level. What may be worse is that concessions may have the consequence of creating expectations where none previously existed. Where territorial devolution goes as far as the establishment of regional institutional structures of representation with some decision-making powers, one adverse effect that can emerge – and has done so, for example, in Quebec, Flanders and Scotland – is that the state has merely created a new and highly visible stage upon which ethnonational politics can consolidate the politics of difference, advance its arguments more publicly, and hence demand further concessions for community and region. Opponents of territorial devolution have rightly identified the risk of its being not a solution to the politics of difference, but primarily the thin end of the wedge.

The second important problem with a territorial strategy is that it cannot be straightforwardly applicable in all situations where the issues and grievances of the politics of identity have been acknowledged by governments and elites. The reason why territorial devolution will not always result in the intended outcome – an outcome that has been described as ethnoregional federalism – where the politics of difference, if not nullified, have been accommodated and removed from the national political arena, again relates to context. Underlying any territorial strategy or option is a confirmation by democratic governments of the ethnonational assumption of congruence between community and territory. Empirical analyses clearly demonstrate that such congruence does not exist everywhere. Where it is lacking, the likelihood of a territorial strategy being rewarded with success can be greatly diminished. In any form of territorial accommodation the grant of devolved authority and autonomy is always geographical: it is to a territory and the totality of the population therein rather than explicitly to an ethnonational group.

A territorial option is therefore much less appropriate in those situations where such congruence is limited or non-existent, for instance where there is but a single territory that is nevertheless inhabited by and claimed as its own by more than one ethnonational community. The instances where this pattern of population and politics exists have constituted the most awkward problems that democratic governments have been called upon to face when they have sought to satisfy the politics of difference. If, for example, a government merely devolves power territorially, it could be accused of ducking its responsibilities, of merely encouraging the rival communities to pursue their arguments and conflicts at the devolved level. Without any safeguards for each community, the end result could well be victory for the stronger or larger, with an intensified discrimination against the losers as a real possibility.

At some point, therefore, a democracy faced with this kind of scenario, if it is committed to achieving a resolution of the issues generated, will inevitably be obliged to consider, as British governments have been in Northern Ireland, some kind of community solution. What is required is an approach that would persuade the rival ethnonationalisms to share authority and autonomy in a proportional manner that nevertheless guarantees the rights and distinctive character of each. The model that has often been advanced as the one which governments in this position should consider is that of consociational democracy.

The thesis for consociational democracy was developed originally as an analytical model of how democratic elites had achieved political stability in divided societies that, because of their divided nature, possessed characteristics highly conducive of instability. The leading democratic cases were held to be the Netherlands, Belgium, Austria and Switzerland. However, the thesis was also prescriptive; it offered, or so its supporters argued, a formula that could be applied to other deeply divided societies.

However, the claim for consociational democracy was based essentially upon evidence from states where the major cleavage lines were religious in nature. How far the consociational model can be applied uncritically to situations where the fundamental differences derive from the politics of ethnonational identity has been a matter of some heated debate. The major point to emerge from this debate is that in ethnonational political disputes there tends to be a much lower level of tolerance and degree of empathy than where economic or religious cleavages predominate. The key factor in that difference again relates to territory.

One central question is not so much how territory is managed, so perhaps leading to a discussion of how a form of proportionality can be built into that management, but who controls it. Because the politics of identity can so easily become a zero-sum conflict, it is much less likely for democracies committed to compromise to be masters of their own fate. Since the early 1970s British governments of all persuasions have followed a broadly bipartisan policy towards Northern Ireland, more latterly with the support of Irish governments in Dublin. The problem has been how to persuade the two communities in the province to accept a compromise that would respect the rights and satisfy the concerns of both. It is in this sense that the 1998 Good Friday Agreement represented a breakthrough: even so, it was almost eighteen months before verbal agreement to talk to each other resulted in the return of some political autonomy to the province. Hence, for a community strategy to work, it might at times seem to democratic governments that all they can do is to encourage and to be demonstrably willing to delegate to the communities as much as possible. The key condition for success, however, is always whether the competing ethnonational communities are willing to accept accommodation and compromise, and are prepared to appreciate that the other sides have genuine cultural and territorial concerns and fears. Even so, where the politics of difference are created by ethnonational communities both residing in and claiming a specific territory, some kind of community approach would seem to be the only option for possible success. Contemporary democracies have ultimately had to accept such a conclusion wherever a straightforward territorial devolution cannot eradicate the roots of unrest.

DEMOCRACY, TERRITORY AND THE FUTURE

While territorial and community routes can be reviewed as general approaches, the alternatives available to democracies are almost always circumscribed by the historical and institutional pattern of centralizing politics within each state. That context shapes both the perceptions and ambitions of ethnonational communities and the mindset of central governments. This makes it extremely difficult for any standard recipe to be developed. What one democracy may regard as a satisfactory means of accommodating ethnonational aspirations, another may reject as something that implies an unacceptable loss of territorial integrity and control. What we are left with is a complex tesseral pattern of politics where ultimately local and regional factors can shape events as much as national ones. Governments, if they were to be honest, have to accept that 'accommodation policies are not always within the gift of the centre' (Mitchell, 1996, p. 33).

The inability of governments in contemporary democracies to enjoy totality of control in disputes arising from the politics of difference, and the nature of the fetters that hamper their freedom of action, relate also to some basic principles of democratic life. These include an effective institutional structure for representation and debate, a broad acceptance that society is pluralistic (with a consequent acceptance of the existence of difference), and tolerance as an essential component of democratic behaviour. Quite often, perhaps, the willingness of contemporary democracy to pursue solutions may have been driven not only by a sense of justice or acceptance of ethnonational rights, but simply as little more than another aspect of everyday pluralist life where political parties and their leaders jostle with each other for political advantage. In states where democratic principles have taken root, such circumstances have served to constrain not only national governments but also ethnonational political movements.

As we move into another millennium, processes of socioeconomic change and accommodationist policies may continue the slow process of ethnonational absorption that has always been present in the past. Even so, democracy will almost certainly continue to be confronted by the politics of difference, and governments will probably continue to endeavour to respond positively to the concerns raised when they deem that some action is necessary. In the past justifications of the nation state were often founded upon the assertion that it was best placed to guarantee the economic health, physical security and cultural heritage of its citizens. Such a premise was always perhaps dubious, but the politics of the last half century have demonstrated that the nation state was a myth, and that as a goal it has maybe been both undesirable and unattainable.

The nature and tempo of recent change has underlined the fact that the context of state, territory and democracy is becoming increasingly internationalized. Whatever guarantees the state may have enjoyed or claimed in the past, they have entered into a period of rapid erosion, helping to shape a world where power is becoming more diffuse and decentralized across a complex array of overlapping and conflicting networks. It is commonplace now to read that the phenomenon of globalization has begun to squeeze the pre-eminence of the state. A multi-angled concept (which is also disputed), globalization has usually been taken to mean, *inter alia*, that the world order of states with rigid territorial boundaries within which each is sovereign is being replaced by one with an absence of overarching order: instead, the future is projected to be one of increasing patterns of cross-cutting loyalties and authority. If this is so, then it carries important implications for democracies and the politics of identity, for it implies a growing dissonance between democratic accountability and the territorial reach of sovereignty. While the future must remain a matter of some speculation, it could well be the case that a more localized particularism and collective identities both within and across states will become more prominent.

Other contemporary events and trends which have impacted upon contemporary democracy include the ending of the Cold War, which has ushered in a new era for physical and collective security, forcing countries to ask what is being defended, and against whom. In Europe, the European Union (EU) has tentatively begun efforts to develop its own policies on citizenship as a plank in its long-term aim to promote a new kind of political cohesion. While the potential impact of the EU upon the politics of identity within its member states may still be largely unknown, substate territories are already catered for within its formal structures; and ethnonational political groups have begun to relate as much to Brussels as to national governments for the realization of their objectives. Immigration from other parts of the world has further transformed democratic societies. The injection of diaspora identities has transformed the cultural complexity of democratic society, extending the degree to which the politics of difference can challenge the equality implicit in traditional notions of democratic citizenship.

What seems to be clear is that these and related contemporary developments pose a continuing challenge to the state imperatives of territorial integrity and legitimacy. They both encourage the politics of difference and endanger the identities from which that politics draws its inspiration. Within this more complex mosaic, democracy and the state may well find it more profitable to pay more attention to collective roots as well as to individual options. As Dahl and Tufte (1974, p. 135) have argued, 'citizenship must have several frontiers simultaneously'. Despite lip service to the notion of the nation state and hence a single dimension of citizenship, democracies have demonstrated an elasticity in expanding individual rights beyond the narrow sphere of political representation. They have, however, found it more difficult to comprehend the cultural and territorial nexus of identity. But the survival of the politics of difference, despite the standardization inherent in democratic consolidation, suggests that both state and ethnonational community may have to persist with patterns of accommodation that incorporate sociocultural and territorial, as well as political and economic, rights and duties within a much more diffuse and multifaceted definition of citizenship. The future colour of the nexus between state, democracy and territory may well be a shifting kaleidoscope of grey; it will not be the black and white vision inherent in the concept of the democratic nation state.

FURTHER READING

Kellas, J.G. (1991) *The Politics of Nationalism and Ethnicity* (Basingstoke: Macmillan). A useful discussion of the meaning of nationalism and ethnicity accompanied by a review of several ethnonational cases, issues and problems.

Laponce, J. (1987) *Languages and Their Territories* (Toronto: University of Toronto Press). An important analysis of multicultural societies and democracies that puts forward the case for ethnoregional federalism as the optimum solution.

Lijphart, A. (1977) *Democracy in Plural Societies* (New Haven: Yale University Press). A presentation of the utility of the consociational democracy model and its applicability to deeply divided societies.

Lustick, I. (1979) Stability in Deeply Divided Societies: Consociationalism versus Control, *World Politics* 31, 325–44. A forceful argument for the necessity of a strategy of containment because an ethnically divided society is inherently conflictual.

Newman, S. (1994) Ethnoregional Parties: A Comparative Perspective, *Regional Politics and Policy* 4, 28–66. A broad survey of ethnoregional parties in contemporary democracies, looking at their organization, strategies and objectives.

Rokkan, S. and Urwin, D.W. (1983) *Economy, Territory, Identity* (London/Beverly Hills: Sage). An analysis of the political mobilization, concerns and options of ethnonational minorities in Western Europe within the framework of a typology of minority predicaments derived from historical processes of state and nation building.

Taylor, C. (1992) *Multiculturalism and 'The Politics of Recognition'* (Princeton: Princeton University Press). An introduction to the difference between and the significance of the politics of universalism and the politics of difference.

Urwin, D.W. (1998) Modern Democratic Experiences of Territorial Management: Single Houses, But Many Mansions, *Regional and Federal Studies* 8, 81–110. A detailed analysis of how modern democratic governments have reacted to ethnonational politics with institutional and policy changes in the area of territorial management.

REFERENCES

Dahl, R.A. and Tufte, E. (1974) *Size and Democracy*. Oxford: Oxford University Press.

Hanham, H.J. (1959) *Elections and Party Management*. London: Longmans.

Huntington, S.P. (1991) *The Third Wave – Democratization in the Late Twentieth Century*. Norman: University of Oklahoma Press.

Laponce, J. (1960) *The Protection of Minorities*. Berkeley/Los Angeles: University of California Press.

McGarry, J. and O'Leary, B. (eds) (1990) *The Future of Northern Ireland*. Oxford: Clarendon.

Mackenzie, W.J.M. (1976) *Political Identity*. London: Penguin.

Mitchell, J. (1996) Conservatives and the Changing Meaning of Union, *Regional and Federal Studies* 6, 30–44.

Mitchell, M. and Russell, D. (1996). Immigration, Citizenship and the Nation-State in the New Europe. In B. Jenkins and A.S. Sofos (eds), *Nation and Identity in Contemporary Europe*. London: Routledge.

Murphy, A.B. (1996). 'The Sovereign State System as Political-Territorial Ideal: Historical and Contemporary Considerations'. In T.J. Biersteker and C. Weber (eds), *State Sovereignty as Social Construct*. Cambridge: Cambridge University Press, pp. 81–121.

Nielsen, G.P. (1985) 'State and 'Nation Group': A Global Taxonomy'. In E.A. Tiryakian and R. Rogowski (eds), *New Nationalisms of the Developed West*. Boston: Allen and Unwin, pp. 27–56.

Schwarzmantel, J. (1991) *Socialism and the Idea of the Nation*. London: Harvester Press.

Taylor, C. (1992) *Multiculturalism and 'The Politics of Recognition'*. Princeton: Princeton University Press.

CHAPTER 4

TRANSNATIONAL MIGRATION, THE LIBERAL STATE AND CITIZENSHIP

Jeroen Doomernik and Roland Axtmann

Mobility is one of the hallmarks of our global age. For example, there is the global flow of visual images and information. There are few inhabited places on earth that are without television and radio, and the Internet and other communication systems such as mobile phones allow ever more people the free exchange of opinions and information unobstructed by censorship. The capitalist mode of production has hardly any rival left and its products are no longer bound by geographical constraints. Capital hardly faces boundaries nowadays and can be transferred from one end of the globe to the other almost instantaneously. Although legally a US company, Nike produces its shoes in South East Asia; Japanese cars are made in Britain; many Fuji films are made in the Netherlands; and one should not forget the global presence of Coca-Cola or McDonald's. The fact that business has become global does not only create increasing flows of products, but it also necessitates the mobility of managers, of specialists, and of those persons who actually transport both these people and the products. For many other highly skilled workers it has become a fact of life that their trade implies a fair amount of travelling: to conferences, business meetings, exchange programmes and the like. In the aeroplanes they use, the rows at the back are crowded with tourists who likewise take frequent trips to distant (and warm) places for granted.

Yet, it is not just members of the transnational economic and political elites and tourists from the rich 'West' that are 'on the move'. David Held *et al.* (1999, p. 303) have summarized the major migration patterns:

> The contemporary era is witnessing a very complex pattern of overlapping and interacting global and regional migratory flows of both an economic and non-economic nature. At the centre of these global flows have been economically driven migrations to OECD countries initially at a regional level, from poorer to richer Western states, predominantly to Western Europe, but they subsequently shifted to North America and Australia. In addition, global migrations have focused on the Middle East. The other large migratory flows have been regional and have developed apace from the 1960s within

South East Asia, western and southern Africa, Latin America and within the Middle East.

We shall concentrate on migration away from poor countries in the 'South' into the 'West'. According to Held *et al.* (1999, p. 312), the estimated total for post-1945 migration to OECD countries was well over 100 million people, which is more than triple the great transatlantic migrations of the 1880s to 1920. The majority of these postwar migration movements took place in the 30 years between 1965 and 1995. In this chapter, we do not wish to discuss the whole range of factors that have caused these developments. However, some particularly important determinants should be highlighted.

The transnationalization of the capitalist economy has not resulted in global economic convergence. For example, discrepancies between per capita income in the highly industrialized world and that in the developing world remain; indeed, in most instances the gap between the two has increased. At the same time, several processes take place in many poorer regions of the world that affect demography, social structure and, ultimately, geographical mobility: improved medical care has greatly reduced the mortality rate, especially among children, which, taken together with high fertility rates, has resulted in extremely 'young' populations and rapid population growth. Only a few decades ago subsistence farming could sustain large parts of the population, but this is often no longer the case partly because of population growth but also partly because traditional farming methods have been replaced by cash-crop agriculture. The latter, furthermore, means vulnerability to fluctuations in world market prices for such products as coffee, rice, and, lest we forget, drugs. It also often means depletion of natural resources like fertile lands and water. Under these circumstances, political unrest is likely to arise and might even lead to the kind of ethnic strife that the world has witnessed in recent years.

As an outcome of these processes, most 'Third World' countries are faced with rapid urbanization as young men and women migrate from the countryside into towns and cities in search for employment and housing that they cannot obtain in rural areas. Already today, the world's largest cities are located in the developing rather than in the industrialized regions. Even though these cities form the economic nucleus of countries they fail to offer meaningful employment or a suitable home to many newcomers. Their rural-to-urban migration may then easily have been merely the first step towards international migration. Given the fact that large numbers of persons belong to this category of young and destitute people, or are on the run from armed conflicts and oppression, the question arises why are not many more on the move. And we may look with similar puzzlement at the countries of the former Soviet Union, where it is not demographic imbalance that is the cause of misery but economic collapse, and surveys show that millions of people would prefer to migrate to the West.

An answer to that question has to be twofold. For international migration actually to occur, some links need to exist between countries of origin and of destination, and the prospective migrants must have the financial means actually to travel abroad (van Amersfoort and Doomernik, 1998). Whereas the latter precondition is commonsensical, the former needs some explanation. There are different types of links. Transport connections are an obvious one. These are not random and tend to be most frequent between countries that have political ties (for example, on the basis of a colonial history) or close economic relations. This is illustrated by the simple fact that the Dutch airline KLM operates a direct line Amsterdam–Paramaribo but not to Gaborone, whereas British Airways flies from London to Botswana several times per week but not to Surinam. As for economic links, one needs only to remember the transnational corporations mentioned earlier and the mobility they generate. Another link between countries is information. A prospective immigrant needs to have some idea about what to expect upon arrival, regardless of whether the image he or she has is correct or not. Information stems not only from the popular media, that often portray 'the West' as populated by prosperous and happy people, but is also conveyed indirectly, for example, in industrial products, and in the form of well-dressed Western tourists with video equipment dangling from their shoulders. All this does not just give prospective migrants an image of what to expect abroad but it might also inspire people who would otherwise not consider emigration to try their luck beyond the borders of their own country.

Arguably the most important link between countries of origin and of (potential) settlement are ethnic communities resulting from previous immigration. They provide knowledge about their country of settlement and their own position in it (often pictured rosier than the facts merit) and may even help fund the actual voyage and assist the newcomers during the first phase of their stay. Moreover, their legal status is of great relevance since most of the highly developed states allow legally settled immigrants to have their spouses and children join them. In short, much immigration is predictable because it is the result of previous settlement or because there are obvious intimate links between countries of origin and settlement.

However, unpredictable immigration has clearly been on the increase during the past decade and can mainly be attributed to asylum seekers and refugees. Their arrival is partly the result of violent conflicts, like the wars in former Yugoslavia, and partly induced by the lack of a viable or attractive alternative for those who simply seek a more satisfactory life. In classical countries of immigration like the United States, Canada and Australia the latter type of migrant may be allowed in to try his or her luck. In most other highly developed nations, however, this is, by and large, impossible. The only legal gate of entry for the majority of immigrants passes through the asylum system.

THE INDUSTRIALIZED STATE'S RESPONSE TO UNSOLICITED IMMIGRANTS

Between early 1992 and the end of 1998 Western European governments were confronted with a total of about three million asylum seekers. The largest influx occurred in 1992 when approximately 700,000 asylum requests were logged, two-thirds of them in Germany. In that country, but also in others that received relatively large numbers of asylum seekers (for example, the Netherlands, France, Sweden and the United Kingdom) a sense of crisis emerged. The state seemed to have lost control and its sovereignty seemed to be under attack (Sassen, 1996). We can identify two basic reasons why most highly developed states see a need to control immigration – to decide who is allowed to enter their territory and settle, for how long, for what purpose and under which conditions. The first reason is closely related to the idea of the nation state. A state is often conceived as belonging to a particular people, the 'nation', and it is then seen to be its right, and even its duty, to keep those out who do not belong. Being unable to stop foreigners from entering the country and thus successfully to confront the challenge to 'exclusive membership' may lead to an erosion of the state's legitimacy (Sassen, 1996). In this view, extending hospitality towards newcomers becomes a privilege, not a right for them to claim.

The second reason why governments see the need to limit the arrival of newcomers pertains predominantly to the political logic of the welfare state. In Western welfare states, every person who legally resides in the country has equal rights to basic support, housing, access to the educational system, health care and so on. Through taxes and national insurance contributions, most adults contribute to the welfare system. Thus problems arise if considerable numbers of new members arrive who have not contributed or may even not do so over a long period of time. Asylum seekers, in contrast to labour migrants, might fall into this category, most certainly as long as their fate has not been decided upon and they are refused entry into the labour market. This reason for restricting the influx of newcomers, be they asylum seekers or other immigrants, appears especially pressing in times when considerable unemployment among those already legally present in a country seems to have become endemic.

States that are signatories to the Geneva Convention relating to the Status of Refugees (1951) and the Protocol relating to the Status of Refugees (1967) have accepted the right of individuals to apply for asylum. The Geneva Convention does not, however, impose a duty on states subsequently to grant protection. This has led to some intricate constitutional and political developments. Germany is a case in point. The German Constitution (the Basic Law) establishes an 'inalienable' right to asylum for all persons who are politically persecuted (article 16a). Hence, the regulation of the immigration of asylum seekers has depended on a political decision as to who qualified as a 'persecuted person'. In order to deal with the considerable influx in the early 1990s, the German government introduced two measures: an amendment of the Basic Law, which now allows the government to keep a catalogue of countries whose citizens are *a priori* considered to be free from persecution, and a catalogue, overlapping with the first one, listing states where a person could have applied for asylum prior to her or his arrival in Germany. These policy changes came into effect in the summer of 1993. Subsequently, the number of asylum seekers in Germany did indeed drop considerably. Over the next few years, most other Western European states devised similar policies in order to keep asylum seekers away from their borders. Meanwhile, most EU member states have harmonized this type of arrangement in the Schengen Agreement and the Dublin Convention. These countries have a common visa policy (for example, for all countries from where many asylum seekers originate) and procedural rules to decide which of the contracting states is responsible for which asylum seeker. In addition, some states have assigned immigration officials to those airports at which asylum seekers are likely to board direct flights. Their task is to assist airline personnel to check the validity of visa and travel documents. Moreover, airlines and other carriers face financial sanctions should they bring persons into the country without duly issued and valid documentation. By imposing such sanctions, states have in effect moved their border controls abroad and have privatized a task commonly performed by civil servants.

We know from previous efforts to curb the numbers of asylum seekers, that the effects of stricter policies wear off after a number of years. Between 1994 and 1996 asylum requests in Western Europe showed a clear downward trend, but in 1997, and especially in 1998, the numbers rose again, when they stood at about 340,000. How can we explain this development? More generally, why can liberal states not prevent unsolicited immigration? We wish to distinguish two sets of reasons, one embracing more 'contingent', the other more 'systemic' factors.

Among the 'contingent' factors, two deserve particular attention. First, although receiving states invest heavily in migration controls, they can never be fully effective in an environment where a premium is put on unobstructed cross-border trade and where tourists or business people expect not to be held up and be inconvenienced by extensive passport checks. Furthermore, the diversity of international travellers has hugely increased:

> Permanent migrants arrive with contract workers. There has been a phenomenal increase in international tourism, asylum seekers, students, family reunions, etc. Increasing numbers and the increasing complexity of these bureaucratic categories have strained the capacities of border control agencies. Tourists can overstay and students can disappear into the population after their course ends. (Held *et al.*, 1999, p. 322)

Second, we must take note that migration has increasingly become a global business (Salt and Stein, 1997). In the past, asylum seekers used to make their way to Europe by and large under their own steam. Nowadays, more often than not, they require help, at times from a professional. This assistance may be relatively marginal, for example from a taxi driver who brings an immigrant to a border and shows him where best to cross. It may, however, also include the entire journey, together with a story to tell that will convince the authorities of the asylum claim. Somewhere between these extremes are migrants who are ferried across the Adriatic in speed boats or put in the back of a lorry on its way from Istanbul to Rotterdam. All these means of assistance have in common the fact that they require investment from the side of the migrant and incur huge profits for traffickers. Arguably, these profits can be larger than those made in the international drugs trade and the criminal organizations see trafficking in humans as a much less risky way of making money. It would therefore appear that states are bound to find it difficult firmly to control immigration and that immigration will just become an ever more expensive affair, both for the migrants and for receiving states. A perverse by-product of this development is that those migrants that governments claim to be willing to protect – refugees as defined in the Geneva Convention – are the ones who are increasingly denied access; for there is no reason to assume that they have the financial means to secure the assistance of a trafficker.[1]

There are also 'systemic' factors that account for the curtailed capacity of liberal states to eradicate unwanted immigration. Christian Joppke has discussed these factors in considerable detail (Joppke, 1998; 1999a). First, as a policy issue, immigration is subject to *client politics*. As Gary Freeman (1995, p. 885) has argued, 'those who benefit from immigration in direct and concrete ways are better placed to organize than are those who bear immigration's costs ... The concentrated benefits and diffuse costs of immigration mean that the interest group system around immigration issues is dominated by groups supportive of larger intakes'. Vote-maximizing politicians, so Freeman argues (1995, p. 886–7), are prone to bow to organized opinion out of electoral interest. Popular opinion, though typically restrictionist, is, on the other hand, less well articulated. Arguably, the liberal immigration policies of the 1960s and 1970s throughout north-western Europe accommodated employers' needs for unskilled labour. Second, such an accommodating immigration policy on the basis of a 'rational' calculation of the costs and benefits of immigration is embedded, according to Freeman (1995, p. 885) in the universalist idiom of liberalism that constitutes 'a strong anti-populist norm that dictates that politicians should not seek to exploit racial, ethnic or immigration-related fears in order to win votes'. This *anti-populist norm*, so Freeman says, induces political elites to seek consensus on immigration policy and to remove the issue from partisan politics. Given the rising electoral support across Europe of populist right-wing parties that mobilize around xenophobic sentiments – and whose leaders may even be well entrenched within the political class, as the example of Jörg Haider and his Freedom Party in Austria demonstrates – the strength and importance of such an 'anti-populist norm' may justifiably be questioned.

Indeed, as Joppke argues, this norm is more firmly enshrined – thirdly – in the *legal process* than in the political discourse; and in order to explain why European states continued accepting immigrants despite explicit zero-immigration policies since the early 1970s, the role of the judiciary has to be analysed: 'In open opposition to a restrictionist executive, which switched from elitist client politics to popular national interest politics, courts invoked statutory and constitutional residence and family rights for immigrants' (Joppke, 1998, p. 271). This legal framework, which gives rights and protection to immigrants, may have domestic roots as in constitutional provisions such as the protection of individuals qua people rather than qua citizens in the American constitution or the extensive human-rights provisions in the case of Germany's Basic Law. Yet, it may also derive from international conventions and agreements, and thus be grounded in international law. We have already mentioned the Geneva Convention on the Legal Status of Refugees (1951). Within the United Nations framework, we should further refer to the Universal Declaration of Human Rights (1948), the International Convention on the Elimination of All Forms of Racial Discrimination (1965) or, more recently, the International Convention on the Protection of the Rights of the All Migrant Workers and Members of Their Families (1990). The Council of Europe and the International Labor Organization have both produced a string of international conventions that are applicable to international migrants. The European Community/Union, too, has issued a series of regulations and directives that are binding for the member states regarding, for example, migrant workers and their families (1976), the rights and status of foreigners (1985) or a Declaration against Racism and Xenophobia (1986).

    Fourth, states' curtailed capacity to foreclose unwanted immigration may be a consequence of long-established, *political-historical relations* between the immigrant-sending and the immigrant-receiving states. Here, the colonial connection is particularly important. As Messina (1996, pp. 143–4) points out,

> [D]espite recent pressures from a wide variety of new immigration sources, more than 70 percent of all foreign residents in France during the early 1990s were either European Community nationals, who by statute enjoy the right of free circulation throughout the EC, or citizens of one of the three North African labor-exporting countries (Algeria, Morocco, and Tunisia) with which France has had close, postcolonial relations. In contrast, only 4 percent of total foreign residents in France in 1991 were citizens of the asylum and refugee-exporting East European countries. Much the same situation obtains in Britain, where over 75 percent of the total ethnic minority population originates from Britain's New Commonwealth and Pakistan, areas previously within the British historical empire. Even as recently as 1991 more than half of all the relatively small number of new immigrants accepted by the British government for permanent settlement in the U.K. originated in the New Commonwealth and Pakistan.

Joppke asserts that, as a result of such political-historical links, elaborate discourses of rights and moral obligations towards specific immigrant groups have developed in each European state. Therefore, the differently developed *moral obligations*, fifthly, help explain variations in European states' generosity or firmness towards immigrants. Putting the colonial connection to one side, Joppke claims that these moral obligations 'are strongest vis-à-vis primary immigrants, who have been actively recruited, and they become weaker vis-à-vis secondary immigrants, who have entered in recognition of the family rights of primary immigrants' (Joppke, 1999a, p. 268). And there is also the sense of 'moral obligation' that may derive from a nation's self-understanding. The asylum provisions in Germany's Basic Law must be seen in the context of the Nazi past; and the immigration and asylum policies of the United States are related to the founding myth of America as an 'asylum of nations' (Joppke, 1999a, p. 268).

THE FUTURE REGULATION OF MIGRATION AND THE QUESTION OF CITIZENSHIP

Obviously, it is hard to foresee in detail how EU- and other industrialized states will shape their immigration policies. Yet, a few trends can be predicted.

States, acting either on their own accord or supranationally within the EU, will be forced to complement external controls (borders and asylum procedure) with internal ones. External controls are likely to be improved through better co-ordination between states, more efficient procedures, and increased attempts to combat the smuggling of aliens and other policing methods. But under conditions of ever increasing global mobility, there are practical limits to how far states can go. The alternative is to intensify internal controls. One mechanism is linked to the operational logic of the welfare state and the scrutiny of entitlement claims. The Netherlands is a forerunner in this field. All administrative databases, for example, those of the Inland Revenue, and the social services, are linked up with the central population register and the register of the aliens police. Where previously immigrants without residence status could apply for tax registration, find legal employment, claim unemployment benefits or social security benefits, they are now excluded from these facilities. These previously invisible immigrants, pushed into the limelight by these measures, appear to be large in number. It also becomes clear, however, that the government is frequently unable to expel them. In many cases these people originate from countries deemed unsafe (such as Afghanistan or Iraq) which makes deportation impossible under the European Convention on Human Rights. In other instances, migrants cannot be expelled because their country of origin refuses to accept them back. The same problem exists when it comes to asylum applicants who have not been granted protection or a residence permit on other, for example humanitarian, grounds. They are no longer entitled to state care but frequently they are not expelled either.

States without a central population register, like the United Kingdom or France, are unable to establish the same type of internal control. They will nevertheless want to exclude undocumented persons from society's core fields. This means they either have to start compiling such a register or devise different kinds of checks. The labour market is the easiest target. Under such a system employers would be required by law to check the residence status of their employees, as is already done in the Netherlands or in the United States. But many other service providers, like schools, hospitals, housing associations would then equally be expected to establish whether an applicant is a legal resident. In countries not used to this, such measures are likely to spark discussion about the risks involved in terms of racial discrimination and threats to privacy, as they have done, and still do, in the USA.

If implemented, these measures have in common that they will produce large quantities of persons who are pushed out of society, left without the means to provide for themselves. But they cannot be sent away either. Immigration is unavoidably part and parcel of our global age. In the coming decades, governments, first and foremost those of welfare states, will have to determine whether they accept the presence of considerable numbers of aliens on their territory, left to fend for themselves at the very margin of society, and thus create a very visible group of new paupers, or to devise creative policies by which to prevent this from happening. In a sense, the challenge is to decide whether immigrants should be seen as 'ethnic minorities' or as 'ethnic communities'. According to Castles and Miller (1993, p. 195), who discuss this distinction, as 'ethnic minorities', 'immigrants are excluded and marginalised, so that they live on the fringes of society', without, ultimately, a rightful place in the political community. As 'ethnic communities', on the other hand, 'the immigrants and their descendants are seen as an integral part of a multicultural society which is willing to reshape its culture and identity'.

At stake in these issues is the political and legal status of immigrants in liberal democracies. In some academic literature in recent years, it has been claimed that a new type of citizenship, 'postnational' in character, has been forming, linked to the intensification of transnational migration. David Jacobson (1996, pp. 8–9) has argued that

> [t]ransnational migration is steadily eroding the traditional basis of nation-state membership, namely citizenship. As rights have come to be predicated on residency, not citizen status, the distinction between 'citizen' and 'alien' has eroded. The devaluation of citizenship has contributed to the increasing importance of international human rights codes, with its premise of universal 'personhood' ... States

must increasingly take account of persons *qua* persons as opposed to limiting state responsibilities to its own citizens.

Yasemin Soysal declared that national citizenship was losing ground to a more universal model of membership that was anchored in deterritorialized notions of persons' rights: 'In the postnational model, universal personhood replaces nationhood; and universal human rights replace national rights ... The rights and claims of individuals are legitimated by ideologies grounded in a transnational community, through international codes, conventions, and laws on human rights, independent of their citizenship in a nation-state. Hence, the individual transcends the citizen' (Soysal, 1994, p. 142; see also Soysal, 2000; Hollifield, 1992, pp. 222–6). As a result of this process, the role and character of the state have changed, and the state is now charged with the institutionalization of international human rights. The basis of state legitimacy has undergone a shift 'from an exclusive emphasis on the sovereignty of the people and right to self-determination ... to rights of individuals regardless of nationality' (Sassen, 1996, p. 95).

There is no denying the political importance of discourses on human rights and the legal significance of human rights in international law and through it, in municipal law. Yet, a number of reservations may be raised against the notion of a 'postnational' citizenship model. Joppke (1999a, p. 273) is right to point out that 'individual rights are not external to, but part and parcel of liberal states. Otherwise one could not explain why human-rights constraints are more urgently felt in the states of the West than, for example, in the migrant-receiving states in the Middle East'. He is also right to remind us that most civil rights – such as freedom of speech or the right to ownership – and social rights – such as entitlement to social 'benefits' – have never been dependent upon 'political' citizenship, but upon lawful residence in the territory of the state and, frequently, labour-market participation. It was the political right to participation in the process of collective self-determination that had been reserved exclusively to the citizen. The important qualification with regard to civil rights pertains to residence and free movement in a state's territory that did not extend to persons, but were reserved to citizens:

> The dramatic moment in the evolution of migrant rights was the decoupling of resident and free-movement rights from citizenship. Only, this was not a postnational moment driven by abstract human-rights considerations. Instead, it was a crypto-national moment that equated long-term residency with *de facto* membership in the national community ... The underlying motif is communitarian, not universalist: migrants are not conceived of as abstract holders of

human rights, but as particular members of a community with historically derived entitlements to due consideration and protection. (Joppke, 1999a, p. 272)

Finally, national citizenship in their 'host' country matters to many immigrants. Indeed, it matters so much that many would wish to possess dual citizenship, both in their 'home' country and in their 'host' country. 'National', not 'postnational' citizenship is a status that many immigrants value and crave. As long as this interest prevails among immigrant populations, and as long as there are no autonomous institutional structures that could enforce entitlements that individuals hold on the basis of human rights, 'postnational' membership is not a viable alternative to national citizenship (Joppke, 1999a, 1999b).

As a result of the influx of tens of millions of immigrants, refugees, asylees, and migrant workers into West European societies after the Second World War, they have become increasingly multiethnic, multiracial, and multicultural. What is at stake is not so much the development of a 'postnational' citizenship, but a 'multicultural' citizenship. It is this question that Barry Hindess addresses in the following chapter.

NOTE

1. It is important to differentiate between the two: asylum seekers are those aliens who hope to find protection under the Geneva Convention but whose fate has not yet been decided upon by the authorities of the receiving state; refugees are those aliens who have been granted protection because they fall under the criteria of the Convention, based on a decision by either the national authorities or a third party mandated to make such a decision, for example the UNHCR.

FURTHER READING

Amersfoort, Hans van and Jeroen Doomernik (eds) (1998) *International Migration: Processes and Interventions* (Amsterdam: Het Spinhuis). Provides a comprehensive theoretical framework for the analysis of international migration flows and their manageability. The volume includes case studies from the Netherlands, Germany, France, Europe in general and the United States.

Castles, Stephen and Mark J. Miller (1993) *The Age of Migration: International Population Movements in the Modern World* (Basingstoke: Macmillan). A magisterial overview of migration processes in the past as well as of possible future trends and the challenges they pose in the main regions of immigration.

Castles, Stephen and Alastair Davidson (2000) *Citizenship and Migration: Globalization and the Politics of Belonging*. Basingstoke: Macmillan. New approaches to citizenship are needed which take account of collective identities and accept that, with growing international mobility, many people now belong to more than one society.

Cornelius, Wayne A., Philip L. Martin and James F. Hollifield (eds) (1995) *Controlling Immigration: A Global Perspective* (Stanford: Stanford University Press). Case studies pertaining to controlling unsolicited immigration in Europe, Japan, and Northern America.

Harris, Nigel (1995) *The New Untouchables: Immigration and the New World Worker* (London/New York: I.B. Tauris (reprinted by Penguin)). Powerful arguments against restrictive immigration policies by showing that labour immigrants in most instances do not compete with native workers. The book further argues that liberal immigration regimes produce higher economic growth.

Jacobson, David (1996) *Rights across Borders: Immigration and the Decline of Citizenship* (Baltimore/London: Johns Hopkins University Press). As human rights and other transnational rights gain in importance, national citizenship loses importance.

Joppke, Christian (1999) *Immigration and the Nation-State* (Oxford: Oxford University Press). In this important study, Joppke focuses on the impact of immigration in the two key areas of state sovereignty and citizenship.

Sassen, Saskia (1996) *Losing Control? Sovereignty in an Age of Globalization* (New York: Columbia University Press). How does labour mobility affect state sovereignty?

Soysal, Yasemin N. (1994) *Limits of Citizenship: Migrants and Postnational Membership in Europe* (Chicago/London: University of Chicago Press). Argues that 'national' citizenship is being complemented, if not replaced, by 'postnational' citizenship.

REFERENCES

Amersfoort, Hans van and Jeroen Doomernik (eds) (1998) *International Migration: Processes and Interventions*. Amsterdam: Het Spinhuis.

Castles, Stephen and Mark J. Miller (1993) *The Age of Migration: International Population Movements in the Modern World*. Basingstoke: Macmillan.

Doomernik, Jeroen (1998) *The Effectiveness of Integration Policies towards Immigrants and Their Descendants in France, Germany and The Netherlands*. Geneva: International Labour Office.

Freeman, Gary P. (1995) Modes of Immigration Politics in Liberal Democratic States, *International Migration Review* 29, 881–902.

Held, David, Grew, Anthony, Goldblatt, David and Perraton, Jonathan (1999) *Global Transformations*. Cambridge: Polity Press.

Hollifield, James F. (1992) *Immigrants, Markets, and States: The Political Economy of Postwar Europe*. Cambridge, MA: Harvard University Press.

Jacobson, David (1996) *Rights across Borders: Immigration and the Decline of Citizenship*. Baltimore and London: Johns Hopkins University Press.

Joppke, Christian (1998) Why Liberal States Accept Unwanted Immigration, *World Politics* 50, 266–93.

Joppke, Christian (1999a) *Immigration and the Nation-State: The United States, Germany, and Great Britain.* Oxford: Oxford University Press.

Joppke, Christian (1999b) How Immigration Is Changing Citizenship: A Comparative View, *Ethnic and Racial Studies* 22, 629–52.

Messina, Anthony M. (1996) The Not So Silent Revolution. Postwar Migration to Western Europe, *World Politics* 49, 130–54.

Salt, John and Jeremy Stein (1997) Migration as a Business: The Case of Trafficking, *International Migration* 35, 467–91.

Sassen, Saskia (1996) *Losing Control? Sovereignty in an Age of Globalization.* New York: Columbia University Press.

Soysal, Yasemin N. (1994) *Limits of Citizenship: Migrants and Postnational Membership in Europe.* Chicago and London: University of Chicago Press.

Soysal, Yasemin N. (2000) Citizenship and Identity: Living in Diasporas in Post-War Europe? *Ethnic and Racial Studies* 23, 1–15.

CHAPTER 5

DEMOCRACY, MULTICULTURALISM AND THE POLITICS OF DIFFERENCE

Barry Hindess

Most contemporary states have substantial immigrant communities, many have indigenous minorities, and numerous others contain two or more distinct national cultures. In the Western democracies governments have, with greater or lesser degrees of enthusiasm, come to adopt policies of practical multiculturalism, thereby acknowledging the reality of cultural diversity among their citizens. Various movements, mostly on the Right, have responded with a politics of national and racial exclusivism, and academics have debated the appropriate forms and limits of citizenship in culturally diverse populations. Elsewhere, as Timothy Garton Ash observes in the case of Central Europe, it often seems that 'the greater the ethnic mix in a post-communist country, the more likely it has been to take a nationalist authoritarian path rather than a liberal democratic one. Those that have done best are also those that are ethnically most homogeneous' (Garton Ash, 1999, p. 22).

It would be a mistake to see the problem that cultural diversity poses for established and would-be democracies as resulting from diversity itself. Most states throughout recorded history, including the few democracies of classical antiquity, have ruled over ethnically diverse populations (McNeill, 1986). Nevertheless, as Will Kymlicka points out, the liberal and democratic currents of modern political thought have 'operated with an idealized model of the polis in which fellow-citizens share a common descent, language and culture' (Kymlicka, 1995, p. 2). While, as we shall see, this ideal has also been disputed, governments and political movements have often made strenuous efforts to ensure a substantial degree of cultural homogeneity in the populations under their control.

If the modern experience of cultural diversity poses a problem for democratic politics, an important part of the reason is that democracy itself has been understood in terms of this idealized model of the *polis*. The first part of this chapter outlines three features of modern democratic thought which together suggest a strong presumption of cultural uniformity: first, the belief that government should be, directly or indirectly, by the people themselves; secondly, the assumption that those who belong to the people are citizens; and thirdly, the peculiar egalitarianism that distinguishes the modern understanding of citizenship from those of classical antiquity and the early modern period. The second part of the chapter shows how the assumption of uniformity has coloured discussion of what, if anything, a democratic government should do about cultural and other differences within the body of citizens. Here we consider three influential perspectives: T.H. Marshall's treatment of the 'social' rights of citizenship, multiculturalism, and the 'politics of difference'. The third and final part of the chapter brings the assumption of uniformity itself into question, drawing on associational pluralism and James Tully's challenge to the 'empire of uniformity'. The effect of this move is to suggest a more complex view both of the modern constitutional state and of the sense in which it can be considered 'democratic'.

DEMOCRACY AND THE RULE OF UNIFORMITY

As a first approximation, we can describe democratic government as being, in the words of Abraham Lincoln's Gettysburg Address, 'government of the people, by the people and for the people'. This formula invites the question of who or what the people consists in, of who belongs and who does not, but it offers no answer: does 'the people' refer to the free, adult residents of a democratic state or only to those who share a more exclusive cultural, ethnic or national identity? If democracy appeals to the idea of government by the people and if membership of any particular people is open to interpretation, and therefore open to political contestation, it is hardly surprising that attempts at democratization following the withdrawal of colonial rule or the collapse of other types of authoritarian government should so often be associated with the rise of ethnic and national chauvinisms.

In fact, however, there is considerably more to the idea of democracy than government of, by and for the people. There is also the fact that 'the people' is thought to consist of citizens, that is, of individuals who play a fundamental part in the government of the state to which they belong. A citizen, Aristotle tells us, is 'he who has the power to take part in the deliberative or judicial administration of any state ... ; and, speaking generally, a state is a body of citizens sufficing for the purposes of life' (1988, III, 1275b, 19–22). There are two rather different elements to be considered here. The first part of Aristotle's sentence indicates that citizens are men who share a privileged and distinctive status within the larger population governed by the state and it defines this masculine status in otherwise universalistic terms, that is, without reference to the particular character of Athens, Sparta or any other state. A state, in

Aristotle's sense, is a democracy if it is ruled by its members, that is, by the citizens as a whole and not just by the one or the few among the citizens. Understandings of democracy and of citizenship have changed considerably since Aristotle's day – with the development of representative government, professional politicians and state bureaucracies transforming the perception of relations between citizen and state – but the central idea remains that a democratic state is one that is ruled, directly or indirectly, by its citizens.

To say that the citizens of a democratic state are both rulers and ruled is to say that the government of the state is the agent of the citizens themselves, that the citizens' obligation to obey its legitimate instructions derives from the fact of their participation in that government. In effect, this is the democratic version of contract theory, of the claim that, whatever its actual historical provenance, the constitution of a modern state can be treated as if it had been established in a single, foundational and continuing act of agreement – a social contract – between the citizens as a whole. This claim, in turn, suggests that a uniform set of laws and conventions for their interpretation should, at some fundamental level, apply equally to all citizens. It is this presumption of uniformity that produces the problem that multiculturalism and the politics of difference seek to address – the problem, that is, of how to deal with the effects of diversity within the overall body of citizens.

The contractarian view is that citizens should see themselves and be seen by others as having agreed to form or to recognize a government and to act according to the laws which that government lays down. This, of course, supposes that citizens already possess what Nietzsche calls 'the right to make promises' (1967, Essay 2, s.2), that they are able to experience their own conduct and the conduct of their fellow citizens as calculable and predictable. It assumes, in other words, that a population of citizens is made up of individuals whose habits of thought and of behaviour have been established through appropriate forms of socialization, education, and training. Since these activities always take place in particular social contexts, this suggests that citizenship will in fact involve a significant degree of particularism, that the citizens of modern democracies will be formed with British, French, American and diverse other national accents. We should not be surprised, then, to find that the idea of a community of citizens governed by laws to which they have, at least in principle, agreed commonly goes hand-in-hand with the idea that the community is also governed by a distinctive culture or way of life – a way of life that has the effect both of regulating interactions between the citizens themselves and of distinguishing them from citizens of other communities. That citizenship has this particularistic side is precisely what is suggested in the second part of Aristotle's definition – which identifies the citizen as belonging to 'a body of citizens sufficing for the purposes of life' – and again by the fact, which Aristotle also noted, that the citizens of a state are generally children of its citizens.

While citizenship with different accents may seem relatively anodyne it is clear that the particularism of citizenship frequently takes a more substantial, nationalist and chauvinistic form. But this particularism also has a further, disturbing, aspect that is less commonly noted in the literature on citizenship. If we regard the universalistic qualities of the citizen as qualities that must always be nurtured in particular cultures or ways of life, then we may also be tempted by the belief that some cultures nurture these qualities more effectively than others. The Greek view that the *polis* is the highest form of political life, for example, suggests the correlative judgement that those who live in different ways, without using the *polis* as an organizing principle, exist at a substantially lower level of civilization. Judgements of this kind have often infected Western interactions with others. In his *Considerations on Representative Government* John Stuart Mill argues that the people of British India were not 'sufficiently advanced … to be fitted for representative government' (1977, p. 567) and that they must therefore be governed in other ways. My point is not to endorse Mill's judgement and others like it but rather to observe that this elitist perception of cultures radically different from one's own – and of those who have been brought up within them – has been a perpetual temptation of democratic thought and, indeed, of Western political thought more generally. It clearly plays a significant part in the politics of all modern democracies, especially in the treatment accorded to non-Western immigrants and indigenous peoples.

This seductive elitism notwithstanding, there is also a sense in which modern understandings of citizenship, and also, therefore, of democracy, are considerably more egalitarian than their earlier counterparts. In the city states of classical antiquity citizenship was a matter of a limited range of statuses within a larger, highly differentiated network of statuses: most inhabitants (women, slaves, resident foreigners) were not citizens, many had no legal standing as independent persons and, in some cases, the citizens themselves were divided into legally defined classes with distinct rights and obligations. In the democracies of the modern period, in contrast, almost all members of the community are regarded as independent persons (children now being the largest single category of exceptions) and therefore as actual or potential citizens, and citizens are no longer divided into legally defined classes or estates.

It is this egalitarianism of the modern view of citizenship that gives the image of a community of citizens governed by shared culture or way of life the particular importance that it possesses in contemporary democratic societies. The assumption, in particular, that the overwhelming majority of the population will be citizens of the state in which they live slides all too easily into the perception of non-citizen residents as an alien intrusion. Both the classical and the modern view of citizenship suggest that it is normal and acceptable for states to discriminate against those who are not their citizens, but the classical view was that non-citizens would always form a substantial part of the state's own population. Although there are significant non-citizen minorities in most contemporary societies, the predominant modern view is that those who live in a state's territory will normally be its citizens, and, conversely, that those who are not its citizens will normally belong elsewhere.

DEMOCRACY AND DIFFERENCE

The predominant modern understanding of democracy, then, suggests that all, or almost all, members of the population of a democratic state will be citizens of that state, that the citizens themselves will belong to the one people, and that they all participate in the same (albeit imaginary) founding contract. As a result, citizens are seen as sharing both the same culture or way of life and the same fundamental rights and obligations in relation to the state: they are all subject to what James Tully (1995) calls 'the empire of uniformity'.

While this understanding of democracy is far from reflecting the actual condition of any democratic state it has nevertheless had a powerful impact on contemporary politics. It has profound and disturbing consequences for the ways in which democratic states treat those who are not their citizens (Hindess, 1998). But what particularly concerns us in this chapter are its implications for the consideration of differences among the citizens themselves. The presumption that citizens participate in a common way of life is not necessarily incompatible with the view that there may be significant differences between, for example, women and men, one city or region and another, urban and rural dwellers, the wealthy and the not so wealthy. It does suggest, however, that some differences will be of a kind that either cannot or should not be accommodated within a democratic community. It has been claimed, for example, that individuals who suffer from certain kinds of disadvantage may thereby be prevented from participating in important aspects of the life of their society, with the result that they are effectively excluded from the full enjoyment of their citizenship. In an influential argument of this kind T.H. Marshall (1950) describes citizenship as involving three sets of rights: the *civil* rights to liberty and equality before the law; the *political* right to vote and to participate in the political process; the *social* right to participate fully in the way of life that is shared by the citizens as a whole. The state has a responsibility, in Marshall's view, to ensure that these rights are secured for all citizens. With regard to social rights, in particular, Marshall argues that the role of government social policy is to ensure that citizens are not in fact excluded from participation in the life of their society by reason of poverty, ill-health or lack of education. On this view of citizenship, the twentieth-century welfare state is an essential foundation for a true community of citizens. Many commentators therefore saw the weakening and partial dismantling of Western welfare regimes during the 1980s and 1990s as a fundamental attack on citizenship itself (King, 1987; Roche, 1992).

Multiculturalism and the politics of difference raise another kind of issue: both suggest that, even with Marshall's civil, political and social rights in place, members of various kinds of minority group can find themselves excluded from the full enjoyment of citizenship. Multiculturalism has been defined in various ways but it refers most commonly to both a doctrine and an area of government policy intended to respond to the fact of national and ethnic diversity among the citizens. The Standing Committee on Multiculturalism of the Canadian Parliament describes it as involving:

> Recognition of the diverse cultures of a plural society based on three principles: we all have an ethnic origin (equality); all our cultures deserve respect (dignity); and cultural pluralism needs official support. (Standing Committee on Multiculturalism, 1987, p. 87)

While recognition of cultural diversity poses no great problem for the comparatively relaxed understanding of citizenship to be found in most modern democracies, the active promotion of cultural pluralism by public authorities is another matter entirely. It is a relatively recent development, dating in most Western societies from the 1960s or even later and, as we shall see, it is also highly contentious, in part because it seems to conflict with the presumption of uniformity.

Before we turn to this issue, however, it should be noted that the three principles taken together strongly suggest that the cultures that are deserving of respect and public support can be identified in terms of their ethnic origin – that, at least for the purposes of public policy, *cultural* diversity and *ethnic* diversity can be treated as if they were more or less equivalent. Will Kymlicka has argued that this focus on ethnic diversity may obscure important differences: 'There are a variety of ways in which minorities become incorporated into political communities, from the conquest and colonization of previously self-governing societies to the voluntary immigration of individuals and families' (1995, p. 11). Kymlicka is particularly concerned to distinguish, in Western societies, between the situations of *national* minorities (for example, Quebecois in Canada, Basques in France and Spain, Scots and Welsh in Britain), *indigenous* communities (for example, Native Americans in the USA and Canada) and minorities resulting from voluntary or involuntary *immigration*. Kymlicka restricts his focus to cultural diversity arising 'from national and ethnic differences' (p. 18), and he insists that these differences are not all of a kind.

The question this raises is why cultural diversity should so often be regarded as a matter of *national* or *ethnic* differences – even though, as Kymlicka acknowledges, there may well be other significant types of cultural difference. An important part of the answer, I suggest, lies in a problematic view of culture both as reflecting the way of life of a singular people (a nation or an ethnic group) and as providing one of the foundations of the rule of uniformity. The problem that multiculturalism seeks to address, then, is that the presence of distinct peoples in the one polity does not sit easily with the presumption that the rule of uniformity has its foundations in the culture and way of life of a singular people. Multiculturalism operates within the limits of this view of culture and aims to finesse the tensions that it produces: to maintain the rule of uniformity while nevertheless ensuring that citizens who belong to minority peoples are not substantially disadvantaged.

Multiculturalism therefore leaves itself open to attack not only from those who fear that the needs of minorities are not being adequately addressed but also from those who fear that its policies will undermine the fabric of uniformity. Before turning to this second line of attack, however, it should be noted that there are disadvantaged groups in contemporary democracies whose problems have nothing to do with the mixing of distinct peoples. Following the appearance of Iris Marion Young's *Justice and the Politics of Difference* (1990) the last part of this title has served to identify an influential style of argument which aims to address this issue directly. The politics of difference incorporates multiculturalism's focus on national and ethnic differences but moves beyond it to insist that, important though such differences are, the exclusive character of the dominant way of life in most Western societies discriminates also against women in general, blacks, gay men, lesbian women, and others who are seen as having deviant lifestyles.

At one level, what is at issue in such discrimination is the failure of policy makers, public service agencies and mainstream political groups to acknowledge the concerns of certain minorities. Young notes, for example, that the norms of deliberation in the contemporary USA 'are culturally specific and often operate as forms of power that silence or devalue the speech of some people' (Young, 1996, p. 123). As a result, even when those from minority cultures are encouraged to participate in public life, their claims will frequently be unheard or misrecognized. What is required, in the first instance, is for the dominant groups to adopt a more open, less exclusive understanding of the citizens' way of life and, in particular, to recognize the speech of various cultural minorities and the norms and values expressed within it.

Young generalizes this last point to argue that, in contemporary pluralist societies, such openness is the responsibility of all participants. Thus, adapting the multicultural prescription to encompass a broader range of differences, she insists that all groups should 'have a commitment to equal respect for one another, in the simple formal sense of a willingness to say that all have a right to express their opinions and points of view, and all ought to listen' (1996, p. 126). The effect of adopting this prescription, Young suggests, would be that all groups would come to understand something of the other perspectives, thereby gaining 'a wider picture of the social processes in which their own partial experience is embedded' (p. 128). The reference to 'a wider picture', the perception of which could be shared, at least in principle, by all participants, invokes yet another version of the image of overarching unity – a unity, in this case, that is expected to be built from a multiplicity of suitably respectful interactions.

It has also been argued that minorities will sometimes require more specific protection, for example, through special provision for minority languages or religious practices. In making his multiculturalist case for such group-differentiated, or 'collective', rights Will Kymlicka is particularly concerned to show that provision of these rights need not be incompatible with the fundamental liberal objective of equal liberty for all citizens – the objective, that is, of securing an underlying uniformity of treatment. He does this by distinguishing between two kinds of collective rights. On the one hand, there are collective rights that enable a group to restrict the liberty of its own members. Kymlicka cites the case of the Pueblo, a self-governing indigenous group in the USA that discriminates against those of its members who have converted to Protestantism, in part by denying them access to housing and certain other benefits. In this case, the collective rights which allow the Pueblo to exercise a substantial degree of internal self-government are also used 'to limit the freedom of members to question and revise traditional practices' (Kymlicka, 1995, p. 40). Collective rights of this kind, Kymlicka argues, should not be provided since they cannot be reconciled with the objective of equal liberty for all citizens. On the other hand, there are collective rights – religious schooling providing an obvious example – that serve rather to protect the distinctive culture of the group and to prevent it from being submerged in that of the larger society to which the group belongs. In Kymlicka's view, rights of the latter kind are not necessarily in conflict with individual liberty but they may also be required for protection of the liberty of members of many minority groups. Indeed, he argues, it is only through participation in their societal culture that individuals are enabled to make meaningful choices for themselves. Thus, to the extent that majority practices threaten the integrity of minority cultures, they can also be seen as undermining the ability of members of these minorities to make meaningful choices for themselves, and therefore, in fact, as encroaching on their liberty. More-over, Kymlicka insists, group-specific rights (such as those regarding the use of minority languages) are often required to secure some approxima-tion to equality of treatment by the state of minority and majority groups. In his view, then, there may be circumstances in which equal liberty for all citizens can be secured only through special public provision for cultural minorities.

In fact, Kymlicka's distinction between two kinds of collective rights is by no means as clear cut as he would have us believe. Public support for religious schools may well, as Kymlicka suggests, help certain minorities to preserve their distinctive character but it will do so by allowing public officials and/or representatives of the minorities concerned to determine the content of their religious education. It is difficult to see how this can be achieved without at the same time producing the very problem that Kymlicka complains of in the case of the Pueblo – without, that is, placing those who speak for such minorities in a position where they might be able to limit the freedom of members 'to question and revise traditional practices' (1995, p. 40). Moreover, as anyone who has lived in or tried to obtain public housing will be aware, the experience of discriminatory action by public officials is hardly restricted to members of national and ethnic minorities. Kymlicka's reference to 'traditional practices' notwith-standing, the problem of state encroachment on individual liberty is one that arises in all areas of public activity and it should not be seen as arising specifically from the provision of certain kinds of minority rights.

If the distinction between two kinds of collective rights is difficult to sustain, where does this leave Kymlicka's argument in favour of special rights for minority cultures? Defenders of the rule of uniformity might be expected to support the contrary view on the grounds that the granting of such rights will tend, as David Miller puts it, to 'ossify group differences, and destroy the sense of common nationality on which democratic politics depends' (Miller, 1995, p. 154). The fact that there are significant minorities in most democratic societies whose members are less than fluent in the language and other practices of the majority invites a response along the lines of Marshall's case for the protection of social rights by the state. The argument, in this case, would be that the state has a responsibility also to ensure that cultural differences do not exclude members of such minority groups from the full enjoyment of citizenship. However, since Marshall treats citizenship precisely as a matter of participating in a common culture or way of life, this argument would imply that the state should aim to assimilate such disadvantaged minorities into the dominant culture – for example, by providing the members of relevant minority groups with remedial classes in the majority language, wheelchair access to public places, and other kinds of assistance so that they may participate in the dominant way of life on something like equal terms. It suggests, in other words, that governments should deal with the disadvantageous effects of cultural pluralism on the civil, political and social rights of minority citizens by integrating them into the majority community.

Multiculturalism's support for collective rights aims, on the contrary, to reinforce, or at least to maintain, separate identities among the citizens. The vulnerability of this strategy to criticism from the empire of uniformity is suggested by Glazer's and Moynihan's observation that the single most important fact about ethnic groups in New York city, 'is that they are also interest groups' (1963, p. 17). Many critics of multiculturalism have agreed, arguing that public support for minority rights amounts to the promotion of sectional interest groups by the state. There are at least two ways in which, from the standpoint of uniformity, this can be seen as leading to a distortion of public life. On the one hand, as Kymlicka argues in the case of the Pueblo, it might be said that interest group organization itself tends to privilege particular groups or factions within the minority concerned. Australian governments, for example, have frequently taken this view, treating leaders of Aboriginal organizations as if they were not truly representative of their communities. On the other hand, following a long-standing liberal concern over the effects of faction in public life, it has been argued that the representation of sectional interests outside of the electoral process leads to the pursuit of those interests to the detriment of the interests of the community as a whole.

In fact, both the liberal case for multiculturalism and the objections just noted are predicated on the same ideal of uniformity. The argument, on the one side, is that provision of cultural rights is required to ensure

uniformity and, on the other, that uniformity is endangered by such
provision. A strong case can usually be made for both of these positions.

PLURALIST DEMOCRACY?

There is another way to approach the issue of diversity, which is simply
to relax the initial presumption in favour of uniformity. The problem is
now less a matter of preserving the principle of uniformity in face of the
unsettling empirical fact of diversity, and more a matter of enabling the
members of a diverse population to live together in peace. What motivates politics, at least within established states, Young suggests, 'is the
facticity of people being thrown together, finding themselves in geographical proximity and economic interdependence ... *A polity consists
of people who live together, who are stuck with one another* (1996, p. 126 –
emphasis added). She goes on to argue that, democracy requires something more than mere coexistence: in addition to the institutional
arrangements of representative government there should also be a practical commitment by all participants to some minimal degree of 'equal
respect for one another' (p. 126). This, as we have seen, appeals to an
image of overarching cultural unity, but it is a unity that is considerably
less substantial than that suggested by most received understandings of
democracy.

Before turning to the redefinition of democracy that is involved here we
should acknowledge an important tradition of political thought that challenges the empire of uniformity. Perhaps the most powerful recent
statement of this challenge is to be found in James Tully's *Strange Multiplicity: Constitutionalism in an Age of Diversity*. The key to the empire of
uniformity, in Tully's view, is the assumption, noted earlier in our discussion of citizenship, that the constitution of a modern state can be treated as
if it were established in a single foundational act of agreement – a social
contract – between the citizens as a whole. This, he argues, denies the
legitimacy of any prior agreement amongst the members of a minority
group to operate according to their own distinctive constitutional arrangements. Thus, while it might be acknowledged that, as a matter of historical
fact, the provenance of constitutional arrangements commonly has a
complex and disordered character, the regulative idea of an imaginary
social contract suggests that a uniform set of laws and conventions for their
interpretation should apply to all members of the population in question.
From this perspective, lack of uniformity within the population and the
territory of a state will be seen as an unfortunate historical residue, a
problem that has to be overcome by the harmonization of laws, the
establishment of a single national language, and measures to combat

resistance to such developments. There may still be room here, as Kymlicka's argument shows, for special provision for minorities, but only within the limits set by the overarching rule of uniformity.

Tully begins his critique by acknowledging the difficulty of establishing a morally defensible framework with which to examine the justice of claims emanating from culturally diverse groups. He observes that an inquiry into justice should first of all 'investigate if the language in which the inquiry proceeds is itself just: that is, capable of rendering the speakers their due' (1995, p. 34). This simple point, frequently overlooked by political theorists, directly challenges the bland assumption – which Kymlicka's discussion, for example, takes for granted – that the conduct of indigenous and other minorities can reasonably be judged according to the liberal standards already embedded in the institutions of the presumed majority. In fact, Tully suggests, if we examine constitutionalism from the perspective of the struggles of Aboriginal peoples, then the empire of uniformity takes on a radically different aspect than conventional accounts of the history of modern political thought would have us believe. First, it appears substantially less attractive: in place of securing the indispensable foundations of a just social order we observe that the empire of uniformity exhibits a studied indifference towards many historical and continuing injustices. Secondly, Tully's examination brings to light the importance in modern political thought of a subordinated, but nonetheless influential style of constitutional thinking – to be found, for example, in the works of Montesquieu and Matthew Hale and again, more recently, in the majority Mabo and Wik judgements of the Australian High Court – a style which sees modern states as consisting of peoples, cultures and ways of life that are, in Young's words, 'stuck with one another'.

Tully's aim is to transform the ways in which we think about constitutional issues in the broadest sense – that is, about the framework of political and legal arrangements within which the people manage their collective affairs. In fact, however, he develops his case for dialogue concerning such arrangements primarily with respect to an important, but nonetheless restricted range of special cases, namely, the struggles of Aboriginal peoples to defend their own constitutional arrangements against the encroachment of the empire of uniformity. While it is easy to see how this approach might be adapted to the situations of national and immigrant minorities it is less clear that it could also be extended – as Tully in fact suggests – to the rather different situations of minorities whose origins are not to be found in the incorporation of members of previously independent groups into a larger political unity.

We can see what is required here by turning to a different version of the pluralist challenge: in this case, to the associational pluralism developed by G.D.H. Cole, Harold Laski and J.N. Figgis and taken up again, in a somewhat revised form, in the recent work of Paul Hirst (1989, 1993). This pluralism shares the liberal view that, as far as reasonably possible, individuals should be free to pursue their diverse understandings of the good life, but it disputes the contractarian conception of relations between citizen and state – the empire of uniformity again – that liberalism derives from that view. Briefly, the argument is that most individual purposes can be pursued effectively only in association with other individuals and that, in any large community, there will be a plurality of purposes that individuals might reasonably wish to pursue. A desirable polity, by this view, would be one that allows, and in some cases actively promotes, the development of associations that enable individuals to pursue their several diverse purposes. The state would, of course, regulate the behaviour of associations, but it would also recognize their autonomy and their right, within limits, to develop in accordance with their own internal decision procedures. Such a pluralism encompasses the positive features of multiculturalism, especially its commitment to the provision of support and protection for indigenous, national and immigrant minorities, while remaining open to the possibility of similar provision for established and emerging minorities of other kinds.

This pluralist challenge to the empire of uniformity has taken us a long way from the view of democracy with which we began. Government of, by and for the peoples, groups and associations who happen to find themselves together in the territory of the one state has little of the appealing simplicity of government of, by and for *the* people of that state – especially when we recall that many of these peoples, groups and associations will have members who inhabit, and may well be citizens of, other states. What is at issue here is nothing less than a major redefinition of democracy. But this point is hardly an objection to the pluralist project: democracy has been redefined before and, as long as the term retains its political salience, it is likely to be redefined again. The most significant changes in the meaning of democracy during the modern period have involved the emergence of representative government and the subsequent move towards full adult suffrage. I have already noted the novelty of the latter. As for representative government, this was not initially regarded as a form of democracy at all. In late eighteenth-century Europe and the Americas, democracy was understood to mean government by the citizens themselves, not government by their representatives and bureaucratic state agencies. Because democracy meant government by the people directly, and because it therefore involved getting the people together in one place, it was not seen as a practicable way of governing any large and populous modern state. Moreover, because the people collectively were seen then – as they often are today – as dangerously unpredictable, democracy was not generally regarded as particularly desirable. Thus, in his contributions to *The Federalist Papers*, James Madison described the American system of representative government as a republic, not a democracy, as a system which had the advantage (as he saw it) of excluding 'the people, in their collective form, from any share' in their government (*Federalist*, p. 63). Today, while the earlier meaning has by no means disappeared, democracy commonly means representative government with full adult suffrage.

In effect, the pluralist argument is that, while still retaining the sense of representative government, democracy should no longer be seen as an affair of a singular body of citizens who together constitute a singular people. Rather it is to be seen as an affair of citizens who constitute a plurality of diverse peoples, groups and associations. One consequence of such a change in the meaning of democracy is that the state could no longer be seen as the central focus of democratic concern: it would be seen, rather, as one significant focus amongst others. Another is that the institutions of representative government should be tempered – as they commonly are in modern democracies – by institutional arrangements of other kinds: a federal system of states, semi-autonomous regions, corporatist interest-group mediation, and more or less self-governing associations of various types. Once the presumption of uniformity has been relaxed there can be few general rules for determining what institutional arrangements might be required to complement those of representative government. It is clear, for example, that arrangements designed to accommodate the concerns of national and indigenous minorities will often have little to offer minorities of other kinds, and that established arrangements may have to adapt as new minorities emerge and older minorities change. Moreover, to say that one set of institutions should be tempered by another is also to say that they should be expected to come into conflict with each other. Here the pluralist arguments in favour of dialogue over constitutional arrangements suggest that the preferred outcome will be some kind of mutually acceptable accommodation, but this may well be difficult to achieve and it may, on occasion, prove to be impossible. If this last case were to arise, the politics of pluralist democracy would then be displaced by a very different kind of political engagement.

I have referred to the pluralist *challenge* to the empire of uniformity: a major redefinition of democracy has been proposed but it is far from being securely established. However, since there are other pressures working in a similar direction – ranging from the emergence of important supra-national and sub-national centres of government to influential arguments in favour of a cosmopolitan democracy (Held, 1995) – it would be surprising if there were to be no significant moves towards a pluralist understanding of democracy. What should be noted in conclusion, then, is that the establishment of a new understanding of democracy does not ensure the elimination of earlier understandings. The idea of democracy as representative government clearly dominates contemporary discussion but the earlier idea of democracy as government by the people themselves has not disappeared – the latter, in fact, provides ammunition for an influential 'democratic' critique of contemporary political arrangements. A similar coexistence can be expected in the present case: while the currency of pluralist democracy is likely to increase, the empire of uniformity has considerable democratic resources at its disposal. It will be a long time before the spectre of government by *the* people is finally laid to rest.

FURTHER READING

Two books by Will Kymlicka provide the best introduction to the debates around multiculturalism and liberal democracy. His *Multicultural Citizenship* presents an influential version of the liberal case for the provision of certain sorts of collective rights for minority cultures, arguing that such provision is required if members of these minorities are to enjoy equal rights with other citizens. Liberals have also argued to the contrary, claiming that such rights are not consistent with the requirements of justice, equal liberty for all citizens and national unity. *The Rights of Minority Cultures* brings together some of the most important contributions to the debates on these issues. Iris Marion Young's *Justice and the Politics of Difference* is the classic text of the politics of difference. Young argues that, even where there is formal equality of citizenship, members of various minority groups may suffer from various forms of unjust discrimination and oppression. Many of the issues she raises are addressed in Seyla Benhabib's edited collection, *Democracy and Difference*, while the closely related question of the recognition of minority values, concerns and institutional arrangements is taken up in the contributions to Amy Gutman (ed.) *Multiculturalism and the Politics of Recognition*. James Tully uses the issue of recognition to develop a powerful argument in favour of pluralism and against 'the empire of uniformity', the view that citizens should have a uniform set of rights and obligations in their relations with the state. Tully focuses primarily on the struggles of the Aboriginal peoples of North America, but he argues that his approach can be generalized to cover other disadvantaged and oppressed groups. William Connolly takes the politics of recognition one stage further by insisting that recognition should be extended to newly emerging identities as well as to established groups. He argues, in effect, not only for pluralism but also, in the words of his title, for *The Ethos of Pluralization*.

Many of the remaining issues touched on in this chapter have been directly addressed in other contributions to this volume and there is no need to provide additional further reading on them here. The most conspicuous exception concerns the implications of the image of the citizen and the democratic ideal of a self-governing community of citizens for the treatment of migrants, especially those who come from parts of the world in which Western notions of citizenship and related political conventions appear to be less than fully developed. The Eurocentrism of Western political thought in general has often been debated. Less often noted are the ways in which romanticized images of the Greek *polis* and the Roman *res publica* have infected both the radical, democratic and participatory, tendencies in Western political thought and the emergence of modern conceptions of people, state and nation. It would be dangerously anachronistic to describe Greek and Roman thinkers as suffering from what we now call ethnocentrism. However, neither their accounts of what it means to be a citizen, of what politics is and what it ought to be, nor their judgements on the ways of life of their neighbours (carefully examined in Hartog, 1988) can be seen as being entirely disinterested. The extent to which our own understandings of democracy and of politics more generally reflect Greek and Roman prejudices is an issue that has yet to be properly explored. Patricia Springborg's *Western Republicanism and the Oriental Prince* provides a provocative counter to the usual treatment of the Greek and Roman origins of political thought, as does Gore Vidal's *Creation*, a novel set in the era of Athenian democracy and written from the perspective of a functionary in the Persian Empire.

REFERENCES

Aristotle (1988) *The Politics*. Cambridge: Cambridge University Press.

Benhabib, S. (ed.) (1996) *Democracy and Difference: Contesting the Boundaries of the Political*. Princeton: Princeton University Press.

Connolly, W.E. (1995) *The Ethos of Pluralization*. Minneapolis: University of Minnesota Press.

Garton Ash, T. (1999) The Puzzle of Central Europe. *New York Review of Books* (18 March 1999), pp. 18–23.

Glazer, N. and Moynihan, D. (1963) *Beyond the Melting Pot*. Boston: Beacon.

Gutman, A. (ed.) (1994) *Multiculturalism and the Politics of Recognition*. Princeton: Princeton University Press.

Hartog, F. (1988) *The Mirror of Herodotus: The Representation of the Other in the Writing of History*. Berkeley: University of California Press.

Held, D. (1995) *Democracy and the Global Order: From the Modern State to Cosmopolitan Governance*. Cambridge: Polity.

Hindess, B. (1998) Divide and Rule: the International Character of Modern Citizenship. *European Journal of Social Theory* 1, 57–70.

Hirst, P.Q. (1993) *Associative Democracy: New Forms of Social and Economic Governance*. Cambridge: Polity.

Hirst, P.Q. (ed.) (1989) *The Pluralist Theory of the State: Selected Writings of G.D.H. Cole, J.N. Figgis, and H.J. Laski*. London: Routledge.

King, D.S. (1987) *The New Right: Politics, Markets and Citizenship*. London: Macmillan.

Kymlicka, W. (1995) *Multicultural Citizenship: A Liberal Theory of Minority Rights*. Oxford: Oxford University Press.

Kymlicka, W. (ed.) (1995) *The Rights of Minority Cultures*. Oxford: Oxford University Press.

Madison, J., Hamilton, A. and Jay, J. (1987/1788) *The Federalist Papers*. Harmondsworth: Penguin.

Marshall, T.H. (1950) *Citizenship and Social Class*. Cambridge: Cambridge University Press.

McNeill, W.H. (1986) *Polyethnicity and National Unity in World History*. Toronto: University of Toronto Press.

Mill, J.S. (1977/1865) Considerations on Representative Government. In J.M. Robson (ed.), *Collected Works of John Stuart Mill*. Toronto: University of Toronto Press, pp. 371–577.

Miller, D. (1995) *On Nationality*. Oxford: Clarendon.

Nietzsche, F. (1967) *On the Genealogy of Morals*. New York: Random House.

Roche, M. (1992) *Rethinking Citizenship: Welfare, Ideology, and Change in Modern Society*. Cambridge: Polity Press.

Springborg, P. (1992) *Western Republicanism and the Oriental Prince*. Cambridge: Polity.

Standing Committee on Multiculturalism (1987) *Multiculturalism: Building the Canadian Mosaic*. Ottawa: Queen's Printer for Canada.

Tully, J. (1995) *Strange Multiplicity: Constitutionalism in an Age of Diversity*. Cambridge: Cambridge University Press.

Vidal, G. (1981) *Creation*. London: Heinemann.

Young, I.M. (1990) *Justice and the Politics of Difference*. Princeton: Princeton University Press.

Young, I.M. (1996). Communication and the Other: Beyond Deliberative Democracy. In S. Benhabib (ed.), *Democracy and Difference: Contesting the Boundaries of the Political*. Princeton: Princeton University Press, pp. 120–35.

CHAPTER 6

CONSTITUTIONAL REFORM AND DEMOCRATIC RENEWAL IN THE UNITED KINGDOM

Michael Dyer

INTRODUCTION

In the White Paper on Scottish devolution, Prime Minister Tony Blair declared: 'The Government are pledged to clean up and modernize British politics. We are committed to a comprehensive programme of constitutional reform. We believe it is right to decentralize power, to open up government, to reform Parliament and to increase individual rights' (*Scotland's Parliament*, cm 3658, p. v). 'The elements are known', he continued, 'A Scottish Parliament and a Welsh Assembly ... an elected Mayor and new strategic authority for London with more accountability in the regions of England ... the incorporation into UK law of the European Convention on Human Rights; Freedom of Information; a referendum on the voting system for the House of Commons.' In his foreword to the same document, the Secretary of State for Scotland claimed: 'The Scottish Parliament will strengthen democratic control and make government more accountable to the people of Scotland' (*Scotland's Parliament*, p. vii).

Taken together, the aspirations and measures outlined by the Prime Minister and other members of the government have been presented as steps towards the creation of a modern democracy. In attempting to establish the validity of such a claim, however, or to evaluate the progress of the project, it is important to stress that institutional change is not necessarily modern or democratic, that modernization does not inevitably promote democratic values, and that it is possible for traditional institutions to be democratized without being modernized. Particularly problematical is the matter of determining what the terms 'modern' and 'democratic' mean in this context, though it might generally be agreed they both have their roots in the eighteenth-century enlightenment: custom and tradition being displaced by reason as the foundation of public institutions, producing coherently integrated political and administrative systems, and government by consent leading eventually to the realization of universal adult suffrage.

The philosophical and practical difficulties in reconciling the tensions within and between the rational-technocratic and consent-democratic strands in political cultures and practices, though not unknown to antiquity, have been clearly evident since the writings of Rousseau and the Federalists, and manifested in the contrast between the Napoleonic and American systems of government. It is important, therefore, to consider whether rational-technocratic constitution-making is possible or desirable in a pluralist democracy. Rational constitutions, however meritorious, are almost inevitably imposed on a society by an individual, or a small elite, reflecting their values and interests. In a fragmenting society, such as Britain, where the decline of deference has challenged the right of elites to establish uniform norms of social behaviour, one might also expect to find the need for a plethora of democratic models to express the political aspirations of its citizenry. It might be argued, therefore, that the most appropriate objective might be less the establishment of a modern democracy than a postmodern democracy in which a variety of disconnected approaches and solutions are allowed to flourish. Whether the British government is currently engaged on such a project is doubtful, though its reforms have produced a variety of approaches and solutions relating to the democratic configuration of the political institutions under its supervision.

A major fault line in approaches towards the construction or reform of democratic institutions and the assessment of their success in achieving democratic ends is the conflict between process and outcome, which has important implications for normative notions of representation, accountability, and the distribution of power. That tension is particularly evident in the struggle between the main influences on Western democratic values, liberal and social democracy. Liberal notions that the power and actions of government should be subordinate to natural rights, especially to private property, contrast with social democracy's classic emphasis on economic equality as the *sine qua non* of political equality. Consequently, whilst the former places heavy emphasis on the importance of (due) process, the latter is focused on what the processes accomplish. Decision-making procedures are of the essence for liberal democrats, for social democrats they are merely instrumental. Liberal and social democrats, therefore, are likely to have different approaches towards the reform of traditional institutions, especially where they have been associated with strong executive rule and the concentration of political power. Indeed, in many respects social democrats are closer to the traditional political Right than liberals in their approaches to government and administration, because both the Left and the Right prefer competent rule to inertia and anarchy. In the UK, neither Labour nor the Conservatives have been temperamentally interested in democracy as process, particularly as the prevailing institutions have demonstrably proved efficacious to their interests, so that their approach to constitutional change has been cautious, pragmatic, unprincipled, and often confusing, preferring to base their popular legitimacy on competent service delivery; rather it has been the Liberal Party by philosophical tradition, historical and contemporary circumstance, that has shown the most interest in democratic constitution-making. Inevitably, as one might expect, different democratic traditions have become cross-fertilized: liberal democrats would insist that good policy is dependent on sound processes, and non-totalitarian social democrats that social democracy cannot be realized without the prevalence of conventional political freedoms, but the antithesis is not easily resolved. At the present time, of course, the pursuit of economic equality is not endorsed by any of the main political parties in Britain, but the dispute as to whether the process or the ability to deliver what the people want is the more important measure of the system's democratic credentials remains a matter of contention. As we shall see, that dichotomy is reflected in recent constitutional legislation.

Arguments over process and outcome are closely linked to the question as to whether democratic government should be the rule of the majority or the rule of the consensus, and the related (though not necessarily so) matter of whether or not democratic government is compatible with geographical remoteness. Consensus democracy is facilitated by electoral systems of proportional representation encouraging the formation of coalition governments, by a *de jure* or *de facto* separation of powers making executives responsible to strong legislatures, and by federalism, in which autonomous state governments and the centre co-operate for mutual advantage. Where the will of national majorities is given greater emphasis, electoral systems are designed to favour the creation of single party legislative control, and subnational authorities are subordinate to the centre. In multinational states, or where identifiable ethnic groups are institutionally recognized, democratic considerations might include local rights of self-government and/or vetoes over the general majority, which are somewhat different from territorial decentralization. The dominant tradition in Britain has been for single party rule at all levels of government, and weak subnational administrations, though the pattern was compromised by substantial administrative devolution to Scotland and the establishment of Home Rule in Northern Ireland, following the creation of Eire. The reforms since 1997, as we shall see, have sustained and extended that pattern, so that differences between England and the other nations have markedly increased.

The great difficulty in assessing the democratic credentials/purposes of the post-1997 constitutional reforms lies in the absence of either an over-arching overt or (apparently) covert strategy. If 'joined-up' government is a feature of the Blair administration, it clearly does not apply in this regard. The willingness of the Labour leadership before the general election to entrust the evolution of its policy on Scottish home rule to the semi-independent Scottish Constitutional Convention, the development of proposals for electoral reform to the Independent Commission on the Electoral System, dominated by Lord Jenkins, a Liberal Democrat, and constructive proposals for reform of the House of Lords to Lord Wakeham, a Conservative, betrays an insouciance bordering on indifference. No attempt has been made to integrate these various reforms. The concrete proposals of the Jenkins Commission are incompatible with the Scotland Act in that Jenkins assumes 72 Scottish MPs, whereas the Scotland Act will reduce their number to around 57. And it is curious, taking the Prime Minister's word at face value, that a *referendum* on electoral reform, whose outcome is presumably uncertain, rather than electoral reform itself, is presented as part of the 'comprehensive programme of constitutional reform'. While the House of Lords recommended by the Wakeham Report includes some regional representation, it is no *Bundesrat*, and while some members are to be popularly elected, it lacks a democratic legitimacy. The various elements, therefore, do not constitute pieces of a jigsaw, but free-standing *ad hoc* solutions to uniquely regarded problems, and as such reflect considerations of statecraft and political management more than principle. It is notable that elements considered integral to the programme in 1997 (Westminster electoral reform, credible House of Lords reform, and genuine freedom of information legislation) have ceased to be so by 2000. As ever, reforms to inhibit executive power that are attractive to oppositions, especially when they have been out of office for a long period and whose leaders lack ministerial experience, lose their lustre with the acquisition of a parliamentary majority. The introduction of devolution is a concession to Celtic nationalism (Scotland and, therefore, Wales), and both domestic and foreign contingencies in Northern Ireland.

Whether the transformation of Britain's baroque democracy into *fin de siècle* rococo is more or less democratic than previously is difficult to establish, but it is certainly not modern. If there is a theme, it is the challenge of devolution (especially in Scotland) to the democratic legitimacy of the Westminster model, and its notions of representation, accountability and the distribution of power.

THE WESTMINSTER MODEL

The practical starting point for any discussion of British democracy is the Westminster model, whose operations have been heavily influenced by its pre-democratic past, most notably by the doctrine of parliamentary sovereignty, established in the late seventeenth century, and the exercise of the Royal Prerogatives, dating from mediaeval times, by the Queen's ministers. Although these traditional arrangements facilitated the development of strong executive rule, political power in the eighteenth century was regarded as balanced between the various powers. The centralization of power, both geographically and institutionally, was largely a function of the democratization of the electoral system. For the successive tranches of new electors, the enlightenment and dictation of the centre was required for the realization of their economic and cultural demands against the hostility and/or inability of local elites to deliver. Nineteenth-century Scottish radicals, for example, looked to Westminster for the removal of the remnants of the pre-1707 Scottish constitution, which was far less popularly based than even the unreformed system south of the border, and the Irish and Scottish peasantry needed Gladstone to impose land reform on locally powerful lairds. More recently, having been denied their civil liberties by a locally devolved legislature, the Roman Catholics in Northern Ireland have had their civil liberties extended through the imposition of direct rule. The notion that geographical proximity is more democratic than government emanating from a somewhat remote capital has not been the dominant feature of the British experience. Moreover, the demand of the working-class electorate for a welfare state not only required action by London, but also a major readjustment to the relationship between the Lords and the Commons in favour of the latter; and while the trade unions have accepted the rule of law, the Taff Vale decision in 1901, a major influence on the emergence of the Labour Party, rendered the working-class movement antipathetic to the rule of lawyers. Neither decentralization nor the separation of powers, therefore, was associated with democratic rule. In the British context, the relationship between democratization and pressures for standardization, economic as well as political equality, implied a critical role for the centre through the assertion of parliamentary sovereignty and the exercise of the Royal Prerogatives by elected politicians.

Executive power has also been enhanced by the operation of the first-past-the-post electoral system because it has mostly produced single party governments, even on those rare occasions when an administration has looked for support beyond its own party. Consequently, the accountability of a government to the legislature has been weak, but its responsibility to the electorate commensurately strong. The unfairness of the translation of votes into seats, therefore, has been offset by a powerful democratic link established between the government and electorate: a relationship consolidated by the vulnerability of administrations to defeat at the polls. Considerations of due process, Freedom of Information Acts, and the role of departmental select committees (assuming their existence is known), are less important than effectiveness. If British government is one of 'elected dictatorship', there is no evidence of its general unacceptability. In short, the system has enjoyed widespread popular consent. Criticisms of its democratic credentials, therefore, ought not to be accepted without careful scrutiny, and distinctions made between proposals designed to improve the system from those which seek to undermine it.

The proposals for reforming the administration of local government are mostly compatible with the Westminster model. The introduction of directly elected mayors is an attempt to revive local democracy by establishing a link between citizens and their elected representative(s), which is clearly lacking at the present time, the concentration of executive power and patronage in the hands of a single person is not too dissimilar from that enjoyed by the Prime Minister, and the subordination of the ward councillors a reflection of the role of parliamentary backbenchers. Ironically, the introduction of proportional representation for the return of councillors, fragmenting power in the council chamber, will probably consolidate rather than weaken the influence of the mayor. Administratively, the development is seen as improving efficiency within local government, enabling decisions to be taken more quickly and for services to be delivered more cheaply. Executive accountability will focus more on the mayoral election than on explanations offered to council committees. Where elected mayors are not introduced, the government is pressing for the replacement of the traditional committee system with a cabinet system, an aspiration dating back to the 1960s. The advantage to Whitehall is that executive mayors would simplify central–local contacts/control, but, as the London case illustrates, popularly elected mayors could become foci of opposition to the policies and standing of national politicians. The realization of a more-than-formal local democracy, therefore, could have important unintended consequences for the territorial distribution of power within the state and political parties.

Reform of the House of Lords and the setting aside of proposed changes to the electoral system have reinforced the *status quo*. The abolition of the hereditary peers was symbolic of a change that had been effected by the Parliament Act, 1911, and the consequently enhanced importance of Prime Ministerial patronage has done nothing to improve its democratic credentials. It is not, however, obviously desirable in democratic terms that the upper chamber should challenge and frustrate the authority of the House of Commons – the government. Even more symptomatic of the government's increasing reluctance to compromise its power is the weakness of its proposals for a greater freedom of information, which is less defensible.

THE CHALLENGE OF SCOTTISH DEVOLUTION TO THE WESTMINSTER MODEL

The democratic integration of the UK was dependent on the ability of the major political parties to mobilize support across the various nations, but from the mid-1960s the gradual decline of Scottish Conservatism and the more fitful emergence of the Scottish National Party threatened the popular legitimacy of the state at a basic level. Consequently, both Harold Wilson and Edward Heath, against the instincts of their Scottish parties and the technocratic thrust of their own local government reforms, were persuaded that a restructuring of the Union might be necessary to sustain consent north of the border. The tortuous politics of devolution in the 1970s need not detain us here, but the failure of the devolution proposals to carry sufficient support in the 1979 referendum was greeted more with relief than anger. Subsequent Conservative general election victories, however, coupled with Labour's seeming inability to win British general elections and the increasing marginalization of Scottish Conservatism, strengthened the demand for a Scottish Parliament, independent or otherwise.

The Campaign for a Scottish Assembly, a pro-home-rule pressure group commanding elite support on the nationalistic centre-left, commissioned its constitutional steering committee, under the chairmanship of Professor Sir Robert Grieve, an academic quangocrat, to produce a *Claim of Right for Scotland*: a list of demands they held that the executive had a duty to concede. (Such 'claims' are rooted in the Presbyterian covenanting tradition, which is a feature of both the Scottish and Northern Irish political culture; and as late as 1950 a Scottish Covenant, somewhat imprecisely requesting a measure of home rule, was signed by approximately two million Scots.) The membership of the steering committee incorporated a mixture of individuals and churchmen, whose status and political connections commanded a certain respect. Amongst their number were Judy Steel (wife of the Liberal leader), Una Mackintosh (wife of the former pro-devolution Labour MP, Professor John Mackintosh), Neil MacCormick (a Nationalist professor of law at

Edinburgh University), Revd Maxwell Craig (sometime Moderator of
the Church of Scotland), Canon Kenyon Wright (an Episcopalian and
later a leading member of the Scottish Convention), Bishop Devine (the
Roman Catholic Bishop of Paisley and Motherwell), and two former
Scottish Office civil servants, Jim Ross (the secretary) and Paul Scott, a
Nationalist. Particularly missing were representatives of the business
community. The committee's report, published in July 1988, was an
uncompromising critique of the Westminster constitution, and was concerned not simply with the territorial distribution of power but the
concentration of power within government and the question of parliamentary accountability.

At the outset, the committee stated: 'The failure to provide good
government for Scotland is the product not merely of faulty British
policy in relation to Scotland, but of fundamental flaws in the British
constitution ... They do not afflict Scotland only ... rectifying these
defects would improve the government of the whole of the United
Kingdom' (*Claim*, 1.2). The English (*sic*) constitution was described as 'an
Illusion of Democracy', because it 'provides for only one source of
power; the Crown-in-Parliament. That one source is now mainly embodied in the Prime Minister, who has appropriated almost all the royal
prerogatives ... Because of party discipline and the personal ambition of
members the consequence is that, so far from Parliament controlling the
Executive (which is the constitutional theory) it is the Prime Minister as
head of the Executive who controls Parliament' (*Claim*, 4.1). Thus, the
Prime Minister enjoyed 'a concentration of power without parallel in
western society'. Furthermore, 'a system which already gives government excessive power adds to that power through the voting system.
Specifically, a large majority may have voted against the Prime Minister
wielding the enormous powers described above, supported by a crush-
ing Parliamentary majority' (*Claim*, 4.5). Taken together the
constitutional provisions 'represent an indulgence to Party dogma and a
hazard to human rights, in particular to the rights of minorities' (*Claim*,
4.8). Relating the general observations to the Scottish context, 'the Scots
are a minority which cannot ever feel secure under a constitution which,
in effect, renders the Treaty of Union a contradiction in terms, because it
makes no provision for the safeguarding of any rights or guarantees and
does not even require a majority of the electorate to override such rights
and guarantees as may once have been offered' (*Claim*, 4.8). It is indica-
tive that the report referred to the American constitution as having been
'framed largely with a view to making such a development, i.e. the
concentration of power in a single person, impossible' (*Claim*, 4.2), and it
is significant that the theme was revisited in the *Epilogue*:

Scotland is not alone in suffering from the absence of consent in government. The problem afflicts the United Kingdom as a whole . . . But Scotland is unique both in its title to complain and in its awareness of what is being done to it . . . These questions will not be adequately answered in the United Kingdom until the concentration of power that masquerades as 'the Crown-in-Parliament' has been broken up. Government can be carried on with consent only through a system of checks and balances capable of restraining those who lack a sense of constraint. (*Claim, Epilogue*)

In response to the *Claim*, a Scottish Constitutional Convention was established in March 1989, including representatives of the Labour Party, Liberal Democrats, the Scottish Trades Union Congress, the Convention of Scottish Local Authorities, representatives of the churches and various civic groups, under the 'Joint Chairs' of Sir David Steel and Lord Ewing, a Labour peer. The refusal of the Conservatives and SNP to participate and Labour's desire to present the Convention process as 'all party' and devolution as 'the settled will of the Scottish people' meant that Liberal Democrat interests had to be accommodated. Indeed, Scottish Devolution was to represent the high water mark of Lib-Lab co-operation over constitutional reform, and was to reflect the liberal critique of the Westminster system. Additionally, there was to be a strong feminist influence, which raised issues of the nature of democratic representation not normally associated with Western democracies.

Crucial to a wholesale reconfiguration of democratic institutions within Scotland was the reform of the electoral system, because 'first past the post' (FPTP) was exceptionally favourable to the Labour Party, underpinning its dominance of local government and Westminster representation. Under FPTP Labour could reasonably expect to win over two-thirds of the seats in the Scottish Parliament with less than 40 per cent of the votes. Although the Liberal Democrats were not disadvantaged by FPTP in Scotland, the introduction of proportional representation, denying Labour a parliamentary majority, promised greatly to enhance their political power, offering the possibility of permanent office in Labour or SNP-led coalition governments. From an early stage the Convention agreed that 'the electoral system should produce results in which the number of seats for various parties is broadly related to the number of votes cast for them' (*Towards a Scottish Parliament*, 1990), and the Scottish Constitutional Commission produced a report in 1994 on the electoral system 'that would offer a clear and radical shift away from the Westminster model' (*Further Steps Towards a Scheme for Scotland's Parliament*, 2.2). The adoption of the Additional Member System, Labour's preferred system of proportional representation following the

Plant Report, ensured that it would be difficult for Labour to win an overall majority, and the most likely administration would be a Lib-Lab coalition or a minority Labour government. The adopted system was also attractive to Labour pessimists who feared the SNP could more easily triumph under FPTP. Importantly, the absence of an overall majority for any party would enhance the desire of the reformers to increase parliamentary accountability.

The Convention also came under great pressure from feminists for gender balance, and initially the Convention had agreed that a statutory obligation should be placed on the parties to offer equal numbers of male and female candidates. Although that was later withdrawn, the Liberal Democrats being opposed in principle, the Constitutional Commission was enjoined

> to make recommendations on gender balance provisions and ethnic minority representation ... based on the Convention's established position that the electoral system for the Scottish Parliament should ensure, or at least take positive action to bring about, equal representation of men and women, and encourage fair representation of ethnic and other minority groups. (*Further Steps*, 3.1)

The report noted that 'the evidence it received was virtually unanimous in agreeing that women and ethnic minorities were inadequately represented in the present Westminster Parliament; and in seeing the creation of a Scottish Parliament as a unique opportunity to start afresh on a fair and equal footing, and to open political debate and decision-making in Scotland to a wealth of human experience at present *unjustifiably* [my italics] marginalized' (*Further Steps*, 3.1). In the event, however, it was decided 'that such a scheme would raise serious civil liberties issues involving the rights of political parties as free and self-organising structures in a civil society' and noted that 'no such statutory system exists in any European democracy' (*Further Steps*, 3.2). Nevertheless, they recommended that each of the parties should be pressured by the Equal Opportunities Commission of the Parliament to make 'the necessary changes in its rules and selection procedures' to meet specified targets of female and ethnic MSPs, and that the Commission be empowered, under 'the provision for "temporary special measures" to redress discrimination contained within the UN Charter on the Rights of Women ... in the event of representation targets not being reached ... to ask the Scottish Parliament to re-examine statutory means of ensuring gender balance and a fair representation of minorities' (*Further Steps*, 3.4). Prior to the first elections, the Labour Party twinned the FPTP constituencies, allocating half to male and half to female candidates, and 'zipped' their lists, alternating males and females. As a result, half the Labour MSPs (Members of the Scottish Parliament) were female, and, although none of the other parties used quotas, a generous number of Nationalist female MSPs ensured that women constituted almost 40 per cent of the new legislature. No attempts, however, were made to secure the return of MSPs from the ethnic minorities, and not a single one was elected. Clearly, the influential feminist lobby had used the representation of ethnics as a cloak to mask their own special pleading, but the implicit ground of their case, that representation should be socially cross-sectional, opens a door to the possibility of intriguing future developments in the determination of the Parliament's composition.

The gender issue, however, was not seen simply as a matter of getting a substantial number of women into the new Parliament, but also as a need to introduce a political culture different from the male-dominated ethos of Westminster.

> The Scottish Parliament should adopt debating procedures and codes of conduct which reflect and promote the best traditions of constructive and consensual debate in Scottish Society. We have received substantial evidence that many women, and some ethnic minority members, are seriously deterred from participation in formal UK politics by the intensely adversarial, partisan and aggressive manner in which it is conducted ... the Scottish Parliament ... through its structures, procedures and Parliamentary culture, [should] avoid the development of such an ethos by adopting a battery of measures designed to minimize social, economic and cultural barriers to women's participation in the Scottish Parliament. (*Further Steps*, 3.4)

For the realization of such 'real changes in the style, atmosphere and decision-making of institutions, women's representation within them has to achieve a "critical mass". An institution with 10% women members remains a male institution ... with 40% women members has to take their distinctive experience and priorities fully into account' (*Further Steps*, 3.1).

The addition of nationalism and feminism to the established liberal critique of the British constitution combined to produce a conviction amongst the reformers that they were engaged not simply in the establishment of a Scottish Parliament, but a redeemed political process. Thus, in presenting their report on procedures for the new legislature, which were to be adopted, the all-party CSG (Consultative Steering Group on the Scottish Parliament) proclaimed, 'Our aim has been to try to capture, in the nuts and bolts of Parliamentary procedure, some of the high aspirations for a better, more responsive and more truly democratic system of government' (*CSG Report*, 1(7)). The policy process was to be more consensual and participatory, and there was to be a quasi-separation of powers. In particular, there was to be a strong committee system in which the roles and functions of departmental select committees and standing committees on legislation were to be combined, exposing the committee stage of bills to specialist scrutiny, and the committees, themselves, were to be empowered to introduce legislation. A high priority was to be given to pre-legislative consultation, which would require the executive both to demonstrate it had consulted affected interests and to justify the need for a particular bill to the appropriate committee before being allowed to proceed. The parliamentary timetable was to be determined by a committee reflecting the party balance in the legislature, not in the government, under the convenership of the presiding officer (Speaker), who, although formally impartial, in certain circumstances could become a rival to the First Minister (Scottish Prime Minister). Frictions, however, were designed not to increase political antagonism but to encourage consensus. As an explicit rejection of the adversarial politics of Westminster, the debating chamber was to be horse-shoe shaped, and 'in keeping with the concept of a family-friendly parliament' (*CSG Report*, 3.3 (12)), the legislature's work would be confined to office hours, with crèche facilities and breaks during the school holidays. It was also considered 'an important principle that the Scottish people should be able to petition the Parliament directly' (*CSG Report*, 3.6 (14)). Individuals were to be given rights of direct access to the legislative process through the committee system, committees were to be peripatetic or based in different parts of Scotland, and formal petitions were to be treated seriously. Given the absence of an overall majority for any party in the parliament, the thrust of these reforms had a reasonable chance of success, particularly if there were to be a minority administration. By and large this model has commanded general support within the Scottish political class. At leadership level Labour and the Liberal Democrats have demonstrated a willingness to co-operate, ideologically the Scottish Nationalists applaud a system that rejects Westminster practices in favour of procedures that feature in European legislatures, and the Conservatives are not entirely unhappy with a structure that makes all parties minorities and gives them parliamentary representation.

DEVOLUTION IN WALES AND NORTHERN IRELAND

Unlike the Scottish Parliament, the Welsh Assembly has not been entrusted with primary legislation, but its manner of election and parliamentary procedures are similar. The Welsh Additional Member System, however, was calibrated to produce a Labour majority, and it was not anticipated that the administration would be any other than single party rule. The culture of Lib-Lab co-operation leading to a climate of coalitionism in Scotland was not a feature of the evolving Welsh political environment, so the failure of Labour to win an overall majority produced a minority administration seeking to govern on Westminster lines, which was at variance with the liberal nature of the devolved constitution. The crisis in Wales following the successful tabling of a no confidence motion in the administration's leadership, illustrated the incompatibility between the Westminster approach and the institutional framework adopted. Moreover, the dissonance between power and responsibility in the Welsh settlement is manifest, so that the determination of accountability between Welsh and UK ministers for policies is proving particularly problematic. Consequently, the Welsh Assembly is emerging more a thorn in the flesh than Edinburgh, because its lack of powers encourages irresponsible opposition to government policy, whereas the Scottish parliamentarians are forced not only to address their own rhetoric but have their opportunities for striking postures vitiated by the necessary consideration of humdrum legislation.

Devolution to Northern Ireland has its own history, which is well known and cannot be dealt with here. It is, nevertheless, instructive to note that the need to reconcile a deeply divided polity has produced a form of consociational democracy at variance with both the Westminster and the Scottish models. Democracy as single party majoritarianism has clearly failed in the province, and even the creation of coalition governments out of 'real' majorities, implicit in the Scottish and Welsh approaches, does not produce the necessary inclusiveness. Instead, recognition of the plural nature of Northern Irish society has come to include proportionate representation in government as well as in the legislature, with ministers choosing their own portfolios as the quota admits them to the cabinet. It might well be argued that this is a logical extension of PR, because it gives office to parties that might otherwise be excluded from the administration (frequently second largest parties), and the proportionate distribution of executive power minimizes the inordinate influence minor parties often exert under such systems. Perhaps the Northern Ireland model might be considered for wider applicability.

Emphasis on the virtues of consensus, particularly evident in the Scottish and Northern Irish approaches to devolution, of course, belies the fragmented nature of their social and party systems. Indeed, they illustrate the maxim that the more adversarial a society, the more its need to minimize disagreement. The English, unlike their neighbours, can endure adversarial politics because on essentials they are united.

DEVOLUTION AND THE ENGLISH REGIONS

Quite how England will respond to the new Celtic institutions is not entirely clear. The anomalous role of MPs from the peripheral nations in relation to English legislation has already been raised by the West Lothian Question, which asks why Scottish Westminster MPs, who cannot vote on those matters affecting their constituents that have been devolved to Edinburgh, can vote on those same matters as they affect England. The present Conservative leadership is proposing that only English MPs should be permitted to vote on peculiarly English matters, effectively transforming the UK parliament into a devolved English parliament for those purposes. Such a resolution, however, could prove somewhat problematical, because the asymmetric nature of devolution implies that the competence of MPs from Scotland, Wales and Northern Ireland would differ. Presumably, the Speaker would have to give a ruling from one bill, or clauses of bills, to the next, indicating which MPs could participate in the process. A further complication is the operation of the Barnett Formula, which determines the size of the treasury block grant available to the Scottish administration. Under its terms, the Scottish block is set by the application of the formula to previously established levels of spending on devolved subjects in England. Consequently, strategic decisions regarding devolved matters are greatly influenced by the English settlement. It would, for example, be almost impossible for Scotland to sustain a National Health Service were England to decide on its abolition, because the resources to sustain it would disappear from the Scottish block. Thus, it might well be argued that Scottish MPs have a legitimate interest in 'purely' English matters because they largely determine the options available to Edinburgh. The West Lothian Question, if not a mirage, is at least as difficult to define as it is to answer.

Although devolution is about recognizing differences, 'local solutions to local problems', it is also about geographical economic inequalities. The realization of Scottish devolution has highlighted the favourable treatment of Scotland under the Barnett Formula, which affords a 20 to 30 per cent per capita advantage to Scotland over the rest of Britain, reflecting not simply a greater need but an advantage over the poorer regions of England and Wales. The Conservatives are likely to exploit this issue as a means of re-establishing themselves as the protectors of English interests, both in areas of net tax contribution (London and the

South East) and in regions of relative deprivation (the North, North West, Yorkshire/Humberside, and the South West). It is notable that the Welsh Conservatives supported a motion of no confidence in the Labour First Secretary for his inability to get an extra £200m of public money from the treasury. Labour MPs and party interests in the North, historically envious of Scotland's advantages and mindful of the new politics in Wales, are likely to demand the introduction of regional assemblies. The outcome will probably lead to greater pressures on public spending, because governments will find it politically easier to increase equality through the allocation of more resources to disadvantaged regions than to redistribute the cake.

CONCLUSIONS

The fiction of parliamentary sovereignty remains in place, but the reality is increasingly difficult to detect and sustain. The Scottish Parliament may be a subordinate legislature, but its political status affords a greater autonomy, the lesser Welsh Assembly cannot be treated with disdain, arrangements in Northern Ireland are subject to endorsement by the Irish Republic and the USA, and even English local authorities, through the introduction of elected mayors, might become significant centres of semi-autonomous local power. Labour's attempt to hold the system together by central patronage has already failed, so that central–local relations under the new dispensation are likely to become more problematical, particularly so if the parties running the regional administrations were to be different from that in control at Westminster, and exceptionally so if the Nationalists were to assume power in Belfast, Cardiff and Edinburgh. Furthermore, the question of democratic accountability is likely to become confused and fudged, because it is not clear whether devolution will result in citizens holding their regional MPs accountable for deficiencies in service delivery, or whether UK politicians, especially the treasury, will be blamed by citizens, goaded by their local representatives, for providing inadequate resources. The lesser their powers, the more the devolved institutions are likely to behave like regional pressure groups than governments. The system does not look particularly stable. A body like the Bundesrat is needed to involve the subnational governments in the formulation of fiscal policy, and to encourage a regional consensus on revenue sharing. Such a development, however, might also require a re-examination of the continuing utility of asymmetric devolution.

While the territorial fragmentation has been the most significant development, there has been a challenge to the Westminster model of representation and decision-making. The Scottish reformers have explicitly pursued a system of checks and balances overtly inspired by the constitution of the USA, effectively ending the likelihood of one-party government and establishing a true accountability between the executive and legislature. The character of the new system was evident in the compromise cobbled together regarding the 'abolition' of student fees in Scotland. Similar developments in Wales have already drawn blood. The introduction of proportional representation was crucial to those changes, and were proportional representation introduced for UK elections the cornerstone of the Westminster model would be removed. British democracy would be operating on a completely different para-digm. Whatever the merits of such a transformation, such a dispensation ought not to be accepted as either modern or as more democratic without debate. The emphasis on 'checks and balances' is based on an historic fear of democratic influence, and its parliamentarism on notions of accountability predating mass electorates. The separation of powers in the USA, commended by the Scottish reformers, has exposed its politics to the inordinate influence of powerful pressure groups, and its citizens have become increasingly alienated from the electoral process. The Westminster model, essentially dating from the 1911 Parliament Act and universal manhood suffrage in 1918, has developed not to frustrate democracy but as a consequence of democracy. It has adapted to political change far better than the older constitution of the USA, and the impor-tance of the link between the electorate and the executive, the crucial element of accountability in mass democracy, was not lost on the French in 1958 nor, more recently, on the Italians, in attempts to make their political institutions more representative. One might argue that the major problem of modern government is not the representation of a fragmented pluralism, but the creation of majorities to confront the excessive influence of sectional interests.

Perhaps more important for the future of democracy in Britain has been the diminution of decisions taken by representative institutions. The granting of independence to the Bank of England has weakened political control over important decisions relating to the economy, the bureaucracies of the European Union increasingly inhibit the compe-tence of the Westminster and the devolved parliaments, and the incorporation of the European Convention on Human Rights into Eng-lish and Scots law has increased the powers of unelected judges. The European Court of Human Rights' views on judicial independence also threaten to restrict the role of the Lord Chancellor. A decision to join the Euro would have a qualitative influence on not only the power of Westminster but the capacity of Britons to make strategic economic decisions. Judges may better secure civil liberties than the Home Secretary and parliamentary statutes, and economic decisions taken by an enlightened technocratic elite may better promote the general good than those taken by a partisan Chancellor of the Exchequer, but they are not democratic in character. The current malaise in the state of democracy in Britain is one that affects the Western world generally, a crisis of confidence in the belief that political power can challenge the economic dominance of global markets in constructing the future. Against that all other issues are secondary.

FURTHER READING

Representative and Responsible Government (Birch, 1964) is the best foundation for understanding the basic issues at stake in the contemporary debate over constitutional reform, because it makes explicit the dialectic between different paradigms of what the British constitution is and/or ought to be; and the *Claim of Right* (Constitutional Steering Committee, 1988) offers a stimulating and provocative liberal critique of the Westminster model. *Constitutional Futures* (Hazell, 1999) provides an excellent review of post-1997 developments and their possible implications, and the journal *Representation* (especially Spring 1999) has sustained a lively academic debate on such matters. On specific issues, the Jenkins Report (Cm 4090-I, 1998) argues the case for electoral reform, though its recommendations have more than a whiff of gerrymandering, and the Wakeham Report (Cm 4534, 2000) highlights rather than resolves the conundrum of reform of the Lords. Particularly helpful for readers focusing on specific matters are the House of Commons research papers, some of which are listed in the bibliography.

BIBLIOGRAPHY

A House for the Future: Report of the Royal Commission on the Reform of the House of Lords, Cm 4534, 2000.
Birch, A. (1964) *Representative and Responsible Government*. Allen & Unwin.
The Constitutional Steering Committee, *A Claim of Right for Scotland: Report of the Constitutional Steering Committee presented to the Campaign for a Scottish Assembly*, July 1988.
Gray, O. and Morgan, B. (1997) *Northern Ireland: Political Developments since 1972.* House of Commons Research Paper, 98/57, 11 May 1997.
Gray, O. (1998) *Cabinets, Committees and Elected Mayors.* House of Commons Research Paper, 93/38, 19 March 1998.
Gray, O. (1998) *The Northern Ireland Bill: Implementing the Belfast Agreement.* House of Commons Research Paper, 98/76, 20 July 1998.
Hazell, R. (1999) (ed.) *Constitutional Futures: A History of the Next Ten Years.* Oxford: Oxford University Press.

The Operation of Multi-Layer Democracy. Scottish Affairs Select Committee, Second
    Report, Vol. I, HC 460-I, 18 November 1998.
Report of the Consultative Steering Group on the Scottish Parliament. The Scottish
    Office, 1998.
The Report of the Independent Commission on the Voting System, Cm 4090-I, 1998.
Representation, Spring 1999, 36(1). (Issue on Devolution and Electoral Change.)
Scotland's Parliament, Cm. 3658, 1997.
The Scottish Constitutional Commission, *Further Steps Towards a Scheme for
    Scotland's Parliament. A Report to the Scottish Constitutional Convention*, October
    1994.
Twigger, R. (1998) *The Barnett Formula*. House of Commons Research Paper,
    98/8, 12 January 1998.
Winetrobe, B.K. (1998) *The Scotland Bill: Some Constitutional and Representational
    Aspects*. House of Commons Research Paper, 98/3, 7 January 1998.
Winetrobe, B.K. (1998) *The Northern Ireland Bill: Some Legislative and Operational
    Aspects of the Assembly*. House of Commons Research Paper, 98/77, 17 July
    1998.
Wood, E. (1998a) *Regional Government in England*. House of Commons Research
    Paper, 98/9, 13 January 1998.
Wood, E. (1998b) *The Greater London Authority Bill: A Mayor and Assembly for
    London*. House of Commons Research Paper, 98/115, 11 December 1998.

CHAPTER 7

MAJORITIES, MINORITIES AND DEMOCRATIC GOVERNANCE: THE DISUNITING OF CANADA?

Peter Leslie

Canada presents the strange case of a fortunate country, the envy of much of the world, that is nonetheless recurrently in danger of breakup. Its credentials as a liberal democracy are solid. As one of the world's oldest federations – after the USA and Switzerland – Canada has had a record of peace and prosperity, democratic governance, and (with some evident blemishes) respect for individual and minority rights; but there has also been a record of political discontent, seemingly on all sides.

Most obvious are the discontents of the province of Quebec, which comprises one-quarter of the population, and is the only province (of ten) to have a French-speaking ('francophone') majority, descendants of the colonists of New France. There is a significant movement in Quebec for political independence. Since 1994 the provincial government has been in the hands of the secessionist *Parti québécois* (PQ), which first held office 1976-85. Twice, a PQ government has called a referendum on sovereignty, although in both cases preservation of the Canadian economic union was envisioned. The first referendum was in 1980, when a proposal for 'sovereignty-association' – political independence, but in economic association with 'Canada' – was rejected by the voters, 60 per cent to 40 per cent. The second referendum, in 1995, nearly broke up the country. A proposal for sovereignty, which would be declared unilaterally if negotiations for economic association failed, was rejected by less than a one per cent margin. The present PQ programme calls for a new referendum during the Party's current term of office, although Premier Lucien Bouchard has made clear that it will be held only under 'winning conditions'. Since support for all variants of the sovereignty option has dropped off considerably since 1995, prospects are that the referendum will be indefinitely postponed, unless the polls show a sharp reversal of the late-1990s trend.

The strength of the independence movement in Quebec is not the only source of strain on the Canadian federation, and on Canadian democracy. Other factors contributing to uncertainty about Canada's future are regional divisions and resentments, controversies over immigration policy and related issues of 'multiculturalism', the discontents and territorial claims of aboriginal peoples, and the structure of the federal system itself.

The last of these factors, the federal structure, may sharpen political conflict in two different ways, even if the roots of conflict are social, cultural, or economic. First, the institutions of Canadian federalism allow for and appear actually to promote a fairly high level of conflict between the federal and the provincial governments, providing an institutional focus and substantial publicity for disaffected groups (Cairns, 1977). Second, majoritarian democracy at the federal level, with strongly disciplined parties and an electoral system that at times has left large parts of the country without any effective voice in governmental decisions, tends to augment regional tensions considerably. Thus an explanation of Canada's present troubles is to be sought in a combination of social forces and institutional design. Canada's geographical position, resulting in the overwhelming economic and cultural presence of the USA, is a complicating factor. In fact, as will be argued below, no discussion of regional and ethnic conflict in contemporary Canada, nor of federal–provincial and interprovincial relations, can afford to neglect one of the dominant facts of Canadian history, namely the continental context – and now the global one as well.

For a foreign observer, for whom the prospect of Canada's splitting up into two or more states is probably neither a dream nor a nightmare, Canada's travails may nonetheless be of considerable interest. Exploring the reasons for present-day strains on Canadian unity invites reflection on the creation, design, evolution, and viability of federal unions and other multi-layered democracies. In addition, a review of proposed changes in institutional design raises interesting questions of democratic theory, or how to achieve balance among social forces within a democratic framework.

NATION BUILDING AND THE ECLIPSE OF 'CANADIAN DUALISM'

Canada is a country built 'in defiance of geography' (Mackintosh, 1923, p. 25). That is because the natural lines of communication in North America run north–south, whereas Canada was built on an east–west axis for political reasons. These included maintaining the British connection after the American War of Independence, and building a country 'from sea to sea' – a country that many hoped would reflect the linguistic and religious dualism of its population. Both aims implied resistance to American conceptions of a 'manifest destiny' – a USA political slogan of the latter nineteenth century – to absorb the whole continent within its borders.

The original step in this country-building process ('Confederation', 1867) involved the federal union of previously separate colonies, but it involved also the division of the largest of them. The Province of Canada was divided into its eastern and western sections, which became Quebec and Ontario. Thus, for Quebec, the significance of Confederation was that it gained a new measure of autonomy. Confederation held out the promise of a country that would respect equally the religious, linguistic, and social legacy of New France – conquered in 1760 – and the British origin of its later colonists. Thus the Canadian federal system was very largely the product of negotiation between political leaders in Canada East and Canada West; it created a form of bicommunal polity (Leslie, 1986) in which the Catholic, French-speaking majority in Quebec had the capacity to develop as a self-governing community, on the basis of laws and customs that had their origins in the pre-conquest period.

Confederation also created the foundations for a transcontinental union. The four-province federation was a country of the Atlantic seaboard and the St Lawrence valley, but almost immediately (1870) it purchased vast lands to the west and north, comprising most of the northern half of the continent. The 'North-West Territories', an area under the control of the British crown, became, in effect, an imperial possession ruled from Ottawa, the fledgling nation's capital. Except for the most northerly zone, these lands were subsequently made into new provinces or annexed to existing ones.[1] The other feature of the process of expansion was the accession of other colonies, beginning with British Columbia (bordering on the Pacific) in 1871. The present provincial and territorial structure is shown in Table 7.1.

The political arrangements invented in Canada were the first to marry Westminster-style cabinet government with a federal division of powers. The essence of this system is that the federal and provincial governments have parallel structures, each with their own list of powers. Broadly speaking, the provinces were assigned jurisdiction over all matters of cultural or social significance. All institutions of direct relevance to the citizen and to the life of local communities (including municipal institutions and functions), were to be provincially controlled. To the Catholic, French-speaking 'fathers of confederation', this was the essential feature of the new country. To those of British origin, however, what was essential was that Ottawa was given the fiscal and legislative powers necessary to develop the national economy, to provide for defence, and to implement treaties entered into by the Empire. On the basis of these broad distinctions, reflected in two lists of exclusive powers and an apparently sweeping federal residuary power,[2] it appeared that a clear

Table 7.1 Canada – provinces and territories

Province/ territory	Area (km²) ('000)[a]	Population[b] '000	%	GDP per capita (index)[c]	Language in home (%)[d] English	French	Other
Newfoundland	405	544	1.8	67	99.1	0.2	0.6
Nova Scotia	55	934	3.1	75	96.0	2.2	1.3
Prince Edward Is.	6	137	0.5	74	97.1	2.2	0.4
New Brunswick	73	753	2.5	78	68.4	30.1	0.6
Quebec	1,542	7,335	24.2	87	10.1	81.9	5.8
Ontario	1,076	11,413	37.7	106	82.4	2.7	12.4
Manitoba	647	1,139	3.8	88	87.3	2.0	8.6
Saskatchewan	651	1,024	3.4	95	93.9	0.6	4.2
Alberta	662	2,915	9.6	122	90.3	0.6	7.5
British Columbia	945	4,009	13.2	95	85.4	0.4	12.1
Nunavut Terr.	2,093	25	0.1	–	–	–	–
Northwest Terr.	1,346	40	0.1	–	–	–	–
Yukon Territory	482	32	0.1	121	94.8	1.6	2.5
Canada	9,985	30,301	100.0	100	66.7	22.3	9.0

[a] Source: 'Facts about Canada: Land and Freshwater Areas', Natural Resources Canada website, http://atlas.gc.ca/english/facts/surfareas.html
[b] Figures are for 1998. Source: 'Population', Statistics Canada website, http://www.statcan.ca/english/pgdb/people/population/demo02.htm
[c] Figures are for 1997. Source: 'Gross domestic product', Statistics Canada website, http://www.statcan.ca/english/pgdb/economy/economics/econ15.htm
[d] Figures are for 1996. Source: 'Population by home language, 1996 census', Statistics Canada website, http://www.statcan.ca/english/pgdb/people/population/demo 29a.htm, ... demo29b.htm, ... demo29c.htm

distinction had been achieved between the responsibilities of the federal government and those of the provinces.

This soon turned out to be an illusion. Both orders of government drew maximally on their constitutional powers to expand their activities, producing overlaps in federal and provincial roles, and resulting in substantial duplication and conflict. Federal–provincial conflicts have been all the more severe, in that the provinces have had no direct role in the formulation of federal policy or the passage of federal laws. Habits of party discipline quickly formed (unlike in the USA), with the consequence that federal parliamentary majorities overrode provincial sensitivities and policy objectives, and provincial legislative majorities backed the provincial governments in repeated challenges to federal power. In the result, the two orders of government, both operating under a majoritarian, winner-takes-all conception of democracy, often work at cross purposes; or, when they co-operate, they may do so because of Ottawa's fiscal *force majeure*.

As a nation-building enterprise with explicitly transcontinental ambitions, Confederation held out the promise of the development of a bi-national state occupying the northern half of the continent. In the only significant settlement in the prairie region, the south-east corner of the present Manitoba, a racially mixed group (French/Indian, generally known as Métis) comprised about half the population, creating the nucleus of a francophone Catholic community. This group, it was thought, had the potential to grow in size through the influx of settlers from Quebec, in which case the future prairie provinces would develop as bicultural communities. Indeed, the federal legislation establishing the prairie provinces of Manitoba, Saskatchewan, and Alberta explicitly provided for the protection of minority religious and linguistic rights. These provisions, however, were quickly overwhelmed (but not judicially forgotten, as became evident during the 1960s) by changing demographic trends, induced by the influx of Orangemen from Ontario and, later, eastern European immigrants who assimilated to the English-language majority. Thus it happened that the Catholic-French population (or now, simply, the francophone community) flourished only within Quebec and, to a lesser extent, within the adjacent territory in New Brunswick and Ontario. Today, about 80 per cent of Canada's francophones live in Quebec, a province in which they predominate by a four-to-one majority.

In ethnic and linguistic composition Canada now exhibits substantial and increasing diversity. As recently as the 1960s, it was common to refer to 'Canadian dualism', implying a majority and a minority defined primarily in terms of language and culture. However, this was never more than wishful thinking, and never strictly accurate; today, it would be widely regarded as an absurdity. There are three good reasons for rejecting the bilingual-bicultural view of Canada. One is that the concept of dualism, and even more so the idea that Canada has been the creation of 'two founding races',[3] entirely neglects the existence of the aboriginal peoples. Their numbers are relatively small, but, as described below, relations between aboriginal and non-aboriginal peoples have become an important and increasingly troubled feature of Canadian political life. The second reason for abandoning the 'dualism' concept is that, territorially, linguistic compartmentalization continues apace; the francophone areas continue to shrink to the Quebec core plus fringe areas in New Brunswick and Ontario. Finally, and dramatically, all major cities in Canada have become, as a result of shifting immigration patterns, 'riotously multicultural' (Cameron, 1990). Thus the older image of Canada as being – outside of its francophone enclaves – predominantly a 'British' country no longer applies. Today, Canada is a British offshoot only within a few smaller cities and in rural, long-settled areas in the Atlantic provinces, Ontario, and British Columbia.

CANADIAN FEDERALISM AND QUEBEC NATIONALISM

Notwithstanding the presence of aboriginals and large numbers of recent immigrants of non-European background, many francophone Quebecers continue to see Canada as a political framework for the co-existence of two national communities, increasingly defined territorially rather than on the basis of language or ethnicity. A multiracial, plurilingual Quebec is one national community; 'Canada' – implicitly, the other nine provinces and the territories – is the other. This is a perspective that is shared by 'sovereignists'[4] and the many federalists who are self-declared nationalists. Both groups tend to view Quebec as a 'distinct society' characterized in part – but only in part – by the public status and the predominance of French. Thus language use, at least in private situations, does not establish the boundaries of the national (Quebec) community; rather, Quebec is a political entity, territorially bounded, in which French is the 'public language'. That means that French is the language in which Quebec does its business: the dominant language for economic affairs, and the sole official language. Quebec nationalists want to preserve and strengthen Quebec as a predominantly francophone society, but they welcome the presence of significant linguistic minorities, anglophone and other ('allophone'), and supports them through the provision of public services, notably health care, in English. (English-language schooling, though, is restricted – see below.)

Contemporary Quebec nationalism contrasts with the French-Canadian nationalism of the pre-1960s era, in which the francophone minorities of other provinces could and did participate (hence earlier notions of 'Canadian dualism'). Contemporary Quebec nationalism is also appropriately distinguished from an ethnic *québécois* nationalism that predominated during the 1960s but has since receded in strength. Today the theme of civic nationalism, denoting a Quebec of racial and cultural pluralism, prevails both in the PQ's official pronouncements and in general francophone public discourse. The basic idea is that immigrant groups necessarily become part of a larger society, even when ancestral languages, religions, and customs remain important in the context of family life and in neighbourhood communities. In Quebec the larger society to which they belong and in which they live their public lives is specifically *québécois*, while in other provinces it is Canadian.

This perception of sociological reality, widely shared among francophone Quebecers, leaves plenty of room for conflicting views of what self-governance within a democratic political system requires or, in a logical sense, implies. There is a gamut of views. The sovereignists – the PQ and its supporters,[5] plus the *Bloc québécois* in the federal parliament – want political independence but preservation of the Canadian economic union. The Quebec provincial Liberals and many other Quebec federalists want expanded powers and financial resources for the province within a decentralized federation. Federal Liberals from Quebec,[6] many of whom are committed to Quebec's being predominantly francophone but not to official unilingualism, find no inconsistency in celebrating federalism as it is. To a large extent, these three groupings are constituted by their inheritance of, or their reaction against, the political philosophy and policies of former Canadian Prime Minister Pierre Trudeau. Trudeau, who dominated the political scene from 1968 to 1984, was a crusader against Quebec nationalism, which he saw as being inherently exclusivist in racial and linguistic terms, as well as politically reactionary (Trudeau, 1968). In its place he advanced a pan-Canadian nationalism, partly economic, combined with a policy of official bilingualism – a policy that, in the latter part of his career, was complemented by the accommodation of aboriginal demands and by support for multiculturalism, or the cultural heritage of diverse immigrant groups.

Trudeau reasoned that if Quebec were to gain powers not exercised by other provinces, a backlash would build up against it. Non-Quebecers, he argued, would come to resent its influence in shaping federal policies and passing legislation that would apply to other provinces but not to it. Thus he became an implacable opponent of 'special status' for Quebec, and of course of *indépendentisme*, which he saw as self-serving for provincial elites and asphyxiating for the society at large. Far better, he said, for Quebecers to participate fully in federal politics and thus also to play an international role, opening up their society to liberal cosmopolitanism. But a necessary precondition for this, he argued, was that the rules of Canadian politics should not be stacked against francophones: hence the policy of official bilingualism that would expand francophone Quebecers' influence, and that of francophone minorities in other provinces, in the Canadian public service and in public life generally. It was a policy that required the development of a Canadian political elite with a bilingual capacity, and would permit the bulk of the population to remain unilingual in either French or English. The latter aspect of the rationale for the policy was, however, never adequately communicated or publicly understood, a failing that contributed mightily to opposition to official bilingualism outside of Quebec.

Ironically, official bilingualism at the provincial level was (and remains) opposed by Quebec nationalists, on the grounds that it would ultimately undermine the position of the French language within the province. The problem has been seen as demographic: a birth rate that has become the lowest in Canada (well below the rate of replacement), combined with the influx of immigrants. Immigration to other provinces reduces the weight of Quebec within Canada as a whole, and immigration to Quebec threatens the predominance of the French language there, if immigrants adopt English rather than French as their public language. The response to this demographic situation has been to claim that Quebec should receive a share of immigrants proportionate to its population – an objective that has been impossible to achieve, as it depends on immigrants' preferences as much as on public policy – and to adopt restrictive language policies in Quebec. Thus, all newcomers, but not anglophones who grew up in the province, must send their children to French-language schools, and commercial signs must be predominantly in French. It was a Liberal premier, Robert Bourassa, who devised the main outlines of this policy in 1974; the PQ strengthened it considerably when it came into office two years later.

In addition to favouring a restrictive language policy, Quebec nationalists – whether sovereignist or Liberal/federalist – demand expanded powers for Quebec, not only in matters of cultural significance but also (as described below) in the economic aspects of governance. With few exceptions, those francophone Quebecers who are not nationalist simply stay out of Quebec provincial politics; if they run for office, almost all choose the federal arena. Or perhaps the generalization should be: francophone Quebecers who want to get anywhere in provincial politics espouse nationalism – whether 'soft' and federalist, or 'hard' and sovereignist. They are trained to it, simply by virtue of acting in the provincial arena.

Differences between the two groups of nationalists have been sharply drawn during the two referendum campaigns, but have not prevented, on numerous occasions, the formation of a common front against Ottawa. This was most dramatically the case in 1981–2, in response to a constitutional initiative launched by Prime Minister Trudeau. The outcome of that initiative was the Constitution Act, 1982,[7] containing two main elements: a formula on the basis of which the constitution could henceforth be amended within Canada, and the Canadian Charter of Rights and Freedoms. The latter empowered the judiciary to pronounce on the constitutional validity of federal and provincial laws on the basis of Charter principles. After federal–provincial negotiations that resulted in several substantive amendments, all provinces but Quebec endorsed the 'new constitution' (actually, an add-on to the existing constitution, not a replacement of it). Quebec accepted the legality of the Constitution Act, 1982, but attacked its legitimacy on procedural grounds, and claimed (accurately) that both of its main features violated and narrowed traditional rights of the Quebec government and legislature (National Assembly). A resolution of the National Assembly protesting the Act was supported by the Liberal Party as well as by the PQ, then in office.

This event has remained pivotal as regards constitutional debate and party politics (both federally and provincially) in Quebec. Mr Trudeau and his followers – he remained, until his death in 2000, an icon among federal Liberals – insist that the assent of the Quebec government was not needed, and that the support of a majority of Quebec (federal) MPs provided adequate legitimation. The provincial Liberal Party has sought a new constitutional amendment that would repair the damage of the 1982 Act, a position also endorsed by the federal Conservatives under the leadership of Brian Mulroney, who became Prime Minister in 1984. When, provincially, the Liberal Party, under Robert Bourassa, assumed office a year later, the way was clear for the negotiation of a package of constitutional amendments that would enable Quebec to adhere to the Canadian constitution 'in honour and enthusiasm', as Mr Mulroney put it. Unanimous agreement among the premiers was secured, in the form of a 'Meech Lake Accord' in 1987. 'Meech', however, failed. A coalition of Trudeau Liberals (including Jean Chrétien, Prime Minister since 1993), various provincial politicians, and aboriginal leaders succeeded in blocking the necessary legislative resolutions. A new attempt, contained in a unanimous federal–provincial agreement in 1992, the 'Charlottetown Accord', also failed; in fact it was rejected in Quebec as well as in most of the other provinces, in a Canada-wide referendum (McRoberts and Monahan, 1993). It is quite doubtful whether any constitutional amendment adequate to obtain Quebec's formal endorsement of the Canadian federal system can ever be achieved. Either Quebec will opt for secession, as it very nearly did (or at least appeared nearly to do) in 1995, or demands for redress of Quebec's constitutional grievances will simply fade into the background.

A major event in the Canadian constitutional drama was a 1998 decision of the Supreme Court on the subject of secession (as described in Leslie, 1999). The federal government asked the court to rule on Quebec's claimed right of secession. In response, the court declared that Quebec does not have a unilateral right to secede from Canada, but that if ever a 'clear majority' of Quebecers opts for secession on the basis of a 'clear question', the rest of Canada would have an obligation to negotiate. This is an obligation that the court declared to be implicit in four principles that 'inform and sustain the constitutional text' – federalism, democracy, constitutionalism and the rule of law, and respect for minorities. The same set of principles, the court unanimously ruled, would govern the negotiations themselves. Accordingly, Quebec could not dictate the terms of secession, which would have to be accomplished through constitutional amendment. Perhaps most crucially, one could not presume that agreement would be reached; secession would not be a foregone conclusion after a clear 'yes' vote. If negotiations failed, and Quebec declared independence unilaterally, the international community would have to decide whether Quebec's action was legitimate.

Of particular interest, in the context of a discussion of democratic governance, is the court's determination, that under international law the right to the self-determination of peoples 'is normally attainable within the framework of an existing state'. The court declared:

> There is no necessary incompatibility between the maintenance of the territorial integrity of existing states, including Canada, and the right of a 'people' to achieve a full measure of self-determination. A state whose government represents the whole of the people or peoples resident within its territory, on a basis of equality and without discrimination, and respects the principles of self-determination in its own internal arrangements, is entitled to the protection under international law of its territorial integrity. (Canada. Supreme Court, 1998, paragraph 130)

How, then, is self-determination to be achieved, if not through political independence? Is the Supreme Court here implicitly describing Quebecers as 'a people'? This is a term the federal government has always resisted, for fear of giving substance to challenges to Canadian territorial integrity under international law. And what, too, of the aboriginal peoples of Canada, and their rights to self-determination and perhaps to self-government? As will be seen in the next section, devising arrangements for the governance of Canada's aboriginal peoples, and defining the extent of their rights under the Canadian constitution, present intractable problems. Those problems arise equally at the levels of democratic theory, of political management, and of individual action.

Before, however, looking at issues relating to aboriginal peoples and their relations with non-aboriginals, it is pertinent to note that there has been a political sequel to the secession case. Both the federal government and the Quebec government tabled legislation in December 1999 to map out a course of action if there is a new sovereignty referendum in Quebec.

The federal Clarity Bill stipulates that Parliament must debate the wording of the referendum question, as published by Quebec, in order to determine whether or not it meets the Supreme Court's requirement that the question be clear. The bill also provides that, if the 'yes' side wins, Parliament is to debate whether or not the majority was a 'clear' one.[8] The court had said that a decision on both matters would have to be made politically. Many, including Prime Minister Chrétien, have argued that a majority of sixty per cent or more should be obtained before negotiations on sovereignty are to be launched; in fact, this view apparently has widespread support in Quebec, even among sovereignists. However, both features of the federal Clarity Bill are anathema to the Quebec government. Its bill affirms the right of Quebecers to determine their own future without interference or supervision from any external government or organization, and stipulates that the outcome will be determined by fifty per cent of the votes plus one vote. Thus, both the federal (Liberal) government and the PQ are visibly positioning themselves for a new showdown on the constitution. It would seem that the federal initiative is actually aimed more at discouraging the PQ from holding a new referendum than at clarifying the rules. It is not even certain that sets of rules will matter much, if Quebec ever does vote for independence – it is unlikely that resolution of the crisis thereby arising would await the outcome of parliamentary debates and protracted negotiations. However, neither the federal government nor the Supreme Court has been willing to admit this, any more than the PQ has been willing to admit that a unilateral declaration of independence would have seriously disruptive consequences for the people of Quebec.

CANADIAN FEDERALISM AND ABORIGINAL PEOPLES

In the secession case, the Supreme Court took the view that francophone Quebecers' full political participation and demonstrably equal status within Confederation is evidence of their historical self-determination, in such a sense as to deny Quebec any right to declare independence unilaterally. However, in the case of another set of national minorities, Canada's aboriginal peoples, full political participation and equal status are far from having been achieved. It is not just that the principles of non-discrimination, equality of opportunity, and self-determination have been inadequately adhered to; on the contrary, law, policy, and practice for many years were based on rejection of the idea that these principles could or should apply to the aboriginal peoples. With few exceptions, at least until recently, Canadian policy makers aimed to marginalize 'Indians' (including Métis and Inuit), or to assimilate them, or to do both in turn. Of course, with assimilation, non-discrimination and equality of opportunity may be achieved, but self-determination becomes irrelevant.

The greater the emphasis, in law and policy, on self-determination, the more important it is to be able to define precisely the relevant group or groups. This is not easy to do in the case of aboriginals in Canada. Of the 1.1 million Canadians reporting aboriginal ancestry, about three-quarters – just under three per cent of the total population – identify themselves as aboriginal. In 1996, about 600,000 were registered under federal legislation as 'Indians'; in addition, there were 210,000 who self-identified as Métis (sometimes described as being of mixed blood, although this is true also of many Indians), and 41,000 Inuit, formerly known as Eskimos. All three groups are defined under the Constitution Act, 1982 as 'aboriginal peoples', whose treaty and other rights are given constitutional protection.

What are those rights? The basic question, which is legal and political, and presents difficult issues of political philosophy, is whether aboriginal peoples ought to have a civil and political status that differs from that of non-aboriginal citizens – and if so, in what respects? Are equality and justice to be achieved by emphasising difference and creating constitutional rights unique to aboriginals, or by eliminating all forms of differential status?

Many aboriginals, it must be noted, experience appalling living conditions and life chances. By the indices employed in the United Nations annual Human Development Reports, where Canada has usually rated first (occasionally second) among countries of the world, aboriginal people lag far behind the Canadian averages. On every measure – life expectancy, infant mortality, suicide rates, alcoholism and drug addiction, educational attainment, employment, nutrition, income, and housing standards – the disparities between aboriginals and others are enormous. Canada's aboriginal peoples experience high rates of economic dependency, destitution, and ill health.

Present-day social problems have deep historical roots. Of fundamental importance has been the impact of European settlement, and the subsequent course of economic development. Prior to the arrival of Europeans, the inhabitants of North America had developed societies based on extensive rather than intensive land use, with cultures well adapted to hunting and gathering. The British crown, which gained a dominant position in North America during the seventeenth and eighteenth centuries, in part by recruiting Indian allies, cast itself in the role of protector of the aboriginal peoples. A Royal Proclamation, 1763, acknowledged the independent status of the Indians, recognized their capacity to conclude treaties of peace and friendship, and provided that no person might presume to buy lands from them; lands traditionally used by Indians could be purchased only by the crown at 'some publick Meeting or Assembly of the said Indians to be held for that purpose' (Canada RCAP, 1996, v. 1, p. 112).

The Royal Proclamation confirmed the validity of existing treaties between the crown and various Indian nations, and set the stage for the negotiation of new ones. The earliest treaties, including those applying to the present-day Atlantic provinces, declared friendship and provided for commercial exchange. Subsequent ones addressed, especially, the issue of lands and land use. Areas suitable for agriculture were opened to settlement by non-aboriginals, in return for which the crown established Indian reserves (areas owned by the federal government and protected from encroachment by non-Indians); it guaranteed hunting and fishing rights both on reserves and within territories surrounding them, and promised various forms of support including cash annuities, supplies of items such as twine and gunpowder, and relief in the event of famine. By 1921, such treaties covered the whole of Ontario and the prairie provinces, and parts of the North West Territories. However, they appear to have been viewed in quite different ways by the signatories on the two sides. The crown viewed them as conferring absolute title to most of the land, for resale or giveaway to settlers, railways, and forestry and mining firms. Aboriginal signatories, by contrast, saw them as establishing a trust relationship, offering continuing benefits and perpetual protection of their lands and of the fish and game they required to support their traditional way of life. It is likely that the written form of the treaties did not correspond to the oral agreements made, a fact that has recently led the Supreme Court to give equal weight to oral tradition (supplemented by the correspondence and reports of colonial officials) and the written treaties themselves. The difficulties of judicial determination of aboriginal rights have, though, been all the greater in those parts of Canada not covered by treaties with land provisions. These areas have included most of British Columbia, parts of the north, and the whole of Canada east of Ontario, although a few modern (post-1970) treaties have been negotiated, particularly in northern Quebec. Many others are in process of negotiation or, in the case of the Nisga'a people of north-west British Columbia, are undergoing ratification.

One of the legacies of the treaties and the policies associated with them is that it has been necessary to officially designate some persons as 'treaty Indians' or 'status Indians'. Thus the Indian Act of 1876 provided for the registration of Indians (some of whom were actually Métis or Inuit), and of their descendants, which until 1985 meant descendants through the male line.[9] Indian status has conferred both benefits and disabilities. For those living on designated reserve lands, Indian status offers entitlements to certain federally provided government services such as education, medical care, and income support, and it also exempts those individuals from most forms of taxation. However, until as recently as 1985, when under the Canadian Charter of Rights and Freedoms discrimination became unconstitutional, status Indians suffered various forms of official discrimination. Until 1960, they were ineligible to vote; until the 1970s they were subject to penalties not applicable to others (for example, regarding the possession and use of liquor). Most outrageously, for about a 20-year period after a Métis rebellion in 1885, status Indians in the western plains area were restricted to reserves unless given a pass. Indians were also discriminated against in economic terms under a variety of federal and provincial laws and policies, preventing Indian communities from diversifying and developing economically.

Aboriginals tend to regard the Indian Act and related policies as both paternalistic and assimilative. Paternalism is obvious; assimilation is a more complex issue. The case for the Act's being assimilative rests on the extent of discrimination that Indian status entailed prior to 1985, together with the opportunity, available to those Indians who met certain educational and linguistic criteria, to opt for enfranchisement. Enfranchisement conferred full citizenship rights, but required those enfranchised to forego the rights and immunities (notably, from taxation) that registration as Indians conferred, at least for those living or working on reserves. The authorities evidently supposed that those Indians who qualified for enfranchisement might be induced to apply, as they could thereby not only escape the disabilities entailed by Indian status, but also acquire individual ownership of a proportionate share of the reserve upon which the family lived. However, relatively few did apply. Psychological factors (identity and heritage) no doubt played a role in this, but another factor, plausibly of equal or greater importance, is that enfranchised persons would forfeit the right to return to their home or ancestral community on a reserve, and thus also to regain entitlements to housing and other benefits. In fact, it has been a common pattern for status Indians to leave the reserve for a time, and subsequently to return, or to adopt a lifestyle that entails frequent sorties from the home community, without ever definitively moving away. Thus, although there is certainly evidence of assimilative intent in the Indian Act and other legislation, the benefits associated with Indian status appear in most cases to have outweighed the disabilities it entailed. The overall effect has apparently been to perpetuate – especially given the extent of economic discrimination against them – patterns of dependency. Easy availability of welfare for Indians living on reserve, a policy legacy of the early 1950s, has strongly reinforced such dependency, contributing to demoralization.[10]

One response to this situation, most clearly formulated in a federal policy statement in 1969, has been to phase out, in parallel, both the disabilities that Indian status has entailed and the entitlements that it has conferred. However, the 1969 White Paper, which announced the abolition of the Indian Act and sought full integration of Indians into Canadian society, provoked a storm of protest among Indian leaders and sympathetic non-aboriginals, and was withdrawn. Since then, the thrust of policy has been threefold: to define and extend the rights of aboriginal persons, to work towards the self-government of distinct aboriginal nations, and to extend the economic base of Indian communities and nations.

A comprehensive set of recommendations outlining such a policy was presented in 1996 by a federal commission of inquiry, the Royal Commission on Aboriginal Peoples (RCAP). The commission noted the existence of between 60 and 80 aboriginal nations, which it defined as 'a sizeable body of Aboriginal people with a shared sense of national identity that constitutes the predominant population in a certain territory or group of territories' (Canada RCAP, 1996, v. 2, p. 166). The RCAP proposed that each of these nations, which average 5000 to 7000 persons, define its own citizenship, and that its citizens also be citizens of Canada. Each nation would be self-governing, although not according to a single, standardized model; each would have its own territory within which it exercised a substantial range of governmental powers and controlled economic development – although the lands in question need not be contiguous and some nation-citizens might live nowhere near their ancestral lands. Most or all aboriginal nations would, in addition, be involved in co-management agreements with other governments and commercial enterprises, to control and direct the economic development of surrounding lands. The expanded land base, said the RCAP, would supply aboriginal governments with revenues, without which self-government would be a sham; even so, for the foreseeable future, such governments would be heavily dependent on annual federal grants. Together, aboriginal governments would constitute a third order of government, constitutionally entrenched, alongside the federal and provincial governments, and interacting with them.

In so proposing, the RCAP was incorporating and extending provisions of the (failed) 1992 'Charlottetown Accord', an agreement among the federal government, all provinces and territories, and the leaders of four aboriginal organizations.[11] The Accord, which addressed the constitutional demands of Quebec, other provinces, and various groups including the aboriginal peoples, provided that the constitution be amended 'to recognize that the Aboriginal peoples of Canada have the inherent right of self-government within Canada ... as one of three orders of government in Canada' (Consensus Report on the Constitution, reprinted in McRoberts and Monahan, 1993, p. 301). It provided that aboriginal legislatures would have authority 'to safeguard and develop their language, cultures, economies, identities, institutions, and tradi-tions; and to develop, maintain and strengthen their relationship with their lands, waters and environment'. By recognizing these rights as 'inherent', the accord provided for judicial determination of the extent of those rights, subject to prior political negotiations, and then – after a five-year delay – to give such negotiations a chance to be brought to fruition. For a variety of reasons, however, these provisions of the accord were contentious even among the aboriginal peoples themselves, and in the ensuing referendum, two-thirds of the voters on reserve rejected its provisions (Long and Chiste, 1993) – along with majorities in most provinces.

The RCAP recommendations were very much in the spirit of the Charlottetown Accord. However, their complexity – complexity that was perhaps inevitable in light of the kaleidoscope of social facts of which the commissioners had to take cognizance – makes both description and critique of the commission's vision a hazardous enterprise. In 1996, not only (as noted above) did about a third of those of aboriginal ancestry not self-identify as aboriginal, but more than 40 per cent of registered Indians in Canada, and more than 60 per cent of those living within a province (not in one of the northern territories), lived off-reserve, mainly in urban areas.[12] All told, in 1991, about a third of those identifying themselves as aboriginal lived in one of twelve major cities (calculated from Canada RCAP, 1996, v. 4, pp. 604, 607). It is also significant that marriages with non-status persons are common: although the RCAP provides no rele-vant data, a 1992 study projects a 62 per cent intermarriage rate among off-reserve status Indians (Clatworthy and Smith, 1992, ii, cited in Cairns, forthcoming 2000).

In light of the diversity of the aboriginal population, it is striking that the RCAP lavished most of its attention on aboriginal nations with a rural land base. It did so on the grounds that the self-government of aboriginal nations, and the control of a substantial territorial base, are essential for traditional cultures to flourish and grow. At the same time, according to the commission, aboriginal communities must be equipped to 'reach out and participate in global society', and aboriginal persons should enjoy 'the same quality of life as other Canadians'. Implicitly, the commission denied that any trade-off between cultural and economic goals need be made; it affirmed, for example, that aboriginal Canadians should be proportionately represented in professional occupations.

Since professional, managerial, and technical occupations are predominately urban, the commission proposed that the powers of aboriginal governments be extended beyond their own territories to cover urban-dwelling aboriginal persons, although only on a voluntary, opt-in basis. Urban aboriginal government agencies would, however, frequently perform their functions – essentially, provision of health, educational, and social services – in relation to a heterogeneous aboriginal population, not in relation to persons from a single aboriginal nation. The commission suggested that through such agencies, and the contacts they would foster among urban-dwelling aboriginal persons, links with traditional communities could be preserved.

This seems, at best, dubious. It is typical of economically disadvantaged ethnic groups – groups defined by some mix of ancestry, language, religion, and a distinctive value-system – that they find it difficult to reconcile economic and cultural goals. They have the problem of eliminating stratification by ethnicity while also achieving separate or distinct cultural development. Failure to do both means assimilation for many, and economic marginalization for the rest. There is an interesting parallel in this respect between aboriginals today and francophone Quebecers of the 1950s and 1960s. At that time, a burgeoning middle class in Quebec came to recognize that cultural preservation was doomed to failure if the society did not modernize economically. The result was the emergence of the new Quebec nationalism (as previously described), the extension of the role of the Quebec government, and the successes of a francophone business class. Thirty years later, in relation to Canada's aboriginal peoples, the RCAP saw precisely the same dilemma, and proposed – under far less propitious circumstances – a parallel solution. The commission stressed the importance of political and cultural self-affirmation (necessarily a collective endeavour), and recognized that for this to occur, extended control of economic resources was required.

In a magisterial review of the RCAP report, political scientist Alan Cairns (Cairns, 2000, chap. 4) notes that the commission gave priority to collective cultural preservation and development, over the goal of advancing individual economic opportunity. In so doing, Cairns says, the commission 'marginalized urban Aboriginals', discounting 'the numerous indicators of Aboriginal urban experience that were superior to the reserve situation'. In fact, 'To the Commission ... the city was not seen positively as a site of economic and other opportunities, but negatively as a vehicle for a "constant barrage of non-Aboriginal values and experiences".' Thus the commission contrasts its vision of 'healthy, sustainable communities that create the conditions for a rounded life', nurtured by the self-government of aboriginal nations, with a scenario of 'forced emigration to the margins of an essentially alien urban environment'.

> The centrality of nation [Cairns writes] meant that the Commission was self-consciously pioneering a contemporary version of a multinational Canadian federalism, one in which the self-governing Aboriginal nation – 'the core around which the Commission's recommendations are built' – was to be the vanguard actor in the revitalization of Aboriginal cultures. Aboriginal peoples are to be part of a 'multinational citizenship.' Canada's 'true vision', accordingly, is a partnership of nations, held together by civic allegiance to the separate nations. This vision has little room for a common Canadian citizenship grounded in individual allegiance, or for the idea of a common Canadian community that is more than the sum of its parts. Nations were the key actors in the past, and should equally be so in the future. The future key relationship, therefore, is nation-to-nation.

One may reasonably raise questions, as Cairns does, about the viability of a complex system of intergovernmental relations involving the federal government, ten provinces, three territories, and 60 to 80 aboriginal nations, especially in view of the financial dependency that is in prospect for aboriginal governments. One may also reasonably be sceptical about the nation-to-nation vision of the RCAP, in light of the urbanization of a third to a half of the aboriginal population, high rates of intermarriage between urban aboriginals and non-aboriginals, and observable patterns of assimilation. Acknowledgement of these problems barely figured in the RCAP report, which concentrated on a single solution to the problems of aboriginal peoples and the negotiation of a new set of treaties between aboriginal nations and the federal and provincial governments.

The treaties envisioned by the RCAP are to set out arrangements for self-government, and to ensure that aboriginal nations have a substantial economic base. This is not a new idea. On the contrary, the negotiation of new or updated treaties has been under way for years, in fact decades – a slow and conflict-laden process driven, in large measure, by a series of Supreme Court decisions beginning in the 1970s. These decisions have expansively defined aboriginal title to lands and resources, as the court discovered entitlements conferred on aboriginal persons by treaties long narrowly applied, or disregarded and virtually forgotten, in terms of federal and provincial law. These treaties, all future treaties and land claims settlements, and other rights (including, it turns out, certain rights enshrined in oral tradition) have acquired constitutional status under the terms of the Constitution Act 1982. Legal immunities to prosecution under fisheries, environmental, and forestry laws and regulations have been recognized or created by the courts, although judgements have still left some room for regulations in these fields that apply equally to aboriginals and to others. Of special significance is the fact that lawyers representing aboriginal interests have been able partially to impede resource development until aboriginal claims have been settled. Thus, through a series of judgements restricting the application of federal and provincial statutes and prohibiting various administrative acts, the courts have been turning up the heat for negotiations to define aboriginal rights in a way that will withstand judicial challenge.

Negotiations for modern treaties, or to settle comprehensive land claims, have entailed considerable frustration for all involved, heightening the potential for future conflict and physical violence. However, there have been tangible results in several provinces and territories (Doerr, 1998). There have been high-profile agreements permitting the development of hydro-electric resources in northern Quebec, an area of over one million square kilometres, and in 1993 agreement was reached to divide the Northwest Territories and establish (given the preponderance of Inuit in the area) an Inuit-controlled government in the new Nunavut Territory, effective 1999.

Of special note is a treaty with the Nisga'a people of north-west British Columbia, signed in 1999 by the federal and provincial governments. The Nisga'a treaty arguably shows, in practice, what the RCAP's broad proposals for nation-to-nation relationships may mean. It is, to say the least, controversial. Proponents see it as a model for future agreements that must be reached if atonement is to be made for past injustices and if a basis for the future economic, social, cultural, and political development of Canada's aboriginal peoples is to be established, as the RCAP has hoped. Critics agree with the treaty's proponents in one respect: that it will be a precedent for many subsequent treaties, covering large parts of Canada. This and any similar future treaties will constitutionally entrench a political status for aboriginal peoples that differs notably from that of other Canadian citizens, for example as regards the extent to which aboriginals are subject to general regulations relating to the management and conservation of fish, game, and forest resources. Treaties on the Nisga'a model will also, evidently, carry far-reaching implications for the development of hydro-electric works, mineral deposits, forests, and oil and gas resources, and for the construction of transportation facilities, especially pipelines. Some welcome this, others are alarmed by it. Perhaps most interesting are principled objections, based on liberal political theory, to the relationship between aboriginal governments or their leaders on the one hand, and both aboriginal and non-aboriginal persons on the other, as enshrined in the Nisga'a treaty (Gibson, 1999).

There are 5000 Nisga'a registered under the Indian Act, of whom 2000 live on a reserve of 62 square kilometres. Under the terms of the treaty, approximately 2000 square kilometres of land, together with ownership of its natural resources, will be transferred to the government of the Nisga'a nation. Over a fifteen year period, the Nisga'a government will receive, in addition, one-time federal grants of $340 million to support economic development and transition, mostly (one may presume) for the benefit of Nisga'a living on Nisga'a lands. If so, there will be upwards of $150,000 per person.[13] In addition, funds supporting existing programmes for on-reserve Indians – health, education, social assistance, and local services – will be transferred to the Nisga'a government, enabling it to take over responsibility for such services as regards both Nisga'a and non-Nisga'a residents. These programmes will cost about $33 million per year, probably at least $15,000 per person, or 60 per cent of the average pre-tax income of British Columbians. In addition, Nisga'a will continue to benefit, as does the existing on-reserve population, from free or heavily subsidized housing. On the other side of the ledger, all Nisga'a will eventually be subject to taxation, as non-aboriginal Canadians are. How significant this is, other than symbolically, will depend on future income levels.

There will be a Nisga'a constitution establishing a general Nisga'a government, four village governments, and three urban locals elsewhere in British Columbia. The general government will exercise extensive legislative powers in relation to Nisga'a lands and those living there. It will be controlled by resident Nisga'a: non-Nisga'a will be ineligible to vote (but must be consulted on decisions affecting them), and only three representatives out of about 30 will be elected by Nisga'a not living on Nisga'a lands. Although the federal negotiator has described the Nisga'a government as similar to 'other local governments in Canada' (Molloy, 1999), the comparison appears false. In Canada local governments are created by provincial governments and are subject to their control, but this is not at all the case with the Nisga'a government. This is a government that has province-like powers vested in it by treaty that has constitutional effect, and in several important fields Nisga'a law will prevail over any conflicting provisions in federal or provincial laws.[14] Thus the treaty takes an important step towards creating a third (aboriginal) order of government, as envisioned in the Charlottetown Accord, and as subsequently recommended by the RCAP.

What is a just agreement, and will be so perceived? What is workable? What will provide the basis for the future wellbeing of Canada's aboriginal peoples, and for good relations between them and non-aboriginal Canadians? These are the questions that are posed by the Nisga'a treaty, presumably a prototype for many future agreements, though each will be specific to the circumstances. Many non-aboriginal Canadians are at least vaguely aware of, and condemn, injustices of the past and social disparities of the present; others, by contrast, denounce judicially recognized immunities and privileges enjoyed by aboriginals, relative to non-aboriginals, as well as the judicial recognition of claims long forgotten or suppressed. As with other constitutional disputes of recent years, notably those relating to Quebec's position in the federation, opinions tend to be shaped by symbolic considerations, ideological predisposition, and emotion. Thus, some non-aboriginals support the generous settlement of historical claims put forward by Indians, Métis, and Inuit. They accept, and even demand, the transfer of substantial resources to aboriginal peoples, as under the Nisga'a treaty, and they endorse the establishment of ethnic governments along the lines, possibly, that the Nisga'a treaty provides for. They welcome the judgements of the Supreme Court that have done so much to force governments to settle aboriginal claims to lands and resources; they celebrate the judicial decisions that have acknowledged and extended aboriginal rights. Others, however, are just as emphatic in rejecting both judicial and political decisions that create or endorse any form of special status for aboriginal peoples; they regard economic arrangements such as those contained in the Nisga'a treaty as unfairly burdensome to taxpayers; and they consider the proliferation of Nisga'a-type governments as absurdly cumbersome and shamelessly lavish in their expenditure of public funds on aboriginal leaders and their battalions of lawyers and professional advisers (Adams, 1999).

To an important degree, the settlement of aboriginal claims and, integral to this process, the creation of a vastly expanded network of aboriginal governments, has been judicially driven. In this sense there is an interesting historical parallel between the extension of aboriginal rights in Canada, and the civil rights process in the USA during the third quarter of the twentieth century. The extension in law of civil rights in the USA began with the Supreme Court's decision in 1954, in the famous case of *Brown vs. the Board of Education of Topeka, Kansas*, initiating the desegregation of the schools. After that, the President and the Congress also came into the picture with the Civil Rights Act of 1964 and a programme of racial integration that included affirmative action; during this latter phase, the courts remained active in supervising the desegregation process to see that it went ahead 'with all deliberate speed'. Thus, in the USA, the Supreme Court has been an important instrument for the redress of long-standing grievances of the country's most discriminated-against minority; in this and other areas, its political role – its involvement in processes of democratic governance – has been remarkable.

In Canada, especially since the passage of the Constitution Act 1982 (which includes the Canadian Charter of Rights and Freedoms), a similarly prominent role has been assumed by the Supreme Court. The actions of the court vis-à-vis aboriginal rights, however, have been based on the very principle that the United States Supreme Court rejected in the *Brown* case, the 'separate but equal' doctrine enunciated by a predecessor court in 1896. The *Brown* case was famous for its declaration that separate education systems (and by extension, separate public facilities of any kind) are inherently *unequal*. In Canada, by contrast, the very basis of court decisions and, in their wake, public policy, has been that institutional structures and individual rights aiming to resist assimilation, and to demarcate aboriginal persons from the rest of the population, are the very basis of justice for aboriginal peoples, the *sine qua non* of equal treatment achieved through nation-to-nation negotiations rather than through a common, undifferentiated citizenship.

REGIONALISM, CONTINENTALISM AND CANADIAN FEDERALISM

Both Quebec nationalism and the claims and identities of aboriginal peoples contribute to the diversity of Canada in evident ways, thereby posing difficult issues of governance and self-governance. However, there is another dimension as well to the diversity of Canada, raising questions of community and governance. This is the regional dimension, complicated, as always, by the dominant position of the USA in North America and the ambivalence of Canadians towards their southern neighbour.

Canada is a regionally diverse country where provincial and even subprovincial identities are strong, where regional economic disparities are considerable, and where regional economic interests have historically diverged. While the federal government has taken primary responsibility for national economic development, successive development strategies have been seen as discriminatory in that they have deliberately sacrificed the interests of the more sparsely settled regions (Leslie, 1987). The essence of federal economic development policy as it took shape in the latter nineteenth century was to promote investment in natural resources industries, expanding this sector and its exports as rapidly as possible, while simultaneously building up a small-scale manufacturing industry to serve the domestic market. This strategy called for vast expenditures on public works, mainly railway building, and for a protective tariff. The tariff was perceived as serving the interests of central Canada (southern Ontario and Quebec), while imposing heavy costs on the rest of the country.

After the Second World War, with the gradual liberalization of world trade, support for industrial development took more active forms. Controls were placed on foreign capital, technological development was heavily subsidized, and steps were taken (ineffectually) towards formulating and implementing an interventionist industrial strategy at the federal level. The apogee of this policy thrust occurred with the run-up in the price of oil during the 1970s, when price controls – supported by an export tax – were placed on the oil and gas industries. Under the National Energy Programme (NEP) of 1980, an attempt was made to place the whole oil and gas industry under federal supervision and control, although ownership of these resources is constitutionally vested in the provincial governments. Ambitious plans for the 'Canadianization' of the industry – one in which foreign ownership ratios were particularly high – were financed out of new taxes (of contested constitutional validity) that gave the federal government a larger share of public revenues from the production of hydrocarbon fuels. The NEP brought Ottawa into direct conflict with the producing provinces, especially Alberta, where the richest oil and gas reserves are located. In the view of Alberta and other resource-rich provinces, their interests were to be subordinated to the needs of central Canada and its manufacturing industry. This perception strengthened the 'hinterland' provinces' determination to wrest more economic power from Ottawa.

Of considerable interest, in terms of regionalism in Canadian politics, is that Quebec, although a beneficiary of the National Energy Programme, sided with the oil-producing provinces in order to support the principle of provincial control of natural resources. Given the labour-intensive and technologically outmoded character of much of its manufacturing industry, Quebec was losing ground to Ontario in continental markets, and had begun to see itself as paying the costs – along with the West and the Atlantic provinces – of federal policies for industrial development. Those policies appeared to benefit only Ontario, and Quebec began to see itself as a hinterland region, subordinate to the urban network centred in Toronto. Quebec began, correspondingly, to view its provincial government as the only effective agent of a badly needed economic transformation. Its strategy was based in part on heavy investment in the resource industries (especially hydro-electricity), and in part on industrial restructuring under the leadership of an emerging class of francophone entrepreneurs, supported by provincial subsidies and tax breaks. Thus Quebec aligned itself with most of the other provinces in demanding an end to traditional federal policies for economic development, and espousal of the principle of continental free trade. A near consensus arose, Ontario alone dissenting, that – in the words of a federal royal commission on the economy, the Macdonald Commission – 'the federal task is to provide [i.e. should be limited to providing, P.L.] a unified national framework for private economic activity and provincial activities to encourage economic development' (Canada RCEU, 1985, v. 3, pp. 149–50).

Such a limited conception of the appropriate federal role in the economy is not only a reaction to past federal policies, it is a natural consequence of the increasing orientation of continental trade flows north–south (internationally) rather than east–west. This shift has been going on throughout the past century, but it has now reached the point where only one province, tiny Prince Edward Island, trades more with the rest of Canada than with the rest of the world (Courchene, 1998) – and that means mainly with the USA. Since the USA takes more than 80 per cent of Canadian exports, rising protectionist sentiment in Congress during the 1980s and a succession of American trade actions against Canada (countervailing duties, often described in Canada as 'trade harassment') fuelled demands for 'assured access' to the American market. This became the rallying call of the Macdonald Commission, and of the government of Brian Mulroney. A free trade agreement was negotiated, and an election in 1988 assured its ratification.

The Canada–USA Free Trade Agreement did not exempt Canada from the application of American trade remedy laws, or the more discretionary forms of protectionism, which was Canada's main objective in the talks. Instead, there is a 'dispute settlement mechanism' to oversee the application of national law in both countries. Both countries retain the power to amend such laws, for example, the rules on countervail, but given the relative size of the two countries this is a power that is more available, in practice, to the USA than to Canada. In return for the removal of tariffs and for the creation of a dispute settlement mechanism (which is of limited but real significance), the USA gained significant concessions on trade in services, and on investment issues. These provisions of the FTA severely limit the regulatory authority of Parliament and the provincial legislatures, and remove most of its capacity to shape or control economic development. The North American Free Trade Agreement (NAFTA), negotiated in 1992, not only extended the FTA to include Mexico, but tightened up its restrictions on the economic powers of government considerably. Multilateral liberalization under the World Trade Organization (WTO) carries on this trend, although it has the advantage for Canada of placing its trade and investment relations with the USA in a multilateral context, somewhat diluting the effects of disparity in size.

In terms of domestic Canadian politics, one effect of continentalization has been that the provinces are increasingly resistant to any federal interference in their efforts to promote economic development, on the basis of the limited tools that the NAFTA leaves under their control. They are anxious to avoid doing anything that might jeopardize their access to the American market, but are much less concerned about antagonizing each other, for example by luring investment from each other on the basis of subsidies and tax exemptions. There is a prospect that interprovincial barriers to trade and investment will in some cases be more extensive than those that exist between Canada and the USA. An Agreement on Internal Trade, the language of which is eerily reminiscent of the NAFTA, was negotiated in 1994 with the aim of ensuring that this possibility did not materialize. However, its language is vague, and the provisions for its enforcement, non-existent. It falls far short of what now exists in Europe under the Internal Market Programme.

The increased regionalization of the Canadian economy has its counterpart on the social side. Far more than in the USA, but less than in Germany or Australia, Canada aims to establish an acceptable 'floor' in standards of public services across the country, and to achieve fiscal equity interregionally. The federal government has assumed responsibility for this. Several federal programmes, notably unemployment (or 'employment') insurance and old age and disability pensions, provide income security or support. In addition, the federal government has encouraged the provinces to establish certain programmes, especially in healthcare, through a system of conditional grants – under these grants, the payment of federal monies is conditional on the provinces' meeting certain federally established criteria, often misleadingly called 'national standards'. It has also transferred federal funds to provincial coffers in order to support post-secondary education and social assistance (welfare) programmes, though without the attempt to control programme design. It has dabbled in housing policy. Most significantly, it has developed a complex system of unconditional fiscal transfers to enable all provinces to provide – in the words of the Constitution Act 1982 – 'reasonably comparable levels of public services at reasonably comparable levels of taxation'. Under federal legislation to meet this objective, the seven 'have-not' provinces – all but Ontario, Alberta, and

British Columbia – receive 'equalization payments' that, in aggregate, amount to nearly 4 per cent of GDP.

In 1990, the net effect of all these forms of interregional redistribution was to reduce the GDP of Alberta, Ontario, and British Columbia by 3 to 5 per cent, and to increase the GDP of the poorer provinces by as much as 33 per cent.[15] During the 1990s, however, all aspects of the fiscal arrangements that have been integral to the functioning of the Canadian federal system came under severe strain. Taxes rose and spending – both the federal government's own programmes, and, even more so, its transfers to the provinces – diminished, as the task of balancing the federal budget, after twenty years of running deficits, was taken seriously in hand. One result was that the provinces, especially the wealthier ones, became more resistant to federal interference in the design of their programmes. Correspondingly, they demanded reductions in federal taxes so they could move into the 'tax room' so created, and finance their own programmes out of their own resources. It appears, though, that if fiscal decentralization on the scale demanded were to come about, the political strains placed on the equalization programme would be intolerable. One can only speculate about this, but it seems likely that the willingness of taxpayers in the wealthier provinces to support fiscal redistribution is contingent on the belief that Canadians, regardless of place of residence, are entitled to certain kinds and standards of public services. If all semblance of national standards disappears – the term is somewhat of a misnomer anyway – there seems little reason to go on supporting, through the agency of the federal government, public services in other provinces. If, in addition, Canada becomes fragmented economically into a congeries of region states seeking to make their own way in an integrated continental economy, it seems hard to imagine how the consensus hitherto supporting interregional redistribution could long survive. The sense that Canada is a national, sharing community may well, then, be dependent on the existence of some form of national economy as well. What is troubling is that 'the Canadian economy' is increasingly, with continental free trade and unimpeded investment flows, a chimera.

DEMOCRATIC GOVERNANCE AND THE FUTURE OF CANADA

Democratic governance in Canada is a delicate balancing act among multiple communities. There is a paradox here. On the one hand, there appears to be widespread commitment in Canada to the principle of majority rule as the sole legitimate basis of democracy, indeed its very essence. On the other hand, Canada is a country where the rigorous and routine application of that principle is deeply offensive to a variety of self-aware minorities. For these groups, dignity and justice demand formal (seemingly constitutional) recognition, in a form that guarantees them – collectively, but some more than others – a substantial measure of control over their lives.

One way of unravelling the paradox is by highlighting the concept of citizenship. Citizenship denotes, in the classic formulation of T.H. Marshall, 'full-status membership in a community' in its civil, political, and social dimensions (Marshall, 1950). Marshall, though, did not face the competing claims of multiple citizenships, or membership in over-lapping communities. In Canada, it is impossible not to do so.

The best-known or most obvious case of overlapping communities concerns francophone Quebecers, most of whom identify more strongly as *québécois* than as Canadian. This, however, is probably less significant than it seems because polls repeatedly find that in other provinces as well – everywhere but Ontario – provincial loyalties or identities are stronger than national ones. The numbers are higher in Quebec, and the feeling of belonging to a distinct national community is evidently (among provinces) unique to Quebec, but the ambivalence of personal attachments is widespread across the whole of Canada. For Quebec, a comedian probably best captured this ambivalence when he quipped: 'What every Quebecer wants is an independent Quebec within a strong and united Canada.' On a par with this, though, are the words of a former premier of Prince Edward Island, who found a wonderful formula for expressing multiple loyalties: 'I'm an Islander first and foremost, but a Canadian above all.'

Probably the best conclusion one may draw is that pollsters who ask about political identities are trying to force people into boxes whose walls they do not normally recognize. With far greater consequences, in Quebec the leaders of the PQ have attempted, in two referendums, to do the same. A very substantial majority of Quebecers say they do not want another referendum, which seems to suggest that most do not want to be forced to choose between Quebec and Canada. Indeed, it is only among a fairly small minority of Quebecers, the most strongly committed *indépendentistes*, that multiple loyalties are rejected, or thought to be incongruous. Strikingly, about half of all Quebecers (including, very possibly, a majority of sovereignists) assume that if the province becomes independent, Quebecers will continue to be Canadian citizens.

In the case of Canada's aboriginal peoples, dual citizenship, as recommended by the RCAP, would have a different significance. It was the commission's suggestion that each of the aboriginal nations should define its own citizenship, and that the individuals so recognized should not only retain full Canadian citizenship, and full rights as provincial residents, but also be able to claim entitlements available only to aboriginal persons. What this may well mean in practice seems to be illustrated by the Nisga'a treaty.

In different ways, three different types of group – supporters of provincial autonomy and policy control (though within limited spheres of responsibility), Quebec nationalists and the 'softer' sovereignists, and proponents of aboriginal citizenship and the self-governance of aboriginal nations – all stake claims that are inconsistent with an undifferentiated Canadian citizenship. And yet those who belong to these groups do evidently see themselves as Canadian citizens, not only in a formal sense, but as persons who are, in every sense, full members of a national community. As such, they see themselves as sharing a common civil status or set of legal rights, as having the right to participate in political decision making equally with others, and as legitimate claimants to similar if not totally standardized social benefits. Canadians evidently expect the federal system to be structured in such a way as to realize these objectives.

In short, Canadians seemingly espouse antithetical views of what is to be expected from their political arrangements: both a common citizenship, and substantial self-governance for communities that are embedded in the larger society and polity. Perhaps a more consensual, less majoritarian, conception of democracy would help resolve the tensions inherent in this situation (Lijphart, 1977). However, acceptance of such a conception of democracy seems unlikely, as both the institutional structures (a Westminster-style parliamentary/cabinet system, and a federal division of powers) and deeply embedded political norms are inconsistent with it. Those norms favour competition and a winner-takes-all attitude over consensus-building and compromise, and they underpin a political system that makes the accommodation of difference, together with the achievement of common goals, extremely difficult.

NOTES

1. Territorial status still obtains north of sixty degrees of latitude. In April 1999 the new Territory of Nunavut, covering the eastern Arctic, was carved out of the Northwest Territories; there are now three territorial governments for a combined population of under 100,000. It is notable that about three-quarters of the inhabitants of Nunavut are Inuit ('Eskimo' is a term no longer used); it is the only part of Canada in which one of the aboriginal peoples constitutes a political majority.

2. Parliament may enact laws for 'the Peace, Order, and Good Government
    of Canada', and it also has 'for greater certainty' the *exclusive* power to
    enact laws in relation to an enumerated list. The provinces have an enum-
    erated list of their own. Initially, only agriculture and immigration were
    assigned concurrently (to both). The courts have paid primary attention to
    the two lists of enumerated powers, and have downplayed the importance
    of the general (residuary) clause. However, where legislation could, with
    equal plausibility, be said to fall under both a federal and a provincial
    enumerated power, concurrency has arisen, with federal laws prevailing
    in case of conflict. See Lederman (1962–3).
3. This phrase was contained in the terms of reference of a federal advisory
    body, the Royal Commission on Bilingualism and Biculturalism, named in
    1963.
4. 'Sovereignists' or 'sovereigntists': those committed to sovereignty or inde-
    pendence. The federal government calls them 'separatists' or – perhaps the
    most accurate term – 'secessionists'.
5. Most business leaders, except for those in smaller enterprises oriented to
    local or provincial markets, are strongly federalist; organized labour sup-
    ports sovereignty, most of its leaders being publicly committed to the PQ;
    rural Quebec is mainly PQ territory, while the Montreal region (containing
    almost half the provincial population), Hull (part of the national capital
    region, the location of many federal government offices and the place of
    residence of many federal public servants), and even parts of Quebec City
    (the provincial capital) vote Liberal in provincial elections, often by large
    majorities. Older francophones tend to be Liberal and federalist, younger
    ones apolitical or *péquiste* (PQ supporters). The PQ is more successful
    among male voters than among females. Anglophones and most allo-
    phone groups, heavily concentrated in the urban areas, are solidly Liberal
    and federalist.
6. The federal Conservative Party, the party of former Prime Minister Brian
    Mulroney (1984–93), scarcely now exists in Quebec, which in federal poli-
    tics divides its loyalties between the Liberals and the *Bloc*. Mulroney's
    ambition was to capture Quebec politically for the Conservatives, essen-
    tially for the first time since the early 1890s, and he briefly succeeded. He
    recruited a group of strong Quebec nationalists, wavering between *indé-*
    pendentisme and federalism, to form the nucleus of his Quebec team. The
    most prominent of this group was Mulroney's long-standing personal
    friend Lucien Bouchard, who became a federal minister. In cabinet, how-
    ever, he felt marginalized. He eventually (1990) resigned, drawing with
    him a rump that became the *Bloc québécois*, committed to supporting the
    independence option in the House of Commons. From this position he set
    about undermining the authority of Quebec Premier Jacques Parizeau,
    displacing him after the 1995 referendum as PQ leader and premier.
7. The text of the Act was contained in an appendix to a statute of the UK
    parliament, incorporating a resolution of the Canadian parliament. The

resolution had been endorsed by the premiers of nine provinces, Quebec dissenting. Although the Supreme Court of Canada subsequently declared that Quebec had never possessed a conventional right of veto, up until 1982 successive Canadian governments had treated Quebec's opposition as fatal to any proposed amendment affecting it.

8. The government of Canada is prohibited under the legislation from entering into negotiations 'on the terms on which a province might cease to be part of Canada' unless the House of Commons has determined 'that there has been a clear expression of a will by a clear majority of the population of that province that the province cease to be part of Canada'. There seems to be room for argument here, that a majority of eligible voters, not merely of votes cast, must be obtained. This interpretation of the wording of the bill is reinforced by the fact that the House of Commons is instructed to take into account not only the size of the majority of valid votes, but the voter turnout.

9. One of the most notorious provisions of the Act, removed with retroactive effect in 1985, was that an Indian woman who married a non-Indian lost status, as did any of their offspring; conversely, a non-Indian woman who married an Indian acquired status, which was passed on to their children.

10. I am grateful to Douglas Brown for this observation, and, in general, for several insightful comments on an earlier draft of this section of the chapter.

11. These were: the Assembly of First Nations (status Indians), the Native Council of Canada (non-status Indians), the Métis National Council, and the Inuit Tapirisat of Canada.

12. Eighty per cent of off-reserve registered Indians were urban-dwellers in 1996; for those identifying themselves as Métis, the figure was 70 per cent. However, it should be noted that the Canadian census defines agglomerations of only 1000 as 'urban'.

13. If all funds were expended on behalf of those living on Nisga'a lands there would be $170,000 per person; if allocated equally to all Nisga'a, the figure would be $68,000.

14. In Canada, when a federal and a provincial law, both otherwise valid, contain conflicting provisions, the courts must decide which law has paramountcy (prevails over the other). Under the Nisga'a treaty, Nisga'a legislation has paramountcy in several fields, including: Nisga'a citizenship and institutions, Nisga'a culture and language, education of Nisga'a children (subject to meeting minimum provincial standards), assets and property excluding intellectual property, land use and resource management and related environmental issues (although federal and provincial standards set a minimum), regulation of trade and commerce, cultural property, and the licensing of aboriginal healers. There are also other areas in which the Nisga'a may legislate, subject to federal or provincial paramountcy, notably: public order (but not the criminal law), traffic and transport, gambling and intoxicants, the solemnization of marriage, and

industrial relations. On Nisga'a lands, most public services are to be delivered, both to Nisga'a and non-Nisga'a, by the Nisga'a government under administrative agreements with the federal and provincial governments (which will pay the bills): this is the case in the fields of health, workforce training, child and family services, and social services including social assistance (welfare). In these cases, non-Nisga'a are guaranteed equal treatment with Nisga'a.

15. Each of the four Atlantic provinces found itself with a GDP at least 16 per cent higher than it would otherwise have been, as a result of the fiscal side of Canadian federalism. It would no doubt be a surprise to most Canadians to learn that Quebec's net position was improved by less than one per cent. These figures were arrived at by subtracting federal tax revenues for each province from all federal expenditures in the province, including federal programme expenditures and transfers to the provincial government. An adjustment was then made to neutralize the effect of the federal deficit that year (Leslie *et al.*, 1993).

FURTHER READING

Cairns, Alan C. (2000) *Citizens Plus: Aboriginal Peoples and the Canadian State* (Vancouver: University of British Columbia Press). Sympathetic towards aboriginal peoples, but strongly critical of the recommendations of the Royal Commission on Aboriginal Peoples.

Canada (1996) *Report of the Royal Commission on Aboriginal Peoples* (Ottawa: Minister of Supply and Services, 5 vols). Presents the case for redressing past wrongs towards Canada's aboriginal peoples through apology, new treaties, and policies for economic development. Comprehensive recommendations for aboriginal self-government on the 'nation' model. Massive, discursive, anecdotal.

Kymlicka, Will (1998) *Finding Our Way: Rethinking Ethnocultural Relations in Canada* (Toronto, Oxford, and New York: Oxford University Press, 1998). A work of political philosophy by a leading thinker on matters of ethnic and linguistic pluralism.

Leslie, Peter M. (1987) *Federal State, National Economy* (Toronto: University of Toronto Press). Explores the linkages between policies for economic development and proposals for reform of Canada's federal system.

McRoberts, Kenneth (1993) *Quebec: Social Change and Political Crisis*, third edition, with a postscript (Toronto: Oxford University Press). A widely read book on Quebec politics, federalist in its political commitment, but sympathetic to Quebec nationalism.

McRoberts, Kenneth, and Patrick Monahan (1993) (eds) *The Charlottetown Accord, the Referendum, and the Future of Canada* (Toronto: University of Toronto Press). A book of essays on Canada's latest attempt at formal constitutional revision, responding to demands from Quebec, from other provinces, from aboriginal leaders, and a variety of social groups.

Monahan, Patrick (1991) *Meech Lake: The Inside Story* (Toronto: University of
  Toronto Press). The most comprehensive coverage available of the Meech
  Lake Accord, negotiated to respond to the constitutional dissatisfactions of
  Quebec, and to reconcile it to the changes in the Canadian constitution
  brought about through the Constitution Act 1982.
Russell, Peter H. (1992) *Constitutional Odyssey: Can Canadians be a Sovereign
  People?* (Toronto: University of Toronto Press). A review of constitutional
  issues in Canada from Confederation (1867) to just before the Charlottetown
  Accord (1992).

REFERENCES

Adams, Stuart (1999) *Understanding the Nisga'a Agreement and Looking at Alter-
  natives.* Vancouver: Fraser Institute, Occasional Paper 17.
Cairns, Alan C. (1977) The Governments and Societies of Canadian Federalism.
  Canadian Journal of Political Science 10: 695–725.
Cairns, Alan C. (2000) *Citizens Plus: Aboriginal Peoples and the Canadian State.*
  Vancouver: University of British Columbia Press.
Cameron, David R. (1990) Lord Durham Then and Now, *Journal of Canadian
  Studies* 25: 5–23.
Canada RCAP (1996) *Report of the Royal Commission on Aboriginal Peoples.* Ottawa:
  Minister of Supply and Services.
Canada RCEU (1985) *Report of the Royal Commission on the Economic Union and
  Development Prospects for Canada.* Ottawa: Minister of Supply and Services.
Canada. Supreme Court (1998) *Re Reference by the Governor in Council concerning
  Certain Questions in relation to the Secession of Quebec from Canada* 161 D.L.R.
  [Dominion Law Reports] (4th) 385.
Clatworthy, Stewart, and Anthony H. Smith (1992) *Population Implications of the
  1985 Amendments to the Indian Act: Final Report.* Perth, Ont.: Living Dimensions
  Ltd.
Courchene, Thomas J. with Colin R. Telmer (1998) *From Heartland to North
  American Region State: the Social, Fiscal and Federal Evolution of Ontario.* Toronto:
  Centre for Public Management, University of Toronto.
Doerr, Audrey (1998) Federalism and Aboriginal Relations. In H. Lazar (ed.),
  Canada: The State of the Federation 1997. Non-constitutional Renewal. Kingston,
  Ont.: Institute of Intergovernmental Relations, pp. 229–43.
Gibson, Gordon (1999) *A Principled Analysis of the Nisga'a Treaty.* Vancouver:
  Fraser Institute, Occasional Paper 27.
Lederman, William R. (1962–3) The Concurrent Operation of Federal and Provin-
  cial Laws in Canada. *McGill Law Journal* 9: 185–99.
Leslie, Peter M. (1986) Canada as a Bicommunal Polity. In C. Beckton and A.W.
  MacKay (eds), *Recurring Issues in Canadian Federalism.* Toronto: University of
  Toronto Press.
Leslie, Peter M. (1987) *Federal State, National Economy.* Toronto: University of
  Toronto Press.

Leslie, Peter M. (1999) Canada: The Supreme Court Sets Rules for the Secession of Quebec. *Publius, The Journal of Federalism* 29.

Leslie, Peter M., Kenneth Norrie and Irene Ip (1993) *A Partnership in Trouble: Renegotiating Fiscal Federalism*. Toronto: C.D. Howe Institute.

Lijphart, Arend (1977) *Democracy in Plural Societies: a Comparative Exploration*. New Haven: Yale University Press.

Long, J. Anthony and Katherine Beaty Chiste (1993) Aboriginal Policy and Politics: The Charlottetown Accord and Beyond. In R.L. Watts and D.M. Brown (eds), *Canada: The State of the Federation 1993*. Kingston, Ont.: Queen's University, Institute of Intergovernmental Relations, pp. 153–74.

Mackintosh, William A. (1923) Economic Factors in Canadian History. *Canadian Historical Review* 4: 12–25.

Marshall, Thomas H. (1950) *Citizenship and Social Class*. Cambridge: Cambridge University Press.

McRoberts, Kenneth and Patrick Monahan (eds) (1993) *The Charlottetown Accord, the Referendum, and the Future of Canada*. Toronto: University of Toronto Press.

Molloy, Tom (1999) Why the Nisga'a Treaty Works. *Globe and Mail [Toronto]* (22 November) p. A19.

Trudeau, Pierre Elliott (1968) Quebec and the Constitutional Problem. In P.E. Trudeau (ed.), *Federalism and the French Canadians*. Toronto: Macmillan, pp. 3–5.

CHAPTER 8

THE STATE, DEMOCRACY AND CITIZENSHIP IN AUSTRALIA

Alastair Davidson

My recent book, which traces the history of citizenship in Australia in the twentieth century, has the title *From Subject to Citizen* (Davidson, 1997a). It describes this progress as positive where both the acquisition of nationality and the rights of citizens are concerned. Its thesis is that the early Australian Commonwealth had been a racist, exclusionary regime based on a blood notion of Anglo-Celtic nationhood. Only those of British stock were welcome. The man who drafted the Constitution, Samuel Griffith, summed up the exclusive communitarianism on Federation day (1901) in these words:

> The whole Empire, the unity of which was never so conspicuously displayed as in the closing year of the past century, is watching the great event of today with sympathetic interest, and he must indeed be churlish who, even though he would have preferred to wait a little longer, will decline to join the rejoicings of an Empire, or refuse his sympathy to the Australian Sons of the Blood in their cheerful acceptance of their manifest destiny . . . Henceforth we are Australians first, then Queenslanders, but always Britons. (*Brisbane Courier*, 1 January 1901)

I argued that that sort of view lasted until the return of the Gough Whitlam government in 1972, when Australia was abruptly dragged into the twentieth century. What prompted the change was the Australian need for labour after 1945. This had resulted in the immigration of a hundred different ethnicities whose sudden presence made it a mockery to demand assimilation to the Anglo national identity before nationality and citizenship rights were granted. In the next eighteen years it became easier and easier to obtain naturalization in Australia. The country became a multicultural society that was proposed as a model for the rest of the world. While Whitlam's attempts to improve citizenship rights, especially for minorities and newcomers, met resistance from the old majority and were only unevenly implemented, there were innovations. A real democracy based on one man, one vote, one value had not been obtained by 1995, but when I finished writing the book, the rights of women, aborigines and ethnic minorities had improved greatly as Australia was hauled into conformity with international norms. I expected that it would only be a matter of time before the one person, one vote, one value principle would also be adopted as a right.

Recent events and research have forced me to revise my optimistic view. Since the mid-1980s a new nationalism has developed (Jayasuriya, 1991). It is not unlike that in other countries, including Britain, France and Germany, in that it has taken on exclusionary anti-migrant and anti-aboriginal forms, and is marked by the introduction of new nationality laws that make it more difficult for immigrants to obtain citizenship. Australia has found her Lepenisme in Pauline Hanson's One Nation party, which has had an alarming success in recent elections, eleven members of Parliament being elected at the last elections in Queensland. The 1993 reform to the Citizenship Act tightened up requirements for citizenship by moving away from the strict *ius soli* which allows anyone born on the national territory to be a citizen regardless of their parent's status. Proposals for reforms in 2001 – while trumpeting a belated acceptance of the principle of dual nationality – show a re-emergence of the notion that Australia belongs to the old Australians who need to defend their patrimony. For example, the environmentalists' argument against further immigration on the grounds that Australia would become overpopulated has been accepted by government spokesmen as reasonable.

Recent research (Dutton, 1998; Hage, 1998; Jackman, 1998) has shown that strong Anglo-Celtic 'white' attitudes are alive, well and growing not only at state but also at community level. Indeed, Hage makes clear that the racist discourse of One Nation is really akin to the taunts of a child in a family whose adults hold the same view in private. He argues that the bad nationalism which colludes with neo-fascism – of which the ruling conservatives have long been suspected – is structurally the same as the good multicultural nationalism which sees 'our' Australia as 'enriched' by newcomers without ever querying the notion that Australia is 'our place'.

This new nationalism could be seen as no more than a knee-jerk reaction to the pressures of a globalization which – on a lived level – combines unemployment and hardship for the old national community with the arrival of great numbers of new sorts of ethnic workforces. Consequently, as it is mere ideological nostalgia for a homogeneous, harmonious world that has been lost and will not return in the new global economic system, the new nationalism might be dismissed as temporary. The approach I adopted in my book, which noted its re-emergence, was that the structural imperatives of globalization would

force positive innovation and override political appeals to a declining
national sovereignty. Following the logic of most commentary on globalization, the imperatives of the global free market were understood as
forcing the development of a state that, in an endeavour to become
competitive, adjusts its norms to imperative international economic
requirements (a 'competition state') and thus ulterior adoption of an
international rule of law (Castles and Davidson, 2000).

On reflection, it seems wiser to consider what logics exist within the
overall Australian state structures, which may give a continuing material
basis to the new nationalism and prevent the positive move from subject
to citizen continuing as it did in the past. These logics will operate even
if the pressure of globalization is in the other direction. The substance of
this chapter is to consider what those structures are and how they
operate. Its theme is that, even if the subject status has been abolished
formally, Australia's particular variety of the Westminster system continues to prevent a move towards a real democratic citizenship. At the
risk of overstating my position, democratic citizenship exists where
people live under laws of their making. This can only occur where they
are the sovereign power in a particular space. In Australia, the practical
conclusion must be that nothing but a radical break with the overall state
structure through a radical new Constitution that does not continue the
previous system will be required to create such power 'from below'. This
seems unlikely given existing political hegemonies.

FROM WESTMINSTER TO AXMINSTER

When the 1901 views of Sir Samuel Griffith cited above are translated
into his view of the British patrimony, the latter reveals itself to be 600
years or more of common law and the system of rule evolved at
Westminster. This structured combination is regarded as without equal
in guaranteeing the rights of the individual subject. The Westminster
system had grown through concessions exacted from a feudal and
absolute monarchy by his lords and notables. This shifted power and
legal sovereignty into the hands of the Parliament, formally the King-in-
Parliament (Low, 1918; Cambridge, 1933). As the franchise was extended
to more and more of the population between 1832 and 1928 and parliamentarians became dependent on electoral support, a practical
democracy with power 'from below' emerged in Britain. The turning
point to democracy is usually located in 1911 when the unelected House
of Lords was effectively subordinated to the elected House of Commons
(Green, 1920). Nevertheless, formal democracy was weak, having
emerged in a piecemeal and *ad hoc* fashion. Unlike European and US

democracies, the people were not made formally sovereign – the King-in-Parliament remains sovereign to this day. This meant that formally the Westminster system makes the state machinery sovereign: the people remain the *subjects* of the monarch and his law is his commands to them. The democratic citizen, as described by Jean-Jacques Rousseau, is not formally included in institutional arrangements.

The admiration for the Westminster model (which extended well beyond the English-speaking world) rested on its capacity to adapt and change without violent revolutionary popular action. Its flexibility owed much to the fact that it was an unwritten combination of common law decisions and 'conventions' of Parliament. After 1840 British imperial possessions were always regarded as heirs legally and politically to that system, which they were all expected to acquire in time: even the non-white Empire. The capital point is that it changed when extended to the colonies – including those of Australia – in the 1850s and continued to grow away not only from the British model but from that of other colonies. The distance is great today between Britain and Australia, New Zealand, Canada and South Africa, all of which were originally based on the system at Westminster. The essence of the system was that it was unwritten and easily adapted to new circumstances. But the system meant that it had to be a sovereign Act of the British Parliament that established a rigid written constitution for Australia. The virtue of flexibility was lost because the constitution became frozen in time. All the defects of the system because of what it omitted then became increasingly obvious. It became known pejoratively as a 'Washminster' (Thompson, 1994) and then an 'Axminster' system (Venturini, 1994). We seek to trace that degeneration in what follows.

SUBJECTS/SUBJECTION

After 1901 Australian discussion of the citizen and democracy followed British practice in focusing on the notion of duties to the state – the Roman tradition of another Empire – rather than on the citizen's right to make the laws under which he or she lives. But in the context of a written constitution the meaning of citizens' rights was much more restrictive than the British. Once it was translated into a written constitution, the practical flexibility was lost since there could not be that practical transfer of power to the people without a series of rebellions like those of British history up to 1688. Rather there was a *formal* omission of the citizen–individual from collective sovereignty. In the Australian constitution of 1901 reference to the citizen was deliberately left out and there is still no formal statement about democracy (Davidson, 1997a). This poses the question of the source of the rule of law, which is essential to any liberal democracy and which has no consensual force without it.

As a written document the constitution had to be interpreted by the High Court for the limits of its powers. This would have been so in all federations. The vast territories of the British Empire had to be federations (even New Zealand considered becoming a federation). Yet, whereas the USA, which was the main model for the Commonwealth of Australia, made clear the sovereignty of the people in its constitution and created a Bill of Rights to which the judiciary could refer for guidance, Australia did not. Indeed, it never has, and until the 1970s it was a canon that such formality was not necessary because the existing system was all that was needed to protect the individual from state tyranny (Menzies, 1967). Since the 1970s even the judiciary, aware of its vast and unaccountable power as the source of the rule of law in the Australian system, has called for a Bill of Rights that establishes citizen inviolability. In 1999 there is still no Bill of Rights.

In sum, the democratic citizen, who was able gradually to emerge, at least informally, in the interstices of Westminster, did not in fact emerge in Australia. Instead there emerged the hybrid of Washington and Westminster, which allowed such power to the judiciary that it had degenerated into the Axminster system, where the state can trample legally on rights recognized elsewhere in the world. In my book I forecast changes in the 1990s on the basis of political trends that depended on international pressure to conform to a rights regime.

Yet, in 1999 there are no signs of change to this structure. Indeed, the negative implications of the failure to change for democracy and human rights for the citizen are dismissed as paranoia. Rather, at the 1998 Convention to discuss the establishment of a republic, which would finally break with vestiges of the monarchical prerogative power, debate was limited to the issue of how to choose the President (Commonwealth of Australia, 1998). Moreover, it was decided that the new President would be chosen by Parliament, not elected by the people. No other failing of the constitution, let alone the absence of a statement and structures to establish popular sovereignty, was even allowed onto the agenda. 'Real' republicans sometimes proposed a vote against change in the 2001 referendum for fear that further reform shall be shelved if the 'minimalist' option of a President chosen by Parliament succeeds. In a strange alliance with supporters of the monarchy against the moderate republicans for whom the end of the monarchy was sufficient, they ensured the loss of the referendum for a republic. At the time of writing, no scholarly analyses of the reasons for voting are yet available but journalistic opinion suggests that many of the public agreed with 'Real' republicans. Certainly many people were not swayed by sophisticated argument that Australia was a republic already despite the formalities of its constitution.

THE PROBLEM

The problem this poses for me is to explain the failure to progress in the way I recently expected. Why have international standards not forced or led Australia away from the undemocratic political residues in its structure? Why are international norms just not talked about here as they are elsewhere, even in the great complacent open republics, the USA and France? The former is, of course, notable for its refusal to sign international agreements, arguing that its rights standards are unmatched or that its national sovereignty would be violated if it adopted such norms.

A preliminary answer is that the limited structure of the debate has been fostered by nearly a hundred years of such a constitution. It shows no sign of changing despite the lip service to the need for an active citizen developed since 1988. That lip service was prompted by the recognition by Labor that the Australian voter was not outraged by the undemocratic 1975 dismissal of the Prime Minister, Gough Whitlam, when he tried to drag Australia into conformity with international norms for democracy and human rights. Rather, so ingrained was the passivity of the subjects – among the few peoples of the world compelled to vote because of their low electoral participation – that they acquiesced easily in what overseas commentators saw as a peaceful *coup d'état*.

Certainly, vast civics programmes were introduced in the mid-1990s by the heirs to the conservative parties who had Whitlam removed using constitutional powers vested in the Governor-General. These programmes were designed to shift responsibilities to individuals and away from the state by emphasizing the duties and obligations of the citizen. The further question is then posed: why have they not succeeded?

An analysis of the intent and content of those programmes, *Discovering Democracy* (Kemp, 1997), reveals an attempt to glorify and not critique Australian political history. This is portrayed as a triumph of democratic principles and human rights – which Australia apparently pioneered – resulting in a system that is superior even to that in Britain. In fact, civics is equated mainly with learning this history and showing, through loyalty to it, how indebted we and future generations are to what our forefathers built (not much mention of the foremothers, though that would not necessarily improve the picture). Little hands-on active participation in running the country is proposed when compared with the civics programmes of France or the USA, or the European Union and Council of Europe (Kemp, 1997; Davidson, 1999).

This bogs Australia down in the 'debt' notion of citizenship (Duchesne, 1997) which makes civic ethics primarily loyalty to our forebears and thus to the community and nation. Any criticism is immediately tainted with disloyalty. It therefore inhibits attention being focused on contemporary problems arising outside the community history. Deciding what should be done by reference to any postnational or global future can only be limited to word games. Solutions are blocked by the structure of reasoning before analysis is even made. Indeed debate about democracy in Australia rarely starts from the question of what is meant by democracy in 2000 but from the assertion that what we have is democracy. Such a position can never result in reform since what we have can never be measured against anything else to see how far it is unsatisfactory.

While similar attitudes can be seen in Britain and European countries more generally, there are two sides to the debate there. There is no real debate in Australia. When debate is called for it is dismissed for pragmatic reasons. In Britain, the former vainglorious assumption that Westminster was superior to all other systems is clearly under challenge and is resulting in changes like the proposed abolition of the House of Lords, the incorporation of the European Convention on Human Rights into the rule of law, the creation of parliaments for Scotland and Wales and even pressure for a written constitution. Progressive Britons might find this typification a little rosy, but it is important that they realize that Britain does look rosy from Australia, because it is giving up its blind attachment to the Westminster model in favour of that imposed by the regional imperatives of Europe.

Again, we see, say, Canadians, evolving away from the Westminster model into a new discourse on politics unimaginable in Australia. While Canada and Australia had had parallel developments since the Durham Report of 1839, the North American colonies had diverged and become much more progressive than the Australian by the twentieth century. Any student of Australian constitutional and international law since 1945 will recall how much Canadian developments served as models that Australia followed after some lapse of time. As a result of an early assertion of international personality, repatriation of its constitution and its 1982 rights charter, Canadian debate about democracy, human rights and the citizen in a country with a colonial past has developed well beyond anything in Australia.

Just how sophisticated the Canadian debate has become is evident from the advisory judgment in *Reference re Secession of Quebec* (treal. ca/doc/csc-scc/en/rec/texts/renvoi. en. txt; compare *McGinty v. Western Australia* 1996: 243c). Advisory judgments are not allowed in Australia despite the High Court being required to make weighty judgment about constitutional matters when dispute arises. The Canadian judges' views are reminiscent of positions found in European rather than British discourse, both in their insistence that democracy is needed to ground rights and vice versa, and their insistence on an open debate (no secrecy) regardless of its effectiveness. Moreover, their decision showed an acute awareness of the place of judicial opinion in a complex structure whose multiple levels would have to be involved. We might say that the judgment endorses all progressive opinion about popular sovereignty: that it is essential and, precisely because it is balanced in many places, it is not the tyranny that conservatives often allege it must become. The Supreme Court of Canada regarded it as necessary to discuss the underlying principles of the constitution comprising federalism, democracy, constitutionalism and the rule of law, and respect for minorities. It argued that federalism starts from a recognition that cultural diversity is enriching and cannot be homogenized à la Renan (Renan, 1992) into a single cultural national identity; it insisted on the virtues of a written constitution for a predictable rule of law especially where limits to sovereignties in the federation are at stake; it defined federation as a form of more democracy in more places, allowing ethnic minorities to manage their own affairs; it affirmed that democracy was the way that the sovereign people exercised its right to self-government at the different federal levels and also established in continuous participation in discussion its consent to the rule of law; and that the latter governed the exercise of democratic legislative will. Finally, it made clear that democracy and its rules identified which majority had to be consulted when the rule of law was to be challenged. No unilateral assertion of, say, the right to secede, was automatically right because it had majority support within a particular constituency. Constitutionalism and the rule of law were as necessary to democracy as the reverse.

In both Britain and Canada we can see that the changes arise from interaction with ideas coming from outside the national political tradition. They are compelled to deal with abstractions like 'democracy'. In Australia, contrarily, no ideas from foreign parts are allowed into the debate. Whereas even in Britain the reality of Europe forces openings to previously anathematized ideas that hark back to Rousseau, Kant and intellectual 'traitors' like Paine, this does not happen in Australia. Because of backward looking stress on 'our' history, which – as practically everywhere – is a vainglorious collective memory totally at variance with the facts, the most that can be done is to pick up on what the Britons are doing that is consistent with the Australian collective memory and style.

IDEAS FROM FOREIGN PARTS

Overall, the ideological hegemony, which goes back to the Australian version of Westminster, results in only that discourse that disempowers the people and encourages the elitist and authoritarian solutions favoured by public policy based on postmodern thought. Thus a close reading of the Constitutional Convention proceedings in 1998 reveals that all debate about multicultural realities and where Australia is going, much less democracy and what it means, was completely shut down (Report, 1998). The majority of the delegates including the moderate republicans and some of the real republicans applied gags or set agenda to prevent such issues being raised. The argument was that the focus should be on the issue of ending the monarchy or even the terms of the referendum would not be agreed upon. The voice of ethnic minorities and aborigines was drowned out by the 'good' nationalists, whose structural position is, as Hage has pointed out, little different from that of Pauline Hanson despite the former's acceptance of multiculturalism as ethnic colour (restaurants, clothes, festivals, cultural life) (Hage, 1998; Jackman, 1998).

To such traditional closures are added their further contemporary extensions. The Labor Party and left progressive forces might be expected to push for popular empowerment and certainly for defence of the minorities. Instead, they shut down all such debate at the Convention and afterwards in favour of the minimalist solution where the Queen is replaced by an Australian President. Indeed, where their 'theory' is advanced it reveals itself to be identical with the right-wing, union-bashing views of the ruling conservative coalition, whose spokesman, Peter Reith, noted this with glee in Parliamentary debate. Three recent books illustrate this assertion (Latham, 1998; Tanner, 1999; Kelly, 1999). The first two are by the putative heirs to Labor leadership and the third by a major newspaper editor whose views are given constant coverage in the press. They pose as exponents of the 'third way', whose postmodern credentials are openly asserted in Britain and North America by, say, Anthony Giddens, but whose first formulation was by Bruno Megret who is effectively replacing Le Pen as leader of French neo-fascism.

Basically, they advance in common a partial view of the new context which Australians face. But they see this as ineluctably imposing a 'competition state' response on the Australian state. They maintain that to be competitive in the global twenty-first century, especially in the

Asia-Pacific region, requires the end of the social or welfare state; the acceptance of the risk society whose main characteristic is unemployment and no guaranteed safety net for citizens. We might see them as rolling back Marshall's view of citizenship in its social dimension and thus proving how much his sociological approach, which saw the war for citizenship as won, was always too apolitical. But they go beyond a refusal to accept a traditional notion of social justice and that all citizens are their brothers' and sisters' keepers. In the selfish individualism (down to voicing disproved idiocies about trickle-down economic effects of rationalization and economic liberalism) which they encourage, a civic ethic of care for the less fortunate is all but replaced with arguments about the need for more 'social capital' and 'trust'. Indeed, Francis Fukuyama is proposed as the philosophical underpinning for one book. The argument of Latham, who puts the most elaborate case, is that the traditional welfare state as a top-down solution is no longer appropriate. The values which make a society cohere to face its challenges are developed in the realm of private associations and not by state policies. This adds up to less investment in areas other than those of education which supposedly allow individuals to cope with rapid and sudden restructuring following the needs of globalization.

But their affirmation that the old national sovereignty and therefore popular sovereignty cannot be maintained in the face of globalization's imperatives, like other proponents of the 'competition state', does not mean that they look to international and global attempts to combat globalization's negative effects. Indeed, they seem unaware that UN indices show that globalization and economic rationalism has brought absolute worsening in conditions of life for 60 per cent of the world's population and, indeed, for Australians themselves. Their reliance on the sort of figures produced in the USA and Great Britain and by bodies like the World Trade Organization (WTO) as well as repetition of clichés like the success of the USA economy allows them to sustain the myth that we must adopt an expert, elitist and non-democratic solution in Australia. This builds easily onto the past Axminster tradition. For example, by use of figures about USA success which occludes the reality that full employment is achieved in the USA (and would be in Australia) by wages so low that in California 74 per cent of applicants for food relief also return themselves as employed (Watson, 1999; Swinburne, 1999), they can paint a positive picture of a disaster in human terms, the triumph of a *capitalisme sauvage*. But it is not the debatable socioeconomic story they tell which is significant. That is told almost universally. Nor is it the competition state scenario. It is their refusal to learn from 'foreign parts' the solutions that re-empower citizens regionally even as citizen power at the nation-state level is reduced (for example, the EU) or globally even as they lose power nationally (Castles and Davidson, 2000). Typically, the index of one of these books does not include the headings: 'citizen', 'human rights', or 'democracy'.

This part of the debate cannot be avoided in Europe and has imposed itself on Britain. If Tony Blair, Bill Clinton, Jacques Chirac and Gerhard Schroeder adopt a 'third way', they are still obliged to seek to empower the democratic citizen and guarantee individual rights. In Australia, consideration of the standards proposed by the Europeans and the United Nations (for example, Global Commission, 1995) are simply rejected – not just ignored. In Australia, getting up to date does not mean re-examining whether Australian national identity and its political forms are deficient. Rather, simultaneously with a definition of national identity as requiring merely commitment to democracy, rights and the rule of law (as was done in the new oath of citizenship in 1993), there is no discussion of the content and substance of the political forms allowed except in the old terms. The mode of discussion at the 1998 Convention was little different from that at the conventions one hundred years earlier. In no way did it reveal that the Australian population comes from myriad civic and political traditions, including democratic traditions much stronger than those of Westminster, even at its best.

The new nationalism builds on such closures. Only the new ethnic minorities and the original indigenous peoples look out to foreign parts for new solutions to the new global world. Indeed, they are obliged to do so to get justice in a world where the old Anglo-Celt nationalists rule at all levels of the polity. The absence of proportional representation of ethnics and other minorities in the judiciary, politics and the administration is less important here – since comparatively it is good – than the fact that members of ethnic minorities are only advanced if they take on the Anglo Westminster discourse, which some do fervently (Davidson, 1997b).

Minorities that wish to preserve their dignity in difference turn outwards for support. Thus aborigines, after a long and futile battle for rights (to land; to culture; to languages) which was nearly always stymied by the courts and Parliament, have now started appealing not only to international law but also directly to the world and European courts for support. Similarly, refugees and boat people, driven forth for myriad reasons from their birthplaces, have had to resort to international tribunals and law to ensure protection of their rights. The local political system defends harshly and against international standards its right to keep such people out on the grounds that this is defending the national citizens' right to maintain control of his and her space.

The aboriginal people, after two centuries of genocide, which was hidden and even ten years ago often denied – any mention of it provoked sanctions, such as threats of dismissal from university posts – forced a grudging acknowledgement by the people who destroyed them and took their land that this had been done. Yet the basis in the common law for such genocidal actions was never acknowledged although it meant that the existing rule of law was incapable of solving the problem. All it could do was replicate the determined two-century-long repression of difference. The hopes that were raised by the Mabo and Wik cases, which finally recognized aboriginal title to land after two centuries when all real property rights had been based on the fiction that Australia was uninhabited and desert when the whites invaded, have been disappointed. In convoluted argument they reversed all previous law by recognizing native title in increasingly wide territorial spaces. But such legal hair splitting has meant little substantial change at a legislative level over the last decade. Nor, in the existing political regime, could a tiny indigenous minority force change politically. At the last federal election the first aboriginal member was elected since a lone predecessor nearly a generation ago.

Indigenous leaders and groups therefore built alliances with peoples like them outside Australia and started to appeal to international tribunals and law as the only way to force justice from the national majority. Quite simply, they recognized that justice cannot be obtained where your oppressors make the decision. It is much better to appeal to people who have no roots in the past to obtain justice (Dodson, 1999). This realization that the best defence of minority community rights is through an appeal to universal standards and not the dangerous path of asserting the right to community difference paralleled that of Muslims in Europe and even the Zapatistas of Mexico. It immediately provoked the response on both sides of the political fence that this was disloyal and treacherous. The overwhelming point of reference for the Australian state clearly remained the communitarian national position.

So, while indigenous minorities were learning that justice cannot be related to any community, the Australian state did not. This was even clearer where refugees were concerned. When such people arrived they were often placed in near-concentration camps in remote parts of Australia. It became almost a policy of the immigration authorities to avoid due procedure required by international convention in considering their cases. They were simply flown back to their countries of origin regardless of what might happen to them there. The most recent example was that of a Somali whose planned return in late 1998 to almost certain death was conducted secretly. The state did its best to ensure that it was not stopped legally by racing through his deportation. Only prompt action by local and international lawyers with links to Amnesty International prevented him being put on a plane until after due consideration of his case had been made (Hamilton, 1999). Aware that the state will try to throw them out regardless – and the case law in this regard has not stopped decisions of state under the extraordinary provisions of the relevant immigration, nationality and citizenship acts – refugees increasingly look to international bodies and conventions for solutions. This way, a dribble of international best practice makes it into the debate through the legal system (Davidson, 1997a). In their case, the accusations of disloyalty levelled at aborigines cannot be advanced. Defence of the national patrimony 'we' have inherited is usually the justification.

Overall, a search for approaches and values other than in the national communitarian tradition of Washminster to solve the problems of globalization is limited to minorities. The overwhelming impression is that progressives in Australia are committed to the communitarian notion that justice can only be established by reference to historical community and not forward-looking universal values. It is on such an approach that all parties from progressives to Hansonites base their right to autonomy and independence. Where innovation or a new state of affairs is recognized it is limited to the economic and social realities of globalization and not to the new ways of empowering people in those new contexts.

The real puzzle about this is why the majority of a population whose conditions of life have sadly declined on economic, social, legal and political levels in the last fifteen years has itself not refused to accept old solutions to new problems. Why, for example, is there no real opposition to the exclusion of discussions about a fundamental revision of the constitution when its supporters make clear that what is at stake is democracy? Why is there no insistence that democracy be discussed; a decision made about what it is today; and steps taken to introduce procedures and institutions to attain it? Statistics show that Australians are unemployed, or underemployed (14 per cent); that globalization has brought a collapse of public facilities, education and health systems, and that more people divorce, take drugs, commit crimes, commit suicide (Australian Bureau of Statistics, 1998; Swinburne, 1999). Recent state attempts to destroy the union movement and to end traditional work conditions brought hundreds of thousands into the streets. The average Australian considers that politicians are completely unprincipled and that the political system does not work. They want elected officials, including an elected President; they want a bill of rights; they want social services. Yet, despite such evidence, what exists is regarded as democratic. Despite huge mounds of evidence that malapportionment is constitutionally entrenched, judicial refusal to state that we should have one vote, one value, and a reality where even querying the system can get a person jailed (*Langer v. The Commonwealth*, 1996), the state is not obliged to change.

So the main explanation for the triumph of the hegemony of state seems to be that it has successfully kept a discussion of democracy out of the public arena without losing its constituency. This makes the real problem not simply a nationalistically myopic leadership whose commitment to 'the way we do things around here' makes them antidemocratic by contemporary standards, but the fact that the Australian people allow them to get away with that when they do not endorse such views. The crucial explanation, it seems, lies primarily in the successful hegemony of state, as I tried to describe it for the nineteenth century in *The Invisible State* (Davidson, 1991). The lack of an organized popular counter-hegemony and the constant defeat of those who try to introduce new ideas into the debate while they are still relevant is central to the ongoing commitment to the overall system. Even academic debate starts by assuming that what exists is democratic. It emphasizes the virtuous role of minority parties of the Senate in controlling lower house majorities, without for a minute adverting to the fact that the Senate is not a democratically elected House (Galligan, 1995; Emy, 1997a and 1997b). Indeed, although One Nation received 14 per cent of the vote in recent federal elections and yet no seats, where a lesser vote got seats for other parties who control a balance of power as a result, no real public objection to the lack of democracy was made. Since the Hansonites advance appalling racist policies, it is considered just that they should have no voice no matter what the price. It should be noted that nothing stated in this chapter denies that sooner or later Australia will come up to date. Rather my concern is that by that time the horse will have long bolted. Intellectually, it is most evident in the dependence of Australians on British and US sources about international political theory. Thus while postmodernism made it into the USA in a distorted form long ago, long after Foucault, Derrida and Lyotard had disappeared from Parisian intellectual debate, the Anglo distortion of 'governmentality' still rules here (Frankel, 1998). It functions as an intellectual justification for the Labor Party writers discussed above and economic rationalism more generally.

The key issue for Australian democracy is whether a viable counter-hegemony in favour of democracy can still be built in conditions of globalization. That that is possible is certainly the belief of the Europeans and of the Global Commission of the United Nations. It can be defended given certain concessions. But the forces blocking it are now immense. Australia experiences those pressures. The first is the loss of all core identities with 'disembedding' and 'distanciation' (Giddens, 1990). These arise from the huge migratory fluxes that leave newcomers forever with multiple identities and attachments (Eade, 1997). If they never feel that they belong in one community only, they are also unable to find a common experience – say, as members of the working class united by their experience of the factory – which would unite them against oppressive forces (Davidson, 1998). No longer are classes – even in themselves – formed by production in advanced societies.

So, the material class-based institutionally expressed conditions for a counter-hegemony based, say, on an international regime of human rights and democracy, do not exist any more. It is tiny ethnic and indigenous minorities who turn to the UN for redress against the injustices caused by the existing hegemonies here. The majority still staunchly refuse to see anything wrong with the system or argue that it parallels realities elsewhere.

ACKNOWLEDGEMENTS

I would like to thank Mike Salvaris, David Hayward and Kathleen Weekley for their comments on this chapter.

FURTHER READING

The following five items cover most of the themes highlighted in the chapter:

Davidson, A. (1997) *From Subject to Citizen*. Cambridge: Cambridge University Press.
Galligan, B. (1995) *A Federal Republic*. Cambridge: Cambridge University Press.
Latham, M. (1998) *Civilising Global Capital: New Thinking for Australian Labor*. Sydney: Allen & Unwin.
Winterton, G. (1994) (ed.) *We the People: Australian Republican Government*. Sydney: Allen & Unwin.
Report of the Republican Convention Old Parliament House, Canberra, 2–13 February 1998, Canberra: Commonwealth of Australia.

In addition, readers may usefully consult the following books:

Chesterman, John and Galligan, Brian (1997) *Citizens Without Rights: Aborigines and Australian Citizenship* (Cambridge: Cambridge University Press). Although the book deals primarily with the situation of aborigines, it also confronts some of the issues thought to be at the heart of a perceived lack of democracy in Australia. In particular, there are two chapters that deal with the Australian constitution and its role in limiting the importance of citizenship and democracy. The book also draws together some of the key problems pertaining to the idea of 'belonging' as a prerequisite to the effective exercise of citizenship.

James, P. (1996) (ed.) *The State in Question: Transformations of the Australian State* (St Leonards: Allen & Unwin). This collection of essays is a postmodern account of the contemporary state of Australia. The book deals critically with a number of themes including labourism, green issues, the welfare state, feminism, foreign policy, sovereignty and territoriality.

McKenna, Mark (1996) *The Captive Republic: A History of Republicanism in Australia 1788–1996* (Cambridge, New York and Melbourne: Cambridge University Press). This book deals with the historical context in which contemporary debates about democracy and republicanism take place in Australia today.

N. Peterson and Will Sanders (1997) (eds) *Citizenship and Indigenous Australians: Changing Conceptions and Possibilities* (Cambridge: Cambridge University Press). The chapters in this book deal with historical and contemporary understandings of aboriginality and the emerging possibilities for indigenous citizenship. The latter section of the book is notable for its emphasis on the role of international law and the concept of aboriginal sovereignty in the contemporary context.

Stokes, Geoffrey (1997) (ed.) *The Politics of Identity in Australia* (Cambridge, New York and Melbourne: Cambridge University Press). The book is crossdisciplinary and covers theories of identity, gender and sexuality, race, place and citizenship and the manifestations of identity through literature and film. Most notably in a number of contributions the argument is made that identity has been manipulated for political ends, the significance of which is not lost on those mobilizing support around constitutional reform and republicanism.

Wiseman, John (1999) *Global Nation? The Politics of Globalisation in Australia* (Cambridge: Cambridge University Press). This book analyses the way in which Australia's current preoccupation with constitutional reform interfaces with forces at work beyond the state. It highlights the contradictory process of globalization and its effect on the nation state through reference to Australia.

BIBLIOGRAPHY

Australian Bureau of Statistics (1998) *Yearbook Australia*. Canberra: Australian Bureau of Statistics.

Cambridge University Press (1933) *The Cambridge History of the British Empire*. Cambridge: Cambridge University Press.

Castles, S. and Davidson, A. (2000) *Citizenship and Migration: Globalization and the Politics of Belonging*. London: Macmillan.

Commonwealth of Australia (1998) *Report of the Constitutional Convention, Old Parliament House, Canberra, 2–13 February 1998*. Canberra: Commonwealth of Australia. Four vols.

Davidson, A. (1991) *The Invisible State: The Formation of the Australian State 1788–1901.* Cambridge: Cambridge University Press.

Davidson, A. (1997a) *From Subject to Citizen: Australian Citizenship in the Twentieth Century.* Cambridge: Cambridge University Press.

Davidson, A. (1997b) Multiculturalism and Citizenship: Silencing the Migrant Voice, *Journal of Intercultural Studies* 18(2): 77–92.

Davidson, A. (1998) A New Global Mode of Production: Achievement and Contradiction. In G. Dow and G. Lafferty (eds), *Everlasting Uncertainty: Interrogating the Communist Manifesto 1848–1998.* Sydney: Pluto.

Davidson, A. (1999) Democracy and Citizenship. In W. Hudson (ed.), *Rethinking Australian Citizenship.* London: Macmillan.

Dodson, M. (1999) Indigenous Peoples and the Globalization of Rights. In A. Davidson and K. Weekley (eds), *Globalization and Citizenship in the Asia-Pacific.* London: Macmillan.

Duchesne, S. (1997) Citoyenneté à la française. Paris: Sciences Po.

Dutton, D. (1998) *Strangers, Citizens, the Boundaries of Australian Citizenship 1901–1973.* PhD thesis. Melbourne: Melbourne University.

Eade, J. (ed.) (1997) *Living the Global City: Globalization as a Local Process.* London: Routledge.

Emy, H (1997a) The Mandate and Responsible Government, *Australian Journal of Political Science* 32(1): 65–78.

Emy, H. (1997b) Unfinished Business: Confirming Australia's Constitution as an Act of Political Settlement, *Australian Journal of Political Science* 32(3): 383–400.

Frankel, B. (1998) Confronting Neoliberal Regimes: The Post-Marxist Embrace of Populism and Realpolitik, *New Left Review* 226: 57–93.

Galligan, B. (1995) *A Federal Republic.* Cambridge: Cambridge University Press.

Giddens, A. (1990) *The Consequences of Modernity.* Cambridge: Polity/Blackwell.

Global Commission (1995) *Our Global Neighbourhood: Report of the Commission on Global Governance.* Oxford: Oxford University Press.

Green, J. (1920) *A Short History of the English People.* London: Macmillan.

Hage, G. (1998) *White Nation: Fantasies of White Supremacy in a Multicultural Society.* Sydney: Pluto.

Hamilton, A. (1999) Compassion on Short Rations, *Eureka Street* (January–February): 6.

Jackman, S. (1998) Pauline Hanson, the Mainstream, and Political Elites: The Place of Race in Australian Political Ideology, *Australian Journal of Political Science* 33(2): 167–87.

Jayasuriya, L. (1991) State, Nation and Diversity in Australia, *Current Affairs Bulletin* (November): 21–7.

Kelly, P. (1999) *Future Tense: Australia Beyond Election 1998.* Sydney: Allen & Unwin.

Kemp, D. (1997) *Discovering Democracy.* Canberra: Department of Employment, Education, Training and Youth Affairs.

Kymlicka, W. (1996) *Multicultural Citizenship.* Oxford: Clarendon.

Langer v. The Commonwealth (1996) 70 ALJR 176.

Latham, M. (1998) *Civilising Global Capital: New Thinking for Australian Labor.* Sydney: Allen & Unwin.

Low, D. (1918) *The Governance of England.* London: Fisher Unwin.

McGinty v. Western Australia (1996) 70 ALJR 200.

Menzies, R. (1967) *Central Power in the Australian Commonwealth.* Melbourne: Cassell.

Renan, E. (1992) *Qu'est-ce qu'une nation? et autres essais politiques.* Paris: Presses Pocket.

Rousseau, J.-J. (1971) *Oeuvres complètes.* Paris: Seuil. Three vols.

Swinburne (1999) *Project on International Index of Social and Civic Health.* Melbourne: Institute for Social Research, Swinburne University of Technology.

Tanner, L. (1999) *Open Australia.* Sydney: Pluto.

Thompson, E. (1994) The Washminster Republic. In G. Winterton (ed.), *We the People: Australian Republican Government.* Sydney: Allen & Unwin.

Tully, J. (1995) *Strange Multiplicity: Constitutionalism in an Age of Diversity.* Cambridge: Cambridge University Press.

Venturini, G. (ed.) (1994) *Five Voices for Lionel: The Lionel Murphy Memorial Lectures.* Sydney: Federation Press.

Watson, D. (1999) WSWS: News and Analysis: North America, shniad@popserver.sfu. ca

CHAPTER 9

POLITICAL PARTIES AND CIVIL SOCIETY IN INDIA

Subrata Kumar Mitra

THE PROBLEM STATED

After five decades of politics based on elections and parties, India continues to offer hope for a democratic future but still with a lingering sense of doubt. The hope arises from the record of achievements since independence. Regular, relatively free and fair elections have been held for practically all the important offices at the national, regional and local levels from 1952 onwards. Participation in these elections has been respectable in comparison to the USA if not to continental Europe. Power has changed hands at the centre and in the regional states frequently as a result of elections, firmly establishing the fact that electoral competition is the only basis of legitimacy in India. These achievements should place India among the stable multi-party democracies of the world. But doubts persist because the political process that underpins the formal structure of democracy is not entirely in harmony with the liberal values essential to democracy.

Ethnic conflict and communal violence which place informal but effective restrictions on free political participation and dialogue are routinely reported in the media in India and abroad. A rough calculation would put the number of Indians living under informal army rule at 40 million people. Even at the national level, democracy all but collapsed in 1975 when Indira Gandhi imposed Emergency Rule.[1] Procedural democracy did bounce back at the central level in 1977 but then, within the short span of three years Indira Gandhi, the unrepentant author of the Emergency was back in power, duly elected as the leader of the majority party in the parliamentary elections of 1980 and appointed to the high office of Prime Minister. The resort to the curtailment of democracy through the declaration of direct central rule at the regional level, a favourite political instrument of Indira Gandhi, had continued during the period when she was out of power. Even in normal times, a number of preventive detention laws, created over the past years to check terrorism, have restricted civil liberties.

India's democratic achievements and her occasional lapse into authoritarian rule, communal riots and mass insurgencies raise two main questions. First, how did a poor society with no democratic tradition of its own succeed in developing and sustaining democratic institutions and why is there such a qualitative variation in the levels of democracy over India's regions? Second, how do elections and political parties affect the existence of a public sphere, indispensable for the creation of a civil society in India? This chapter draws on constitutional and policy innovations under British rule, institutional innovations facilitating party competition and public opinion with regard to some key divisive issues in India today in order to answer these complex questions. Crucial to the latter are data with regard to public opinion and attitudes which are derived from a survey of the Indian electorate.[2]

DEMOCRATIC DEVELOPMENT UNDER COLONIAL RULE

The functioning of political parties is crucial to the arguments of this chapter. As intermediaries between state and society in their capacity as agents of articulation and aggregation of interests, political parties have played a crucial role in the process of political transformation in India. Considering that political parties are often seen as typically Western political institutions, their role in facilitating the interaction of the modern state and traditional society in India extends the scope of the comparative analysis of party systems.

The party system and elections in India are based on single-member constituencies, first-past-the-post system of plurality voting, a parliamentary and federal form of government and a bicameral legislature at the centre. The leader of the majority party or coalition in the lower house forms the government. The President of the Republic normally plays the ceremonial role of a formal head of the state. With minor differences, these rules resemble the British system of parliamentary democracy. Most of these political institutions, adopted from the constitutions and practices of the leading democratic states of the world, have facilitated the growth of party competition and popular participation in India. Their transparency and effectiveness are further guaranteed by the existence of a free press and a watchful and independent election commission.

Despite similarities of procedure, one should not forget the tremendous differences of historical trajectories that mark the growth of modern political institutions in the West and their introduction into India. Thus for example, the British House of Commons and the party system are the product of the great economic and social changes that rocked society and state in the eighteenth and nineteenth centuries and produced the political basis for the extension of franchise to the working classes, minorities and finally to women. India did not go through a similar historical experience. The familiar sequence of the early stirring of the industrial revolution, the radical changes in agriculture, migration and the evolution of the working-class movement for the extension of suffrage did not occur in India prior to the introduction of universal adult franchise and a competitive party system in one fell swoop at independence. Having become a state when the British left, India's leaders strove to build a nation – democratic, secular and industrial – in the pattern of European stable democracies. The attempt by the post-colonial state to reverse the historical sequence of industrialization, secularization, and regional integration, which had led in the West to the growth of institutions of liberal democracy such as parties, elections and universal adult franchise, was heroic and, in historical hindsight, fraught with danger. As we see in numerous examples from Africa and Asia, this attempt led to the tragic collapse of liberal democratic institutions with much disorder, loss of life and the rise of authoritarian rule. Hence the puzzle: why did multi-party democracy apparently take root in India and how do her people cope with Western-style political parties and elections?

Part of the explanation of this puzzle lies in the history of political developments in India during the last six decades prior to independence in 1947. A brief perusal of the interaction of the British Raj and Indian resistance to it during this crucial period reveals that conditions for the emergence of political parties were steadily improving (Brown, 1985). Partly under the impact of utilitarianism but mostly as a matter of expediency, the British had started experimenting with limited self-rule in issues of minor importance such as municipal administration by the 1880s. This formed part of the British strategy of ruling India with the help of Indian intermediaries, in this case selected by a very restricted electorate of urban, rich and loyal subjects. The Indian National Congress was set up in 1885 by Sir Alan Octavian Hume, a retired British civil servant, in order to present Indian interests to the British crown in a systematic and organized manner. The Congress soon became the leading voice of the growing middle class and the liberal professions, constantly clamouring for more jobs under the colonial government and for greater political participation. The successive Acts of the British Parliament in 1909, 1919, 1935 extended the franchise and brought an increasing number of Indians into the scope of party politics albeit with restricted participation.

The process was not as effortlessly incremental nor linear as it may sound. Periods of extension of franchise and co-operation between colonial rulers and elected representatives were interspersed with ruthless suppression and imprisonment of political leaders. The Congress Party itself was often divided in its opinion between collaboration with colonial rule and radical resistance to it in order to fight for full and immediate independence. Gandhi brought these two strands together in his strategy of non-violent non-co-operation and built a powerful mass movement that united the peasantry and the national bourgeoisie under the banner of the Congress Party. By the 1930s, however, the national movement was split once again, this time on the issue of religion. The majority of Muslims, under the leadership of the Muslim League, had started agitating for an independent homeland for the Muslims of the subcontinent. As a result, when independence finally arrived in 1947, British India was partitioned into India and Pakistan. The Congress Party under Nehru inherited power in a smaller but politically and religiously more homogeneous country, with their links to the constituents intact. This was not the case in Pakistan where the Muslim League, victorious at last, took power, but only at the cost of abandoning its political hinterland in northern India which blighted the growth of a competitive party system in Pakistan.

This brief historical background partly explains the relative ease with which India developed electoral democracy and a competitive party system in contrast with Pakistan. Universal adult franchise was introduced in 1952, and both the non-democratic Left and non-democratic Right were able to compete equally with the centre and moderate Left and Right for political power through elections. At independence, the electorate consisted of large numbers of voters who had not experienced direct British rule and were stepping out of Indian princely rule (there were about six hundred such princely rulers whose territories merged with India or Pakistan at independence) straight into popular democracy. Such a sudden expansion in participation could have been a recipe for disaster both for parliamentary democracy and political order. But, although the partition of British India into independent India and Pakistan was marked by unprecedented communal violence, parliamentary democracy, thanks to the continuity of the institutions of state and the structures of leader–constituent relations, parties and elections, subsequently became part of the political culture of post-independence India. Participation has steadily gone up, increasing, for example, from 45.7 per cent in the first general election to the Lok Sabha (the lower house of the Parliament) held in 1952 to 62 per cent in the twelfth general election, held in 1998. Participation in elections has been widely spread across all social strata, and in urban areas as well as villages. The level of participation of women, former untouchables, and aboriginals does not lag far behind that of the national average.

How does India combine the functioning of elections based on single-member constituencies and a franchise based on the one-person-one-vote principle with the existence of castes, tribes and other groups structured according to collective and social identities? The answer to this apparent contradiction lies in the fact that elections and party competition in India have played a double role by empowering both individuals and groups and thus leading to the continuous creation of new groups and short-term coalitions. Rather than inhibiting the growth of party competition, social conflict, which has become interwoven with political conflict, helps deepen political partisanship. Elections with limited franchise under British rule facilitated political transition by acting as the institutional context in which power was transferred by the British rulers to elected Indian leaders. After independence, the same process accelerated the pace of social change, leading to a second phase of political change when the generation that was identified with the freedom movement was replaced by younger leaders, many of whom came from upwardly mobile, newly enfranchised, lower social classes.

At independence, the introduction of universal adult franchise empowered underprivileged social groups with a new political resource. The right to vote by secret ballot, exercised at a polling booth conveniently located at a public place where one could vote freely, created an environment that was helpful for political participation. The right to vote freely, thanks to the presence of specially recruited election officers, acted as a direct challenge to the dominance of the upper social strata. The newly mobilized lower castes and minorities felt empowered thanks to the value of the vote. Since the literature of modernization, both general and specific to India (Huntington, 1968; Harrison, 1960) warns against the disorder that follows rapid expansion of participation in traditional societies, the question that we need to raise here is why did the social pyramid not break chaotically?

Social mobilization and its political containment appear to have taken place in India as two independent but ultimately convergent processes. While the pace of social change has been accelerated through social reform legislation, recruitment of new social elites into the political arena and the political mobilization through electoral participation, their overall impact on the stability of the political system has been moderated by the existence of political intermediaries and parties at the regional and local levels. The process has been described by Lloyd and Susanne Rudolph (1967) as vertical, differential and horizontal mobilization.[3] Typically, as the marginal social groups discovered the negotiable value of the vote during the early years after independence, they became avid players in the political arena at the local and regional levels. Established

Jajmani systems – reciprocal social bonds based on the exchange of service and occupational specialization – broke down to create new groupings. Secondly, caste associations, based on shared social and economic interests emerged as links between parties and society (Mitra, 1994a). This has created a useful room to manoeuvre in the middle in the hands of national, regional and local elites (Mitra, 1991).

These innovations have been possible in India because of three factors. First, the Gandhian legacy, which informed the state and the political process, took the shape of a two-track strategy, namely accommodation of interests located at the broad middle of the political system and repression of those at the extremes on the part of the state and institutional participation and rational protest on the part of the society (Mitra, 1992). The second factor is the ability of the national and regional elites to transfer substantial power to elected village councils known as *panchayats*. The third was the presence of the Indian National Congress, a national movement turned into one dominant party, promoting democracy and containing its excesses during the formative years after independence to act as an agent of social change without disturbing political stability.

THE EVOLUTION OF THE PARTY SYSTEM SINCE INDEPENDENCE

A competitive party system provides the crucial backdrop to the political articulation of competing interests. As such, it is an important indicator of a functioning civil society. Party competition creates the political space in which social groups come together in order to engage in competition for the allocation of scarce public resources and for the assertion of their collective identity and values in the public sphere. A non-competitive party system denotes the existence of social closure, a restricted public sphere, and of elite values and interests that are above politics. The absence of a party system altogether denotes the absence of an effective and enduring basis of a dialogue and transaction between social interests and the state.

The party system of contemporary India is the result of the six decades of growth under British rule prior to independence. Its institutional base has been considerably reinforced with the political mobilization of all sections of society in the course of the last five decades. It is a fairly complex system, which specialists of comparative party systems find hard to characterize because of the continuous and influential presence of the Congress Party in the national political arena, the emergence of a powerful Hindu nationalist movement, the world's longest elected

communist government at the regional level and the occasional lapse
into authoritarian rule. The picture becomes much clearer if we divide
the post-independence period into one of the 'one-dominant-party system' period (1952–1977) and its transformation into a multi-party system
(1977–1999).

The One Dominant Party System, 1952–1977

The Indian National Congress, successor to the anti-colonial Freedom
Movement, was the ruling party during this period both at the centre and
in India's states except Kerala, which was briefly ruled by the communists in the 1950s. Parties of the Left and Right routinely took part in
elections which were, by and large, both free and fair, but the fragmented
character of the opposition and the combination of the first-past-the-post
system of voting in single-member constituencies systematically resulted
in a Congress majority in the legislature. This hegemonic position of the
Congress has caused this period to be described as the period of one-
party dominance (Mitra, 1994b). The main ideological doctrines of the
Congress Party such as secularism, democratic socialism and non-
alignment constituted the main parameters of the policy process during
this period. The opposition parties were present as active players in the
Parliament and in national politics but their role was confined to influencing policy from the sidelines of the institutional process rather than
making policy and alternating with the Congress Party in power.

The challenge to the dominance of the Congress Party had already
become clear in the fourth general election of 1967 when the first
coalitions of the Left and Right took place at the regional level, leading to
the breakdown of the dominance of the Congress Party in several states.
These opposition coalitions were successful in some states like in Kerala
and West Bengal and became the basis of the beginning of a multi-party
system, with the Congress alternating with other political parties and
coalitions very much like a normal political party. At the national level,
however, the Congress Party continued to rule, albeit with a reduced
majority. The situation changed radically after the split of the Congress
Party in 1969 into the Congress (Requisitionist) and the Congress (Organization). The faction led by Indira Gandhi, referred to as Congress (R),
brought about radical changes in the programme of the centrist Congress
Party. A number of new, Left-leaning policies like the nationalization of
banks, abolition of the special privileges of Indian princes and closer ties
with communists were reinforced with a more forceful populist leadership style. These policies brought the Party great electoral success in 1971
but led to the corrosion of its organizational links with the electorate.

In retrospect, the 1967–77 period can be thought of as a period of transition from one-party dominance to multi-party democracy. The setback suffered by the Congress Party in the election of 1967 demonstrated the vulnerability of the centrist Congress to broad electoral coalitions of the Left and the Right. After its initial setback, however, Congress, under Indira Gandhi's forceful leadership, turned its new policy of radical, populist leadership into its main asset. Its initial success in the 1971 election was further reinforced in the assembly elections of 1972 when Indira Gandhi transformed India's successful intervention in the Liberation War in East Pakistan – which led to the birth of Bangladesh – into the electoral platform of the Congress Party. However, the radical rhetoric rebounded on the Party when a number of interest groups including industrial workers, railway employees and students started political agitation. The culmination of this period of unrest was the authoritarian interlude of 1975–7.

The period of Emergency Rule was imposed by the President on the advice of the Prime Minister under Article 352 of the constitution in June 1975 as a temporary measure against rising lawlessness. The conditions that facilitate the functioning of party competition such as free assembly, participation, freedom of information and movement were drastically curtailed. General elections were postponed and the term of the Parliament was extended. Although the regime of Indira Gandhi claimed that the Emergency was brought about to ward off grave threats to the unity and integrity of India, it was more likely a response to the challenges to her rule. Elections were announced in 1977 when the regime received the impression that because of a significant increase in law and order, food supply and general prosperity, the election would lead to a victory for the Congress Party. However, as the results of the 1977 parliamentary elections show, that was far from the case. The Congress Party was punished by the electorate for the authoritarian excesses of the Emergency in terms of a net fall in the percentage vote for the Congress from 43.7 per cent to 34.5 per cent. But, even more important was the drastic decline in the number of seats, from 352 to 154, reducing it to a minority in the Lok Sabha for the first time in the post-independence history of India.

The Formation of a Multi-party System, 1977–1999

The general elections of 1977 ushered in a new period in Indian politics. Since then, Indian politics have entered a period of broad-based coalitions forming part of an unstable multi-party system. During the second party system, India has witnessed a situation where relatively stable multi-party systems at the regional level find themselves within an unstable multi-party system at the national level. The gap between the Congress and the vote share of the largest non-Congress party or coalition has steadily narrowed following the election of 1984, which, in view of the sympathy wave in favour of the Congress, led by Rajiv Gandhi following the assassination of Indira Gandhi, has been thought of as a deviant election, temporarily obscuring the secular decline of the Congress. Although governments have been relatively short-lived during this period, rather like under the Fourth Republic of France, governmental instability has coexisted with policy stability. When new cabinets are constituted with the same ministers or ministers committed to the same policies, policy stability is maintained despite governmental change.

PARTY COMPETITION AND INTEREST ARTICULATION

It was not deliberate colonial policy to develop a competitive party system in India, but the policy of ruling India through indigenous intermediaries whose character gradually changed in keeping with the pace of rising political consciousness was certainly one of the contributing factors to the growth of a party system in India. This political class of intermediaries was greatly expanded with the pace of political mobilization of a wider range of social groups and interests after independence. The ultimate expression of the plural character of Indian society was a multi-party system. What keeps the party system socially anchored and reasonably stable?

Political Parties and Social Cleavages

A stable multi-party democracy is based on an effective linkage between social cleavages and political parties. The nature of the party system typically follows the complexity of social cleavages. Political systems with the first-past-the-post system, where social class constitutes the main cleavage, tend to develop two-party systems. Those with other cleavages such as religion, language and region in addition to social class produce more complex multi-party systems. India's multi-party system exhibits the effects of multiple cleavages (Downs, 1957). The Congress Party, occupying the ideological centre of Indian politics, functioned during the period following independence from British rule as a catch-all party (Kirchheimer, 1966) cutting into all social cleavages. However, with greater political consciousness and mobilization of new interests the situation has become much more complex. Religion, at the heart of the controversy about the secular credentials of the state in India, divides the electorate into those who are for a closer relationship between Hinduism and the state and others who wish to retain the wall of separation between religion and the state. On this issue, during the recent elections, the Bharatiya Janata Party closely identified itself with a strong 'Hindu' position as compared to the National Front and the Left Front who allied themselves on a 'secular' agenda. However, as we shall see below, notwithstanding the fiery rhetoric of some of their leaders, a broad consensus appears to run through the supporters of all political parties, which facilitates the creation of broadly based coalitions and the convergence towards moderate policies.

Broadly Based Sense of Political Efficacy

Established patterns of party-cleavage linkages would be an attractive alternative to non-democratic alternatives only if individuals who constitute those social cleavages perceive political parties as efficient instruments for the articulation of their interests. The survey data, reported in Table 9.1, provide adequate evidence that such a sense of efficacy is present in large sections of the Indian electorate. When asked 'do you think your vote has effect on how things are run in this country, or, do you think your vote makes no difference?' a majority of the

Table 9.1 Effectiveness of vote

Respondent's vote	1971	1996
Has an effect	48.3	59.4
Makes no difference	16.2	21.3
Don't know	35.2	18.9

Vote has an effect (%)	
Illiterate	47
Scheduled tribes	48
Older (> 56 years)	52
Hindu	58
All	**59**
Scheduled castes	60
Muslim	61
Young	61
Urban	64
Men	66
College and above	79

national sample asserted that their vote has an effect on the political state of affairs in the country. The percentage of such people has gone up from about 48 per cent in 1971 to about 60 per cent in 1996. Interestingly, however, the number of those who do not believe that their vote has any effect has also gone up, from 16 per cent in 1971 to 21 per cent in 1996. The explanation for this comes from the fact that over the past 25 years there has been a steady growth in political consciousness. As a consequence, the percentage of those who could not answer this question about personal efficacy one way or another has gone down from 35 per cent in 1971 to 19 per cent in 1996.

Like participation in different electoral activities, here too we find that the lower social orders have less confidence in their votes. Women and older people also belong more or less to this group. The well-educated and people from higher income groups report a greater sense of efficacy. It is important to note here that even at its lowest, the sense of efficacy is still respectably high. Even among the illiterate, close to half hold their vote as efficacious. Unlike what one is often led to believe, the scheduled castes (former untouchables) and minority communities like Christians and Muslims are not far behind the national average. Most important for us, among 'partisans' – those who say that they have voted for one of the major parties – the figure for 'my vote has an effect' is higher than the national average.

Political Legitimacy

If the existence of a sense of efficacy at the micro level is a necessary condition for the effectiveness of a multi-party system, then the perception of the system of competing parties and elections as legitimate constitutes a sufficient condition. The larger implications for the relationship between efficacy and legitimacy should be clear by now: an efficacious electorate that does not hold the party system as legitimate would look for other institutions to articulate and aggregate their interests. Political parties are one of the main agencies available to people to enable them to articulate and aggregate their demands, censor errant officials and seek to influence public policy but they are not the only ones. The same arguments have been made for the justification of military intervention, for the political role of the church, *mullahs, sadhus, bhikkhus* (respectively denoting religious leaders from Islam, Hinduism and Buddhism who have been increasingly playing aggressive roles in South Asian politics), students and Left radicals.

In order to measure the perception of the effectiveness of political parties as an integral part of the structure of parliamentary democracy in

Table 9.2 Better government without parties, assemblies and elections?

	1971	1996
Yes	14.2	11.4
No	43.4	68.8
Can't say or don't know	41.5	19.8

Government not better without parties, assemblies and elections (%)

Illiterate	61
Older (> 56 years)	63
Hindu	68
All	**69**
Young (< 25 years)	71
Muslim	72
College and above	74

India, the following question was asked: 'Suppose there were no parties or assemblies and elections were not held – do you think that the government in this country can be run better?' The responses show how much significance people attach to the system that provides a basis for their direct participation in it. When asked to conjecture about a situation where the electoral option is not available, the national sample overwhelmingly rejects a future without parties and elections. Significantly, this percentage has gone up from the relative low of 43 per cent in 1971 to 69 per cent in 1996 (see Table 9.2).

The young (71 per cent), the educated (74 per cent) and the urban people constituting the group called 'opinion makers' have come out overwhelmingly in favour of sustaining the system. More importantly, they are also joined, at least on this indicator, by Muslims (72.4 per cent) and Christians (72.5 per cent), but interestingly, not by Sikhs, who, at 63 per cent, are 6 per cent lower than the national average. The positive evaluation of the political system based on parties and elections by the better informed and the minority Muslims reinforces the picture of steady empowerment of the electorate through participation in electoral politics. Support for India's political system based on parties and elections (higher among Muslims than the national average but significantly lower among Sikhs) can be explained by referring to the political context of Punjab. In contrast to the other regions of India, Punjab has seen the steady decline of democratic rule, the rise of the military and, eventually, one of the longest periods of direct rule from Delhi.

Deeply Seated Conflict on Values and Civil Society

Societies that are deeply divided on the core beliefs that underpin political life cannot sustain an effective articulation and aggregation of interests through the intermediation of political parties. In order to measure popular perception of such deep value conflicts and the position that political party supporters take on them, four questions were asked in the national survey of 1996 with regard to the perception of the demolition of the Babri Masjid at Ayodhya, the choice of negotiation as against military suppression of the conflict in Kashmir, India's attitudes towards Pakistan, and the issue of a common Personal Law with regard to property, marriage, succession, divorce for the whole of India as opposed to different religious communities having their own specific laws in those matters.

The results of this investigation show that Indian opinion is far more inclined towards tolerant pluralism than is commonly supposed in the international media (Mitra and Singh, 1999). For example, on the Babri Mosque, from all those who express an opinion on the issue, 64 per cent do not believed that the demolition was justified. Social elites and other articulate groups such as 66.2 per cent of urban dwellers, 67.5 per cent of graduates and 63.8 per cent of Hindu upper castes found the destruction of the mosque unjustified. Similarly, on the issue of Kashmir, 33.3 per cent are for a resolution of the issue by negotiation, a percentage which goes up to 74.5 per cent when we exclude those who do not have an opinion on the issue. The same positive attitude of religious and regional reconciliation within India is also reflected in attitudes towards Pakistan. Those who suggest that India should make more efforts to develop friendly relations with Pakistan outnumber those who suggest the opposite or do not have an opinion on the issue. Once again, if we exclude those who do not have an opinion on the issue, then the percentage of those in favour of friendly relations towards Pakistan goes up to 72 per cent. Similarly, on the issue of Personal Law, an impressive 44.5 per cent of the total sample or 60 per cent of the opinion holders say that every community should be allowed to have its own laws to govern marriage and property rights. Against this, only 30.1 per cent say the opposite and the rest, that is 25 per cent, fail to express any opinion on it. It is true that the Muslims have lent greater support (66.9 per cent) to the idea of having or continuing with a separate civil code, but the fact that their stand is also supported by Hindus makes a strong case for continuing with present law.

Judging from the above, there is considerable support within the electorate for tolerant pluralism in India. Of course, there is greater sensitivity among Muslims for their own community to have the right to define the scope of their social institutions similar to other minority communities, also concerned about their Personal Law. However, this position is supported by a considerable section among Hindus as well as across the broad spectrum of India's political parties, including the supporters of the Hindu nationalist Bharatiya Janata Party (BJP).

The divergence of views with regard to value conflict within each political party is another interesting finding to emerge from the analysis of the survey data from 1996. Even among the supporters of the Bharatiya Janata Party, a quarter of the respondents found the demolition of the Babri Mosque unjustified as compared to 40 per cent who thought it justified. Negotiation in Kashmir received more support from voters of the BJP (35 per cent) as opposed to the BJP advocates of suppression (17.5 per cent). Forty-two per cent of the BJP supporters would have India make efforts to be friendly towards Pakistan as opposed to 23 per cent who disagree with the idea. Finally, 40 per cent of BJP supporters see no difficulty with each community having its own Personal Law as opposed to 36 who plead for the one state, one nation, one law variety of hard nationalism.

THE GREY AREA OF MULTI-PARTY DEMOCRACY IN INDIA

Does support for a competitive party system in India come across as an act of faith on the part of the electorate or, rather, a limited commitment, conditional on performance? The question arises from the fact that Indira Gandhi, the unrepentant author of the 1975 Emergency was actually brought back with popular acclaim in 1980 when the Janata Party, who were the heroes of the anti-Emergency movement, failed to deliver stable, efficient and honest governance. In this section we shall explore the reasons for the possible doubts about the stability of multi-party democracy in India. Once again, India is not alone. In historical and comparative perspective, the collapse of an established party system is known to have occurred when it fails to accommodate the interests of an important emerging social group, or fails to aggregate the interests of groups who are articulate and assertive about their demands.

High Trust in Institutions but Distrust of Politicians

The impression of broad value consensus among urban, educated and politically active persons in India is further reinforced from the data with regard to trust in institutions. When asked: 'How much trust/confidence do you have in different institutions of India?' the results show relatively high trust for the main institutions of the state such as the election commission (46 per cent – a great deal of trust), the judiciary, and local, regional and central governments, in decreasing order. But trust in those responsible for running those institutions, such as elected representatives, politicians and government officials, and the police (13 per cent – a great deal of trust) is much lower.

High Efficacy in the Context of Low Institutional Legitimacy

A situation where individual voters are assertive about their identity and interests but do not have a great deal of confidence in elected representatives and civil servants does not augur well for multi-party democracy. A stable democracy would require reasonably high performance on both dimensions, namely a situation where a substantial proportion of the people feel personally efficacious and, at the same time, hold the system to be legitimate. In a situation where low efficacy and low legitimacy are the rule, one can have little reason to expect a functioning multi-party democracy. In a context of high legitimacy and low efficacy one can expect an authoritarian regime with limited participation. The fourth case, where personal efficacy overtakes system legitimacy, opens up the field for intervention from outside the party system from potential challengers to multi-party democracy such as protest movements, the church, students, the army – in fact any organized group with the means to convince the masses that they can deliver better results.

The negative evaluation of government officials and the police on the one hand and the plethora of corruption and other scandals involving political leaders on the other explain the uncertain feeling many Indians have about their own political system. In order to test the strength of association of efficacy and legitimacy, these two variables were cross-tabulated. The results are presented in Table 9.3.

We learn from the cross-tabulation of efficacy and legitimacy that the

Table 9.3 Cross-tabulation of efficacy and legitimacy (%)

	Legitimacy		
Efficacy	Low (%)	Medium (%)	High (%)
Low	5.4	8.3	1.1
Medium	15.4	41.5	4.8
High	4.0	14.3	5.2

Kendall's tau b 0.17, N = 9589

overall relationship between the two is positive although the strength of association is rather low. This helps provide the necessary and sufficient conditions for the existence of a multi-party democracy in India. The 'centre' is occupied by a core group of people, constituting 41.5 per cent of the population, who are moderately efficacious and hold the system to be moderately legitimate. The main sources of challenge to the stability of the system comes from those at the bottom left corner of Table 9.3, namely, the 4 per cent who are highly efficacious but for whom system legitimacy is at its lowest, 15.4 per cent who are moderately efficacious but hold system legitimacy to be low and 14.3 per cent who are highly efficacious but hold system legitimacy to be only moderate. But, balancing them are about 14 per cent of the Indian population, occupying the top right corner of the table, where legitimacy overtakes efficacy. These findings, indicating the presence of potential rebels as well as acquiescent 'subjects' who defer to authority, provide some new insights into both the stability of multi-party democracy in India as well as the sources of its vulnerability.

CONCLUSION

In their efforts to achieve a quick transition to democracy, many post-colonial and postrevolutionary societies have accelerated the pace of political mobilization, only to discover subsequently that these attempts have brought to the fore political demands from social groups long suppressed by alien rulers or politically oppressive regimes, leading to violent ethnic strife and political disorder. The democratic structure itself has often been the first victim of the radical aspiration of the masses. These failed attempts show that political mobilization may be a necessary but not a sufficient condition for a representative democracy. The growth of a competitive party system and the existence of inter-party consensus on key issues affecting civil liberties are crucial facilitating conditions for a transition to democracy and civil society. The party system, in turn, is effective and seen as legitimate only in so far as it succeeds in getting itself accepted by society as an effective means for the articulation and aggregation of demands. Failing this, politically mobilized groups have every incentive to turn to other agencies like the army, the clergy, radical groups of the Left or the Right and last, but not the least, to mob violence, none of which has a proven record of an abiding commitment to civil society.

From electoral data and results of opinion surveys, multi-party democracy appears to have struck root in India. This is seen particularly from the linkage of partisanship and social cleavages, a broadly based sense of political efficacy and legitimacy, and cross-cutting value conflicts and partisanship. Nevertheless, some doubts about the stability of multi-party democracy linger on, reinforced by such events as the national Emergency of 1975–7, the destruction of the Babri Mosque in 1992, continuing communal conflict and the subnational movement in Kashmir. The danger to multi-party democracy from these issues is muted because, as we have seen in the survey data, opinions within India's political parties as well as social groups on these crucial issues are divided, with a substantial percentage of respondents within each major political party, as well as across major social groups in general, showing their commitment to tolerant pluralism in India.

The survey data provide useful insights into a possible solution to the essential tension between majoritarian democracy and civil society in multiethnic societies. By opting for an interparty consensus on tolerant pluralism, India's voters have shown themselves capable of avoiding the extremes of both a naive advocacy of national values as well as a mechanical insistence on essentialized, universal human rights as the basis of civil society. This pragmatic pluralism, the policy of 'live and let live' and, above all, the ability of India's social groups to put themselves in the position of other communities, and to devise the rules of communal accommodation as the basis of the creation of a public space for a common citizenship, provides a contrasting picture to the media images of the decay of civil society and the rise of intransigent and unaccommodative fundamentalist movements in India.

Local and regional breakdowns in democracy are common in many postcolonial and postrevolutionary countries. The issue is, why do they not become cumulative or terminal in India? As we have already seen from the survey data, there is a significant number of individuals who feel themselves to be efficacious but do not accord a great measure of legitimacy to the institutions of the state, or to political parties, as the most effective instruments for the implementation of the popular will. This provides some insights into these grey areas of Indian democracy. It can be suggested that the breakdown of democracy is a manifestation of attempts by political actors to bring pressure on the system. As long as the system responds, either through policy change or by the change in the rules of the game, the process of democratic politics bounces back. Research on the potential for a responsive political system to gain strength from protest movements and the ability of the Indian political process to accommodate 'rational protest' as a complement to institutional participation provides an additional explanation to the resilience of multi-party democracy and civil society in India.

NOTES

1. The constitution of India provides for temporary suspension of popular rule in the centre as well as in the states in extreme cases when lawful government is no longer possible.
2. The survey was conducted through face-to-face interviews during May–June, 1996, in the aftermath of the eleventh parliamentary elections. A representative sample of about 10,000 adults was interviewed by investigators from the Lokchintan, a group of scholars based at several Indian universities and the Centre for the Study of Developing Societies, Delhi. The 1971 survey, conducted by the same institute, was based on a sample of 5500 persons.
3. According to Rudolph and Rudolph (1967), vertical mobilization refers to political linkages that draw on and reinforce social and economic dominance. Horizontal mobilization takes place when people situated at the same social and economic level get together to use their combined political strength to improve their situation. Differential mobilization refers to coalitions that cut across social strata.

FURTHER READING

Austin (1966) is an excellent secondary source on the making of India's constitution and the major institutions of India. Kothari (1970) is still one of the finest comprehensive books on Indian politics. Butler *et al.* (1995) is a very useful source of data on Indian elections and the institutions that sustain the electoral process. Mitra and Singh (1999) complement the statistical data with the findings of a survey of the Indian electorate, conducted in 1996. More generally, Almond and Verba (eds) (1989) is an excellent source of the concepts that underpinned the modernization approach to the study of the politics of post-colonial societies and the recent debate about their continued applicability. And Diamond, Linz and Lipset (eds) (1989) is one of the most discussed books on democracy in poor countries.

BIBLIOGRAPHY

Almond, Gabriel and Sidney Verba (eds) (1989) *The Civic Culture Revisited.* London: Sage.

Austin, Granville (1966) *The Indian Constitution: The Cornerstone of a Nation.* Oxford: Oxford University Press.

Brown, J. (1985) *Modern India: The Origin of an Asian Democracy.* Delhi: Oxford University Press.

Butler, David, Ashok Lahiri and Prannoy Roy (1995) *India Decides: Elections 1952–1995.* Delhi: Books and Things.

Diamond, Larry, Juan Linz and Seymour Martin Lipset (1989) *Democracy in Developing Countries.* Boulder, CO: Lynne Rienner.

Downs, Anthony (1957) *An Economic Theory of Democracy*. New York: Harper & Row.

Harrison, Selig (1960) *India: The Most Dangerous Decades*. Delhi: Oxford University Press.

Huntington, Samuel P. (1968) *Political Order in Changing Societies*. New Haven: Yale University Press.

Huntington, Samuel P. (1996) *The Clash of Civilizations and the Remaking of the World Order*. New York: Simon & Schuster.

Kirchheimer, Otto (1966) The Transformation of Western European Party Systems. In Joseph LaPalombara and Myron Weiner (eds), *Political Parties and Political Development*. Princeton: Princeton University Press.

Kothari, Rajni (1970) *Politics in India*. Boston: Little Brown.

Rudolph, Lloyd and Susanne Rudolph (1967) *The Modernity of Tradition: Political Development in India*. Chicago: University of Chicago Press.

Mitra, Subrata K. (1996) India. In Gabriel Almond and Bingham Powell, Jr. (eds), *Comparative Politics Today*. New York: HarperCollins.

Mitra, Subrata K. (1991) Room to Maneuver in the Middle: Local Elites, Political Action and the State in India, *World Politics* 43.

Mitra, Subrata K. (1992) *Power, Protest, Participation: Local Elites and the Politics of Development in India*. London: Routledge.

Mitra, Subrata K. (1994a) Caste, Democracy and the Politics of Community Formation in India. In Mary Searle-Chatterjee and Ursula Sharma (eds), *Contextualising Caste: Post-Dumontian Approaches*. Oxford: Blackwell, pp. 49–72.

Mitra, Subrata *Sociological Review* (1994b) Party Organization and Policy Making in a Changing Environment: The Indian National Congress. In Kay Lawson (ed.), *How Political Parties Work: Perspectives from Within*. Westport: Praeger.

Mitra, Subrata K. (2000) Politics in India. In Gabriel Almond, G. Bingham Powell, Jr., Kaare Strom and Russell J. Dalton (eds), *Comparative Politics Today: A World View*. New York: Addison, Wesley, Longman.

Mitra, Subrata K. and V.B. Singh (1999) *Democracy and Social Change in India*. Delhi: Sage.

Moore, Barrington (1966) *Social Origins of Dictatorship and Democracy: Lord and Peasant in the Making of the Modern World*. Boston: Beacon Press.

CHAPTER 10

THE PROSPECTS FOR SUSTAINABLE DEMOCRACY IN POST-APARTHEID SOUTH AFRICA

Thembisa Waetjen and Martin J. Murray

One cannot say the ANC [African National Congress] government failed. However, it has not achieved all it set out to do. (Justice Malala)[1]

On 10 May 1994, Nelson Mandela was sworn in as South Africa's first truly democratically elected president. This momentous occasion, following as it did in the wake of nationwide elections held two weeks earlier on 26–28 April in which almost 20 million South Africans of all races went to the polls to select a new government, symbolized one of those rare historical moments signalling the triumph of the human will over the blanketing forces of oppression. Taken together, these watershed events signalled the crowning achievement of an exhaustive four-year period of intense and often acrimonious negotiations during which representatives of numerous political parties and organizations achieved what many political theorists had long dismissed as virtually impossible – to bargain their way voluntarily out of a stifling system of white minority domination, and frame a new interim constitution. Despite widely divergent outlooks at the outset of 'talks-about-talks', which began in earnest in early 1990, the two main antagonistic political blocs – one led by the African National Congress (ANC) and the other by the National Party – reached a political settlement that was underpinned by a surprising degree of consensus on the ground rules for peacefully resolving political differences in the 'new South Africa'.

Seen within the wider-angle lens of the continuing tragedy of much of the African continent, what has happened in South Africa is truly remarkable. From start to finish, this brokered transition to majority rule can be characterized, albeit with some exaggeration, in the words Mandela himself used, as a 'small miracle'. The dismantling of the last remnants of the apartheid system, including the erasure of the legalized fiction of 'independent' and 'self-governing' homelands, the revamping of racially defined state bureaucracies, and the annulment of the tricameral Parliament, marked the demise of white minority rule. The decisive historical moment came with the April 1994 'liberation election', a coded term whose basic reference point in this context was comparison with decolonizing elections elsewhere in Africa, pivotal events that signified emancipation from white colonial rule, the triumph of African nationalism, the achievement of political independence, and progress towards self-determination. Long ostracized by world public opinion as a racist, 'pariah' state without moral standing, South Africa was suddenly cast in a new, more favourable light. Almost without exception, commentators characterized the birth of majority rule, in the words of two particularly exuberant observers, as 'one of the most extraordinary political transformations of the twentieth century', where the people 'have defied the logic of their past, and broken all the rules of social theory, to forge a powerful spirit of unity from a shattered nation'.[2] Analysts across the ideological spectrum embraced South Africa's political transition as an exemplary case of how resolute leaders can set aside their self-interest and personal agendas in order to achieve the greater 'common good' of social harmony and political stability in a continent and a world greatly divided by racial, ethnic, and religious strife.

MAPPING THE 'NEW SOUTH AFRICA'

South Africa after apartheid is an especially ideal case by which critically to examine the limits and possibilities of democratization because it is a peculiar example of a political transition from authoritarian rule that occurred under conditions not widely thought conducive to democracy – deep cleavages along ascriptive lines, a long tradition of autocratic rule, a relative underdeveloped 'civil society', low levels of political tolerance, economic stagnation, and a high degree of socioeconomic inequality. In the main, the scholarly literature produced during the apartheid years perceived the South African situation as intractable, where political differences were largely regarded as irreconcilable and racial divisions were seemingly unresolvable. Knowledgeable observers across the political spectrum long expressed great pessimism about South Africa's future and the prospects for a democratic settlement. The centrifugal tendencies towards continuing 'low intensity' warfare, unbridled anarchy, ethnic strife, and racial violence seemed to overshadow the desire for social cohesion and political stability. The fact that South Africa was perceived not so many years ago as a least likely case for democratization makes it an important if not crucial case for analysis. Studying the democratization process in South Africa after apartheid provides a particularly fruitful setting for analysing the politics of 'divided societies' and assessing the ways and means of managing deep-rooted ethno-racial conflicts by creating the institutional framework conducive to the emergence of a new democratic political order.

There is no denying the dramatic turnabout that has taken place in South Africa since the transfer of political power to the ANC-dominated government. Under the able leadership of President Nelson Mandela, the ANC government oversaw the adoption and implementation of a new democratic constitution, side-stepped the disruptive threat of the *revanchist* Afrikaner far Right, brokered a political settlement in QuaZulu/Natal that resulted in greatly diminished violence, took the first tentative steps towards upliftment of the 'poorest of the poor', undertook the reorganization of the existing departments and agencies of the state administration, launched the Truth and Reconciliation Commission (TRC) to investigate violations of human rights during the apartheid era, and incorporated former guerrilla armies of the ANC and the Pan Africanist Congress (PAC) into the revamped South African National Defence Force (SANDF).[3] Yet placed in a wider historical context of politics in sub-Saharan Africa where backsliding from democratic pledges is a common occurrence and one-party states represent the normal state of affairs, one must not take at face value the assumption that democracy is a *fait accompli* once honest elections have taken place. South Africa's peculiar combination of class and racial divisions, taken together with extreme social inequality and a long tradition of autocratic rule, stand in the path of the consolidation of democratic achievements. While there is the shared belief that the clock cannot be turned back, there is little consensus on the substance and meaning of democracy in the 'new South Africa'.[4]

CHALLENGES FOR DEMOCRATIC CONSOLIDATION

The transition and consolidation to a parliamentary form of liberal, multi-party democracy has not been a smooth and uninterrupted process, but instead has been marked by contradictory impulses pulling the social fabric in many different directions. These do not make South Africa unique, but there are aspects of these contradictions that stamp the political transition with a historically specific peculiarity in comparison with other countries undergoing similar experiences.[5] To be sure, the 1994 landslide electoral victory of the ANC alliance marked the triumphant culmination of a long, and often bitter, struggle against white minority rule. Five years later, the equally overwhelming electoral victory of the ANC and the 16 June 1999 inauguration of President Thabo Mbeki to replace the retiring Nelson Mandela confirmed the depth of popular support for the tripartite alliance.[6]

In the main, scholars agree that the consolidation of stable multi-party democracy in post-apartheid South Africa rests on four interrelated cornerstones: (1) socioeconomic recovery and growth, (2) revamping state institutions and establishing new rules of governance, (3) the development of an embedded, robust 'civil society', and (4) the emergence of a vibrant grassroots political culture that ideally fosters respect for the rule of law, encourages tolerance of difference, and promotes the active participation of citizens in democratic ('nation-building') processes that affect their lives. But they do not agree on the relative importance of these four conditions, or how they relate to each other.[7] What kind of political transition has taken place in South Africa, and what is the peculiar balance between rival social forces at this historical conjuncture? What are the prospects for enduring political stability? What opportunities exist within the framework of an emergent liberal democracy for a genuine assault on the country's longstanding socioeconomic inequalities? By necessity, answers to these questions are at best provisional and tentative, yet they may provide some useful insights into where South Africa might be heading and why.

DEMOCRATIC CONSOLIDATION AND ECONOMIC GROWTH

Post-apartheid South Africa is a racially divided, highly stratified social order, characterized by extreme polarities in wealth, income, and opportunity. Despite rich resource endowments, accumulated wealth, a developed transportation system, a substantial built environment, a sophisticated financial and banking system, and a solid infrastructure, unemployment and persistent poverty have changed very little. South Africa's peculiar dependence upon its gold-centred mineral-industrial complex has created severe handicaps for capital restructuring and a full-scale integration into the world economy. Long protected behind apartheid-era tariff barriers and isolated by the international sanctions campaign, manufacturing industries have only a limited capacity to respond to the new international division of labour, grounded as it is in the highly competitive global marketplace of post-Fordist flexible specialization.

The prospects for socioeconomic revitalization in post-apartheid South Africa depend upon overcoming a wide range of existing contradictions, cleavages, and conflicts. One source of tension pits an entrenched white oligarchy against an aspiring black middle class comprised of nascent entrepreneurs, high-ranking state officials, and technically trained professionals. Demands for the socioeconomic upliftment of the black majority, debates over affirmative action, and calls for 'black empowerment' reflect longstanding socioeconomic cleavages. The virtually all-white business class is a highly cohesive social group that jealously guards its power, privilege, and wealth. Corporate leaders rely on a complex network of business associations and personal networks to protect their propertied interests and insulate themselves from unwanted outside interference. Formidable barriers to entry – structural as well as sociocultural – prevent aspirant black entrepreneurs from participating in the business world as equal partners.

A second source of tension exists between large-scale employers and the organized labour movement. With an elaborate system of cross-holding and pyramiding of shares, coupled with such features as interlocking directorates, ownership of firms in South Africa has remained concentrated in a few hands, thereby enabling small groups of business executives to maintain a firm grip over huge conglomerates. This type of business organization – characterized by the virtual fusion of ownership and control – contrasts sharply with patterns established elsewhere in the North American, European, and East Asian core areas of the world economy. Despite the recent fanfare over the 'unbundling' of these vertically integrated cartels, a handful of large corporate groups controls the lion's share of the capitalization of the Johannesburg Stock Exchange (JSE), and dominates nearly every product market of the domestic economy, from mining and manufacturing to finance and services, and in both capital- and labour-intensive sectors. Ultimate control remains in the hands of a small coterie of extremely wealthy families.

Around two-fifths of those workers formally employed belong to a trade union. By mid-1999, there were 481 registered trade unions in South Africa, a more than 100 per cent increase in little over two years. Many of these are understaffed and cash starved, with small memberships and little political influence. In the main, these independent trade unions cluster around three labour federations. The Congress of South African Trade Unions (COSATU) operates as the labour wing of the tripartite alliance that includes the ANC and the South African Communist Party (SACP). The membership of COSATU has increased by 40 per cent since 1991 to 1.8 million, and its affiliates are concentrated in those sectors that include blue-collar, unskilled, and semi-skilled industrial and service workers. The National Council of Trade Unions (NACTU) mirrors COSATU in many ways, yet with a fluctuating membership of around 300,000 workers and with its roots in black consciousness and Africanist ideologies. Lastly, the Federation of Unions of South Africa (FEDUSA) – also with a membership of around 300,000 workers – is primarily a confederation of skilled, white-collar, and salaried wage earners.

The democratic *apertura* triggered intense debate in the trade union movement over the proper course of action that would best secure the interests of workers against the extraordinary concentration of power and wealth in the hands of a deeply entrenched white oligarchy, and would ensure the institutionalization and consolidation of working-class achievements during the anti-apartheid struggle. This controversy over an institutionalized role for labour and capital in the formulation of economic policy – 'bargained corporatism', as Baskin termed it – signalled a strategic revision of trade union thinking.[8] This turn towards a more co-operative *modus vivendi* with large-scale employers marked a shift away from the non-co-operative shop floor militancy that characterized the anti-apartheid struggles of the 1980s. Advocates of 'strategic unionism' called for a strong, interventionist state both to offset the undue power of the corporations and to help workers organize themselves collectively to press their demands. They further argued that participation in state-sponsored forums like National Economic Development and Labour Forum (NEDLAC) gave the organized labour movement a 'voice' in influencing macroeconomic policies, and strengthened the hand of workers to fend off retrenchments and to protect wage gains. In contrast, sceptics warned that social contracts binding labour, business, and the state in a rule-governed bureaucratic framework weakens the organized labour movement by forcing trade unions into compliance with 'business-friendly' policies without sufficient reciprocity.

In South Africa as elsewhere, the unrelenting globalizing pressures of worldwide market competition – made even worse by the lifting of apartheid-era tariff barriers and trade liberalization – has weakened the bargaining power of organized workers. Under these sociohistorical circumstances, it is not surprising that trade unions enter into provisional alliances, both among and between themselves and with political parties, as means to ends and not ends in themselves. The alliance with the ANC has enabled organized workers in COSATU to secure palpable benefits they might fear to lose if the ANC leadership turned to organized capital for its political support. Forging a stake in the existing political order looks like an attractive option, especially under conditions where the property-owning classes are increasingly well organized and hence capable of delivering plausible threats to whittle away at the shop floor gains made during the turbulent decades that preceded the collapse of white minority rule and the demise of apartheid. In the main, political commentators gravitate between two extremes: portraying the organized trade union movement as a pampered, privileged labour aristocracy, on the one hand, and a genuine social movement struggling to secure the rights of workers, on the other.

A third source of tension exists between the so-called 'haves' and the 'have nots'. The collapse of white minority rule and the demise of the apartheid system accelerated processes of social differentiation that has led to 'new winners' (an emergent black bourgeoisie, along with an upwardly mobile black skilled labour force and middle class) and 'new losers' (a growing underclass of poor and unemployed, in both rural and urban areas). Existing socioeconomic inequalities are rooted in differential access to resources like property, cultural capital, skills, and other endowments. Uneven possession of these resources impedes life chances on the market and, correlatively, places structural limits on opportunities for upward mobility and socioeconomic advancement. Growing differentiation of the labour market has resulted in increasing social stratification in the 'new South Africa'. In the urban and periurban areas, black townships are no longer undifferentiated social spaces characterized by endless monotony. Pockets of affluence have come into existence. Displays of conspicuous consumption offer visual proof of slow but steady social differentiation of black households.[9] At the same time, the exponential growth of the 'informal economy' – where millions of formally unemployed people eke out daily existence in 'penny capitalist' microenterprises – provides ample testimony to deeply embedded impoverishment. Structural inequalities find expression in the extreme disparities between town and country, between impoverished shanty-towns blossoming on the fringes of cities and elegant suburbs replete with social amenities, between the employed and unemployed, and the differentiation between resource-rich and resource-poor regions.

MOVING THE LEFT TO THE RIGHT[10]

In a real sense, the political transition in South Africa represents a clear example of what Samuel Huntington has called 'transplacement', or a dramatic shift in political alignment where 'the dominant groups in both the government and opposition come to realize that they are incapable of unilaterally imposing their own solution on the body politic'.[11] Put broadly, the negotiation process that began in 1990 and culminated with the April 1994 elections brought the main political protagonists together in a shared quest for political stability and social order. The *modus vivendi* between National Party reformers and ANC moderates not only side-lined radicals and extremists in both camps, but also created space for the emergence of a political centre where none had existed before.

The broad-based anti-apartheid movement underestimated the capacity of organized capital – large and small – for developing and sustaining a mutually beneficial compromise between the entrenched white oligarchy and aspirant property-holding black elites. During the period of heightened political turmoil and incipient guerrilla war, working-class intellectuals did not believe such a broadly based class compromise was possible in the first place. Hence, they devoted little time or energy to critically assessing the conditions under which this blending of interests was likely to emerge. The growing affinity between the largely white business class and the ANC-led government is perhaps the most visible expression of what Jean-Francois Bayart has called the 'reciprocal assimilation of elites'.[12] Because of their overriding interest in averting social conflict and overcoming political disorder, the propertied and privileged classes have accepted (albeit sometimes begrudgingly) the tutelage and authority of a relatively powerful state with ANC notables in charge of day-to-day governance.

The belief that there is a direct linkage between capitalism and liberal democracy had gained widespread currency in South Africa and has given new legitimacy to the norms and values of private proprietorship and market-oriented political reforms. According to the faithful who preach the gospel of entrepreneurialism, the most effective alchemy for bringing about the reciprocal assimilation of old and new elites can be found in a convergence of interests around property, privilege, and wealth. In this view, the pursuit of socioeconomic self-interest not only effectively disciplines the passion for raw autocratic power that motivates so much political ambition, but also provides the point of departure for a mutually rewarding compromise between an entrenched white oligarchy and an emergent restive black middle class, two groups that otherwise have very little in common. The animating *leitmotif* of this doctrine is that this spirit of acquisitive capitalism, by extolling the virtues of proprietorship, provides an underlying moral authority that imposes its own self-regulating normative order on 'civil society'.

Business interest groups have assiduously courted the ANC leadership, and this strategy had paid rich dividends. Leading corporate executives have become the staunchest supporters of the ANC, praising its moderate course of action and making substantial campaign contributions to the organization. The ambitions of the entrenched white oligarchy are clear: to incorporate a black professional managerial elite as a subaltern group within an expanded hegemonic bloc organized around a defence of rooted material interests. South Africa's leading companies have embarked on an adept strategy of accommodation and co-option, introducing 'affirmative action' plans, inviting black notables to sit on their enlarged boards of directors, 'Africanizing' their corporate images, and engaging in public acts of philanthropy and charitable good deeds.[13]

The 'new men and women of power' occupying key posts in the upper echelons of the state administration have responded favourably to these overtures, adopting root and branch such neo-liberal policies as artificially high interest rates and other strict monetarist measures, trade liberalization, and the dismantling of state monopolies and their sale to private bidders. Within two years of taking office, the ANC policy makers quietly jettisoned the social democratic Reconstruction and Development Programme (RDP), and substituted the 'investor-friendly' Growth, Employment, and Redistribution (GEAR) programme. Despite the protestations of the ANC's alliance partners, the ANC senior leadership adopted a whole range of socioeconomic programmes in line with neo-liberal orthodoxies, thereby pulling the party towards the centre of the political spectrum, and marginalizing the radical, populist, and socialist currents in its ranks.

STATECRAFTING: GOVERNANCE AND ACCOUNTABILITY

In order to understand the consolidation of democratic rule in the 'new South Africa', it is necessary to draw attention to the techniques of governance rather than looking at the interests that shape and constrain the exercise of state power. The legitimating premise of South Africa's first post-apartheid political regime was that at some future date those who had been disadvantaged under white minority rule would experience improvements in the conditions of their daily existence. From the outset, the ANC government set out to redefine the nature of statecraft by institutionally refashioning the state administration and to introduce new modes of political rationality. The 'new men and women of power' in the executive, legislative, and judicial branches of government brought a new style of 'doing politics' that is exemplified by their commitment to such issues as gender equality, individual rights of self-expression, and civil liberties.

Strictly speaking, the exercise of political hegemony requires the active or passive consent of the governed who, by means of a pliable mixture of persuasion and force, come to accept the overall legitimacy of the established social order along with their subordinated position in it. Achieving political stability requires more than restoring order. The continuity of democratic elections in South Africa does not itself guarantee relatively stable political equilibrium and containing social conflict within manageable parameters. The opening of the political system to new social and political forces has created space for new democratic norms and values, but it has also spawned new kinds of licence and 'anti-social' behaviour.

Since taking office, key ANC leaders have repeatedly lashed out at anarchy, corruption, crime, rent boycotts, unauthorized land invasions, and illegal strikes. In February 1995, Mandela opened Parliament with a harshly worded statement chastizing those who subscribe to a 'culture of entitlement' and who 'misread freedom to mean license', warning ANC supporters not to expect an immediate outpouring of material benefits from the new government.[14] Despite its political legitimacy, the ANC leadership continues to face an uphill battle in disabusing its hardened grassroots supporters, schooled in the bloody township battles of the 1980s, that disruptive tactics are no longer appropriate and viable means of popular struggle. Curbing politically related violence depends upon the ability of the new government to foster a spirit of political tolerance and to instil a respect for the police and the courts, both of which have long been associated with apartheid overrule. It also requires disarming political factions and criminal syndicates, rooting out the remaining covert 'third force' elements that are bent on political destabilization, and instituting professional policing.[15]

Nepotism, favouritism, and patronage can easily metamorphize into more egregious kinds of self-enrichment. While a great deal of the political corruption that exists in post-apartheid South Africa is inherited from the past, new kinds of official abuse of public office have come into existence. The promise of 'clean government' has been marred by charges of widespread financial impropriety, outright fraud, bribery, extortion, misappropriation of funds, and pilferage of state property.

Prominent anti-apartheid activists have in some cases disturbingly strayed from their stated political principles. The case of Alan Boesak is an illustrative example. A former leader of the ANC-aligned United Democratic Front in the Western Cape and an ordained minister in the Dutch Reformed Church, Boesak was convicted of misappropriating huge sums from overseas donors and redirecting them for his personal use. During his trial, a number of key ANC figures, including Justice Minister Dullah Omar and Nelson Mandela himself, came to Boesak's defence, suggesting that the charges against him were politically motivated. Official tolerance for corruption – especially for those persons with 'struggle credentials' – undermines public confidence that the ANC is genuinely concerned with its promise of public accountability.

On the broader front, longstanding defiance of official authority and the rule of law has also spawned its own corrupting influences. These assume myriad forms, including squatter camp slumlords who rule their turf with an iron fist, local gangs who operate with virtual impunity in some areas, and criminal syndicates that specialize in gun-running, drug trafficking, car theft, and bank robbery. Post-apartheid South Africa has acquired a reputation as the world's most violent country outside a war zone. After the 1994 elections, crime skyrocketed. South Africa has a murder rate of 58 per 100,000 people, a figure more than eight times higher than in the USA. With a rape taking place every 30 seconds, women's organizations report that half of all South African women can expect to be sexually assaulted during their lifetime. Car hijackings and robberies are frequent occurrences, with a car stolen every 10 seconds and a home robbed every 11 minutes. The police report that there are 1,155 organized syndicates engaged in drug smuggling and a further 278 gangs specializing in other sorts of criminal activities. In 1998, the telephone company lost more than $7.5 million to thieves in the burgeoning scrap metal business who absconded with its newly installed copper cables.[16] These statistics paint a disturbing picture. Crime – and the fear and distrust it breeds – has become perhaps the most important rallying point for political parties and organizations that oppose the ANC. By adopting a 'tough on crime' stance, the Democratic Party in particular tapped into the fears – real or imagined – of the white electorate.

CIVIL SOCIETY AND CITIZENSHIP

By and large, political theorists suggest that in the wake of the transition to democracy a vibrant 'civil society' ideally fills the vacuum left by the retreating authoritarian state apparatuses. They look upon 'civil society' – a notoriously imprecise term – as an arena of voluntary associational life, the birthplace of 'pressure groups' that act as counterweights to authoritarian impulses, and the seedbed of democratic social movements hostile to illiberal state interference. The consolidation of liberal democracy depends in large measure on a strong 'civil society' where voluntary associations generate cross-pressures to moderate the crystallized power of ascriptive identities. But this idealized view must be tempered against a sanguine assessment of the centrifugal forces that reinforce old sociocultural fissures and create new ones. In post-apartheid South Africa, progress towards stable multi-party democracy is certainly handicapped due to the historically grounded obstacles to open and responsive governmental institutions.

A central question for political theory focuses on what makes democratic institutions stable and effective, open and responsive, representative and fair, transparent and accountable. 'Making democracy work' – to use Robert Putnam's apt phrase – requires the installation of political institutions, like systems of multi-party electoral contestation, that ensure accountability, responsiveness, and representation.[17] These institutional arrangements work to deepen democratic practices by creating mutually acceptable 'rules of the game' within which political actors must operate in order to accomplish their goals. They must be strong and effective in order to prevent cliques from usurping or abusing political power. The consolidation of liberal democracy also involves strengthening political infrastructure guaranteeing due process, protecting civil liberties, and promoting the rule of law. It also means establishing new modes of governance that are transparent, inclusive, and responsible to shifting coalitions and constituencies.[18]

Democratic theorists have recently turned their attention to how democratic practices might be made more substantial and effective through greater efforts to include a variety of disadvantaged groups for which the formal promise of democratic equality has masked continued exclusion and marginalization. Proponents of what has been termed 'deliberative democracy' argue that something more than interest-group bargaining is both possible and desirable, 'a transformative politics that extends the range of potential solutions', in order to ensure equal rights of citizenship.[19]

These theoretical debates are particularly relevant in the South African context, where the conjoined issues of affirmative action, socioeconomic 'upliftment', and 'economic empowerment' are at the centre of political controversy. Liberal political commentators, especially those linked with the Democratic Party, the New National Party, and the Inkatha Freedom Party, caution against 'too much' state interference, and argue in favour of allowing self-regulating markets to rectify existing imbalances. In contrast, critics of market-driven approaches to 'upliftment' contend that only deliberate state intervention can even the 'playing field' between the white minority and the black majority.[20]

In South Africa as elsewhere, the transition to democracy has unleashed countervailing tendencies where pressures towards greater inclusion and homogenization are matched by forces of exclusion and fragmentation. The process of inclusion is not a smooth and continuous one. With the expansion of the perimeter of legitimate politics, previously inchoate social groups discover shared grievances, create collective identities, establish common political agendas, and lay claim to entitlements. Yet, ironically, this process of enlarging the 'political community', and redrawing political boundaries by providing access to previously denied resources, creates new classes of outsiders. Opening the political system to new voices, interests, and constituencies ultimately means excluding others.[21] The formal ingredients of democracy provide little solace to the millions who lack adequate housing, healthcare, potable water, and decent jobs. In a similar vein, the failure of the state administration to provide even a minimum standard of services results in fragmentation, which in the most extreme version, resembles a veritable 'war of all against all'. The twin processes of 'exclusion and fragmentation' undermine the ability of political parties and the state administration to organize any long-term articulation linking 'the public realm', 'the citizens', and 'the people' within a stable political order.[22]

NATION-BUILDING AND THE POLITICS OF INCLUSION AND EXCLUSION

The content and meaning of a 'South African' national identity must be continually created and reproduced through language, institution-making, and cultural practices. 'Nation-building' requires the implantation of a political culture that stresses inclusion and participation of an informed citizenry, tolerance of rival points of view, and respect for human rights. It demands a genuine commitment on the part of an alert citizenry to view themselves as active participants in an 'imagined community' of fellow South Africans. The idealized notion of a 'rainbow nation' rests on the premise that citizens of the 'new South Africa' share a common interest that is enriched, rather than fragmented or diminished, by differences of cultural heritage, race and ethnicity, gender, and religious belief.[23]

One of the most hotly contested debates in democratic theory revolves around the thorny issues of political legitimacy and minority rights, and whether the fair representation of disadvantaged groups requires their guaranteed presence in elected assemblies. Some theorists suggest that in 'plural societies' divided along religious, racial, or linguistic axes the 'winner-take-all' practice of simple majority rule is both unfair and undemocratic. As Lijphart puts it, 'majority rule is not only undemocratic but also dangerous, because minorities that are continually denied access to power will feel excluded and discriminated against and will lose their allegiance to the regime'.[24] These scholars further hypothesize that stable democratic government requires guaranteed protection of minority rights to guard against the threat of exclusionary practices associated with the tyranny of the majority.

The implementation of inclusionary democratic practices is especially salient in post-apartheid South Africa, where issues like regional autonomy and federalism, constitutional protection for basic civil liberties, 'traditional leaders' and ethnic identities, national language, and cultural heritage, are burning political issues. The politics of inclusion – non-racialism, political tolerance, coalition-building – must be matched against abiding exclusionary practices, such as racial discrimination, sexism and homophobia, political intolerance, and ethnic competition and strife.

In a country where *differences* operated as the grounds upon which sustained and violent oppression took place, there are many questions about how diversity can be adequately acknowledged without becoming the pivot for new forms of discrimination and prejudice. The transition to democratic rule in South Africa has been accompanied by the rising influx of foreign immigrants – many illegally – who have streamed into the country in search of economic opportunities or political refuge. It is ironic that this so-called 'alien invasion' has prompted rising xenophobia and scapegoating, where foreigners are blamed for crime and disease, and taking jobs away from worthy South African citizens.[25] Under apartheid, cultural and racial identities had very real, material consequences, and the reversal of these cleavages defies simple solutions. Many people who self-consciously attach themselves to various racial and ethnic identities as cultural markers regard the idealized notion of a 'rainbow nation' as an empty phrase that denies the specificity of their interests and concerns. *Revanchist* Afrikaner separatism, narrowly focused 'tribalist' loyalties, all manner of chauvinistic ideologies, and exclusivist ethnic identities are powerful forces tearing at the social fabric and impeding progress towards the universalizing ideals of 'nation-building'. Once they are mobilized into action, these crystallized identities become sources of fragmentation, discord, and distrust. In arguing that Afrikaners as a cultural minority in the 'new South Africa' require special forms of protection, the Freedom Front has effectively borrowed the language of 'cultural recognition' from established liberal discourse to gain legitimacy for its idea of a separate *volkstaat*.[26] Originally fashioned as a 'tribal' identity under apartheid rule, Inkatha-inspired Zulu nationalism cuts against the grain of 'anti-tribalist' liberation politics. Chief Mangosuthu Buthelezi has repeatedly employed the discourse of Zulu 'tradition' to tap into the alienation felt by poor and marginalized rural people who came to believe that the largely urban-identified ANC had failed to address their material and political interests.[27] The recently revived coloured identity has given rise to an emergent 'brown nationalism'. Muslim clerics in the Western Cape have fostered a version of Islamic fundamentalism. These culturalist expressions are centripetal forces that operate as counterweights to the idealized notion of a 'rainbow nation' with a single national identity.[28] Rural people – and especially women – living under the authority of chiefs and customary law have not fully shared the fruits of all-inclusive citizenship rights.[29]

CONSOLIDATING DEMOCRATIC RULE IN THE
'NEW SOUTH AFRICA'

Over the course of its first five years in office, the ANC leadership gravitated between idealism and accommodation. Despite its electoral promises of delivery of jobs, services, and access to resources denied the black majority during the apartheid years, the ANC government came face-to-face with a number of significant obstacles that prevented its officials from implementing a progressive social agenda. Confronted with powerful propertied interests at home and international capital abroad, ANC policy-makers moved away from their initial social-democratic impulses and adopted instead market-driven policies designed to maintain business confidence. The ANC government inherited an entrenched civil service, a bloated bureaucracy packed onto the payroll during the heyday of apartheid overrule, and one that had operated for years at the behest of the ruling National Party. Because these civil servants owed their primary loyalty to the old regime, they were suspicious if not openly hostile to the new government. Another impediment to delivery has been the chaotic state of affairs at the provincial and local levels of government. In order to root out incompetence and to eliminate duplication, almost every branch, agency, and department of government must be overhauled, their resources rechannelled, their goals redirected, and their chains of command re-organized to meet the entirely new challenges of the post-apartheid era.

The defining feature of the transition to democracy has been the charismatic leadership of President Mandela. Mandela is rightly credited with placing moral principle above political expediency, with setting a high ethical standard for elected officials, and for preparing a smooth political transition after his retirement from public office. Yet, ironically, moral strength can also be a political weakness. Mandela's personal loyalty to 'old guard' ANC exiles prevented him from replacing those cabinet ministers or other key bureaucrats who failed competently to carry out their assigned tasks with more capable figures.

To a significant degree, the strength of the ANC has been helped considerably by the weakness of opposition parties. In the national elections of 2 June 1999, the ANC once again scored an impressive victory, taking 266 parliamentary seats, or one seat short of the magical two-thirds majority that would have given the party the *carte blanche* power to amend the constitution. The desire to frustrate, if not reverse, the fortunes of the ANC binds the destiny of the parties in opposition who fear that South Africa may become a *de facto* one-party state under the unwelcome dominance of the ANC. By winning 38 Parliamentary seats with around 10 per cent of the popular vote, the Democratic Party (DP) replaced the New National Party as the 'official opposition'. Under the fiery leadership of Tony Leon, the DP sharpened its market-oriented message, but failed to broaden its appeal beyond the disgruntled white electorate. The Inkatha Freedom Party followed with 34 seats. Yet with an appeal couched in the lexicon of 'Zulu nationalism', the Inkatha Freedom Party cannot expand much beyond its support in KwaZulu/ Natal and amongst Zulu-speaking migrants in the urban townships. Despite its efforts to reinvent itself as a fervent advocate of multi-party democracy and its successful appeal to the coloured electorate in the Western Cape, the National Party – renamed the New National Party – is haunted by its dreadful apartheid past. Under the leadership of Roelf Meyer and Bantu Holomisa, the United Democratic Movement (UDM) cobbled together an alliance of political mavericks and tapped into whatever disenchantment there is with the ANC amongst the black electorate. Organizations of the socialist Left and those inspired by radical nationalism – notably the Pan Africanist Congress (PAC) and Black Consciousness-oriented Azanian People's Organization (AZAPO) – failed miserably to develop a coherent programme and a workable strategy effectively to challenge the enduring faith in the ANC.

On balance, the failure of the lilliputian parties in opposition to mount a serious challenge to ANC dominance provides President Thabo Mbeki with an unprecedented opportunity to carry out his party's programme without serious interference. Whereas Mandela focused on reconciliation and forgiveness, Mbeki has promised deliverance on the ANC's promises of jobs, security, and peace.[30] Yet the end of legal disenfranchisement does not automatically guarantee a full-scale assault on deprivation and impoverishment. 'The American civil rights movement provides a cautionary tale', two astute South African political observers suggest; 'tragedy overtakes apparent success if economic rights are not pursued after political rights are won'. Despite pledges to the contrary, 'political freedom can exist surrounded by economic misery'.[31]

FURTHER READING

Fine, Ben and Zavareh Rustomjee (1996) *The Political Economy of South Africa: From Minerals-Energy Complex to Industrialization* (Johannesburg: Witwatersrand University Press). This book traces the long history of the political economy in South Africa with special emphasis on the structural weaknesses, crisis points, and contradictions.

Lodge, Tom (1999) *Consolidating Democracy: South Africa's Second Popular Election* (Johannesburg: Witwatersrand University Press). A timely, provocative analysis of the context for South Africa's second democratic elections, this work takes up questions about the electoral system, the nature of voters and voting, and the campaigns and ideologies of the main political parties.

Marais, Hein (1998) *South Africa: Limits to Change: The Political Economy of Transition* (London: Zed Books). This book chronicles the transition to democracy in South Africa and addresses why it is that the new government, led by the ANC, has adopted conservative economic policies and has been unable to break the boundaries of change erected by the privileged classes.

Maré, Gerhard (1993) *Ethnicity and Politics in South Africa* (London: Zed Books). Here is explored the question of ethnic identity as a mobilized political force operating against broader conceptions of political identity and practices. It specifically examines the case of mobilized Zulu identity promoted by Inkatha, while addressing broader theoretical questions about the nature of ethnic nationalism.

Marks, Shula and Stanley Trapido (1987) *The Politics of Race, Class, and Nationalism in Twentieth Century South Africa* (London: Longman). This classic anthology brings together social history and political analysis providing important insights on South African society and politics over time.

Murray, Martin (1994) *The Revolution Deferred: The Painful Birth of Post-Apartheid South Africa* (London: Verso). A comprehensive, critical analysis of the period of rapid political change in South Africa, this book surveys the key events, organizations, and outcomes in the struggle against the apartheid state.

Walker, Cherryl (1990) *Women and Gender in South Africa to 1945* (CapeTown: David Phillip and London: James Currey). An edited collection that addresses the gendered history of this region with special attention to how political and economic transformations in the nineteenth and early twentieth century affected women's social position. This book provides crucial and fascinating background reading, and enables an understanding of politics beyond the formal spheres of parliamentary power.

NOTES

1. Justice Malala, Down with the People, *Sunday Times*, 21 March 1999.
2. Patti Waldmeir and Michael Homan, A Powerful Spirit of Unity, *Financial Times*, 18 July 1994, p. 1.
3. Ian Liebenberg (1997) The Integration of the Military in Post-Liberation South Africa: The Contribution of Revolutionary Armies, *Armed Forces & Society* 24(1): 105–32.
4. Ian Shapiro (1993) Democratic Innovation: South Africa in Comparative Context, *World Politics* 46(1): 121–50; John Saul (1997) Liberal Democracy vs. Popular Democracy in Southern Africa, *Review of African Political Economy* 72: 219–36; Hermann Giliomee (1995) Democratization in South Africa, *Political Science Quarterly* 110(1): 83–104; and W. Van Vuuren (1995)

Transition Politics and the Prospects for Democratic Consolidation in South Africa, *Politikon* 22(1): 5–23.

5. This idea is borrowed from Alexander Johnston (1994) South Africa: The Election and the Transition Process – Five Contradictions in Search of a Resolution, *Third World Quarterly* 15(2): 187–8.

6. The tripartite alliance comprises the ANC, the South African Communist Party (SACP), and the Congress of South African Trade Unions (COSATU).

7. Heribert Adam, Frederick Van Zyl Slabbert (1997) *Comrades in Business: Post-Liberation Politics in South Africa*. Cape Town: Tafelberg; John Brewer (ed.) (1994) *Restructuring South Africa*. New York: St Martin's; Glenn Adler and Eddie Webster (1995) Challenging Transition Theory: The Labour Movement, Radical Reform, and the Transition to Democracy in South Africa, *Politics and Society* 23(1): 75–106; Ken Cole (1994) *Sustainable Development for a Democratic South Africa*. New York: St Martin's; Barry Munslow and Frank Fitzgerald (1994) South Africa: The Sustainable Development Challenge, *Third World Quarterly* 15(2): 227–42; and P. Fitzgerald, A. McLennan and B. Munslow (eds) (1995) *Managing Sustainable Development in South Africa*. Oxford: Oxford University Press.

8. Jeremy Baskin (1993) *Corporatism: Some Obstacles Facing the South African Labour Movement*. Johannesburg: CPSR Report No. 30.

9. See Philip Harrison, Alison Todes and Vanessa Watson (1997) Transforming South Africa's Cities: Prospects for the Economic Development of Urban Townships, *Development Southern Africa* 14(1): 43–60.

10. This phrase is borrowed from Mick Moore (1997) Moving the Left to the Right: Populist Coalitions and Economic Reform, *World Development* 25(7): 1009–28.

11. Samuel Huntington (1991) *The Third Wave: Democratization in the Late Twentieth Century*. Norman, Oklahoma: University of Oklahoma Press, pp. 152–3.

12. Jean-Francois Bayart (1993) *The State in Africa: The Politics of the Belly*. New York: Longman, pp. 150–79.

13. Rajen Harshe (1994) New South Africa: Ironies and Challenges, *Economic and Political Weekly*, (1 October): 2591–2; and (1995) Black Business in South Africa, *African Business* (June): 8–9.

14. Paul Taylor (1995) Mandela Scolds Blacks on Violence, *Washington Post* (25 February).

15. Tom Lodge (1999) Blame Violence on the Politics of Life and Death, *Sunday Times* (21 March).

16. South Africa: Hyjacked by Crime, *African Business* (April 1998): 25–6; *Los Angeles Times* (26 May 1999); and Wilf Nussey (1995) After Apartheid, Hope and Decay, *Guardian Weekly* [London] (19 November).

17. Robert Putnam (1994) *Making Democracy Work: Civic Traditions in Modern Italy*. Princeton: Princeton University Press.

18. Barry Weingart (1997) The Political Foundations of Democracy and the Rule of the Law, *American Political Science Review* 91(2): 245–63.
19. Anne Phillips (1995) *The Politics of Presence*. Oxford: Clarendon Press, p. 148.
20. See, for example, The Risks of Redistribution, *Financial Mail* (13 February 1998).
21. Charles Maier (1987) makes this argument in *Search of Stability: Explorations in Historical Political Economy*. Cambridge: Cambridge University Press, pp. 263–4.
22. See Francisco Panizza (1993) Democracy's Lost Treasure, *Latin American Research Review* 28(3): 375–6.
23. Douglas Booth (1996) Mandela and Amabokoboko: The Political and Linguistic Nationalisation of South Africa?, *Journal of Modern African Studies* 34(3): 459–77.
24. Arend Lijphart (1984) *Democracies: Patterns of Majoritarian and Consensus Government in Twenty-one Countries*. New Haven: Yale University Press, pp. 22–3.
25. Brij Maharaj and Rinku Rajkumar (1997) The Alien Invasion in South Africa: Illegal Immigrants in Durban, *Development Southern Africa* 14(2): 255–73.
26. Aletta Norval (1998) Reinventing the Politics of Cultural Recognition: The Freedom Front and the Demand for a *Volksstaat*. In David R. Howarth and Aletta J. Norval, *South Africa in Transition: New Theoretical Perspective*. New York: St Martin's Press, pp. 93–110.
27. Gerhard Maré (1992) *Ethnicity and Politics in South Africa*. London: Zed Books; Morris Szeftel (1995) Ethnicity and Democratization in South Africa, *Review of African Political Economy* 60: 157–76; Gerhard Mare and Georgina Hamilton (1987) *An Appetite for Power: Buthelezi's Inkatha and the Politics of 'Loyal Resistance'*. Johannesburg: Ravan; and Mary de Haas and Paulus Zulu (1994) Ethnicity and Federalism: The Case of KwaZulu/Natal, *Journal of Southern African Studies* 20(3): 433–46.
28. Rachel Prinsloo (1997) Disintegrations: The Politics of Coloured Identity, *Indicator SA* 14(3): 24–7.
29. See Tshidiso Maloka and David Gordon (1997) Chieftainship, Civil Society, and the Political Transition in South Africa, *Critical Sociology* 22(3): 37–56.
30. Mark Gevisser (1999) Seeking South Africa's Dream, *The Nation* (7 June): 19–22.
31. Kader Asma and Ronald Roberts (1994) Apartheid Lives On, *New York Times* (29 October).

CHAPTER 11

A FUTURE FOR DEMOCRACY IN RUSSIA?

Klaus von Beyme

INTRODUCTION: THE BURDEN OF FOUR COMMUNIST LEGACIES

'Transitology', as the study of the transition to democracy, was accompanied by a paradigm change: grandpa's institutional political science saw a comeback in a period when the arrogance of some champions of rational choice paid back to the behaviouralists what they once had done to the institutionalists in political science. *Constitutional engineering* as a catchword took up rationalistic ideas of the Enlightenment when constitutions were sometimes considered coherent all-embracing systems of elements neatly fitting into one another. But after the waves of de-democratization in the twentieth century, we know that coherent constitutions and systems can be made by revolutionary force. The costs are high: the formal constitution plays only a propagandistic role and the nicely fitting elements of the totalitarian system disintegrate after three generations. At the end of the system, the monolith of totalitarian dictatorship was a 'loosely knitted anarchy' of countervailing power centres. Whereas Carl Joachim Friedrich in 1965 still believed that totalitarian systems end only by *debellatio* from outside – which was true of the fascist regimes – the Soviet Union, the most fiercely armed system in world history, disintegrated without daring one shot, although its power would still have been sufficient to resort to the Chinese solution at Tienamen Square. Spain's Franco dictatorship was the first case to show that an initially quasi-totalitarian system abdicated after Franco's death without an upheaval. No wonder that Juan Linz, Alfred Stepan and many others tried to explain the whole transition of Samual Huntington's 'third wave' according to the Spanish model. This worked in systems where a *dictablanda* had substituted the *dictadura* in a phase of 'liberalization', such as in Poland and Hungary. It did not apply to the mode of transition by collapse as in Czechoslovakia or the GDR. It worked still less in the third mode of transition with a certain continuity of the elites and 'the system', such as in Romania, Serbia or most of the CIS states that had belonged to the Soviet Union (with the exception of the Baltic states). Russia was a deviant case in several respects:

1. In spite of a certain continuity of the system, it had experienced a period of liberalization under Gorbachev when 'glasnost', *the liberalization of the public discourse*, undermined 'perestroika' as a way of transition by radical reform, according to models such as Atatürk's Turkey or the Meiji restoration in Japan. Gorbachev, despite his many virtues, failed to recognize two facts: that the Leninist one-party rule was no longer feasible and that the centrifugal forces in the Soviet federation demanded radical reform and true autonomy. Some parts of the elites knew already in 1988 that the Baltic states could no longer be integrated in a Soviet federalist system.

2. The Soviet Union was the *centre of a huge Empire*. Gorbachev was too much absorbed with upholding the disintegration of the COMECON and the Warsaw Pact in order to take the necessary radical steps in domestic affairs.

3. Even after the disintegration of both the Empire and the Soviet Union there was the problem of Russian hegemony within the remainders of the *federation*. It is not by chance that the Russian Communists tried to impeach Yeltsin in early 1999 for – among other 'crimes' – having blown up the former Soviet countries in a loose confederation, the CIS. The *ideological vacuum* after the erosion of Marxist-Leninist thought was filled less with *civil society* devices – as in East Central Europe in the time of the hegemony of forum-type confederations of democratic forces – but by a search for *nationalist identity*. Neoslavophile thoughts – Solzhenitsyn's *Rossiya v obvale* (1998) was typical, though marginal in this debate – and rivals of *Eurasian myths* about a special mission of Russia (excluded from Europe) between Asia and Europe sprang up. Even the professional journals such as *Polis* and *Socis* are a frustrating source for Westernizers and Western observers who look for a truly modernized social theory to democratic transition. Nevertheless, these journalistic exercises in 'populist' philosophy were probably necessary to satisfy an intelligentsia which even in opposition was imbued by Marxist-Leninist ideas about a 'special mission of the intellectuals'. Russia had little tradition in civil society in its intellectual history. The democratic camp of liberals and democratic *narodniki*, until 1917, were torn to pieces between the camps of the Neoslavophile Vekhi movement and the dictatorial minded Marxists and anarchists. The 'new Vekhi' movement is still stronger in the debates on Russian identity than the true Westernizers. There was a 'sociological association' under the name of the most prominent liberal sociologist Maxim Kovalevsky. But Westernizers were too uncritically absorbed by the ready-made models of the Chicago-boys to look for the Russian roots of an idea of civil society.

Nevertheless, two achievements are noteworthy in this period of intellectual confusion. The *institution-making* process included much work on Western institutions, but the final result of a *three-quarter-presidential system* was *sui generis* in Russia. There was no time in a period of breakdowns to study thoroughly Western experiences. Already, under Gorbachev, the leading institutes of the Academy were torn to pieces by orders from the government for briefing them one day on American federalism, the next day on Scandinavian ombudsmen or German constitutional courts and the week after on the transition of Western nations to the welfare state.

Institution building in a transition with much continuity on the elite level is a power struggle. It came hardly as a surprise that the elements of parliamentary government and a plurality electoral system advocated by the Communists in order to save their power position did not neatly harmonize with elements of semi-presidential systems and a variation of proportional elections. The latter combination was *per se* thought to be a very unfavourable device by many Western scholars such as Arend Lijphart or Juan Linz.

The illiberal dangers of an attempt to save as much of Russia's grandeur as possible has not led to very uncivil actions. Lebed operated in the dominantly Slavic parts of Moldavia, but he did not try to become a Russian Garibaldi to save the Slavic irridenta and no other Russian Garibaldi landed with troops on the Crimean peninsula or the Eastern Ukraine to liberate the predominantly Russian population in these areas. The division of the fleet was achieved by negotiation. Despite much latent and open nationalism among the intellectuals, none of Russia's 23 frontiers – only three of them were considered as justified from the ethnic point of view – was redrawn by force by the Russian government (Kreikemeyer and Zagorsky, 1997). The carnival of declarations of sovereign states within the Russian federations was outmanoeuvred in rather a civil way. The notable exception is Chechnya – oddly enough another main point in the impeachment move by the negative coalition of Communists and Nationalists in the Russian Duma against Yeltsin.

4. The revival of an 'enlightened neo-institutionalism' – as it was styled without modesty by its torchbearers – opted for the *primacy of institutional and political consolidation in open confrontation with older sociological modernization theories*, which shared with Marxism the *emphasis on economic transition to market society*. Only some Marxist rational choice scholars such as Adam Przeworski were sceptical about democratic institution-building on the basis of a deeply etatist and underdeveloped economy. Most political scientists were impressed by Brazil, which

discarded the assumptions of modernization theories as well as *dependencia* theories and dared to usher in democracy without a sufficient per capita income (sometimes defined at the level of about $5000–6000). The Linz-Stepan school again preferred Spain as a model – sometimes overlooking the fact that, already in the time of sclerosis of Franco's regime, Spain was smoothly being transformed into a Westernized open economy by technocrats and Opus Dei elites.

In Russia, all attempts to create a more decentralized and liberal economy since Khrushchev's experiment with 105 *Sovnarkhozy* had failed. The huge country had no hope of being integrated quickly into an open globalized economy. Russia is still an 'invited observer' among the seven great economic powers. Remainders of dreams of autarchy were less easy to overcome in an economy with no hopes to enter the European Union, hopes that the Visegrad group of states could entertain.

The new paradigm of *consolidology* instead of *transitology* that developed in the mid-1990s was hardly applicable to Russia. My hypothesis is that the contradictions of the political *system inédit* in Russia would cause much less damage if the problems of economic transition would have been solved to the same extent as they had been in Poland or Hungary. History teaches that systems can live with many institutional shortcomings when the economy prospers as in the Federal Republic of Germany. In such a case one can complain about the incapacity of the political system to reorganize a more satisfying balance between the units of the federation or the executive–legislative relations, but the system functions nevertheless and can even dare to ignore the chances of an opportunity to reorganize its institutions so frequently demanded at the occasion of the merger of the two German states. If the Communist-Nationalist coalition gets a hold of the Russian presidency and keeps its majority in the Duma in the year 2000, they may re-parliamentarize a semi-presidential system somewhere at the level of the French Fifth Republic and Poland after Walesa. But this would hardly solve the problems of a stagnating economy. This is the reason why the evaluation of chances for a Russian democracy has to start with the economic burden of democracy in Russia before examining the stages of consolidation.

THE HEAVIEST BURDEN OF COMMUNIST LEGACIES: A STAGNATING ECONOMY

Survey studies show in most of the transitional societies that the citizens are more ready to internalize the democratic rules than the rules of a capitalist society (von Beyme, 1996, pp. 76ff.). Hardly any of the countries are satisfied with the economic transition. Nevertheless, Russia has a much harder burden to carry than most former communist systems outside the Soviet Union. Only a comparison of the achievements can show how far various economies have advanced on the road to a functioning market economy. Initially the degree of privatization was used as an indicator. The success of a big push strategy or a gradualist transition have been most widely debated. Poland was more successful with Balcerowicz's strategy of a big push than Gaydar in Russia. But there is no longer an ideological war over the alternatives of private or public economy, big push or gradual transformation. Most of the former Soviet republics had no chance for a big change. Privatization of enterprises in the hands of nomenklatura elites or even mafia entrepreneurs does not really transform an economy into a market society of the Western type. Structural changes, consolidation of the state budget, fighting inflation, stabilizing the extractive capacity of the political system in terms of taxes, unemployment growth, development of investments and per capita income are more telling indicators than the big alternatives of the initial economic debate.

If we compare the figures of transitional economies (Table 11.1), Russia belongs to those countries that did not keep up radical measures. The inflation rate is an indicator. Russia did comparatively well with an inflation of 1353 per cent in 1992 and 28 per cent in 1998. Russia did better than the Ukraine (30 per cent) and Romania (50 per cent in 1998), but not as well as Czechia (8 per cent in 1998) and Hungary and Poland (13 per cent in 1998). Half-hearted measures of reform policy show themselves also in the consolidation of state budgets. Russia (–6 per cent) together with the Ukraine (–6.1 per cent) and Bulgaria (–5 per cent) ranks in the lower part of a ranking scale. Russia is the classic example of a *managerial privatization and lobbying* in exchange for subsidies for exports, credits and exemption from taxation (Aslund, 1995; Schleifer and Treisman, 1998, pp. 21ff).

Russia has a fairly good record in privatization and creating a modern balance between the three sectors of the economy. The 'gradualist laggards' (Commander and Tostopiatenko in Zecchini, 1997), such as Russia (11.0 per cent in 1998) and Romania (10 per cent) kept unemployment below the average in Eastern Europe, even below Poland (13 per cent). But Czechia (4.5 per cent) and Hungary (10.5 per cent) show that more radical market economies can do as well or even better. Russia is, however, no model, because it has few unemployment benefits compared to the Visegrad states (Müller, 1998, pp. 194f.). The growth rates of Russia (1998: 2 per cent, 1991: –12.9 per cent) demonstrate that the 'worst is over', even in Russia. However, at the end of the 1990s, *growth* is still below most other countries with the exception of Romania.

Przeworski suspected (1991, p. 191) that the 'East' may become the 'South' of the developing countries. This seems to be the case in the South of the East (Bulgaria, Romania) but it does not necessarily apply to a highly industrialized country such as Russia – at least in many sectors. The arms industry was in crisis. But Russia is again one of the most important exporters of arms in the world. Even India continues to rely on old established exchanges with Russia, because of better prices than the West can offer. Nevertheless, according to the data on per capita income, compared to the US dollar, Russia ranks between Panama and Venezuela (Müller, 1998, p. 200). But this ranking should not be overrated because Russia, unlike Venezuela, has more to offer than oil and agricultural goods.

Russia is such a huge area that the rates of foreign investments can hardly be compared to the Visegrad states ($4.4 billion in 1996: OECD, 1997: p. 127). The problem remains that modest foreign investments do not equal out the losses by capital secretly escaping to foreign banks, according to estimates about $50 billion in 1996 (*Transition*, vol. 8, no. 3, p. 10; Müller, 1998, p. 201). The foreign debts in some countries of Eastern Europe have increased to dimensions of the Third World (Bulgaria $102 billion, Hungary $58 billion). But Russia ($25 billion) is below the much smaller country Poland ($31 billion) and has far greater natural resources to rely on. The state's role in investment is increasing (in 1997: 426, and in 2000: 573.1 trillion Rbs) (OECD, 1997, p. 129).

But even when the 'worst is over' in terms of economic growth, the spillover effects of economic transition to political consolidation are minimal if the state – as in Russia – proves to have little capacity to increase its tax income. In Russia, the taxes in per cent of the GNP fell from 41 per cent (1989) to 28 per cent (1994) – by far the lowest extractive capacity of any transitional state in Eastern Europe. The share of a second economy evading taxes in Russia – according to calculations of the World Bank – is 40 per cent (1994). Only the Ukraine was above this level, even if the figures for Romania (17 per cent) and Bulgaria (29 per cent) are open to doubts.

Moreover, the changes do not indicate a peaceful political development when social inequality increases to the extent it does in Russia. Even in the old Soviet Union, 20 per cent of the population at the beginning of perestroika (1985) lived below the poverty line (Matthews, 1986, p. 26). The World Bank calculated the percentage of people living below the poverty line at 35 per cent (Table 11.1). Only Hungary ranks at the same level. The figures are meaningless, however, if we do not correlate them with the system of social security. It is developing in Hungary, but stagnating in Russia. In times of the highest inflation rate

Table 11.1 Indicators of economic development in Russia compared to other systems on the road to market economy

	Russia	Ukraine	Poland	Czech Republic	Hungary	Romania	Bulgaria
Real GNP (% of change) 1999	-7.0	-3.6	4.7	0.5	4.3	-2.0	3.7
Share of the private sector	1991: 10	1991: 8	1991: 42	1991: 16	1991: 30	1991: 23	1991: 17
GNP occupation	1996: 70	1996: 48	1996: 60	1996: 74	1996: 73	1996: 50	1996: 45
	n.d.	1991: 3	1991: 54	1991: 16	1991: 48	1991: 34	1991: 10
		1994: 10	1995: 63	1995: 65	1995: 60	1996: 62	1996: 41
Share of sectors in % of GNP	1995:	1994:	1994:	1995:	1995:	1994:	1994:
agriculture	15	14.3	6.0	5.2	7	20	14.7
manufacturing	38	42.4	38.0	41.0	34	38	33.6
service sector	53	30.3	56.0	53.8	59	22	51.7
Balance of budget	1996: -6.0	1997: -6.1	1997: -3.0	1997: -2.0	1997: -5.1	1996: -2.0	1996: -5.0
Inflation	1991: 93	1991: 94	1991: 76	1991: 57	1991: 34	1991: 161	1991: 333
	1998: 28	1998: 11	1998: 12	1998: 11	1998: 14	1998: 59	1998: 22
Unemployment	1992: 4.9	1992: 0.3	1992: 13.6	1992: 2.6	1992: 13.2	1992: 8.4	1992: 15.2
	1998: 11.0	1998: 12.0	1998: 13.0	1998: 4.5	1998: 10.5	1998: 10.0	1998: 17.0
Growth	1991: -12.9	1991: 11.9	1991: -7.0	1991: -14.2	1991: 11.9	1991: -12.9	1991: -11.7
	1998: 2.0	1998: 4.0	1998: 6.0	1998: 3.0	1998: 3.5	1998: 0.0	1998: 5.0
Investments 1996 compared to 1989 in %	30.9	26.9	116.1	121.5	91.1	68.6	55.8
GNP 1996 compared to 1989	56.5	40.3	104.5	88.1	86.9	88.2	68.9
GNP per capita compared to	17.8	10.1	21.2	34.4	23.5	15.8	16.9
US $*	2240	n.d.	2790	3870			

1994
1995

Foreign debts % of GNP	25.4	21.2	31.4	20.4	58.7	23.5	102.7
Balance of imports and exports and foreign transfers related to GNP % 1997	2.5	-3.3	-9.5	-8.5	-3.0	-6.5	7.0
Taxes in % of GNP							
1989	41	26	41	62	59	51	60
1994	28	42	46	51	52	33	38
% of population below poverty line	25 / 35 (World Bank)	21.1	13	10.8	35	n.d.	19.5
% of second informal economy	1994: 40	46	15	18	29	17	29

* Greece: 8210; Portugal: 9740; Spain: 13580

Sources: DIW et al. (1997) *Wirtschaftslage und Reformprozesse in Mittel- und Osteuropa.* Bonn, BMW; OECD (1997) *The Russian Federation.* Paris; World Bank (1999) *World Economic Outlook.* Washington (May); Salvatore Zecchini (ed.) (1997) *Lessons from the Economic Transition. Central and Eastern Europe in the 1990s.* Paris: OECD; Klaus Müller (1998) Postsozialistische Krisen. In idem (ed.) *Postsozialistische Krisen.* Opladen: Leske & Budrich, pp. 177–249; Finanzbericht 1999. Bonn, BMF.

(1992–4) pensions grew only from 4 to 4.5 per cent of GNP. Moreover, we have to correlate these figures with the increase in prices for consumer goods. The OECD has calculated that the state subsidies for these goods were cut down to half of the former level. The figures for unemployment are 'normal', but they do not uncover the structural problems. In some regions, women constitute 70–80 per cent of the unemployed (Rzhanitsyna and Sergeeva, 1995, p. 60; Sillaste, 1994, p. 21). The employed workers and civil servants are not always better off. Only 40 per cent in 1996 received regular payment. It is a miracle that the Russian army – sometimes waiting for its salaries for months – has not yet challenged the 'only (democratic) game in town'. The only officially tolerated compensatory system is a private smallholding agriculture (*lichnoe podsobnoe khozyastvo*). In a survey, 19 per cent of the rural population was living on small agriculture for subsistence, without contributing to the market (Voz'mitel', 1994, p. 50).

Individualization and *stratification* are quickly progressing and a new class of *bisness-meny* (businessmen) is forming, that does not avoid conspicuous consumption (as mostly happens in the West) thus creating social hatred (von Beyme, 1998). The gini-index of inequality in Russia rose from 24.0 (1988) to 49.6 per cent (1993). The upper stratum, which constitutes 20 per cent of the population, has a 38.7 per cent share of the income and consumption of the nation (World Bank, 1997; Müller, 1998, p. 210). The fraction of winners of the transformation is extremely small and elitist in Russia.

Whereas the three West European transitional economies in the 1970s (Spain, Portugal and Greece) did extremely well in catching up with help from the European Community, Russia will have to live with one-fifth of the per capita GNP (in American dollars) of Spain. Even Czechia gets one-third and Poland about one-fourth of the Spanish level.

THE UNFINISHED PERIOD OF DEMOCRATIZATION AND INSTITUTION-BUILDING

Institution building is the main task in the period of democratization. If we could believe that Yeltsin's constitution of 1993 was the final solution for the system, then this process was rather short – shorter than in Poland (1989–97) or Hungary (1989–?). The ex-communists normally defended the old constitution because the 'government by assembly' corresponded to their own notion of power. The Party in 1991 still existed but the power of the president of the Party had eroded and a new power centre had formed around the chairman of the parliamentary assembly. It was interesting to see how little the rebel communists during the attempted coup were accustomed to constitutional change in the Soviet Union. When, after the coup d'état of August 1991, Yanaev gave his first press conference and was asked whether Gorbachev would remain party chairman, he tried to evade the question: the insurgents had no clear idea how to proceed.

Democratization of authoritarian empires in the first stage normally meant *parliamentarization*. Autocratic regimes in the nineteenth century had avoided the development of a government responsible to Parliament and certainly avoided full democracy (the Meiji restoration in Japan, Bismarck's constitution of 1871 in Germany). Democratization was thus a process that had to pass the stage of parliamentarization. This line was followed even in Czarist Russia. In the changes of 1989, a struggle for parliamentary government was no longer necessary, as it had been in the monarchies of the nineteenth century. The rules of parliamentary government had even been inserted on paper in the socialist constitutions. The parliamentary movement had only to vitalize the text of a constitution which in many cases was still valid, especially in Russia until the end of 1993. In December 1989, the only missing requisite of parliamentary government, which was then introduced via constitutional amendment, was the vote of censure. It was limited to a majority of two-thirds and its legal consequences remained without regulation. In March 1990 an amendment was introduced that forced a government to resign after the acceptance of a vote of no confidence. But the parliamentary system in the British tradition was soon developed into a French type of semi-presidential government, with a president in a council of ministers and a double responsibility of government before the President as well as before Parliament. The President's power increased, but his right to issue decrees was limited. It was subject to the budding system of judicial review by the constitutional court.

Parliamentarization called for the initiative to strengthen Gorbachev's powers as well. In September 1990, a law for a limited duration enlarged the competences of the president. It has frequently been dubbed *Ermächtigungsgesetz*, bringing to mind Hitler's bid for wider powers in early 1933. In the draft for a Union treaty, similar tendencies were visible and mobilized against the Russian opposition. The second amended draft of March 1991 was meant to serve as a blueprint for a new Soviet constitution. *Presidentialization* of the executive made headway. Members of the council of ministers no longer needed endorsement but only consent of the Supreme Soviet. How this was meant to work in case of conflict remained obscure. The reduction of the presidium of the Supreme Soviet to a mere parliamentary chairmanship was the necessary consequence of the presidentialization process.

A normal system did not develop, however; too many exceptions to the rules were admitted. By amendment to the constitution in March 1990, the president was elected by the Congress of People's Deputies and not by the people. Yanaev as vice-president was also installed by this exceptional procedure, an act with severe consequences as the vice-president became the leader of the coup d'état against the president.

Parliamentarization and presidentialization were followed by a third process, *federalization*. In March 1990 the presidential council was dissolved and was substituted by a deliberating body under the same name of *federative council*. In December 1990 the new body received powers which made those of the Congress of People's Deputies redundant. All of the Republican presidents of 20 autonomous republics, which partly had been elevated to the Status of a 'Union Republic', were represented. The delegates of eight autonomous Republics and ten autonomous national districts were allowed to participate only in questions that directly concerned their territories.

Gorbachev also failed to opt early enough for a confederation of states as a device through which to save the Soviet Union. The president lost himself in tactical manoeuvres without a clear concept. He claimed not to have ordered the intervention in the Baltic states (which is likely) and he pretended not even to know about the intervention (which is most unlikely). But the failure of this rollback policy in the progress of confederalization gave Yeltsin more chances to gain profile as a reformer. Gorbachev was doomed to end as a kind of 'Kerenskij of the perestroika period'. The power to act at Union level had withered away in the three conflicts between parliamentarization, presidentialization and confederalization and between the three men Gorbachev, Yeltsin and Ryshkov. No institution building in accord with an overarching concept was possible at Union level.

The fight of competing forces for institution building was not over after the end of the Union. The conflict over a new constitution for Russia was fiercer than the old quarrels between Gorbachev and Yeltsin. Parliament under Chazbulatov even imposed on Yeltsin the question that was put to the people in a referendum. The result of the referendum of March 1993 was celebrated as a victory for both sides. On the whole, it was more important for strengthening President Yeltsin.

In 1992 an official draft of the constitution was drawn up by a constitutional commission. Headed by Oleg Rumyantsev, it provided a semi-presidential federative republic with a two-chamber system which was to replace the old competition between the Congress of People's Deputies and the Supreme Soviet. This draft was met with criticism by the Chairman of the Supreme Soviet. An alternative draft was put

forward by the Movement for Democratic Reforms under Anatolij Sobchak, Mayor of St Petersburg. Inspired by the writings of Andrey
Sakharov, this draft emphasized the importance of human rights and the
rights of ethnic groups. Yeltsin's adviser, Shakhraj, launched a third draft
which took America's presidential system as a model, including a true
balance of power with the right to veto and no possible dissolution of
parliament. None of the three drafts, however, was accepted by the sixth
People's Congress, and the official draft was only accepted 'in principle'.

Yeltsin looked for a way out of the deadlock by proposing a referendum, although, legally, only the Congress had the right to initiate one.
A strange dual system developed. The constitutional committee had the
task of working on a new constitution and amending the old one
(between 1978 and December 1992 this happened nine times). The
committee tried to find a compromise between the future norms and the
actual reality of the constitution. The Seventh Congress in December
1992 abolished certain powers of the President, which the Fifth Congress
had granted him for one year. In this conflict the compromises were
again without precedent in the history of parliamentary government: the
President needed consent not only for the Prime Minister but also for the
three most important departments (foreign affairs, internal affairs,
defence). The responsibility of the ministerial council to Parliament was
strengthened. The Eighth Congress in March 1993 further limited the
extraordinary powers of the President and even initiated an impeachment, which was only avoided by a tiny majority of the votes.

In March 1993 the Constitutional Court ruled on the conflict that
existed between the executive and legislative branches: the President's
proclamation to the people violated nine articles of the constitution and
some regulations of the then union treaty and the law on the referendum.
The President was isolated from the parliamentary majority and from his
vice-president, Rutskoj. Room for manoeuvre for the President could
only be restored by mobilizing the people and its parts, the Republics.
But mobilizing the Republics involved risks. Some announced that they
would not implement a referendum on their territory. The threat was
carried through only in Chechnya, however. Some territories, as well as
St Petersburg, added questions of their own to the official questionnaire.
The referendum of April 1993 exposed certain misconceptions: that the
President had no confidence within the population and most of the
citizens would remain at home (62 per cent of the population actually
participated). Confidence in the President – the first question on the
questionnaire – was expressed by 58.8 per cent of the voters and only 32.8
per cent demanded a new election of the president.

The real miracle was that the economic and social policy of the President, which was very unpopular according to public opinion polls, was supported by a small majority (52.7 per cent). Not only did Yeltsin do well – his adversaries also had their victory: only 42.9 per cent voted for a new election of the People's Congress. Each side in the conflict had announced reservations. Yeltsin held in advance that the majority for the question of confidence would be tantamount to a support of his view on the constitutional question. Chasbulatov, on the other side, had announced that even a confidence vote for Yeltsin would not be able to derogate the existing constitution – which was legally correct. Yeltsin's support was about 60 per cent of the 60 per cent of those who actually went to the polls, which was tantamount to slightly more than one-third of the whole population – not a very impressive result. In international comparison this is, however, a situation which an American President or British Prime Minister in a system of winner-takes-all meets quite frequently. What the people really meant can only be interpreted by the public opinion polls, but they are incomplete. In March 1993, 47 per cent of those interviewed in Moscow endorsed a strong presidential government for Yeltsin (Wishnevsky, 1995, p. 6). At that time, however, Moscow was not representative of the mood in the rest of the country.

The conflict between Yeltsin and Chasbulatov was a reminder of the conflicts between Gorbachev and Lukyanov in the first period of transition. Neither side was able fully to benefit from its part in the victory of the referendum. Yeltsin could have used this victory to his advantage if he had been able to link the support for his person to an acceptance of his constitution, but the Ninth Congress prevented the legal acceptance of this kind of juncture. On the other hand, the Constitutional Court had prevented the Congress in the first two questions during the referendum from demanding an absolute majority of the electors. The Court, however, upheld the necessity of an absolute majority for questions three and four. This was one of the reasons why quick elections were impossible. One way out of the deadlock seemed to be bargaining, but Chazbulatov's support in the Congress was diminishing in May 1993. The other way out would have been to bypass Congress by the convocation of a constitutional assembly, which Yeltsin indeed called for on 5 June 1993. Chazbulatov insisted on Parliament's rights to decide on the constitution. His escape was the invocation of the constitution-making power of the people. Both sides mobilized and Chazbulatov called for an assembly of 2000 deputies of the legislatures of various levels. Yeltsin, on the other hand, was wavering between three scenarios:

- the constituent assembly;
- a second referendum;
- a newly elected parliament.

A referendum would have secured the most complete democratic legit-imization. The new Parliament was a concession to the constitutional doctrine of the post-communists and was risky because the President could by no means be sure that his majority would prevail in the elections, as was proved by the results of December 1993.

In July 1993 the constitutional committee accepted the President's draft of a constitution, but there was still no clear scenario on how to legitimize it. Yeltsin remained silent on what he would do if the parlia-mentary majority rejected the draft of the constitutional committee. The President weakened his position in the conflict because of a badly prepared reform of the rouble. The people were upset and the parliamen-tary opposition grew stronger. In August 1993 Parliament tried again to submit the president to parliamentary resolutions on many questions. In December 1992, Yeltsin had conceded the right of the assembly to co-determine the distribution of the most important portfolios. He did so in order to prevent the toppling of his Prime Minister, Gajdar. Soon there-after he discovered that Gajdar could not be held in office, but his concessions to the other side remained valid. The President was in a very awkward position and announced elections for a new Parliament in autumn 1993. He did so, though, only in a half-hearted way, in order to avoid elections against the will of Parliament. The Republics and the Federative Council were used to secure legitimacy for new elections as well as for a new constitution.

The territorial units upon which Yeltsin called could no longer be manipulated at will and it was not only the ethnic minorities who were active. It had also been foreseen that predominantly Russian territories such as Siberia and the Far East would develop a consciousness of their own. By mid-1993, there were 90 legal state-like entities within the Russian Federation, if we include Tatarstan and Chechnya, which had already declared their independence. Moscow and St Petersburg plus 67 regions and autonomous districts asked for autonomy. Theoreticians of Russian federalism would have preferred a federal state of 25 entities. But *homelandization* was progressive and overruled experiences with a working federalism. Russian federalism created an asymmetric system. No devolution scheme as in Britain or Spain was put into operation so the tendencies of equalization for the units prevailed.

Democratization and federalization have rarely been combined in a har-monious way. Federalism in Russia had various aspects: within the

Russian Federation, for example, the President tried to compensate democracy by granting more federalism. In relationship with other Republics of the former Soviet Union and within the Commonwealth of Independent States (CIS) Yeltsin tried increasingly to get rid of the rights of co-determination in the various republics. A CIS was possible only as a consensus of the elites. When Yeltsin had the consent of the presidents of the other Slavic Republics, he sometimes cut out reforms that had already been accepted by the Russian Parliament without consulting his Parliament again (Veen and Weilemann, 1993, p. 77). Parliaments of the CIS were normally reduced to ratifying agreements drafted by the heads of state. Confederalization within the CIS began to counterbalance federalization within the Russian federation.

By 1993, the Russian people were so tired of the constitutional conflicts that almost half of the citizens interviewed (47 per cent) were ready to leave the final decision to the constitutional committee. Only 15 per cent insisted on the Congress's prerogatives and 17 per cent wanted another institution to decide (RFE/RL, 1993, No. 29, p. 14). The President could deduce from this that a solution made by the government would be acceptable to the people.

The constitutional conflict was possible because no clear party structure prevailed in either Congress or the Supreme Soviet. One of Yeltsin's mistakes was that he started to co-operate with the Centrist camp too late. The great opportunist Chazbulatov used his capacity as a scholar most aptly to deduce his respective political line from scientific insights. In the discussion on the project of the constitution he described three systems (parliamentary, semi-presidential and presidential) without indicating a clear preference (Proekt konstitutsii, 1993, pp. 61ff.), but on other occasions he fought for his favourite type of 'government by assembly' as long as he was in charge as Chairman of Parliament.

The doctrine of *parliamentary sovereignty* was renewed and deduced from the 'depth of national psychology' (ibid., pp. 19ff.). He anticipated that two oppositions, on the Right and the Left, would strengthen the Centre. However, historical experience teaches that the Centre disintegrates in a severe conflict between two camps. Even Western commentators in this conflict were heavily biased towards Yeltsin's position. Grudgingly, they accepted all of the President's moves, although by December 1993 it was by no means clear that a fair and free climate for elections had been created in such a short time after the call for new elections. The bloody conquest of the 'White House' was also accepted by many of his supporters, although his initial strategy of 'wait and see' and wearing down the resistance of his enemies, such as Rutskoj and Chazbulatov, seemed preferable. Yeltsin came through victorious but it was a disastrous Pyrrhic victory, as a result of which he became hostage to the military and the federal units that had helped him.

The electoral campaign was short and unfair. The President changed the rules of the game several times. Distortions could not be excluded and rumours of irregular voting in distant districts have never been falsified. It was a little unnerving that the results from distant areas all passed through the President's office before being published. The quorum of 50 per cent for the constitution was doubtful even on the evening of election day. Electoral turnout was 55 per cent – a figure much doubted in Russia.

Yeltsin had changed certain articles of the constitution shortly before election day. Of those who went to the polls, 58 per cent accepted the constitution. This was hardly a referendum in favour of democracy because the figure included the votes of Zhirinovskij's followers. Zhirinovskij considered this constitution to be a good instrument for himself and recommended his group to vote 'yes'.

The election led to a stronger polarization of the blocs. The Centre was weaker than in the old Supreme Soviet. The three democratic lists had fragmented the potential for reforms. The group of Sobchak were only able to enter the Duma (the people's chamber) via direct mandates, similar to Volskij's Centrist group which remained below the 5 per cent threshold. The 'women' seemed to tip the balance, but it was uncertain whether they would vote with the opposition. There was no doubt: Yeltsin had not attained his most important goal of securing a majority for his reform government.

In many budding democracies there were two elements that prevented a high concentration of power, *federalism* and *judicial review*. Both elements were developed in Russia, but without truly moderating presidential power. The *federalism* of 89 territorial units contains very unequal 'states' and 'regions'. The division of competences in the constitution seems to be exhaustive, but the power of implementation and the distribution of finances – normally the key to a functioning federalism – was not sufficiently regulated. The subnational units remain dependent on the President. They have considerable autonomy in some areas, but they frequently use it not in the sense of German *Bundestreue* (loyalty to the federation) but for regional autarchy in the economy and for blocking the flow of market forces throughout the union. The second federal chamber has some powers, but it can hardly be used against the centre in favour of the periphery because too many governors are represented who depend on the president who appointed them.

The Constitutional Court was a cumbersome innovation in Russia and underwent several severe crises. The first crisis began in November 1991 and lasted until October 1993. The second stage began when a new court of nineteen (instead of thirteen) members in 1995 under Vladimir Tumanov began to consider concrete cases. The previous period under Valery Zorkin has been dubbed the 'romantic phase' when the separation of powers was taken literally. Some of its decisions, such as the compromise on the Communist Party, were considered as a wise decision to reconcile the two political camps (Nikitinsky, 1997, p. 84). The Court is an important element of symbolic politics on the road to a *Rechtsstaat* – but not yet the *pouvoir neutre* within the system.

CONDITIONS OF CONSOLIDATION IN RUSSIA

Economic prospects are dim in Russia. Some observers blame the failure of institution-building for this economic lag. The history of democratization of the Russian system, however, rather suggests that similar contradictions prevailed in both subsystems, the economic as well as the political one. During the three stages of transition, liberalization, democratization and consolidation in the first two periods did not achieve what one would be led to expect according to the sequence specified by Philippe Schmitter.

Liberalization took place under Gorbachev, but hardly contributed to a set of feasible institutions. *Democratization* took place under Yeltsin, but did not develop a system that would lay the fundaments for consolidation. *Consolidation* research has stressed four levels of consolidation:

- *Constitutional consolidation* at the polity level (constitutional order). This happened in the third and fourth wave of democratization rather quickly, even though sometimes 'finishing touches' to the constitution had been necessary (Portugal, Poland, not yet finished in Hungary).
- *Representative consolidation* at the level of parties and interest groups. The party systems were affected by long-lasting restructuring.
- *Behavioural consolidation* at the level of 'informal' actors, such as military, entrepreneurs or radical groups.
- The level of the *consolidation of civil society* usually takes a generation, as the second wave of democratization in the twentieth century has shown in Italy, Germany, Austria and Japan.

The checklist of consolidation should not be applied too literally to Russia.

1. Two elections have been held without violence from below. The

elections were seen by Western observers as not having been systematically manipulated. The elections were free, but the electoral battle was
largely unfair (Butenschön and Beichelt, 1996).

2. The *acceptance of a change of power* by the political parties and the
president has not yet been proved. *Alternation* – as in Bulgaria (1991,
1995), in Czechia (1998), in Slovakia (1998), in Hungary (1994, 1998), in
Romania (1996) – has not yet taken place. It was difficult enough to
convince Yeltsin that he should integrate a few ministers from the
Communist-Nationalist opposition in one of his cabinets.

3. *Volatility should normalize after the post-founding elections.* The Russian
system, however, has broken the impact of voting on the government on
three levels. Voter volatility in the elections of 1995 was high because
only four parties survived on the lists. But these figures are misleading
because so many independent candidates were directly elected. The
parallel (or segmented) system (the Germans call it *Grabensystem* because
there is a gap between two different types of deputies) tries a middle
road between proportional and plurality systems. It was considered as a
compromise with the old communist elites, which preferred the absolute
majority voting systems (as in Russia in March and April 1990). The
parallel system initially benefited, on balance, the new democratic forces.
The conservative groups (Communists, Agrarian and Nationalists)
remained underrepresented. The shortcomings of party consolidation
were, however, hardly a consequence of poor 'electoral engineering'
because the parties remained personalistic, clientelistic and did not really
develop into modern Parliament because the threshold, though they
received only 52.9 per cent of the votes on the lists. Almost half of the
votes for candidates on the lists were lost – not a very legitimizing result
(Nohlen and Kasapovic, 1996, p. 80). The direct mandates in the parallel
system even out these losses to a certain extent. Seven more parties
entered Parliament in addition to 94 independents.

When an electoral system is tested, three main requirements make up
the yardsticks:

- *representation* of groups and strata;
- *concentration* of parties;
- *participation* of electors.

Only the third function is fulfilled by the Russian system in a satisfactory way (Nohlen and Kasapovic, 1996, p. 188). Elections in Russia
so far did not determine the strength of the parliamentary groups. There

is a *high volatility of the elected* as well. Thirty-five party members are
needed to get assignment for committees and other privileges. In 1995,
only four parties qualified for the Duma privileges as a direct result of the
elections. One-hundred-and-forty-two Duma independent deputies and
members of eighteen minor groups were initially without recognition as
parties in Parliament. This led to a huge migration of deputies between
the parliamentary groups (Sobyanin, 1994; Ware, 1995). About one
hundred Duma deputies switched affiliations in the weeks between the
election and the inauguration of the new parliament. Only the democratic group Yabloko and the misnamed Right-wing extremist Liberal
Democrats under Zhirinovskij remained basically unchanged in their
size. The Communists lent deputies to their satellite groups, the Agrarians and the women – a kind of communist multi-party system
(Oleshchyk and Pavlenko, 1997, p. 16). Our Home Russia, as a government party, integrated 11 deputies. Two large groups, such as the
Russian Regions and Power to the People, were artificially created by
independents and small parties. An election that was formerly only
slightly democratic had thus quite different consequences (White *et al.*,
1997, p. 238f.). This powerlessness does not encourage professionalization of parliamentary work. Regulation of lobbying is incomplete. The
government does not introduce sufficient well-prepared bills as it does in
other consolidating semi-presidential systems (Ware, 1995, p. 273f.;
Hahn, 1996).

But there was less harm done than one could expect. The huge powers
of the President and the erosion of parliamentary legislation by presidential decrees gave Parliament and the voters much less power than
they should normally have.

4. *Large parties are hostile to the system.* The Russian case is unique. About
two-thirds of the Duma is hostile to the democratic government – as long
as it remains democratic. In the presidential elections in the first round of
1996, the two major hostile leaders received 32 per cent (Zyuganov,
Communist) and 5.7 per cent (Zhirinovsky, Liberal Democrat). If Lebed
(no party 14.5 per cent) had not been motivated to join the Yeltsin camp
temporarily, Yeltsin would hardly have been able to increase his share of
votes in the second round from 35.3 per cent to 53.8 per cent. Yeltsin was
able to organize his campaign as a referendum on Communism rather
than on his own record and was lucky enough to find with Zyuganov a
counter-candidate who misunderstood the political orientation of the
pool of 'new voters'. The Communists, however, have learned a lesson.
The Communist Party is still an anti-system party. Its political and
economic agenda are fundamentally at odds with the liberal blueprint

for marketization and democratization (Hashim, 1999, p. 87). When during the next presidential elections, probably in the year 2000, the charismatic Yeltsin effect can no longer be mobilized, the camp hostile to the democratic *facade democracy* may well get a majority. The end of post-communism has been predicted for the year 2000 (Pastukhov, 1998, p. 70).

5. There are *no consolidated parties*. Russia developed *parties without a system* because they have only an indirect impact on the government. The parties – with the exception of the Communists – have no stable member-ship, a weak organization, the tendency to develop a 'somebody-ism' instead of a programme. They are present only in big cities. They hardly penetrated the rural areas and the ethnic regions and republics (Ish-iyama, 1996, p. 410). *Factionalism* is developed to the extent that no stable units of parties can be traced. The necessary division of labour between interest groups and parties is hardly developed. Women and Agrarians served as satellites of the Communists – as in the old days when mass organizations performed their function of a 'conveyer organization' in a Popular Front-type of Communist organizations. *Coalition-building* capacity is not yet demanded because of the extensive powers of the President.

6. *A division of labour between parties and interest groups* is blurred by elite networks of the new nomenclature. On the one hand, the Communists – as in the old regime – strengthened themselves in parliamentary repre-sentation by co-operating with functional groups such as farmers and women's organizations. On the other hand, a new form of lobbyism has developed. There are few social organizations that try to lobby state agencies; rather, it is political actors in government and administrations that organize state lobbyism (Mögel and Schwanitz, 1996). Mafia net-works are frequently used as a link (Kravchenko, 1996).

Parties try to participate in the process of legislation, but most of the time they are outmanoeuvred by decrees of the President, which fre-quently serve the organized interests. There are three types of decrees that have been counted in 1994–6: in three years the President issued 953 normative, 2575 non-normative (law-implementing) and 1544 secret decrees (Parish, 1998, p. 119). In comparison, only 425 federal laws were promulgated. The decrees according to the constitution should not contradict federal laws (Art. 90,3) which, however, is quite frequently the case. In the war in Chechnya, for example, Yeltsin has not respected the article (88) that forces him to inform Parliament about emergency measures.

7. An important criterion for the consolidation on the level of parties, organized groups and elites is *democracy as the 'only game in town'* (Linz). It is quite amazing that the military so far has not tried to play another undemocratic game. Apparently the Communist tradition of the military recognizing the political leadership of the system is still strong in Russia – even when the lower echelons of the military are poorly paid or not paid at all. But even if no other game is played on the surface (after two coups have failed against Gorbachev and Yeltsin), other games work below the facade of democracy: Mafia elites blackmail the state, evade taxes (Table 11.1 shows that Russia has the lowest extractive capacity of all the states in the new East European democracies) and *state lobbyism* creates a kind of new confederation of elites. This is certainly also due to the incapacity of the political system to consolidate the legal system. We know from other mafia-type elites in history – from the Medici in Florence down to the rubber barons in the USA in the nineteenth century – that they want to become legal and honest entrepreneurs. But some Russian business elites have confessed that this is not yet possible in Russia because of the precarious legal system. The nomenclature elites have reproduced themselves even in the younger generation (Hanley, 1995, p. 668). Hardly any new social groups managed to get into the command positions.

The democratic process is undermined by bypassing the formal legal institutions of decision-making. The *new nomenclature* prefers to make the state's important political decisions in secret (Koshkarev and Narzikulov, 1998, p. 85). Some analysts, however, justify this practice because a more open procedure might undermine democracy still more. The 'come-back of the nomenclature' is said to have saved Russian society from a social cataclysm and facilitated the relatively smooth transition from state socialism to semi-democratic society (Lapina, 1996, p. 28).

Surveys in Russia do not show a deep internalization of democratic values (White *et al.*, 1997, p. 134). Only 8 per cent of Russians believe that they have more influence in the new regime. This is the lowest percentage for all the new democracies in Eastern Europe. Surveying public opinion in Russia is surveying a 'representation of formlessness', which changes from survey to survey (Alexander, 1997). The majority of citizens in Russia does not favour dictatorship but prefers 'a strong man' to lead the state and to restore 'law and order' (Preissler, 1997, p. 33). Democracy is more frequently associated with positive than with negative values. But it is still a problem for most Russian respondents in surveys on attitudes towards democracy that no politician – whether from the government side or the Nationalist or Communist opposition – has a statistically significant positive relationship with people's feelings that the country was on the road to democracy. There is a striking absence of leadership in Russia (Pammett, 1999, p. 59).

Russian government is still heavily involved in the economy and its social expenditures are still well above the average for transitional economies (Shevtsova and Bruckner, 1997, p. 17). The government remains oversized. The National Security Council is hard to control and has been compared to the old Politburo. Civil society is still under-developed. The acceptance of democracy is not guided by the concept of participatory democracy (Kreikemeyer, 1998, p. 316).

Consolidology developed many concepts of imperfect democracy that contain elements of truth for Russia: *delegated democracy* (O'Donnell), *uncertain democracy by default* (Whitehead), *defective democracies* (Merkel) which are characterized by a fairly satisfactory process of democratic participation but a defective *Rechtsstaat*. Russia, however, developed a deficiency on the level of efficacy which has been dubbed *anocracy* (Ted Gurr) – a mixture of autocracy and anarchy that is unique in Eastern Europe.

FURTHER READING

The following books cover many of the topics addressed in this chapter:

Barner-Barry, Carol and Cynthia A. Hody (eds) (1995) *The Politics of Change: The Transformation of the Former Soviet Union*. New York: St Martin's Press.

Bower, Mike and Cameron Ross (eds) (2000) *Russia after the Cold War*. London and New York: Longman.

Colton, Timothy J. and Robert C. Tucker (eds) (1995) *Patterns in Post-Soviet Leadership*. Boulder: Westview Press.

Eckstein, Harry *et al.* (1998) *Can Democracy Take Root in Post-Soviet Russia? Explorations in State-Society Relations*. Lanham: Rowan & Littlefield Publishers.

Holmes, Leslie (1997) *Post-Communism: An Introduction*. Cambridge: Polity Press.

Lane, David (ed.) (1995) *Russia in Transition: Politics, Privatisation and Inequality*. London: Longman.

Lane, David (1999) *Transition from Communism to Capitalism*. Basingstoke: Macmillan.

Lapidus, Gail W. (ed.) (1995) *The New Russia: Troubled Transformation*. Boulder: Westview Press.

Kirkov, Peter (1998) *Russia's Provinces: Authoritarian Transformation versus Local Autonomy?* Basingstoke: Macmillan.

Nagy, P.M. (2000) *The Meltdown of the Russian State: The Deformation and Collapse of the State in Russia*. Cheltenham: Edward Elgar.

BIBLIOGRAPHY

Alexander, James (1997) Surveying Attitudes in Russia: a Representation of the Formlessness, *Communist and Post-Communist Studies* 30, 107–27.

Aslund, Anders (1995) *How Russia Became a Market Economy*. Washington: Brookings.

Beichelt, Timm (1997) Nochmals zu den Wahlen in Rußland. Waren sie demokratisch? *Osteuropa* 47, 116–28.

Bell, Claudia (1997) *Der fiskalische Föderalismus in der Russländischen Föderation*. Baden-Baden: Nomos.

Butenschön, Marianna and Beichelt, Timm (1996) 'Frei gewählt, aber unfair gekämpft'. Wahlbeobachtung in Wologda, *Osteuropa* 46, 483–6.

DIW *et al.* (1997) Wirtschaftslage and Reformprozesse in Mittel- und Osteuropa. Bonn: BMW.

Filippov, Mikhail and Shvetsova, Olga (1999) Asymmetric Bilateral Bargaining in the New Russian Federation, *Communist and Post-Communist Studies* 32, 61–76.

Gnauck, Gerhard (1997) *Parteien und Nationalismus in Russland*. Frankfurt: Lang.

Hahn, Jeffrey W. (ed.) (1996) *Democratization in Russia: The Development of Legislative Institution*. London: Sharpe.

Hanley, Eric (1995) Russia – Old Wine in a New Bottle? The Circulation and Reproduction of Russian Elites, 1983–1993, *Theory and Society* 24, 639–68.

Hashim, Syed Mohsin (1999) KPRF Ideology and its Implications for Democratization in Russia, *Communist and Post-Communist Studies* 32, 77–89.

Ishiyama, John T. (1996) The Russian Proto-Parties and the National Republics, *Communist and Post-Communist Studies* 29, 395–411.

Koshkarev, Tatiana/Narzikulov, Rustam (1998) Administrative Chaos and the Nomenklatura's Revenge, *East-European Constitutional Review* 7, 84–8.

Kravchenko, A.J. (1996) Lobbizm vo Rossii: etapy bol'shogo puti, *Socis* 4, 3–11.

Kreikemeyer, Anna and Zagorsky, Andrey V. (1997) *Russlands Politik in bewaffneten Konflikten in der GUS*. Baden-Baden: Nomos.

Kreikemeyer, Anna (1998) *Friedensfähiges Rußland? Die Transformation Rußlands und seine Rolle im gesateuropäischen Kooperations- und Integrationsprozeß aus der Sicht der politischen Theorie des Friedens*. Hamburg: Ad Fontes Verlag.

Lapina, Natalia (1996) *Die Formierung einer neuen russländischen Elite*. Cologne: Berichte des Bundesinstituts für ostwissenschaftliche und internationale Studien, vol. 7.

Matthews, Merwyn (1986) *Privilege in the Soviet Union*. London: Allen & Unwin.

Mick, Christoph (1994) Probleme des Föderalismus in Rußland, *Osteuropa* 44, 611–29.

Mögel, Nicola A. and Schwanitz, Simone (1996) Staatslobbyismus – eine Form der Interessenvertretung in Rußland, *Osteuropa* 46, 987–1004.

Müller, Klaus (ed.) (1998) *Postsozialistische Krisen*. Opladen: Leske & Budrich.

Nikitinsky, Leonid (1997) Interview with Boris Ebzeev, Justice of the Constitutional Court of the Russian Federation, *East European Constitutional Review* 6, 83–8.

Nohlen, Dieter and Kasapovic, Mirjana (1996) *Wahlsysteme und Systemwechsel in Osteuropa*. Opladen: Leske & Budrich.

OECD (1997) *Economic Surveys: Russian Federation*. Paris: OECD.

Oleshchyk, V.A. and Pavlenko, V.B. (1997) *Politicheskaya Rossia god 1997: Partii, bloki, lidery*. Movsow: Izdatelstvo Moskva.

Ordeshook, Peter C. and Shevtsova, Olga (1997) Federalism and Constitutional Design, *Journal of Democracy* 8, 27–42.

Pammett, Jon H. (1999) Elections and Democracy in Russia, *Communist and Post-Communist Studies* 32, 45–60.

Parish, Scott (1998) Presidential Decree Authority in the First and Second Russian Republics 1991–1996. In Shugart, Matthew and Carey, Hohn (eds), *Executive Decree Authority*. Cambridge: Cambridge University Press.

Pastukhov, Vladimir (1998) The End of Postcommunism: Perspectives on Russian Reformers, *East European Constitutional Review* 7, 64–70.

Preissler, Franz (1997) *Demokratische und autoritäre Einstellungen in der russländischen Gesellschaft: Eine Studie zur politischen Kultur*. Mannheim: FKKS 14.

Przeworski, Adam (1991) *Democracy and the Market*. Cambridge: Cambridge University Press.

Remington, Thomas F. *et al.* (1994) Transitional Institutions and Parliamentary Alignments in Russia 1990–1993. In Remington, Thomas F. (ed.), *Parliaments in Transition*. Boulder: Westview, pp. 159–80.

Rzhanitsyna, D.S. and Sergeeva, S.P. (1995) Zhenshchiny na rosslyskom rynke truda, *Socis* 7, 57–62.

Schleifer, Andrei and Treisman, Daniel (1998) *The Economics and Politics of Transition to an Open Market Economy*. Paris: OECD.

Shevtsova, Lilia and Bruckner, Scott A. (1997) Where Is Russia Headed? Toward Stability or Crisis?, *Journal of Democracy* 8, 12–26.

Sillaste, G.G. (1994) Sotsiogendernye otnosheniya v period sotsial'noy transformatsii Rossii, *Socis* 3, 15–22.

Sobyanin, Alexander (1994) Political Cleavages among Russian Deputies. In Remington, Thomas F. (ed.), *Parliaments in Transition*. Boulder: Westview, pp. 181–215.

Solnik, Steven (1998) Explaining the Failure of Liberal Statebuilding. Russia over the Edge, *East European Constitutional Review* 7, 70–2.

Solzhenitsyn, Alexander (1998) *Rossiya v obvale*. Moscow: Russiky put'.

veen, Hans-Joachim and Weilemann, Peter (Hrsg.) (1993) *Rußland auf dem Weg zur Demokratie?: Politik und Parteien in der Russischen Föderation*. Paderborn; München u.a.: Schöningh.

von Beyme, Klaus (1996) *Transition to Democracy in Eastern Europe*. Basingstoke: Macmillan.

von Beyme, Klaus (1998) *Reformpolitik und sozialer Wandel in der Sowjetunion (1970–1988)*. Baden-Baden: Nomos.

Voz'mitel', A.A. (1994) Sotsial'nye tipy fermerov i tendentsii razvitiya fermer-skogo dvizehniya, *Socis* 10, 43–50.

Ware, Richard (1995) Transferability of Parliamentary Experience: The Russian Example, *Journal of Legislative Studies* 1, 264–82.

White, Stephen *et al.* (1997) *How Russia Votes*. Chatham: Chatham House.

Wishnevsky, Julia (1995) Russian Constitutional Court: A third branch of Government? *East European Constitutional Review*, 2(7), 1–12.

World Bank (1999) *World Economic Outlook*. Washington: International Monetary Fund.

Yavlinsky, G.A. (1997) Where Is Russia Headed? An Uncertain Prognosis, *Journal of Democracy* 8, 3–11.

Zdravommyslova, Olga (1996) Die Privatisierung des Lebensstils in Rußland. In Glatzer, Wolfgang (ed.), *Lebensverhältnisse in Osteuropa*. Frankfurt: Campus, pp. 55–66.

Zecchini, Salvatore (ed.) (1997) *Lessons from the Economic Transition: Central Eastern Europe in the 1990s*. Paris: OECD.

CHAPTER 12

DEMOCRACY AND CIVIL SOCIETY IN CENTRAL AND EASTERN EUROPE

Mary Kaldor and Zdenek Kavan

It is often stated that the 1989 revolutions contained no new ideas. For instance, the French historian Francois Furet wrote: 'With all the fuss and noise not a single new idea has come out of Eastern Europe in 1989' (quoted in Dahrendorf, 1990, p. 23). Timothy Garton Ash, in his eyewitness account of the 1989 revolutions, said much the same thing. 'The ideas whose time has come are old and familiar ones. (It is the new ideas whose time has passed.)' (Garton Ash, 1999, p. 154). And Jürgen Habermas noted 'a peculiar characteristic of this revolution, namely its total lack of ideas that are either innovative or oriented towards the future' (quoted in Halliday, 1999, p. 53). The stated general aims of most of the postcommunist regimes in this region – the establishment of a free market economy and of democracy and return to Europe – tended to strengthen this assumption as they were largely interpreted in the West as indicating that these countries had embarked on the path of transforming themselves into Western-type societies – a process that would require these countries to learn from the West and to adopt Western institutions and practices. Most of the Western assistance was indeed geared towards this outcome and the process of enlargement of Western institutions to accommodate new members from the Eastern part of Europe was perceived largely as a process of change in the East and not as requiring any fundamental reconsideration of Western institutions and practices.

This chapter starts with a different assumption. The variety of ideas that emerged from the Central European dissident movements in the 1970s and 1980s and that had been developed in a dialogue with Western social movements had a significant impact not just on the postcommunist transformation in these countries but also on the thinking among social movements and non-governmental institutions (NGOs) elsewhere and have contemporary relevance. These ideas centred on a new understanding of citizenship and civil society, on transnationalism or internationalism at the level of society, and on the coming together of peace and human rights. It is worth noting that in the postscript to the new tenth anniversary edition of his book *We the People*, Timothy Garton

Ash somewhat revises his opinion as to whether there were new ideas. What was new, he now says, was the method – the non-violence, the self-organization, the readiness to compromise – the 'how' and not the 'what' of the revolution. But, as we shall argue, the 'how' is a crucial component of new ways of thinking about politics in our contemporary situation.

The reconstructed concept of civil society and the related conceptualization concerning 'anti-political politics' was central to the way that democracy and democratization were conceived at this time. It is also apparent, however, that these ideas and practices, influenced as they were by the particular circumstances of the advanced 'actually existing socialism', contained a number of weaknesses that became manifest when confronted with the forces of neoliberalism, which temporarily came to dominate after the 1989 revolutions. In this chapter, we shall concentrate on analysing the relationship between civil society and democracy, in both theory and practice, in the Central and Eastern European area and draw some conclusions as to the relevance of these ideas and practices for contemporary politics in Europe.

One further preliminary remark is warranted. In most accounts of the 1989 revolutions rather little attention is paid to agency. Most explanations focus on the economic and moral bankruptcy of the communist regimes and the coming to power of Gorbachev, sometimes the effect of Reagan's nuclear policies is also included as an explanation. Undoubtedly, these factors were important. But the first factor, the economic situation, is insufficient as an explanation; it explains the context but not why the revolutions happened. And while the role of individuals in history can be important, no single individual can bear the weight of the 1989 revolutions. Hence, in this chapter, we pay particular attention to agency – the actions and thinking of the actors who actually carried out the revolutions in the period immediately preceding 1989. Finally, particular attention will be paid to Central Europe and to Czechoslovakia and its successor states especially as an analysis of democratic transition in those postcommunist countries most suited to this process would reveal the complexities and difficulties involved in postcommunist democratization most clearly.

IDEAS AND PRACTICES BEFORE 1989

In Central and Eastern Europe, ideas about the crucial importance of citizenship and of civil society for the development and maintenance of democracy, emerged from the dissident movements, but have their antecedents in the reform movement in the 1960s. The origins of the reform movement in the 1960s lay in the failure of the centralized systems to modernize the economy and to deal with the effects of the scientific and technological revolution and, in particular, to deal with the fast developing information technology (Richta, 1969). Some critiques went beyond the economy and addressed the question of state power, the tendency of any system of political power towards corruption and of the individual's civic responsibility to stem this process. For instance, L. Vaculik argued at the Czechoslovak Writers Congress in 1967 that in totalitarian systems where the power of the regime remains unchecked, citizenship is non-existent and the system breeds fear, political apathy and dependence on ever more corrupt political leadership. The reconstitution of real citizenship is, therefore, vital. Such ideas found their way into the reform programme in Czechoslovakia in 1968, which promised to revitalize the elective organs of the state and guarantee a full range of human rights to facilitate full participation of citizens in a genuine and pluralistic public sphere – pluralistic at least in the sense of facilitating and tolerating a multiplicity of competing ideas and interests.

As a result of the Soviet military intervention, the failure of these reforms ushered in a period of a deeply conservative anti-reformist purge of all social, political and economic institutions. Conservatism became the dominant force in most of the communist regimes and radical reform was off the agenda (with the exception of Poland during the *Solidarity* period). The communist regimes became more and more empty of any real ideological content and their efforts to appease their disgruntled populations took the form of a peculiar social contract where, in exchange for their political passivity and apathy and expressions of conformity symbolized by ritualistic affirmations of faith in the system and all its works, people were promised work security, bearable standards of living and relative non-interference in their private sphere. For the majority of the population this led to a kind of inner immigration into the sphere of privacy and domesticity, a sphere devoid of any traces of real citizenship.

The Soviet invasion of Czechoslovakia in 1968 dealt a deathblow to the hopes of reforming communism – hopes harboured until then by many socialists in both East and West. It was an 'existential shock', as the East German writer Christa Wolf was later to say ('Flesh Ties', *New Statesman*, 23 February 1990). And Leszek Kolakowski, the Polish philosopher and commentator on Marxism, wrote that communism 'ceased to be an intellectual problem, and became merely a question of power' (quoted in Crampton, 1994, p. 341). Both the invasion and the subsequent 'normalization' meant that the main form of opposition in most of the communist countries was no longer radical reformism but individual dissent. Most dissidents saw themselves not as precursors of a political movement but as individuals who wanted to retain their personal integrity. Dissidence was about the dignity of the individual as much as about politics.

The dissent that emerged in these circumstances was heterogeneous but relatively small in size. International developments such as the Helsinki Accords of 1975 provided some stimulus. The initial reaction in East European opposition circles was negative. Western leaders were seen to be embracing Soviet leaders, and the commitment to human rights was thought to be purely cosmetic since the communist regimes developed 'thousands of artfully contrived methods for skirting human rights obligations'. However, Helsinki did have a positive effect in that by 'confirming the outcome of World War II [it] served to rid the Soviet Union of its old obsession about external threats, and this subsequently had a positive effect on its attitude to detente' (Simecka, 1989, p. 363). The human rights part of the Accord did also provide a legitimate framework for making civic demands upon the government and did provide a common ground for agreement among the politically disparate groups of dissidents.

'Anti-political politics' became the somewhat loose label that applied to a range of ideas that emerged in the 1970s from Central Europe and found their best known expression in the work of Adam Michnik in Poland, Gyorgy Konrad in Hungary and Vaclav Havel in Czechoslovakia. There were some important differences between them at least partly due to the differences between the countries concerned. In Hungary, for instance, where reformism from above persisted in some form or other until 1989, Konrad developed a concept of anti-politics that was less concerned with developing a 'parallel polis', a community of truth, than with ways of exercising control over politicians and the state. Thus he considered anti-politics to be the 'rejection of the power monopoly of the political class and if the political opposition comes to power, anti-politics keeps at the same distance from, and shows the same independence of the new government' (Konrad, 1984). Some tension between the state, which tends to be expansionist in its activities, and society is presupposed and the task of anti-political politics is to keep the state to what it should do. For Michnik, the Polish experience of 1956 and the Czechoslovak experience of 1968 indicated that change (reform) was possible but that it was fragile and had its limits: the ruthlessness of the repression suggested that revolutionary change was not possible. Thus 'an unceasing struggle for reform and evolution that seeks an expansion of civil liberties and human rights is the only course East European dissidents can take. The Polish example demonstrated that real concessions can be won by applying steady public pressure on the government' (Michnik, 1985). Through self-organization it was possible to create autonomous spaces in society up to the limits imposed by the 'Brezhnev doctrine' – the threat of Soviet intervention. Michnik thus rediscovered the term 'civil society'. But he used it in a new way, not merely as denoting a rule of law and the institutions to check the abuses of power by the state, but placing the emphasis on self-organization, autonomy, solidarity and non-violence. Of course, nothing is really new; Michnik's concept of civil society was probably closest to that of De Tocqueville. Nevertheless, in the context of the overbearing state and the emergence of new groups and movements, the term had an entirely new resonance, as a political aspiration and technique and not just as an analytical tool.

Havel's conceptualization, influenced by the harsh forms of Czech normalization, involved an acute analysis of power in late communist society. It recognized that power was not entirely monopolized by the government and that the governed were not entirely powerless. In such a society, Havel argued, everybody tended to be implicated in the process of reproducing power and power relations. By participating in the ritualized acts of obeisance, people helped to reinforce the rules of the game and to create pressure on everybody else similarly to conform. This process was, of course, reinforced by threats, although these remained relatively low-level ones. In Havel's view the main function of Charter 77, the Czech dissident organization formed in the aftermath of the Helsinki Accord for the purpose of human rights advocacy, was thus to break the game by showing that compliance in this game is not necessary and that one does not have to live a lie (participate in something one does not believe in). Living in truth in this sense is not an epistemological position but a refusal to participate in the game that is designed to reinforce the regime. Chartists could thus serve as moral examples to the rest of society. Not only did they reveal that alternatives were possible, but they generated, in fact, some sense of obligation for the rest to accept responsibility for their actions and their consequences (Havel *et al.*, 1985). It is noteworthy that this proposition to moral leadership was criticized by some, particularly on the Left. The other aspects of Havel's position generated greater agreement. Although he formulated a critique of politics in general, he was fundamentally concerned with post-totalitarian society. The idea of pushing back the state into much narrower spheres than those occupied by the communist state was shared by all the Czech dissidents. This required the establishment of a proper public sphere in which individuals acted as citizens rather than as servants of the regime. Civil society based on a variety of civic initiatives and actions is such a public sphere in which solidarity is created and a sense of real community arises. The 'parallel polis' is the emergent civil society in the post-totalitarian states. This civil society is non-political only in the narrow sense that it does not involve competition for political power.

This encouragement of civic initiatives, activities and solidarity had an international dimension, too. The Chartists recognized that domestic repression had an international aspect as it was based on frequent consultations and common action of European communist regimes to suppress particularly unwanted developments in any one country of the Eastern Bloc. The Chartists asserted, therefore, that co-operation across the frontiers in the region was the best defence for the civic and human rights movement. A dialogue was also opened with the Western peace movement. Civic rapprochement across the East–West divide required a common struggle for the development of such public spaces in the East that were already available in the democratic West as a matter of course. Accordingly, the struggle for human rights had to be placed at the centre of the agenda. Furthermore, it was considered essential that the Western movements should recognize that a struggle for peace in Europe required a struggle for democracy throughout the whole of Europe. The extent of the ensuing co-operation should not be overstated. Not all Western peace campaigners came to support this position and a number of Eastern dissidents remained suspicious of the peace movement as being insufficiently anti-Soviet. Nevertheless, arguably, this collaboration generated the seeds of a more genuinely pan-European transnational civil society.

These ideas reflected a new reality in Central Europe – the emergence of social movements and citizens groups. The best known were Charter 77 in Czechoslovakia and Solidarity in Poland; but there was also Swords into Ploughshares in the GDR and the Dialogue Group, a young people's peace group in Hungary. Some opposition to the regimes also came from the emergent Green movement. Given the scale of the ecological disaster in the area, it is, in fact, not surprising that a number of Green groups emerged in the early 1980s. There were also some elements of counter-culture that began to emerge among the young that generated some forms of civic activism. In the late 1980s, a second generation of groups developed. These included Frieden und Menschenrechte ('Peace and Human Rights') in the GDR, Wolnosc I Pokoj ('Freedom and Peace') in Poland, several small peace groups in Czechoslovakia such as the Independent Peace Association or the John Lennon Society, and the Danube Circle and FIDESZ (the young democrats) in Hungary. The spread of these groups, however small, helped to undermine the regimes. The regimes depended on total control, but small autonomous spaces were multiplying in civil society. These groups helped to organize the mass demonstrations and participated in several countries, along with the earlier generation, in the Round Table talks.

As the 1989 revolutions brought dissidents, at least temporarily, to power it is worth at this stage to identify some of the weaknesses of their position. The first and most obvious one is that, with the exception of Poland during the Solidarity years, the dissident movement remained relatively small and communicatively isolated from the rest of society. Even in Poland the mass participation in Solidarity was of a relatively short duration and did not quite succeed in inculcating new patterns of civic behaviour among the majority of the population. The revolutions themselves were, with the exception of Romania, non-violent and relatively brief and the end of the communist era tended to be negotiated between the respective sets of elites (communist and dissident). Hence, even though there was mass participation in the revolutions themselves (such as demonstrations), there was insufficient experience with the involvement in the public political sphere. The political apathy inculcated in the people in the decades of communist rule could not be entirely swept aside in one fell swoop of the revolution. This suggests that it was going to be difficult to develop a firmly rooted civil society. Secondly, as was to be expected, the dissidents were concerned with ways to constrain state power and thus remained largely focused on the political sphere. They did not develop a clear and coherent position on the political economy. As we shall show below, this proved to be a fatal weakness in the conflict with the economic neoliberals. The opposition to the state also tended to lead to the formulation of civil society as being in opposition to the state. While this would largely have been the case in the late communist regimes, it proved to be a simplification and not entirely practicable under postcommunism.

DEMOCRACY AND CIVIL SOCIETY UNDER POSTCOMMUNISM

The weaknesses cited above quickly became apparent after the revolutions. In Czechoslovakia, the formation of the mass organization of citizens – the Civic Forum – and its victory in the first elections in 1990 was greeted by the new foreign minister as indicating that civil society was now in power. This optimistic view clearly neglected the problem of how civil society becomes firmly established and how it can cope with the emerging plurality of interests. It should be contrasted with the very much more pessimistic view of Ralf Dahrendorf who estimated that the process of developing a democratic civil society would involve such profound cultural and social psychological changes that it would take generations.

The process of establishing democracy in the region had to face a number of difficulties. The process of democratization was just one of a multiplicity of processes of radical change to which these societies were being subjected. The interconnectedness of these changes placed extra strains on these societies' capacity to develop democratic frameworks. The demise of communism also created an ideological vacuum that, in some places more than in others, led to the revival of nationalism and to some difficulties in developing a non-discriminatory civic basis for democracy. A further obstacle was the lack of democratic traditions, and particularly the relative lack of experience with democratic practice, coupled with the historically strongly developed 'etatist' tradition. Furthermore, the cultural traditions in the region were authoritarian. Deference to the authority of office, and particularly to the authority of hierarchically constructed knowledge, was not conducive to the construction of an open public discourse, which depends on a degree of tolerance of diversity and the acceptance of the possibility that one's own position is wrong. Last but not least, these societies faced a major difficulty in coming to terms with their past and achieving a rational synthesis of demands for the preservation and publication of memory with justice and fairness. The quasi-judicial procedure entailed in the lustration process served neither purpose well as it involved a very inadequate form of selection and legitimation of data as well as violating some of the principles of natural justice. Crucially, however, the process with its relatively narrow identification of the 'guilty men' allowed the rest to avoid facing their own responsibility for the deeds of the previous regime.

All of these obstacles help to explain the slow process towards democratization. But another factor was also important – something that is also experienced in the West and South. The demise of communism marked the opening up of these countries to the process known as globalization. The democratic revolutions occurred at the very moment when the autonomy of the state was being undermined by integration into the world economy. Thus democratic choices that could now be made were, at one and the same time, being constrained by limits on the state's freedom of manoeuvre, especially in the realm of economic strategy.

The debate about economic strategy in the aftermath of 1989 rapidly crystallized into a confrontation between the radical position demanding swift liberalization and privatization and the position arguing for a more gradual approach, the latter being favoured by the majority among the former dissidents. The radical position adopted by the neoliberals had a profound impact on the strategy of political change and on the position taken by governments towards the development of civil society. Its consequences in Czechoslovakia were a loss of power by the former dissidents and their replacement by younger professionals. The crucial and possibly somewhat paradoxical aspect of the neoliberal position – given that the neoliberals argued for the need to push the state out of any significant involvement in the economy – was the stress put on maintaining a strong and highly centralized state. The requirement of speed and the sweeping nature of the changes that these radical economic policies were to bring about required in their view that, at least for the time being, the government's ability to introduce and fully implement such changes was not to be compromised by any form of political decentralization. This included any form of empowerment of civil society with its potential to voice conflicting demands and interests necessitating discussion and compromise. The political transformation, according to the neoliberals, was to follow the well-tested experience of the West and was to be based on the establishment of a pluralistic party political system. The parties themselves would not be real sites of discussion and compromise, but merely instruments for the conquest of power by a small group of party leaders. Citizens' participation would be largely fulfilled by their periodic participation in elections. The idea of active citizenship and of civic initiatives was considered virtually synonymous with irrational meddling. The different positions on citizenship taken by the neoliberals and representatives of the civic position were well illustrated by the public debate between Havel and Klaus in the Czech Republic in 1994 in which Klaus made it clear that he viewed the citizen as a free individual who enjoys certain rights and Havel argued that the citizen should also be actively involved in communal life.

The neoliberal position was strengthened by the support it received from authoritative Western institutions such as the IMF and from the way it could claim to occupy the grounds of economic orthodoxy, going, in fact, as far as accusing their opponents of lack of professionalism. These economists even utilized their non-involvement in the dissident movements to their advantage by stressing that their professionalism was enhanced by remaining in their jobs as experts unlike the dissidents who, in their view, had become deskilled during their years in opposition. In Czechoslovakia, the political position of the neoliberals was strengthened by the support from the majority of the new arrivals on the active political scene who saw the old dissidents as obstacles to their ambitions and who attempted to enhance their positions by adopting rather crude forms of Manichean anticommunism which implied that any nuanced position was socialist or even communist in reality. This

simplification of the public discourse, symbolized by the adoption of
new laws on lustration – the purging of public institutions – and
criminalization of the previous communist regime was not conducive to
the development of a democratic, non-authoritarian political culture.

The challenge to the emergent civil society and to civil society ideas
came not only from the neoliberals but also from the reformed communists and nationalists. Regimes dominated by leaders such as Iliescu in
Romania, Lukashenko in Byelorussia, Meciar in Slovakia and the Milo-
sevic regime in Yugoslavia, displayed hostility towards civil society,
although for reasons somewhat different from those of the neoliberals.
These were largely quite authoritarian regimes, which utilized forms of
populism, including the manipulation of nationalist feelings, to create
and maintain clientelistic regimes with strong centralized control. They
perceived civil society as a threat to their positions and tried their best, if
not to suppress it then at least to hinder its development.

We should note that the postcommunist developments in the region
could in some ways be seen as the final triumph of nationalism. The
multiethnic states disintegrated either violently or peacefully and this
could not but imply that, after the demise of communism, nationalism
was the most potent ideological force in the area. This makes the position
that stresses the civic as against the ethnic principle more difficult to
prevail. This can be demonstrated by analysing the constitutions of the
new states where references to the civic principle are severely compromised by an ethnic approach to citizenship or the question of official
language (Czech Republic, Slovakia, Estonia). Furthermore, the problem
of minorities has not been successfully resolved in this area and, as the
treatment of the Roma minorities indicates, racism has not been eradi-
cated in Central Eastern European cultures. The attempt to build a wall
separating the Roma from the Czech community in a north Bohemian
town in 1999 illustrates the acute nature of the problem.

Those who favoured radical market reforms saw themselves as democrats. But democracy was conceived as a formal set of values, a method of
selecting and legitimizing rulers who could implement what were considered to be necessary economic reforms. In all the postcommunist
Central and East European countries outside of the former Commonwealth of Independent States (CIS) impressive strides have been made in
developing the institutions and rules of formal democracy – pluralistic
party political systems have been developed, new constitutions including bills of rights have been passed, the military and security services
have been brought under civilian control, the judiciary and the media are
independent of government control, and elections are free and fair (see
Kaldor and Vejvoda, 1999).

For this democracy to become rooted and habitual in the postcommunist cultures democratic habits and frames of mind needed to be
developed. A well-functioning civil society is indispensable to that
project. If the process of globalization constrains the autonomy of states,
it also helps to open up autonomous spaces in society, even in the most
authoritarian regimes. Closed societies are no longer possible. Practically
all these countries experienced a significant growth of the 'third' or non-
profit-making sector with a considerable annual increase in the number
of NGOs. The social movement development seems less impressive, but
even here we see the appearance of some new movements (women/
feminism) and some growth in others (Greens). The growth of this sector
has to do with a number of factors some of which are specific to the
countries concerned, but some of it has to do with the support that the
development of civil society, and particularly its organized aspects
(NGOs), have received from Western public institutions (the EU PHARE
programme, for instance) and private foundations (George Soros, for
instance).

The nature of civil society and its impact on the development of
democracy varies considerably in the area. It could, for instance, be
argued that the development of civil society has been a greater success in
some of the countries with a noticeable democratic deficit than in some of
the less problematic ones. It could certainly be argued that the well-
organized Slovak 'third' sector was quite instrumental in bringing about
the end of the Meciar regime in Slovakia, being more politically effective
than the bickering and disunited political opposition. Similar claims can
be made about the Romanian 'third' sector and the outcome of the 1996
elections there. In Slovakia, in particular, the organizational 'know how'
and close co-operation with the 'third' sector was, paradoxically, facilitated by the efforts of the Meciar government to deprive this sector of its
autonomy. It seems clear that particularly in the advocacy-oriented
organizations, the central purpose of which is the public advocacy of
particular values, ideas and policies, participants do not just facilitate the
transfer of democratic values and ideas such as those of human rights to
the rest of the population through overt public education campaigns but
they themselves learn the nature of democratic civic practice, the value of
reflexive discourse, of negotiation and of co-operation. It is interesting to
note in this context that both in Romania and in Slovakia the hardcore
'third' sector activists came to be associated with a number of NGOs
widening the network of organizations and spreading organizational
'know how'. The capacity of such advocacy organizations as the Pro
Democracy Association in Romania to recruit supporters and volunteers
further facilitates the spread of democratic 'know how' (6000 volunteers

were recruited for its monitoring of elections in 1996, for example). The primary goal of this organization is citizens' participation in public affairs, and for this purpose the association has engaged in numerous activities and projects involving public education such as publication of information and educational materials, and organization of public debates, colloquia and meetings. The association also monitors government activities and lobbies for change of legislation particularly in the human rights area. A good example of an advocacy NGO in Slovakia is SKOI (Permanent Civic Institute Conference). This Civic Institute had its roots in the original civic organization in Slovakia in 1989, Public Against Violence, and had some links with the parliamentary democratic opposition, particularly the Democratic Party, the Christian Democratic Movement and the Hungarian Independent Initiative. Their project was fully focused on the weakest aspects of Slovak democracy – lack of public awareness, political apathy and even cynicism, deficits in democratic practice, racism and, particularly, culturally inherited antisemitism. One of their core projects aimed at establishing democratic civic clubs holding regular meetings in most of the urban centres. They have surpassed the 20 towns they have specified in the project and have already established 50 of them. In each of these places, local activists are responsible for the organization of meetings on important aspects of civic culture and human rights with well-known persons and experts. Attendances have varied so far between 30 and 400. The attendance of these meetings has increased markedly after the abortive referendum in 1997 which clearly made people angry. Another successful NGO of this type in Slovakia is the Milan Simecka Foundation. This foundation was established in 1991 as a Czechoslovak foundation by people from the Civic Forum in the Czech part of the Federal Republic and from People Against Violence in Slovakia. This is a civic advocacy group mostly involved in various projects of civil education particularly in the human rights area. Though they were not associated with any political party this was one of the foundations treated with the greatest animosity by the Meciar government due to its standing, particularly among the urban elites, and its independence. It has to be said that most of the founders and members of the board of directors were known for their opposition to this government (Kaldor *et al.*, 1997).

Somewhat more problematic is the development of professionalization in this sector and the shift of emphasis from social movements to NGOs. On the one hand, professionalization increases the effectiveness of the organization in some areas of its activities and is a prerequisite for its autonomy, but it can also detract from the voluntaristic, civic initiative-based side of its work, on the other. The more the organization begins to resemble a commercial organization and is driven by considerations of effectiveness as against public spiritedness, the less obvious is the democratic benefit. This leads to another problematic issue. In a number of the postcommunist states and particularly the poorer ones in which the state's provision of welfare has declined, there has been a significant increase in service-providing organizations in this sector – according to some of the latest statistics, the majority of NGOs in Russia and a significant proportion of NGOs in Bulgaria are service providers. According to a recent report on the 'third' sector in Russia, 30 per cent of the Russian NGOs provide social services, 24 per cent provide self-help, 10 per cent law consultancy and 5 per cent education (Mersijanova, 1999). In Bulgaria, 18 per cent provide cultural and recreational facilities, 17 per cent education and science, 7 per cent health services, 8 per cent housing services, 8 per cent legal assistance and 4 per cent social assistance. There is little doubt that these organizations perform sterling and much-needed work, but the question is whether this might not further encourage the process of transfer of responsibility for welfare from the state, and thus in some ways from society as a whole to a voluntary provision partly financed by the private sector. Ferenc Mislivetz describes this process somewhat sadly in the following terms:

> A new world was created by the middle of the 1990s: the world of professional NGOs, civil organizations and foundations. Most of these NGOs take over some of the responsibilities of the state, and they do not have particularly warm feelings about the civil ethos or new forms of cooperation. Those civil organizations, however, who carry out their work in the fields of human rights, minority questions, education, culture and the protection of the environment, have every right to regard themselves as institutions of civil society. (Mislivetz, 1999, p. 229)

This implies a conceptualization of civil society as a public sphere of civility located between the state, the family and the market. However, as will be argued below, a hard and clear demarcation of this sphere as separate from the state, market and family does not quite work, as a degree of overlap exists between them.

The relationship with the state or some other powerful political agency still remains one of the central issues for the democratic development of civil society. The extreme example of the violent disintegration of society in the former Yugoslavia, which rendered the developing civil society powerless, shows that the conceptualization of civil society as standing largely in opposition to the state and having as its main task the exercise of constraints upon that state was at best a simplification. It appears that

democracy requires a more co-operative relationship between civil society and the state in which the latter is necessary for the provision of a
secure framework within which civil society can flourish. It also provides
the means for the implementation of the public will that emerges from
the discourses in civil society. Constraint upon state power is thus only
one of the functions of civil society. But the example of service provision
also suggests that civil society does not stand in isolation from the market
but is also intertwined with it and this raises the issue of what democratic
control could be exercised over the market and what is the degree of
appropriate civil society penetration of it. This is to say that the service
providers among the NGOs, at least those that still involve voluntary
social action – even though, as Mislivetz suggests, less clearly identifiable
with civic ethos – or even the environmental NGOs, engage in activities
that either directly or indirectly involve the market.

    Even a brief consideration of the history of postcommunist transition
in recent years suggests that the original contention that civil society was
vital for the development of democracy, and citizenship must not be
reduced to rights alone, was correct. The process of establishing a
functioning civil society in societies that were not just made politically
apathetic by decades of communist rule but that also developed through
an overdependence on the state and thus had strong elements of authori-
tarianism built into their culture is, however, proving much more
difficult. It must be recognized that the majority of the populations in the
area are primarily concerned with issues of economic wellbeing and law
and order rather than with democracy and civic engagement. It is to be
acknowledged that the value of democracy itself has not yet become
firmly rooted in most of the countries in the area and that a significant
economic decline could still jeopardize democracy. The sizeable nostalgia for the lost securities of the communist past is also not to be
underestimated. It is also clear that mass forms of civic engagements –
such as the creation of sizeable social movements, for instance – is still, at
best, a matter for the future. It will come about not just as a result of civic
education, but also as a result of the recognition by the citizens themselves that civic engagement is more than an altruistic form of social
engagement. In the long term, it is a much more effective means of
realizing individual interests than the untrammelled expressions of
individualism prevalent today. Nevertheless, the very existence of a
significant 'third' sector and the growing transnational links within that
sector, prevent the totalitarianism of the past. The combination of neoliberalism and nationalist populism, as well as the weakness of the rule of
law, has created a new dark post-totalitarian phenomenon. The idea of

civil society, and indeed transnational civil society, has turned out to be no less relevant in this new post-1989 globalized context.

FURTHER READING

Havel, V. *et al.* (1985) *The Power of the Powerless.* Ed. by John Keane (London: Palach Press). This is a collection of essays representative of debates in Charter 77 in the late 1970s. The essays by Havel and Kusy, in particular, raise innovative conceptualizations of the systemic practices leading to public participation in the reproduction of the oppressive power of the state under late state socialism and analyse the role of civil society and of citizenship in challenging this system.

Michnik, A. (1985) *Letters from Prison and Other Essays* (Berkeley: University of California Press). In a series of essays written between 1976 and 1979, and particularly in the essay on A New Evolutionism, Michnik formulated an influential argument concerning the importance of civil society. In the view put forward he argued that constructive change of the communist regimes occurs when reforms from above are complemented by civil society pressure from below.

Konrad, G. (1984) *Anti-Politics* (London: Quartet Books). The third of the influential dissident Central European texts on the importance of civil society for the process of democratization. Konrad argues that due to the essential corruptibility of all power it is vital that anti-political politics arising out of a developed civil society operates as a constraint on the power of the state not just under the conditions of late communism but also subsequently.

Keane, J. (ed.) (1988) *Civil Society and the State* (London: Verso). This influential collection of essays covers three related issue areas – the modern philosophical tradition regarding the relationship between the state, democracy and civil society; the relationship between Western states and civil societies; and the Eastern states and the re-emergence of civil society.

Kaldor, M. and Vejvoda, I. (eds) (1999) *Democratization in Central and Eastern Europe* (London: Pinter). In this collection the progress of democratic transformation in Central and Eastern Europe is analysed and assessed. The approach adopted is based on a distinction between institutional and legal frameworks of democracy (formal democracy) and the development of democratic values, culture and behavioural patterns (substantive democracy).

BIBLIOGRAPHY

Crampton, R.J. (1994) *Eastern Europe in the Twentieth Century.* London: Routledge.

Dahrendorf, R. (1990) *Reflections on East European Revolutions.* London: Chatto & Windus.

Garton Ash, T. (1999) *Uses of Adversity.* Harmondsworth: Penguin.

Havel, V. *et al.* (1985) *The Power of the Powerless*. Ed. by J. Keane. London: Palach Press.

Halliday, F. (1999) *Revolution in International Relations*. London: Macmillan.

Kaldor, M. (1999) Transnational Civil Society. In T. Dunne and N. Wheeler (eds), *Human Rights and Global Politics*. Cambridge: Cambridge University Press.

Kaldor, M. and Vejvoda, I. (1999) Democratization in Central and East European countries: an overview. In M. Kaldor and I. Vejvoda (eds), *Democratization in Central and Eastern Europe*. London: Pinter.

Kaldor, M., Wilke, P. *et al.* (1997) *Final Report: Evaluation of the Phare and Tacis Democracy Programme 1992–1997*. European Commission of the European Union.

Kavan, Z. (1999) Anti-Politics and Civil Society in Central Europe. In M. Shaw (ed.), *Politics and Globalisation*. London: Routledge.

Konrad, G. (1984) *Anti-Politics*. London: Quartet Books.

Mersijanova, I.V. and collective (1999) Organy Mestnovo Samoupravlenia i Negosudarstvennye Nekomercheskie Organizacii: Otnoshenia Partnerstva, Novosibirsk: Associacia Sibirskikh i Dalnevostochnykh Gorodov.

Michnik, A. (1985) *Letters from Prison and Other Essays*. Berkeley: University of California Press.

Mislivetz, F. (1999) *Illusions and Realities*. Szombathely: Savaria University Press.

Richta, R. and collective (1969) *Civilizace na rozcesti-spolecenske a lidske souvislosti vedeckotechnicke revoluce*. Praha: Svoboda.

Simecka, M. (1989) From Class Obsessions to Dialogue: Detente and the Changing Political Culture of Eastern Europe. In M. Kalder, G. Holden and R. Falk (eds), *The New Detente: Re-thinking East–West Relations*. London: Verso, p. 363.

CHAPTER 13

BETWEEN THE LOCAL AND THE GLOBAL: DEMOCRACY IN THE TWENTY-FIRST CENTURY

Paul Hirst

Until the First World War democracy was conceived almost exclusively as an issue of the form of government within individual sovereign states. The international order was generally perceived as a world of autonomous states, interacting externally at their borders in terms of commerce and foreign policy. The principle of democracy was also widely assumed to be coincident with nationalism. Nations were the primary demos, and the right of nations to self-determination was a central part of democratic thought. That right could lead to demand for either national secession from an existing state or the unification of hitherto separate territories into a new nation state. The result of such processes, however, was still a sovereign state, free to govern by popular decision within its borders. Before 1914, most states were either autocratic or had a narrow basis for representation, or placed important aspects of government beyond the control of elected representatives. Many states were also multinational and/or colonial empires, denying rights of secession to subordinate nations or excluding the colonized population from political participation.

DEMOCRACY AS AN INTERNATIONAL ISSUE

Thus the democratic agenda could be seen as twofold: the extension of political rights within states and the extension of statehood to peoples. The aftermath of the war transformed the issue of democracy. On the one hand democracy was internationalized. The new international liberalism (identified with the American President Wilson) aimed not only at national self-determination and domestic democratization, but also at a new international order. States would not only be self-governing but would adhere to certain fundamental principles: non-aggression, the gradual elimination of colonialism, and the protection of minority rights within national states. Advocates of the League of Nations (created after the Allied victory in 1918) saw it as the beginning of a world government that would replace the old international anarchy. It would ensure collective security, promote international co-operation, and oversee the government of mandated colonial territories and the rights of minorities in the new nation states of Central and Eastern Europe. The League made strong claims against traditional notions of the rights of sovereignty, and, had it succeeded, would have introduced new international norms as the universal basis for legitimate government.

On the other hand, democracy was both radically redefined and challenged. Before 1914 most radical political groups, including most European socialists, had accepted representative democracy and parliamentary government either as politically desirable or as pragmatic necessities. Now, however, 'bourgeois' democracy was confronted by confident and aggressive political doctrines that aimed to replace it with 'higher' forms of government. These doctrines became embodied in states and political parties committed to the destruction of the existing liberal order. The USSR and its allied communist parties claimed that democracy based on *soviets* was superior to one based on multi-party elections to a representative parliament. Fascist ideas challenged democracy as such in favour of the leadership principle. The USSR sought to create a new world order based on proletarian internationalism. The fascist powers sought revision of the 1918 settlement and to destroy the League. For the *revanchist* powers, the League was regarded not as high minded but as no more than a cynical device to protect the interests of the 'have' powers against the losers and the disappointed in 1918. Thus 'the democracies' quickly switched from being a hegemonic force immediately after the war to being a small and embattled group of states in the collapsing liberal international order after the Great Crash of 1929 and the Nazi victory of 1933. The issue of democracy had been internationalized in a new way. The isolationism of the USA and the political feebleness of Britain and France fatally weakened the defence of the Wilsonian new order. In the 1930s, 'bourgeois democracy' was but one element in a three-cornered contest for international hegemony between liberal, fascist and communist powers. To many intelligent observers it seemed as if the democratic states were doomed (Mazower, 1999).

The conflicts of the 1930s destroyed the League, and undermined its pretensions to set norms for and to intervene in the internal affairs of states. However, in a way that would have seemed incredible in 1939, the Second World War vastly strengthened the liberal democracies. The Allied victory not only physically destroyed their fascist enemies, but also undercut the legitimacy of fascist doctrines, which claimed superior military prowess over the weak democracies. Victory renewed the vigour of liberal democratic doctrine and the sense of purpose of representative governments. The falling out of the Western and Soviet powers in the Cold War further served to strengthen the international solidarity and co-operation of the democracies. The major democracies –

including the successfully reconstructed liberal states of Italy, Japan, and West Germany – united against the Soviet Bloc. In a different conjuncture, democracy once again became an issue dividing groups of states.

Membership of a bloc changed the relation of the democratic Western countries one to another. They were now linked in a close and highly integrated series of military alliances, the chief of which was NATO. This was a more real and effective system of collective security than the League. These states were also linked in the new institutions of the post-1945 international economic settlement: the Bretton Woods monetary system and the accompanying institutions of the IMF and the World Bank and the new liberal trade regime of GATT. The democracies in continental Europe were further integrated by the formation of the European Communities from 1952 onwards. Democracy could no longer be regarded as a domestic issue. It divided states on an international basis into the democracies and their communist opponents and this in turn radically altered their domestic politics. The post-1945 transformation radically changed the relationship between the nation state and its international environment. It created a supranational political system in which states were the members. States banded together and, in partnership with the new international agencies, they acted to govern a wider economic and social system. This system could best be seen as a quasi-polity. It had common decision-making institutions like the NATO council or the G7, and its component members (its 'demos') were states. The USA had created this system, its power underwrote it and it was vastly influential within it, but it was also bound by membership and by the rules of the game it had brought into being. This could best be described as 'embedded liberalism' (Ruggie, 1983). America was a member of an ongoing association of states, taking part in various fora, and not a crude hegemon, an uncommanded commander.

The most signal failure of the new international order was the replacement for the League, the United Nations. It was endowed by its supporters with many of the same ideals as the League and proved almost as big a failure judged against those standards as its predecessor. Advocates of world government placed a touching faith in the principle of a comprehensive international institution. Yet they mostly ignored the true success story of post-1945 international governance, that was the complex of functionally specific supranational institutions created and controlled by the Western powers. The UN suffered from a double political failure. Crippled by the antagonistic interests of the superpowers, the Security Council could achieve little. Dominated by the mass of non-aligned and often non-democratic states created by decolonization, the General Assembly had little legitimacy, however large the majorities for its resolutions. Despite the failure of the UN, the Western democracies had built for themselves and their clients an international order far more integrated and densely governed than any previous system. This meant that key states could no longer treat external relations as 'foreign policy'; it had become part of their practices of governance and transformed their political agendas.

The collapse of communism after 1989, and the equally significant parallel retreat of the dictatorships that the West had supported as 'bulwarks against communism' in Africa, Asia and Latin America, led to a world in which a large number of states either have become formally democratic or were attempting the transition to democracy. In less than half a century democracy had gone from being an internationally embattled doctrine to being the only legitimate political system available. It had no credible alternatives: failure to achieve the transition to multi-party elections was a sign of economic backwardness, social fragmentation and political failure. This widespread diffusion of representative government made democracy much less significant as a distinguishing feature between states. What now differentiated governments was not the presence of formal democratic institutions but wider values and social practices. The line between the 'old' democracies and the rest was drawn in terms of economic prosperity and governmental competence. The USA, the EU, and Japan set the agenda for international governance. They exclusively control many of the key institutions, like the G7 or the OECD, and they dominate others, like the WTO or IMF, whose governing bodies are in theory more inclusive.

The present situation in international governance is viewed very differently by opposing groups of commentators: some view it negatively and others see it as offering prospects for building greater democracy beyond the nation state. Some critics argue that democracy has triumphed in nation states just when they have ceased to have scope for effective decision-making about the things that matter. Economic globalization is held to have reduced the powers and roles of governments, and thus the ability of domestic majorities to affect policy. Authors like Greider (1997), Gray (1998) and Martin and Schumann (1997) take variants of this view. Power is now seen to be in the hands of essentially undemocratic bodies, supranational institutions or transnational companies. Where states do have influence, it is confined to the large rich countries. It is claimed that such countries are under the control of internationalized technocratic and corporate elites that set the domestic political agenda and take the lion's share of national income. The masses can vote for what they like, but the international markets and the key elites will decide what happens. Democracy no longer really subjects the political agenda to the test of a popular mandate; rather, it now provides no more than formal legitimacy for politicians who look elsewhere to decide what the issues are. No wonder, it is claimed, that political participation by citizens is declining and apathy increasing. Millions have received the vote just when it does not matter. The critics might invoke the old Brazilian proverb that states, 'if shit were valuable the poor would be born without arseholes'.

Other commentators are, by contrast, optimistic and see advantages in the process of globalization that has taken the problems to be managed beyond the nation state. They see prospects for further political development in the widespread diffusion of democratic institutions and values. Thus David Held (1995) argues that we need to construct a 'cosmopolitan democracy' beyond the nation state. This complex of institutions would seek to tackle world problems like global economic flows and the global environmental crisis with new forms of supranational governance. These would be based on a revitalized United Nations. These ideas seek to overcome the democratic deficit that they accept is inevitable at the national level by building inclusive democratic institutions of larger scale and linking them to local forms of participation.

Are the assumptions of both the negative and positive views of globalization and democracy true? Has economic globalization actually taken place? Has it diminished the role of the state? Have institutions of supranational governance reduced the scope of national sovereignty? Are international agencies beyond accountability? Are transnational companies and world financial markets beyond effective public regulation, whether at national or international level? Have states been sidelined by markets, and, therefore, have national politics and the conflict between states been replaced by world market forces as the factor which decides the fate of nations?

HOW REAL WAS SOVEREIGNTY?

The great problem with the argument that democracy was possible in the past when the nation state was sovereign but is undermined by the process of globalization is that neither part of the proposition holds water. States were not sovereign in quite the way that many people think and globalization is not the force that it is widely claimed to be. It is quite true that before 1914 there were very few international institutions and that states were the primary international actors. But states did not enjoy an absolute sovereignty. The scope of national policy was limited by the fact that states were small public spenders: about 10–15 per cent of GDP on average in 1914, as against about 30 per cent in the 1960s and 40+ per cent today. The main liberal states were committed to the doctrine of *laissez faire*, that is that they should interfere as little as possible in their domestic economies and that they should permit free international commerce by private citizens. The pre-1914 international economic system was highly developed, open and integrated, even by today's standards. Trade flows, capital flows and labour migration grew steadily throughout the nineteenth century and in many respects have still not been surpassed today. The UK's merchandise trade to GDP ratio of 44.7 per cent in 1913 was still not equalled in 1994, when it stood at 42.6 per cent. Lest Britain be thought an exception, the figures for France and Germany were only marginally higher in 1995 than in 1913: France at 35.4 per cent in 1913 and 36.6 per cent in 1995 and Germany at 35.1 per cent in 1913 and 38.7 per cent in 1995 (Hirst and Thompson, 1999, Table 2.3, p. 27). The surge of capital exports by leading foreign investor countries like Britain and France in the period just before 1914 has not been equalled since (at one point the UK was investing 9 per cent of GDP abroad). The nineteenth century was the great age of mass migration: between 1815 and 1914 an estimated 60 million people left Europe to settle overseas (Segal, 1993, p. 16). The gold standard, widely adopted after 1870, in which national currencies were pegged to gold and freely convertible into gold, was at least in theory a self-equilibrating international system. Governments had to take measures to adjust the domestic economy to restore the external balance, adjusting interest rates and cutting public spending accordingly (Eichengreen, 1996).

States appeared to be more 'sovereign' than this in the 1930s, but this was as a consequence of both their foreign trade and their domestic economies being severely depressed. Greater local control was gained at the price of the loss of prosperity. The attempt to restore the liberal pre-1914 regime of free trade and the gold standard after the end of the First World War was a failure. The Great Crash of 1929 led to widespread withdrawal from the gold standard and the adoption of protectionist tariffs on foreign goods. States competed to control declining markets and imposed restrictions on the movement of relatively scarce capital. It would be a mistake to see the 1930s as a dramatic leap in the governance capacity of the state, rather than as a change in the policy environment and in regulatory objectives. The liberal era before 1914 also involved deliberate public policy to sustain its institutions no less than when states after 1929 began to try to manage the economic crisis by additional domestic controls. *Laissez faire* was a political choice. In the mid-nineteenth century Britain deliberately adopted free trade and accepted the costs, tolerating those powers like Germany that maintained tariffs.

As Karl Polanyi (1944) argued, the free market both nationally and internationally was built by strong state intervention, dismantling traditional institutions of economic regulation. One could argue that attempts by modern day economic liberals to deregulate domestic economies and to promote the liberalization of external trade and capital movements are an analogous phenomenon. The nineteenth-century liberal state was powerful, but it chose to use public policy to promote non-state activities. 'Globalization' is similarly a project of elites (using international agencies and national governments) to deregulate the international economy.

In the period before 1914, although the international system was primarily made up of states, individual states were constrained in both their structure and behaviour by the basic characteristics of the system. States were internationally sovereign to the extent that they were recognized as such by other states, and to obtain that recognition required their adherence to a wide range of internationally accepted norms. States that did not behave in conformity with those norms were sanctioned by the states system. Political entities that did not exhibit the characteristics of modern statehood were not treated as members of the international system. The doctrine of non-interference in the internal affairs of other states was generally accepted but on the assumption that states were organized in a certain way and behaved as they should. The range of intervention in other political entities' affairs was probably as wide in the pre-1914 system as it is today. Today, of course, the old international law doctrine of non-intervention in domestic affairs has been supplemented and in part overridden by the new law of international human rights, but states in the past intervened differently and for different reasons.

Full statehood only applied unambiguously to European states and their offshoots. Other political entities might legitimately be the object of intervention by European powers. As international commerce grew and was removed from the mercantilist shackles of an earlier era, the international rights in trade of states and private citizens, and the legitimate objects of trade and acceptable commercial practices, were all gradually defined. Thus piracy was coherently defined and eliminated by vigorous international action in the nineteenth century (Thomson, 1994). Political entities that harboured pirates, like Algiers, were suppressed. The slave trade was outlawed as legitimate commerce. Slavers could be lawfully searched and seized on the high seas, whatever flag they were flying. States were obliged to respect the right to trade and the property of foreign traders. Often this was little more than a cloak for commercial imperialism, as with the Opium Wars fought by Britain to open up the Chinese market or American and British pressure on Japan to permit foreign trade. States that defaulted on their foreign borrowings were subject to sanctions far more draconian than those of the IMF, thus Britain and France took *de facto* direct control of Egypt's public finances after 1881.

The Great Powers, after the Vienna settlement of 1815, attempted to maintain order in Europe by common agreement wherever possible. The Concert of Europe was a conservative ideal of inter-state co-operation, but seeking consensus was as much a reality as conflict in the relationship between states for most of the nineteenth century. In the 1890s this system broke down and Europe divided into two rival alliance systems centred on Germany and Austria-Hungary, and France and Russia respectively. The powers frequently co-operated with one another to settle disputes between lesser states, and in particular to manage conflicts arising from the decomposition of the Ottoman Empire. They also tried to settle disputes over colonial territories between themselves by negotiation and mediation. The powers may have sought to practise *realpolitik* but almost all had to take account of public opinion, particularly strong support for national unification movements and liberation struggles against the Ottomans. In this sense the powers took some account of human rights, perhaps no less actively and only slightly more cynically than the Western states do today. Thus Britain, France and Russia intervened in favour of the Greeks at Navarino in 1827, destroying the Turkish fleet. At the Congress of Berlin in 1878 the powers adjusted the borders of the states emerging from Ottoman rule. The Treaty of London in 1913, which tried to do the same for the Balkan War of 1912, failed and led to a new conflict. Dayton and Rambouillet are thus far less remarkable than they might seem.

In this sense the period between 1914 and 1945 could be seen as the exception in the international system. It was a period of stand-alone sovereignty and intense inter-state conflict sandwiched between two long periods of international liberalism and inter-state co-operation, at least on the part of the Western powers. If we accept this view, then the period between 1945 and 1973 can be seen as the key phase of the reconstitution of international liberalism. This was accomplished by active institution building, led by the USA, and by renewed and rapid growth in world output and trade. The period between 1973 and the mid-1980s can be seen in contrast as one of turbulence and transition, occasioned chiefly by the two OPEC oil price rises of 1973 and 1979. If controls on capital movements were widely abandoned after the late 1970s, then the reason was primarily the growth of large external dollar balances by the OPEC countries and the large Japanese trade surplus. Middle Eastern and Japanese capital flowed to Europe and the USA, thereby offsetting the effects of trade flows. Capital controls could only have been maintained if trade between the major regions of the world had remained roughly in balance.

The purpose of the section has been to question a simplistic 'before' and 'after' view of sovereignty. The system was more regulated by international norms before 1914 than is often believed. States were more capable actors than many who judge by the period between 1930 and the 1960s now suppose.

HOW REAL IS GLOBALIZATION?

Globalization is a word used so often and so indiscriminately that it is essential to define what one means by it. If globalization merely means, as it often does, growing levels of international trade and investment between distinct nations, then we have seen that there is nothing remarkable about it. For example, international trade grew at 9 per cent per annum on average between 1950 and 1973, which compares favourably with trade growth during 1980–1995. However, globalization is frequently taken to mean something quite different, that is, a recent process (beginning in the last two decades) in which national economies are dissolving into closely integrated world markets for goods, investments and short-term financial flows. Such an economy is supposed to be dominated by world market forces that are beyond the scope of regulation of either national governments or international agencies. If a new international economy of this kind existed, then economics would have sidelined politics, and the issue of democratic control would be irrelevant.

An international economy with high and growing levels of trade and investment between national economies is compatible with the continued existence of effective national economic governance and with scope for greater control by supranational agencies, underwritten and rendered accountable by member states. A truly globalized economy should show evidence of the following:

- rapidly escalating trade to GDP ratios;
- the dominance of production and distribution by truly transnational companies, which trade and produce across the globe as economic advantage dictates, which have a multinational management, and no distinct national base;
- that national capital markets are dissolving, local investment being increasingly determined by global flows of foreign direct investment;

- that short-term financial flows are completely internationalized, dictate real economic performance, and are beyond the control of central banks, whether acting alone or in concert;
- that there are radical shifts from established centres of economic power as capital markets switch resources to new locations that exhibit greater competitive advantage, typically from the traditional Western manufacturing countries to newly industrializing countries.

On most of these dimensions the evidence does not support the strong globalization thesis. It is impossible to present more than the barest summary here (for a fuller account see Hirst and Thompson, 1999). We have seen above that trade to GDP ratios for most advanced economies (with the exception of the USA) are either lower or not significantly greater than they were in 1913. Again most major companies are multinationals and not true transnationals, that is, they operate from a distinct national base in one of the three rich regions of the world – Europe, Japan and North America – and use subsidiary and affiliate companies to produce and trade abroad. Doremus *et al.* (1998) show the persistence of distinct national corporate structures and strategies in the three main regions. Typically the advanced countries' multinationals sell about 60–70 per cent of their output in their home country/region and have between 70–90 per cent of their assets there too (Hirst and Thompson, 1999, Tables 3.8–3.10, p. 82). The key test of the transnationalization of production is the share of the output of foreign subsidiaries and affiliates in GDP: this rose from 5.2 per cent of world GDP in 1982 to 6.7 per cent in 1990 and then fell back to 6 per cent in 1994 (Hirst and Thompson, 1999, Table 3.11, p. 85). This hardly shows a vast move by major companies away from their national bases.

Foreign direct investment (FDI) flows are also highly concentrated between the three major blocs of Europe, Japan and North America – between 1991 and 1996 these three accounted for 60 per cent of world FDI, down from 75 per cent in 1980–91. However, these flows are highly cyclical. In the early 1990s Europe and Japan were in recession and FDI flows to Asia were booming. Since the Asian crisis that began in 1997, this situation has changed radically and flows have reversed. The advanced world will continue to produce the great bulk of world output and to recycle the majority of FDI between its three main centres. In 1996 the three major rich regions of the globe represented 74.9 per cent of world GDP and 66 per cent of world export trade (Hirst and Thompson, 1999, Tables 3.3 and 3.4, p. 73). In 1996, the high income economies ($9,363+), 15.6 per cent of the world's population, accounted for 80.6 per cent of world GDP and the remaining 84.4 per cent of the world's population received less than 20 per cent of world income (the bottom 56.2 per cent of people just 5.4 per cent of world income) (Hirst and Thompson, 1999, Table 3.5, p. 74). Wealth and output remain as concentrated as ever; globalization is not shifting trade, investment and output away from the G7 countries.

Capital markets remain stubbornly national, too. About 90 per cent or more of investment in the advanced countries is still domestically sourced. The share of FDI in gross fixed capital formation demonstrates this: in Japan in 1994 it was 0.1 per cent, in the USA in 1995 5.9 per cent and in Germany 1.7 per cent in 1995. Equities are still predominantly held nationally: in 1996 foreign holdings of equity in the USA were 5 per cent, in Japan 11 per cent and in both Germany and the UK 9 per cent. Banks have very distinct national patterns of foreign borrowing and lending, showing the persistence of national strategies rather than an integrated global system. This varies from very low values for the foreign assets and liabilities of banks such as the USA (2.6 per cent and 8.2 per cent respectively in 1996), to medium values like Japan (13.8 per cent and 10.6 per cent respectively in 1996), to high values such as the UK (47 per cent and 48.8 per cent respectively in 1996) (Hirst and Thompson, 1999, Table 2.11, p. 46).

Short-term capital flows have grown dramatically, are a recent development (since the 1970s) and have the potential to be highly destabilizing. The paradox is that they contribute very little to real economic performance. This has especially been the case with emerging markets. Here long-term FDI can significantly add to national economic performance by providing access to new products and production technologies. Short-term funds may contribute little. As Montes (1998) shows, such short-term lending may have little effect on growth rates: in Indonesia 1 per cent and in Malaysia 1.5 per cent, whereas in Thailand (the point of origin of the Asian crisis) the impact of these flows actually reduced growth by 0.6 per cent. In Malaysia and Thailand the efficiency of investment (that is, the ratio of investment to real GDP growth) fell. Thus those developing countries that exposed themselves to such flows did so for no benefit, the effects of the crisis rapidly dwarfed minor gains in rates of GDP growth. The principal sources of these short-term funds were the European and Japanese commercial banks. They stampeded into Asia with net inflows of $24 billion in 1994, $49.5 billion in 1995 and $55.5 billion in 1996, and then fled in a herd panic in 1997, with a net outflow of $21.3 billion (Wolf, 1998, p. 22). Critics of the financial markets often portray developing countries as the victims of speculative attacks. In the Asian crisis the problems were created less by active and malevolent speculation than by unthinking panic, reacting to real economic problems but in a way that was both disproportionate to the scale of the problems and in the negative effects it produced. Nevertheless, some Asian countries were relatively unaffected by the crisis because they had not engaged in extensive foreign borrowing (Taiwan), or had non-convertible currencies (China), or had very deep financial markets that could weather the impacts (Singapore). Thus developing countries do have options: they are not inevitably victims of global market forces. They could, for example, adopt a variant of the Chilean policy that puts obstacles in the way of short-term loans, whilst not penalizing long-term investment.

The international financial markets now dwarf real trade flows and FDI. Much of this is repeated 'churning', seeking gains on imperfections between different markets and utilizing assets derived from national financial institutions to do so. Such pure financial dealing is not generally in the interest of manufacturing companies, and often rebounds on the more traditional parts of financial institutions that provide the resources for the riskier trades. Such markets are a threat not only to emerging economies but also to the developed countries through backward link-ages from crises in emerging markets. Soros (1998) argues that this large volume financial trading is a source of fundamental instability in the modern capitalist system. Exchange rate volatility is the lesser part of the problem. Generally, the markets move in to force the adjustment of an unsustainable exchange rate, as was the case with 'Black Wednesday' in 1992 when Britain was driven from the ERM. The real problem is the transformation of derivatives trading from a hedge against volatile market movements into a speculative instrument and a source of vola-tility in its own right. The potential for danger is shown by the near collapse of the massively overexposed Long Term Capital Management, which had positions outstanding with liabilities some 250 times its assets. A crisis was prevented by prompt action orchestrated by the US authorities, but the potential for such firms crashing, bringing down other institutions to which they are indebted and starting a chain reac-tion, is very real. This is not something that is exclusively the result of 'globalization'; rather it is an intrinsic feature of ill-organized and weakly regulated capitalist markets. In the aftermath of the 1929 Great Crash, the US government put extensive controls in place domestically to prevent such overexposure and contain backward linkages. The issue now is to agree a firmer international regulatory regime between the major finan-cial centres and to impose compliance upon offshore trading centres. The world financial system is fragile, but so far co-ordinated international action by the principal central banks has prevented major contagion effects from the Russian, Brazilian and Long Term Capital Management crises. The greatest believers in *post hoc* public intervention are commercial bankers about to get their fingers burnt. They are less keen on extended prudential regulation. Nevertheless, the possibilities of greater and more active governance are there; to implement them requires both a sense of urgency and a degree of extended co-operation by the regulatory authorities.

Thus international financial markets do pose problems but not insuperable ones. It is necessary to put tighter rules in place about the type of trades that are possible, the institutions allowed to undertake them, the internal governance structures of those institutions, and their permitted asset-liability ratios. This is regulation to structure markets, rather than to achieve some specific desired outcome in terms of price movements. It is not impossible for public authorities, however, to intervene in markets and prevent them getting out of hand. Singapore acted to prevent its property market from turning into an unsustainable bubble. The Hong Kong authorities actively intervened to support the stock market during the 1997–8 crisis.

States are not, therefore, powerless to control financial markets, given sufficient resources and prudent policies. International co-operation between national authorities could curb the worst kinds of speculation. The world economy is not ungovernable in the way the more extreme advocates of the fashionable thesis of globalization suppose. There is a price for such extended governance: IMF support requires OECD taxpayers to be prepared to foot the bill. Co-ordinated action by national central banks likewise requires public money to be mobilized to bail out fools and rogues and it involves quick intergovernment decisions that cannot be referred to national parliaments for ratification. Such co-operation may seem to limit national democratic 'sovereignty'. But the alternatives are worse. Stand-alone policies in the 1930s gave rise to national action, but co-ordinated international action may have avoided the crisis that made such actions necessary. International governance, as we shall see, does not necessarily weaken states.

THE OLD SOVEREIGNTY AND THE NEW

When the concept of state sovereignty was developed in the sixteenth and seventeenth centuries, sovereignty was conceived as something that could only be exclusively possessed. That is, sovereignty was conceived as a fixed quantum of power. The struggle for such power was a zero-sum game and whatever power a given holder amassed diminished the stock of power available to others. The sovereign was conceived as an uncommanded commander, who gave orders but did not receive them

(Bodin, 1576; Hobbes, 1651). In a sense this was true, because central administrations were appropriating governance capacity from regional parliaments, towns and local nobles. These local bodies lost powers we now think to be exclusive to the national state: to tax, to raise armed forces, to make laws and exercise justice, to declare war, and to make treaties. This process of centralization was violently resisted on a wide scale, sometimes successfully, as with the revolt of the Netherlands, and sometimes unsuccessfully, as with the localist and noble rebellion in France called the Fronde (1648–53).

Some analysts argue that a similar process of redistribution of governance capacity is taking place today and the victims are no longer local powers but the previous victors, the sovereign territorial states. The new victors are world markets, transnational companies and the international technocracy. Power is shifting from political institutions to economic ones and from elected to unelected decision makers. The problem with this view is that the nature of sovereignty has changed radically and it is misunderstood if conceived in Bodinian terms as a fixed quantum. Some, like Cerny (1998), accept that structures of power are changing, but they see that change as a shift back to a more polycentric world like that of the Middle Ages. He sees the future as a 'durable disorder' in which both public and private powers proliferate and compete. Similarly, Susan Strange (1996) envisages a 'retreat of the state' in the face of markets, private governments and supranational institutions.

Undoubtedly, governance is becoming more complex: states are sharing governance with supranational agencies (both public and private), with regional governments, and with 'non-governmental' organizations. This does not imply a world like the Middle Ages in which powers could overlap and compete to perform the same functions. The reason is simple: modern economies, unlike medieval society, are characterized by a complex division of labour that creates extended interdependencies. Unless that division of labour is regulated to minimize unintended consequences and unacceptable outcomes, it will tend to unravel with effects that are disproportionate to the causes of the initial disorder. Crucial to such a division of labour is the confidence that remote links in the chain, of which actors have no personal knowledge, will hold. That is why incompetent derivatives traders and corrupt Russian central bankers have to be rescued from the consequences of their folly; they are part of a web of interdependence and others who are neither incompetent nor corrupt will suffer if they are not bailed out. We need, therefore, a division of labour in governance that parallels that in the economy. There is a degree of co-ordination necessary at international, national and subnational levels, and between public and private bodies, that ensures that there are no major 'gaps' in governance. If the gaps widen too much, then governance is lost into the gaps and control over activities is lost to the extent that social actors face incalculable uncertainty. Such uncertainty leads to inactivity, undermines markets and kills economic growth. Such things are no more tolerable now than was piracy in the nineteenth century.

Such a division of labour in governance is currently highly imperfect, but the rudiments of it do exist. The question is whether the sharing of the tasks of governance with other agencies seriously weakens the power of the nation state? The answer is that if sovereignty is defined as governance capacity, then a general increase in capacity consequent on the co-operation of agencies at several levels not only adds to the total governance available in the system but makes most (if not all) members of the system more effective in governing the functions specific to them too (Hirst, 1998b). Consider the case of the European Union (EU). As Milward (1992) points out, the creation of the European Communities actually strengthened the member states by stabilizing and controlling their external environment: enhanced economic growth, trade, peace and stability made it easier for states to govern within their territories. If the modern state is primarily an economic management and public service agency, for which the ability to provide a secure environment for private economic actors and to deliver welfare services to citizens are the crucial standards of measure of its governance capacity, then that state can *gain* in sovereignty whilst accepting the need to co-operate with other governing powers. Imagine that, instead of creating the EU, Europe's nation states had attempted go-it-alone policies centred on the protection of national markets. Can we suppose that economic growth would have been higher, the macroeconomic environment more manageable, or national public services better? The answer is obvious: the state would have been struggling to provide national solutions to problems that were the more difficult because it didn't share power and hence had less control.

International governance thus need not weaken states. Power is not a fixed quantum. The state is not merely a beneficiary of the new division of labour in governance – it is pivotal in securing that division. As we shall see below, this is because the state is territorial and, if legitimate, it is the link between the different levels. It can give appropriate powers to regional governments and quasi-governmental agencies. It can both underwrite international governing bodies and render them indirectly accountable to national populations. The state has attributes other agencies do not have, and this makes states indispensable in the constitutional ordering required by the new division of labour between governing powers. Of course, co-operation does limit the parties involved in certain ways. All such arrangements are balances of advantage and constraint. I argue that states have generally gained more than they have lost in governance capacity by entering into such arrangements. States have entered into common governance systems since the beginning of the international system of states. For example, monetary systems like the gold standard, Bretton Woods or the euro impose constraints on national policy, but they remove others, and one should not forget the constraints imposed by volatility in periods of apparently stand-alone floating currencies. Again, since the International Telegraphic Union of 1865, states have evolved the common rules and international standards that make communications networks possible. The network could not exist without the consent of its members and their ongoing support, but who imagines that the constraints of the rules reduce the capacities of the system and the overall benefits to its members of control through communication?

DEMOCRACY AND INTERNATIONAL INSTITUTIONS

International institutions can be made accountable, but only through certain nation states. Democracy above the nation state is deeply problematic, especially if it is conceived in ways analogous to democracy at nation-state level. The worthy idea of a cosmopolitan democracy is impossible. This is for the simple reason that the inequalities between the world's nations are so great that no common interest is possible. The United Nations, in particular, is a poor basis for enhanced democratic international governance. The simple reason is that the vast majority of the world's states are so poor that they cannot will the means to any major ends that they decide to pursue in common. The rich states, by contrast, who have the means, will not concede the power of decision over them to the majority of poor states. Majorities in the General Assembly, even after the widespread diffusion of democracy, are often made up with votes from countries that are not democratic, like the Sudan or Afghanistan, and thus have no legitimacy with the mature democracies.

Effective international governance thus turns on the institutions created and/or sustained by the wealthy states such as the IMF, WTO or NATO, and on the host of specialist public, quasi-public and private bodies that regulate specific activities and trades, like the BIS or INMARSAT. How are such bodies rendered accountable? Only through the rich and governmentally competent states that make up the governing councils of international agencies or that exercise a supervisory role over quasi-public or private bodies. States still matter for both governance and democracy, because they are the primary source of legitimacy for such bodies. States are territorial. We do not live in a borderless world but in one rigidly divided into state territories. Major states control populations and define citizenship even more rigorously than in the past. Nation states, therefore, above all other bodies, are the exclusive representatives of the populations of the world on an ongoing basis. That makes them different from international agencies or regional governments, from companies or trade associations, and from NGOs. Democratic governments can credibly speak for their populations, since they are legitimated by majority vote. Democratic governments know that the international commitments they enter into will, by convention, be honoured by successor administrations. Other states know this too and can thus accept such commitments as binding. Democratic states, because they abide by the rule of law internally and accept decisions against them in the domestic courts, also tend to abide by international law and to respect international agreements. Without this lawful behaviour of states as members of the international society, international law would have little force and international governance above the level of the sovereign state would be virtually impossible. In this sense, democracy is vital to extended international governance, not as cosmopolitan or global democracy, but as democratic practices within states that make wider institutions both possible and legitimate.

This gives the democratic nation state a crucial role in elaborating and sustaining the division of labour in governance between international, national and regional levels mentioned above. The state can do this because it is the primary agency for creating constitutional order. The state is the pivotal political body in the new complex system of governance because only it can lend its legitimacy to supranational bodies and only it can adjust the distribution of power within the national territory to permit effective regional and other forms of governance. Complexity in governance, far from undermining the national state, is predicated upon it.

This does not mean that the accountability of supranational agencies is easy to achieve. Democratic control is always problematic at any level of government. It is difficult enough to make a city council responsive to the wishes of the majority of local citizens, let alone make a world agency like the IMF accountable through their member states to their citizens. We have to accept that there is no single world political community – complexity in governance means that accountability and legitimacy at the international level have to be at best very indirect, through the actions of state officials who are in turn answerable to local representatives.

International agencies are best viewed as quasi-polities; their governing councils are assemblies in which the representative members are states. That is why democratic states are the key to the effectiveness of such quasi-polities: they have primary legitimacy, and their agreement provides secondary legitimacy to the policies of such bodies. Whether there is genuine accountability to domestic constituencies depends crucially on the attitudes of ministers and state officials. The problem is less that accountability is structurally impossible, than that such personnel have seen such activities as an arcane domain peculiar to them and, whilst a core part of domestic politics, not something to bother the electorate with over much. This is a hangover from the world of the old sovereignty and the logic of reason of state. The other reason why there has been so little conflict and calling to account between states and international agencies is because the supranational technocrats have perceived the world in much the same (economic liberal) way as national level politicians, central bankers and business executives. The IMF, for example, has traditionally encountered little opposition to its policies from its core G7 supporters. When the IMF applied its policies to weak and often undemocratic African states, then few bothered to question it. Yet its policies have often been questionable. Why, for example, should a loan to Hungary be made conditional on major cuts in housing subsidies? Increasingly it will face problems as many of the governments it will deal with will be democratic and have firm support for distinctive national policies. The backlash in South Korea against the IMF's initial conditions in the aftermath of the Asian crisis was very vigorous: the government was democratic, the people fiercely nationalistic and the country had industrialized on a path very different from Anglo-Saxon economic liberalism. As more states become prosperous democracies and join the OECD, the IMF will have to look to the legitimacy of its policies and arrive at a broader and more inclusive definition of what is acceptable, reflecting increasing differences in economic institutions and values on the part of the member states.

States are not equal. In this sense the formal theory of sovereignty in international law is of little use when dealing with the realities of the new sovereignty and the division of labour in governance. Effective international governance depends on a core of wealthy democratic states underwriting the institutions in question. Such states will seldom defer on a key issue to the wishes of the majority of poor states, where the interests of the two groups diverge. Effective governance is undemocratic on a global scale, because it is exercised by, and in the main for, a minority of the world's population. But there is no effective democratic alternative to this state of affairs. Many of the poor states are either not democracies or very fragile and imperfect democracies, and they cannot be taken to speak for their peoples. Thus their international commitments, even if they are reliable (undemocratic regimes often persist), are not legitimate. The problem is that if the decisions of the major international bodies are too biased toward the narrowly defined interests of the rich countries then, whilst they may be legitimate domestically, they will be illegitimate on a world scale. This is nowhere clearer than in the area of environmental pollution where the powers like the USA refuse effective controls on energy emissions and the rich countries generally refuse to pay for measures of environmental protection in the South.

The problem with global democracy is not ungovernability brought on by economic globalization and the weakening of the state, but inequality on a world scale and radical differences of interest between states and between their populations. Democracy requires a substantial measure of homogeneity in the demos, and our world has such extreme differences in both wealth and values as to make the acceptance of global majority decision on the part of the populations of the mature democracies inconceivable. These differences currently can only be managed by negotiation, not resolved by majority will. A solution requires less self-interested policies by the rich democracies; only this will make their effective international governance legitimate in the long run. It also requires a degree of realism by the representatives of the poorer states and on the part of the NGOs who are vocal in advancing their claims. That the present distribution of world income is morally unjustifiable and that the poor deserve better are morally unchallengeable claims, but they are political and economically difficult to deliver on. There are no easy routes to prosperity for the poorer countries and fundamental limitations to the willingness of the populations of the advanced countries to make sacrifices in the interests of fairness. This is not an easy conclusion. The world is much less integrated than the extreme globalizers think, and, for that reason, both more governable than they claim but also less easy to do so democratically.

FURTHER READING

On the general concept of sovereignty see Krasner (1988). On the formation of the sovereign territorial state and its triumph over rival forms of political organization see Spruyt (1994) and Ruggie (1993). For a challenging critique of the notion that a coherent 'Westphalian states system' was created after 1648, see Krasner (1993, 1995). For a defence of the saliency of the Treaty of Westphalia in building sovereignty and of the international origins of national sovereignty see Hirst (1998a). For an attempt to show that sovereignty was less exclusive in the past than is widely imagined and that it is less undermined by the processes of globalization than is often thought see Krasner (1999).

On the fashionable notion of the retreat of the state in the face of the pressures of globalization see Camilleri and Falk (1992), van Creveld (1999), Horsman and Marshall (1994), Sassen (1996) and Strange (1996) for a representative sample of views.

On the debates about the extent and nature of economic globalization see Boyer and Drache (eds) (1996), Dicken 3rd edition (1998), Held *et al.* (1999), Holden and Bellamy (eds) (1999), and Michie and Grieve-Smith (eds) (1998).

REFERENCES

Bodin, J. (1576) *On Sovereignty* Ed. J.H. Franklin. Cambridge: Cambridge University Press.

Boyer, R. and Drache, D. (eds) (1996) *States against Markets*. London: Routledge.

Camilleri, J.A. and Falk, J. (1992) *The End of Sovereignty*. Aldershot: Edward Elgar.

Cerny, P. (1998) Neomedievalism, Civil War and the New Security Dilemma: Globalization as Durable Disorder, *Civil Wars* 1, 36–64.

van Creveld, M. (1999) *The Rise and Decline of the State*. Cambridge: Cambridge University Press.

Dicken, P. (1998) *Global Shift*. London: Paul Chapman. (Third edition.)

Doremus, P., Keller, W., Paul, L. and Reich, S. (1998) *The Myth of the Global Corporation*. Princeton, NJ: Princeton University Press.

Eichengreen, B. (1996) *Globalising Capital: A History of the International Monetary System*. Princeton, NJ: Princeton University Press.

Gray, J. (1998) *False Dawn: The Delusions of Global Capitalism*. London: Granta.

Greider, W. (1997) *One World Ready or Not: the Manic Logic of Global Capitalism*. New York: Simon & Schuster.

Held, D. (1995) *Democracy and the Global Order: From the Modern State to Cosmopolitan Governance*. Cambridge: Polity.

Held, D., McGrew, A., Goldblatt, D. and Perraton, J. (1999) *Global Transformations*. Cambridge: Polity.

Hirst, P. (1998a) The International Origins of National Sovereignty. In Paul Hirst, *From Statism to Pluralism*. London: UCL Press, chap. 14.

Hirst, P. (1998b) The Eighty Years Crisis 1919–1999 – Power, *Review of International Studies* (special issue) 24, 133–48.

Hirst, P. and Thompson, G. (1999) *Globalisation in Question*. Cambridge: Polity.

Hobbes, T. (1651) *Leviathan* (ed. M. Oakeshott). Oxford: Basil Blackwell.

Holden, B. (ed.) (2000) *Global Democracy: Key Debates*. London: Routledge.

Horsman, M. and Marshall, A. (1994) *After the Nation State*. London: Harper-Collins.

Krasner, S.D. (1988) Sovereignty – An Institutional Perspective, *Comparative Political Studies* 21, 66–94.

Krasner, S.D. (1993) Westphalia and All That. In J. Goldstein and R.O. Keohane (eds), *Ideas and Foreign Policy*. Ithaca, NY: Cornell University Press.

Krasner, S.D. (1995) Compromising Westphalia, *International Security* 20, 115–51.

Krasner, S.D. (1999) *Sovereignty*. Princeton, NJ: Princeton, University Press.

Martin, H.P. and Schumann, H. (1997) *The Global Trap*. London: Zed Books.

Mazower, M. (1998) *Dark Continent: Europe's Twentieth Century*. London: Allen Lane.

Michie, J. and Smith, J. Grieve (1998) *Globalization, Growth and Governance*. Oxford: Oxford University Press.

Milward, A. (1992) *The European Rescue of the Nation State*. London: Routledge.

Montes, M. (1998) *The Currency Crisis in SE Asia*. Singapore: Institute of S.E. Asian Studies.

Polanyi, K. (1944) *The Great Transformation*. Boston: Beacon Press (1957 edn).

Ruggie, J.G. (1983) International Regimes, Transactions and Change: Embedded Liberalism in the Post War Economic Order. In S.D Krasner (ed.), *International Regimes*. Ithaca, NY: Cornell University Press, pp. 195–231.

Ruggie, J.G. (1993) Territoriality and Beyond: Problematising Modernity in International Relations, *International Organisation* 47, 134–72.

Sassen, S. (1996) *Losing Control: Sovereignty in an Age of Globalization*. New York: Columbia University Press.

Segal, A. (1993) *Atlas of International Migration*. London: Hans Zell.

Soros, G. (1998) *The Crisis of Global Capitalism*. London: Little Brown.

Spruyt, H. (1994) *The Sovereign State and Its Competitors*. Princeton, NJ: Princeton University Press.

Strange, S. (1996) *The Retreat of the State*. Cambridge: Cambridge University Press.

Thomson, J.E. (1994) *Mercenaries, Pirates and Sovereigns: State-Building and Extra-territorial Violence in Early-Modern Europe*. Princeton, NJ: Princeton University Press.

Wolf, M. (1998) Flows and blows *Financial Times*. March 3, p. 22.

CHAPTER 14

THE EUROPEAN PARLIAMENT AND DEMOCRACY IN THE EUROPEAN UNION

Julie Smith

The European Parliament (EP) is part of a unique experiment in regional integration. Other countries have attempted to co-operate, but none have developed such a well-defined institutional order as the European Union (EU). The Parliament itself is unique by virtue of being the only directly elected transnational parliament, part of an attempt to extend to a European level representative democracy, which had emerged alongside the nation state in the nineteenth century. Over the years the EP's powers and influence have increased considerably, yet at the same time mutterings about a 'democratic deficit' in EU decision-making have been increasing. This chapter considers the nature and functions of the European Parliament, its role in the democratic functioning of the EU and how far it can help overcome the democratic deficit.

WHY A EUROPEAN PARLIAMENT?

Following the Second World War there was a great move towards co-operation between European states seeking to ensure that future war between them would be inconceivable. Opinions differed as to the nature such co-operation should take: Britain and the Scandinavian countries favoured co-operation between sovereign nation states, whereas several continental states, actively supported by the USA, sought much closer ties in a process that came to be called European integration. The intergovernmental Council of Europe, established in 1949, reflected the rather limited British and Scandinavian approach, albeit with a symbolically important parliamentary assembly. Several other treaties seeking to bring their signatories even closer together were signed in the 1950s, most notably those establishing the European Coal and Steel (ECSC), Atomic Energy (Euratom) and Economic Communities (EEC) comprising France, Germany, Italy, and the three Benelux countries.[1]

These treaties created various institutions, although the institutional framework did not follow any clear pattern; it was, and remains, in the words of William Wallace (1983), 'less than a federation and more than a regime'. Key institutions included the High Authority of the ECSC and the Commissions of the EEC and Euratom (these three bodies merged in 1967 to form the Commission of the European Communities), the Councils of Ministers of the three Communities, the Court of Justice and the Common Assembly, which began to call itself the European Parliament in 1962, although its name was not officially changed until the 1986 Single European Act came into effect.

Two strands of opinion underlay the creation of the Common Assembly: federalist idealism and the need to make the High Authority accountable. For the federalists, a parliament would give the necessary trappings of democracy to the constitutional order they sought. However, by the time the Communities were created, the federalists had already lost momentum, hence the Common Assembly was more a democratic add-on than part of a federal model. David Marquand, for example, has argued that the European Parliament was:

> a decorative afterthought, added to the building because the architects feared that its design might otherwise be unpopular. Yet, in adding it, the architects implicitly accepted – or at any rate made an important concession to – a quite different, more political, at least quasi-federalist, conception of what integration was about ... The logic of the decision to create the European Parliament, in short, ran counter to the logic underlying the rest of the system. (Marquand, 1979, p. 82)

Pragmatists, including for these purposes one of the founding fathers of European integration, Jean Monnet, were won over to the idea of an assembly by the recognition of the fact that the High Authority would have certain sovereign powers and therefore needed to be kept accountable. Bringing the people into the integration process was not at the forefront of Jean Monnet's approach to integration, however (see Featherstone, 1994; Wallace and Smith 1995).

Provision was made in the Treaties for direct election to the Assembly. However the concept of a directly elected parliament was highly contentious – for realists, notably the French Gaullists, the idea of a parliament above the national level was a nonsense. Such a body, they argued, would have no authority, since, as Michel Debré put it, 'in political life there are only national realities in Europe' (quoted in Smith, 1999, p. 44). That said, however, they seemed to oppose direct elections for precisely the reasons the federalists advocated them, namely that they would indeed confer legitimacy on the integration process.

In the early years of European integration, the existence of the Assembly ensured a measure of indirect representation – MEPs had normally been elected at the national level and sat in national parliaments, enhancing the links between the national and European levels and hence fostering a better understanding of European issues among national politicians.[2] Over the years, however, popular support for European integration seemed to recede, hence calls for direct elections to the EP were based, at least in part, on the idea that they would foster renewed support for the European Communities (see, for example, the 1976 Tindemans Report on European Union).

It took 22 years for elections to be introduced; only after the demise of General de Gaulle did the Council make progress in fulfilling the treaty commitment to hold direct elections and even then it was not clear that they served the purposes the founding fathers intended. The introduction of direct elections in 1979 ensured direct representation and brought about the trappings of democracy at the European level. However, EP elections have fared less well in enhancing the legitimacy of the European integration process. Voters have shown little interest in elections that have typically focused on national issues and been fronted by national politicians, leading authors such as Reif to describe them as second-order elections (Reif 1984 and 1985, Reif and Schmitt, 1980). Moreover, rather than gaining momentum, interest seemed to wane as turnout declined in each set of European elections.

The European Parliament gradually accrued power and influence before 1979; its role has altered almost out of all recognition since the mid-1980s. Yet, this did not translate into greater respect for the Parliament or even significantly enhanced publicity. Commentators continued to consider EP elections to be second order and voters continued to abstain. In part, this behaviour might be attributed to the working procedures of the EP, which can render it difficult for the outsider to follow.

WORKINGS OF THE EP

The work of the European Parliament is complicated by its multinational composition and the fact that its seat is divided between Brussels and Strasbourg, necessitating a considerable amount of expensive and unnecessary travel between the two cities. The regular journey is costly and time-consuming and serves only to further popular perceptions that the European Parliament (and by extension the entire European Union) is one long gravy train, contributing to a sense of alienation and reducing the legitimacy of a body that was intended to represent the peoples of Europe. For some MEPs the requirement to hold twelve plenary sessions a year in Strasbourg is perceived as a deliberate attempt by the Council to weaken its position. In practice, all the institutions are affected, since Commissioners have to travel to Strasbourg regularly to address the

Table 14.1 Allocation of seats to member states

Country	No. of seats
Austria	21
Belgium	25
Denmark	16
Finland	16
France	87
Germany	99
Greece	25
Ireland	15
Italy	87
Luxembourg	6
Netherlands	31
Portugal	25
Spain	64
Sweden	22
UK	87
Total	626

Parliament and answer parliamentary questions, and members on national governments are also frequent attenders.

Allocation of Seats

The EP has expanded from 142 members in 1958 to 626 in 1995, as a result both of repeated enlargement of the European Union and of a decision to expand the EP at the time of the first direct elections. Seats in the EP are allocated to countries according to their size under a system of 'degressive proportionality', which overrepresents smaller member states: Germany has 200 times as many citizens as Luxembourg, but only sixteen times as many seats. Yet despite being overrepresented in terms of its ratio of seats to votes, Luxembourg with just six MEPs tends to pay little attention to the EP – with less than 1 per cent of the total seats, Luxembourgers realize that there is little scope for their MEPs to have a significant impact in the EP. This is also perhaps true for Ireland and is likely to engender similar responses in other small countries such as Malta and Slovenia, which hope to join the EU in the early years of the twenty-first century.

With the prospect of further EU enlargement, the Treaty of Amsterdam set a ceiling of 700 MEPs, to avoid the EP becoming increasingly unwieldy in an enlarged Union. However, for this provision to be maintained after the first wave of enlargement, member states will have to produce a new formula for the distribution of seats. Any reform would entail a reduction in the number of MEPs for most existing member states and is thus likely to meet serious opposition. Thus, at the time of writing it was unclear how the question would resolve itself.

Languages

The multinational nature of the EU is rarely seen as clearly as in the number of official languages: eleven for fifteen member states. Whereas the Commission and the Council accept the use of English, French, and more recently German, as working languages, all eleven official languages are used by the EP in both plenary sessions and committees. This has serious financial implications – since there are 110 language permutations, numerous interpreters are required. Perhaps more importantly it means debates can be rather stilted. To date, the occasional suggestions that the number of official languages be cut have been rejected out of respect for the right of MEPs to be able to communicate in their own languages: representatives of 'the peoples' cannot be expected to be competent in foreign languages. Moreover, any talk of reducing the number of official languages inevitably touches on national sensitivities, with representatives of small member states, notably Greece, particularly averse to the idea that they might lose their official language.

PARLIAMENTARY GROUPS

Members of the EP sit in transnational groups with representatives of fraternal parties from across the EU, rather than in national groups. Parties from the three largest party families – Social Democrats, Christian Democrats, and the Liberals and their allies – formally established themselves as transnational party federations in the 1970s in the run-up to the first direct elections. Now formally constituted as transnational *parties*, the Christian Democrats' grouping, the European People's Party (EPP), the Party of European Socialists (PES) and European Liberal, Democrats and Reform Party remain essentially *umbrella organizations*, as is the Federation of Green Parties of the European Union.

Those MEPs who are elected as representatives of a constituent party of any of the transnational parties/party federations will sit with that party's group in the European Parliament (see Table 14.2).[3] In addition, the British Conservatives sit with the EPP Group as allied members, although the Conservative Party has eschewed membership of the EPP party organization. Membership of these groups is rather fluid, partly because national parties sometimes decide to switch allegiances during the course of a Parliament; the Portuguese Social Democrats, for example, left the ELDR Party and hence the ELDR Group to join the EPP in 1996.

There are several other groups in the European Parliament, which tend to coalesce only after the European elections. They are typically more heterogeneous than the established party groups and do not campaign on common manifestos. Some of these groups come together primarily to reap the benefits (financial, secretarial and administrative, not to mention committee positions) accruing to groups, given the requirement that they must be a certain minimum size, the precise minimum depending on how many different member states' parties are represented in them. Such groups must, nevertheless, have some affinity – as France's National Front leader, Jean-Marie Le Pen, and the Left-wing Italian former commissioner Emma Bonino discovered in the wake of the 1999 EP elections, when their attempt to form a technical group was rejected precisely because they asserted from the outset that the fact they were co-operating should not be taken to mean that their parties had anything in common.

One noticeable feature of the EP groups since 1994, is the emergence of anti-European factions. In the early years of European integration when the Assembly was an appointed chamber, MEPs were typically pro-European, being by and large a self-selecting group. This was even more true after the introduction of direct elections, when it was almost exclusively pro-European politicians who would stand for the EP. Indeed, with the exception of Denmark, where voters had a choice between pro- and anti-integration parties from the time of the 1972 referendum on accession, one criticism frequently levelled against EP elections was that they offered voters no choice on European integration.

The pro-European consensus was partially challenged by the communists and in the 1980s by the emergence of several far-Right parties, but these choices entailed voting for extreme parties. The situation changed in the wake of the 1992 Treaty on European Union. The 1994 elections saw success for the French Euro-sceptic 'L'Autre Europe' list of Philippe de Villiers and the late Sir James Goldsmith, whose MEPs formed the core of a new anti-European group, the Independent Europe of Nations. Renamed the Union for a Europe of Nations, this group persisted into the 1999–2004 Parliament, though with a slightly different set of constituent parties. A second Euro-sceptic group, the Europe of Democracies and Diversities Group (EDD), was created in 1999, comprising the Danish and Dutch Euro-sceptic parties that had previously been in the I-EN, along with three members of the UK Independence Party and six pro-hunting French members elected under the label 'Chasse, Pêche, Nature, Traditions'.

Table 14.2 Party Groups in the European Parliament as at November 1999

	B	DK	D	GR	E	F	IRE	I	L	NL	A	P	FIN	S	UK	Total
EPP/ED	6	1	53	9	28	21	5	34	2	9	7	9	5	7	37	233
PES	5	3	33	9	24	22	1	17	2	6	7	12	3	6	30	180
ELDR	5	6			3		1	8	1	8			5	4	10	51
Greens/EFA	7		7		4	9	2	2	1	4	2		2	2	6	48
EUL-NGL		1	6	7	4	11		6		1		2	1	3		42
UEN		1				12	6	9				3				30
EDD		4				6				3					3	16
IND	2				1	6		11			5				1	26
Total	25	16	99	25	64	87	15	87	6	31	21	25	16	22	87	626

Source: European Parliament (1999)

EPP/ED	Group of the European People's Party and European Democrats
PES	Group of the Party of European Socialists
ELDR	European Liberal, Democratic and Reformist Group
GREENS/EFA	Greens and regionalists
UEL/NGL	Confederal Group of the United European Left/Nordic Green Left
UEN	The Union for a Europe of Nations
EDD	The Europe of Democracies and Diversities Group
IND	Independents

At one level the changing nature of EP party groups would seem to be reflecting greater diversity among voters, with some members keen advocates of deeper integration and some strongly opposed to any further integration. However, this masks serious flaws of EU-level democracy: firstly, voters supporting many of these parties have no idea before the elections which groups their MEPs will sit with – a Dane voting for the People's Movement against the EU will not necessarily have any interest in the pro-hunting lobby so strongly advocated by the French members of the group. Moreover, whether voters actually do have a choice on European issues depends on where they live. By 1999, it was still almost impossible for voters in some member states to register their scepticism or opposition to further integration. Thus, the apparent opening up of the party system within the EU remained something of a chimera.

By the year 2000 the dominant groups within the EU were those comprising parties of the centre-left and centre-right that reflected traditional social and political cleavages at the national level. Arguably such cleavages were outdated in the member states. Certainly, they seem at first sight ill-suited to the life of the EP and of the EU more generally. However, when one considers the burgeoning legislative agenda at the European level, covering the internal market, environmental policy and consumer protection, as well as social policy, then the traditional Left-Right socioeconomic choices available begin to make more sense even at the European level. The lack of choice on the nature of the European Union may matter less than the opportunity to vote for the type of Europe one wants – one guided by welfarism or one guided by liberal economic values. Indeed, as the role of the EP has expanded over the years, such pragmatic voting would seem appropriate.

POWERS OF THE EUROPEAN PARLIAMENT

It is frequently asserted or assumed that the European Parliament has few powers and little influence. However, while this was true initially, by the year 2000 repeated treaty reforms, custom and practice had altered its role beyond all recognition.

The Common Assembly of the European Coal and Steel Community as established by the 1951 Treaty of Paris had few powers – it had the right to dismiss the High Authority by a two-thirds and absolute majority of its members, but no right to nominate its successor. Nor did it have any legislative powers. When the European Economic and Atomic Energy Communities were created in 1957, the European Parliamentary Assembly was expanded from 78 to 142 members. The newly expanded

Assembly could sack the commissions and was also granted the right to be consulted on legislation. However, since the commissions enjoyed considerably fewer powers than the High Authority, in some ways the Assembly's supervisory power was rendered commensurately less important.

Over the years the Parliament has seen its powers vastly increased: first with the introduction of budgetary powers in 1970 and 1975; then in the legislative sphere with the introduction of a right of amendment via the co-operation procedure in the Single European Act (SEA) and a right of co-decision under the Treaty on European Union (TEU). In each case, the EP's increased role was the corollary of changes elsewhere in the Community/Union. Its budgetary powers, for example, stem from the introduction in 1970 of Community 'own resources'. This method of financing the Community entails money going automatically to the EC without national governments or parliaments explicitly voting on the resources. This meant that there would be no obvious method of ensuring accountability at the national level. Some democratic accountability was seen as desirable and the then-appointed European Parliament seemed the natural body to undertake this task, representing as it did the 'peoples of Europe'.

Subsequently, the EP's powers of amendment and veto were introduced in response to the extension of qualified majority voting (QMV) under the provisions of the SEA and TEU. When decisions are taken by QMV in the Council, individual member states can be outvoted and there is little national parliaments can do to ensure accountability. By giving the European Parliament the power to amend legislation it seemed to the drafters of the SEA that a measure of parliamentary democracy would be maintained. Yet, paradoxically, despite this new provision, the period after the SEA witnessed the greatest expression of concern about a loss of democracy in European decision making. In 1988, the EP defined this so-called 'democratic deficit' as:

> the combination of two phenomena: (a) the transfer of powers from the Member States to the European Community; and (b) the exercise of these powers at the Community level by institutions other than the European Parliament, even though, before the transfer, the national parliaments held power to pass laws in the areas concerned. (Toussaint Report quoted in Bogdanor, 1989, p. 203)

From 1993, the co-decision procedure introduced by the Treaty on European Union gave the EP greater influence in certain policy areas. Initially limited to policies associated with the internal market, the procedure was extended considerably by the Treaty of Amsterdam, with further extension in prospect as a corollary to a probable extension of qualified majority voting expected to result from the 2000 Intergovernmental Conference (IGC).

In addition to legislative powers, the European Parliament wields considerable powers in relation to the EU's bureaucratic and executive body, the European Commission, including the right to throw out the entire Commission, a power that, to date, MEPs have not used. There is no provision to censure individual Commissioners and originally no guarantee that the member states would not merely reinstate the sacked Commission, so it was long assumed that this was a 'nuclear weapon' that the Parliament would never actually use. Over the years there were some abortive attempts to throw out the Commission, which had little chance of success, serving merely to highlight the weakness of the EP (see Westlake, 1994, p. 28). This was all to change in 1999, however.

The Commission disburses the Community budget, but the European Parliament has the right of discharge – the power to agree that the Commission has satisfactorily completed its task. In December 1998 it became clear that there were problems with the 1996 budget and MEPs tried to censure the Commission. After three months of investigation, the Commission finally resigned *en masse* in March 1999 amid allegations of cronyism and mismanagement, jumping before MEPs could push them. Although the EP had not actually sacked the Commission, the episode was vitally important in demonstrating that the EP can hold the Commission accountable, thus rendering the EU system apparently more democratic. Ironically, this was not reflected in the EP elections barely three months later. Rather than turning out in force to elect members of a powerful institution, voters abstained in very large numbers, in part it seems because they tarred MEPs with the same brush as the Commissioners they had rejected.

The Treaty on European Union gave the Parliament the right to be consulted on the Council's nominee for Commission President and the right to give its assent to the incoming College of Commissioners (something that MEPs had been doing informally for years). MEPs rapidly altered their Rules of Procedure to maximize the benefits of this new power. Accordingly in 1994 they held a vote on Jacques Santer's nomination as President prior to the vote on the whole College of Commissioners, which although it had no legal standing was important as it was unlikely that a President-designate could have persisted in his/ her candidature had the EP voted against them. This practice was formalized in the Treaty of Amsterdam, which also gave the Commission President-designate a say in the composition of the Commission, thus offering the EP some prospect of affecting the makeup of the Commission in due course.

In fact, the Commission resignation in March 1999 altered the expected pattern of appointment. A successor to President Santer, former Italian Prime Minister Romano Prodi, was nominated at the Berlin Summit in March 1999 and accepted by the outgoing Parliament in May. Although the incoming Parliament (elected in June 1999) still undertook the Congressional-style hearings of commissioners-designate that had been introduced in the wake of the TEU, the fact that President Prodi had already been appointed prevented the incoming Parliament from exerting as much influence as it might otherwise have done. However, by the time of the hearings in September 1999, it had already become clear that Prodi intended to ensure fellow commissioners were more accountable than their predecessors and each of them told MEPs that they would resign if requested to by the President. The Commission thus seemed to have become more accountable than had previously been the case.

The situation post-Amsterdam still fell short of a parliamentary system where the executive (Commission) emerges from the legislature and the Parliament still lacked the right of legislative initiative. Nevertheless, repeated treaty reforms had certainly enhanced the EP's role in EU decision-making to the point where, in many ways, the EP is at least as powerful as most national parliaments in Western Europe, the main difference lying in perceptions of their respective roles: the powers of national parliaments are frequently overestimated as a result of centralization and accretion of powers by national executives. However, while the EP's influence in the decision-making process of the EU was greatly enhanced, this was not matched by a comparable increase in popular support for the EP or a belief that Europe had become any more democratic. On the contrary, national politicians and voters continued to pay scant attention to the EP, raising questions about how far such elections do in fact confer the democratic legitimacy usually assumed.

DEMOCRACY IN THE EU

EP Elections

Member states consistently failed to agree on a common electoral system and by 1999 there were sixteen different electoral systems in force for the EP elections (Britain and Northern Ireland have different systems). This contributed to a situation where the elections are often seen primarily as a series of fifteen separate national contests. Thus there is little incentive to campaign at the European level, resulting in the emphasis being placed on national contests, with national politicians playing a leading role. The problems have been compounded by the fact that the transnational parties are essentially only co-ordinating bodies for like-minded parties, lacking the resources to engage in intensive campaigning at the European level. In reality, as Klaus Welle of the EP would argue, it makes sense for election campaigns to be run at the national or even a subnational level, since this allows for the most effective distribution of resources. Nevertheless, such arrangements give rise to continuing assertions that EP elections are second order, changing little. This might not matter were it not for the parallel claims that there is a democratic deficit in EU decision-making. The standard argument put forward by MEPs is that granting the EP more powers will help overcome this deficit. If, however, it seems that voters are not interested in EP elections, doubt is cast on the legitimacy of the body elected and of the EU more generally.

Democracy Beyond the Nation State

The European Parliament has played an increasingly important role in European decision-making since its inception as the Common Assembly in 1952. From being merely a consultative body, it has become a co-legislator with the Council of Ministers in some policy areas.[4] Yet, the enhanced role of the EP does not go very far towards giving citizens of the Union a say in EU decisions for a variety of reasons, some related to the EP's position within the Union's decision-making framework, some related to the internal workings of the EP and its party groups, and some related to the relationship between the Union and its citizens. All of these fundamentally affect the nature of democracy within the European Union, distinguishing it from democracy in national or subnational political arenas.

Various problems are associated with extending democracy 'beyond the nation state'. The concept of democracy is itself contested: at the most fundamental level it has to be seen as 'government by the people', but this begs the questions 'Who are the people?' and 'What does it mean "to govern"?' Both questions may appear facile until one begins to realize the difficulties that have surrounded the creation of European 'citizenship'. Within existing nation states there is usually relatively little dispute about who is a citizen (even if there are serious disputes about who *should* be a citizen), but at the European level it is much harder to formulate any sense of identity or community beyond the essentially formal provisions of Article 8 of the TEU. Formal declarations of citizenship do not necessarily lead the 'citizens' to identify with the European

Union; identity still seems to reside primarily at the national or subnational level (Everts and Sinnott, 1995). Moreover, in the case of the European Union opinions differ on whether the European Parliament is or should be the only locus of legitimacy – many would argue that the Council of Ministers, composed of representatives of democratically elected national governments, is in fact a democratic body and one that, moreover, represents the interests of the member states rather effectively. Members of national parliaments also seek to play a key role in decision-making, because they are directly elected and, arguably, much closer than MEPs to the people. National MPs and MEPs tend to see their roles as competitive, but in practice there is considerable scope for co-operation. Neither can hold both the Council and the individual member governments accountable, working together they can do so far more effectively. This is something that MPs are gradually coming to accept, albeit reluctantly. It is essential to find ways of ensuring the accountability of decision-makers, but it is not clear that existing patterns of democracy as practised at the national level, or as they are advocated by some at the European level, can be or should be replicated 'beyond the nation state'; new practices might be necessary. How might the situation be altered?

AMENDING THE STATUS QUO

One answer, which is no longer adequate, is that the powers of the European Parliament should be increased. The Single European Act, the Treaty on European Union and the Treaty of Amsterdam all contributed to creating an EP that enjoys significant powers – greater in many ways than those of most national parliaments (see Norton, 1990a and 1990b and Smith 1999, chapter 4). At the time of writing, it seemed that discussions about extending the scope of qualified majority voting in the Council, which were on the agenda of the 2000 IGC, would lead to a concomitant extension of the EP's right of co-decision. Moreover, MEPs have repeatedly altered their own practices and Rules of Procedure to maximize their influence across the range of EU policies, for example pushing for aspects of foreign policy with financial implications for the EU to be tackled through the normal EU budgetary procedure, thereby ensuring a greater role for the European Parliament in the area of foreign policy than that envisaged by the treaties.

Admittedly the EP does not have the right of legislative initiative, but then neither do many national parliaments. There are few compelling reasons to increase the legislative powers of the EP beyond the extension of co-decision; it would be far more effective to make people – national politicians, civil servants and journalists as well as the voters – aware of the powers the Parliament has than to confer any new powers at this stage. Over the years MEPs have become increasingly skilful in maximizing their influence by judicious use of their powers and have gradually won considerably more media coverage than in the past, especially at the time of the Commission resignation.

The resignation of the entire College of Commissioners does raise the question of whether MEPs should be allowed the right to censure individual Commissioners, something they themselves had previously rejected as detrimental to Commission collegiality (Westlake, 1994, p. 27). The idea has some merit – MEPs might well have been satisfied by the resignation of the individuals most heavily criticized by the Report of Independent Experts, Edith Cresson and perhaps Manuel Marin, rather than by the whole Commission. However, this would arguably go against the ideas of collective Commission responsibility.

In fact, it is the nature of appointment which needs more careful consideration. Despite changes under the Treaty on European Union and the Treaty of Amsterdam, the Parliament still has only the right to accept Commissioners nominated by national governments. Admittedly the provisions for the Commission President to be consulted on the appointment of his colleagues could in future enable MEPs to make clear to him/her that certain nominees would be unacceptable. Yet, even if MEPs were able to influence the composition of the incoming Commission either behind closed doors before the official nomination procedure or formally by vetoing some or all of the Commissioners-designate, the outcome would still be far removed from the electorate. The links between EP elections and the composition of the Commission would remain too weak for voters to feel that they have any significant impact on the dynamics of EU decision-making. Certainly the first elections after the Treaty of Amsterdam came into effect did not show any signs that this was changing. What alternative models might we then adopt?

MODELS OF DEMOCRACY FOR THE EU

Is parliamentary democracy the way forward or are other models more appropriate for a united Europe? Are there any pre-existing models for European democracy or do we need to create new ones? Have attempts to reform the European institutions to enhance democracy been too hidebound by traditional models of democracy, based on the experiences *within* rather than *beyond* the nation state? Do we need to go beyond traditional parliamentary, presidential and semi-presidential systems?

My preferred solution looks rather similar to an existing model: the composition of the Commission should depend on the results of European elections. The best way forward would be for the College of Commissioners, reduced to maybe fifteen members, to emerge from the EP. This would have the combined effect of giving the Commission a virtually direct mandate from the people and of cutting the state–Commissioner links.

It comes rather close to some types of parliamentary democracy, with the executive emerging from the legislature, as is the case in Great Britain. It would be relatively easy to operate and has the advantage of fitting with existing practice in some countries, making it easier to 'sell' the idea to voters in the member states. Of course there are drawbacks. It inevitably means that some states will not have a Commissioner, which, although it should not be a permanent occurrence for any state, may turn out to be a problem for small states such as Luxembourg and later Slovenia or Malta. However, the overrepresentation of such states in the European Parliament and in votes in the Council (regardless of whether by unanimity or QMV) means that their interests would continue to be well represented within the European institutions. Moreover, national political parties are typically members of the transnational political parties/party federations and would thus have a forum in which to voice their opinions, not least in drafting the transnational party manifestos on which European elections are fought. In any case, one frequently forgotten point is that Commissioners are officially independent of national ties once they take office; formally breaking the state–Commissioner link would merely strengthen this independence.

A further implication of this change would be a rebalancing of the powers and influence of the Community institutions. The Commission would enjoy enhanced legitimacy, which would strengthen it in relations to the Council of Ministers. At the same time the Commission would be reliant on the European Parliament to keep it in office, thus rendering it relatively weaker compared to the EP. Inevitably, whether these changes would be good or bad depends very much on one's ideas about European integration.

One clear advantage of breaking the state–Commissioner link would be to impede the dangers of cronyism with which some members of the 1994–9 Commission were tainted. There would be less incentive for second-rate candidates to be accepted because the previous gentlemen's agreement that states do not reject candidates nominated by other states (already weakened in 1994 when the then German Chancellor, Helmut Kohl, vetoed the candidature of Dutch premier, Ruud Lubbers, and British Prime Minister, John Major, went on to veto his Belgian counterpart, Jean-Luc Dehaene) would simply no longer be relevant.

CONCLUSIONS

There is not only one way to democracy in a united Europe. I have put forward one model that I think would offer a greater degree of legitimation for the European Union; I do not claim that it is the only one, but I think it is the best. Direct election of the Commission or the Commission President would offer a clearer focus to European level elections, which would arguably make it much easier to interest voters in the European politics.[5] The danger of that option, however, is that there might be excessive emphasis on the candidates' nationalities – would British voters really be happy to vote for a German candidate or Frenchmen for a Belgian, even if they represented a party family that the voters supported?

There are, of course, those who favour an even more intergovernmental approach, giving more power back to the Council of Ministers and the European Council, on the grounds that these institutions are composed of national politicians, so that legitimacy is indirectly conferred on the decision-making process.[6] Complaints that this gives too little power to parliamentarians could be countered with the claim that improved patterns of scrutinizing European legislation within national parliaments would help overcome the problem. However, unless there was a move back towards unanimous voting in the Council, this argument collapses in the face of the argument put forward at the time of the Single European Act and that underlies one aspect of the current democratic deficit – national parliaments might be able to hold national ministers accountable, but if the latter can be outvoted because qualified majority voting is in force, the parliamentarians will not be able to affect the outcome.[7]

Neither of these scenarios is likely to result from the 2000 Intergovernmental Conference. The challenge for national politicians and MEPs is to ensure that significant reforms are undertaken. A barely changed version of the status quo is *not* the way to democracy in a United Europe. The European Parliament can lead to a democratically legitimate Europe, but this is not automatic – it will require clear thinking and radical reform of the existing institutional framework.

ACKNOWLEDGEMENTS

Parts of this chapter were originally presented as 'Why the European Parliament Cannot be a Model for Transnational Democracy' at the SGIR-ISA Third Pan-European Conference, Vienna 16–19 September 1998, and 'The Dream of a European Parliament: Is there only one way to democracy in a United Europe?' at the Democracy in Europe and the European Parliament Conference organized by the Information Office of the European Parliament for Austria and ECSA Austria, Vienna, 19–21 May 1999. The author is extremely grateful to John Pinder for his invaluable comments on this latter paper.

NOTES

1. The TEU brings together the European Economic Community, renamed the European Community (EC), the ECSC and Euratom to form the first pillar of the European Union (EU), established in 1993. The Communities and later Union increased from the six member states in the 1950s to fifteen by 1 January 1995 with further enlargement in prospect.
2. Clearly an onerous burden on MEPs forced to travel frequently between their national parliaments, the European Parliament and their constituencies, the dual mandate did have certain advantages in terms of socialization or Europeanization.
3. It is important to bear in mind that the parties and party groups are separate organizations. The groups are financially stronger than the parties and are not bound by them.
4. Or, as Otto Schmuck (1989) has put it, 'from a forum for discussion to a co-player' in European politics.
5. For a discussion of these ideas see Vernon Bogdanor (1986).
6. This line of argument is somewhat flawed by the fact that some national ministers are appointed rather than elected.
7. The only counter to this would be if, based on the demands of their MPs, ministers repeatedly resorted to claims of national interest, thus allowing them to invoke the Luxembourg compromise. However, to date this has not really happened.

FURTHER READING

Corbett, Richard (1998) *The European Parliament's Role in Closer EU Integration* (London: Macmillan). Gives a fascinating overview of the EP's role in pushing the integration process.

Corbett, Richard, Francis Jacobs and Michael Shackleton (2000) *The European Parliament* (London: Cartermill, 4th edition). The most comprehensive guide to the European Parliament, its powers, influence, and formal and informal practices. It also covers the electoral and party political dimensions.

Hix, Simon and Christopher Lord (1997) *Political Parties in the European Union* (London: Macmillan). This offers the best overview of party political cooperation at the European level.

Lord, Christopher (1999) *Democracy in the European Union* (Sheffield: Sheffield Academic Press). Considers the issues discussed in the present chapter from a

conceptual perspective, considering the nature of 'authorization', 'representation' and 'accountability'.

Pinder, John (ed.) (1999) *Foundations of Democracy in the European Union: From the
Genesis of Parliamentary Democracy to the European Parliament* (London: Macmillan in association with the European Cultural Foundation). Comprises a
series of essays looking at the evolution of European democracy, highlighting
differences in the democratic experiences of several European states.

Reif, Karlheinz and Hermann Schmitt (1980) Nine Second-order National Elections – A Conceptual Framework for the Analysis of European Election
Results, *European Journal of Political Research* 8, pp. 3–44.

Smith, Julie (1999) *Europe's Elected Parliament* (Sheffield: Sheffield Academic
Press). Gives an overview of the origins and developments of the EP and
analyses the first four sets of direct elections.

Westlake, Martin (1994) *A Modern Guide to the European Parliament* (London:
Pinter). Offers a comprehensive and accessible account of the workings of the
EP and its role in EU decision-making.

BIBLIOGRAPHY

Bogdanor, Vernon (1986) The Future of the European Community: Two Models
of Democracy, *Government and Opposition* 21, 161–76.

Bogdanor, Vernon (1989) The June 1989 European Elections and the Institutions
of the Community, *Government and Opposition* 24, 199–214.

Bogdanor, Vernon (1990) *Democratizing the Community*. London: Federal Trust for
Education and Research.

Chryssochoou, Dimitris N. (1998) *Democracy in the European Union*. London:
Tauris Academic Studies.

Corbett, Richard (1998) *The European Parliament's Role in Closer EU Integration*.
London: Macmillan.

Corbett, Richard, Francis Jacobs and Michael Shackleton (1995) *The European
Parliament*. London: Cartermill International, third edition.

European Parliament (1999) *New 1999 Political Formations in the European Parliament*. Brussels: European Parliament, PE 280.807.

Everts, Philip and Richard Sinnott (1995) Conclusion: European publics and the
legitimacy of internationalized governance. In Oskar Niedermayer and
Richard Sinnott (eds), *Public Opinion and Internationalized Governance*. Oxford:
Oxford University Press.

Featherstone, Kevin (1994) Jean Monnet and the 'Democratic Deficit' in the
European Union, *Journal of Common Market Studies* 32, 149–70.

Hix, Simon and Christopher Lord (1997) *Political Parties in the European Union*.
London: Macmillan.

Lord, Christopher (1998) *Democracy in the European Union*. Sheffield: Sheffield
Academic Press.

Marquand, David (1979) *Parliament for Europe*. London: Jonathan Cape.

Norton, Philip (1990a) Parliaments: a Framework for Analysis, *West European Politics* (special issue on 'Parliaments in Western Europe') 13, 1–9.

Norton, Philip (1990b) Conclusion: Legislatures in Perspective, *West European Politics* 13, 143–52.

Niedermayer, Oskar and Richard Sinnott (1995), Democratic Legitimacy and the European Parliament. In Oskar Niedermayer and Richard Sinnott (eds), *Public Opinion and Internationalized Governance*. Oxford: Oxford University Press.

Reif, Karlheinz (1984) National Electoral Cycles and European Elections 1979 and 1984, *Electoral Studies* 3, 244–55.

Reif, Karlheinz (ed.) (1985) *Ten European Elections*. Aldershot: Gower.

Reif, Karlheinz and Hermann Schmitt (1980) Nine Second-order National Elections – A Conceptual Framework for the Analysis of European Election Results, *European Journal of Political Research* 8, 3–44.

Schmuck, Otto (1989) *Das Europäische Parlament: vom Gesprächsforum zum Mitgestalter europäischer Politik*. Bonn: Institut für Europäische Politik.

Smith, Julie (1999) *Europe's Elected Parliament*. Sheffield: Sheffield Academic Press.

Tindemans (1976) Report on European Union (*EC Bulletin Supplement* 1/1976).

Wallace, William (1983) Less than a Federation, More than a Regime: the Community as Political System. In Helen Wallace, William Wallace and Carole Webb (eds), *Policy Making in the European Community*. Chichester: John Wiley, pp. 403–36.

Wallace, William (1996), Government without Statehood: the Unstable Equilibrium. In Helen Wallace and William Wallace (eds), *Policy-Making in the European Union*. Oxford: Oxford University Press, pp. 439–60.

Wallace, William, and Julie Smith (1995) Democracy versus Technocracy, European Integration and the Problem of Popular Consent, *West European Politics* 18, 137–57.

Westlake, Martin (1994) *The Commission and the Parliament: Partners and Rivals in the European Policy-making Process*. London: Butterworths.

CHAPTER 15

CHALLENGES TO DEMOCRACY IN AN AGE OF GLOBALIZATION

Benjamin Barber

To assess the challenges presented to democracy in an age of globalization where the traditional context for democracy – the nation state – has witnessed an erosion of its sovereignty is to pose a novel set of questions. For in rendering national boundaries porous, globalization has had a serious impact on political economy as well as political systems. However, before facing those challenges, I wish to revisit an ancient dilemma concerning the nature of democracy itself.

STRONG DEMOCRACY VERSUS REPRESENTATION

To begin with, it may be useful to offer an elementary definition of the well-known distinction between representative and participatory or direct democracy – or what I called in the book by that name, strong democracy. Those engaged in governance, whether in the private sector, civil society, or the public sector, need to remember that representation and the representative system have always been parts of a bitter compromise in the history of democracy. Democracy originated in rustic, bucolic republics, in simple principalities in the ancient world, in places where a small group of citizens – often to the exclusion of many others – comprised the *polis*. For the communitarian citizenries of the ancient world were limited in compass, usually based on the enslavement or economic servitude of some and the systematic exclusion of others. The ancient Athenians managed both to disinherit women and immigrants ('resident foreigners') from citizenship and at the same time enslave the local population to give themselves the leisure to govern. However, and this is the point of the distinction, for those who were citizens, governance was understood as an exercise in self-government, in doing for yourself all of the tasks of a republic from military service to office holding (in many cases, by sortition or lottery).

This direct engagement by citizens in the work of government remained the primary approach to democracy in the ancient world until the Roman republic began to extend its boundaries to include an empire too large to afford self-government. With a European and North African empire there were simply too many people from too many diverse cultures to permit strong participation. At that point, citizenship itself was transformed from active engagement into a matter of passive rights, of law, of civic identity. By the end of the Imperial era, nearly everybody in Europe could count themselves as 'citizens' of the Roman Empire. Yet imperial citizenship had become an identity so thin, so widespread, that it meant almost nothing, conveying few rights and still less real civic power to those who met the formal definition of citizen. It was an empty status – cynics might say rather like citizenship in some mass industrial democracies today. For democracy in modern nation states, where we are encompassing and inclusive in our definition, has depreciated and watered down the concept of citizenship so much that citizens on the whole think little of the few marks of citizenship that remain. Hence, the appalling decline of voting in the USA from figures in the late 1950s of 72 per cent or better to the startlingly modest figures today of under 50 per cent in presidential elections and as little as 35 per cent in Congressional elections. Or take the results in the recent European elections where many national populations participated at rates less than a third of the eligible electorate. Moreover, when voter turnout in the USA and increasingly in Western Europe are parsed demographically, the out-comes are even more alarming.

Those who most need to vote to overcome disempowerment in fact vote the least. Numbers decline when we look at the young, the poor and people of colour – less than one-quarter of these groups participate regularly in elections. In Sweden, there is a 'crisis' in democracy being explored by a parliamentary commission on democracy and a new 'minister of democracy' focused on non-participation of new citizens – immigrants with the most to gain through engagement. Finally, then, not even voting – a residual category in thin, representative democracies – is much practised. The power that subjects die for in the struggle to acquire democracy seems to lose its value once acquired, as the behaviour of citizens in Russia and Eastern Europe suggests. Even those who exercise the vote manifest the cynicism and alienation that typifies non-voters, using their vote to 'sweep the rascals from office' or to enact 'term limits' that paralyse effective government and hobble deeply distrusted representatives.

The alienation of citizens from the professional governing classes is a hallmark of behaviour throughout the Western democracies. Public sec-tor employees and politicians no less than resentful citizens have experienced this deep alienation. Public servants flee Congress and parliaments, no longer willing to make the sacrifice of 'service' to the common good. This would not surprise eighteenth- and nineteenth-century critics of representation like Rousseau and Robert Michels. Rousseau argued in *The Social Contract* that representation was incompatible with real political liberty – you had to participate in governance in order that, in obeying government, you could remain free. Michels insisted in his great study *Political Parties* (1911) that under representative government 'liberty disappeared with the ballot into the ballot box'. The architect of the so-called iron law of oligarchy assumed that, from the moment a democratic electorate chose a delegate, the delegate would become increasingly distanced from his constituents. The gap grows and grows until, in the course of a representative's tenure, he is perceived as (and to some degree becomes) one more oligarch from whom constituents can only feel alienated. And so elections become a matter of a frustrated public ready to throw one gang of representatives out and vote another gang to power, in an ongoing cycle of futility that turns citizens into spectators and spectators into sceptics about democracy. The cycle of futility has grown shorter in recent years. In less than a year, German voters enamoured of Gerhard Schroeder's Social Democrats have turned on him with a vengeance, turning local Social Democrats out of office throughout Germany's provinces and cities. The interval of civic satisfaction has been reduced to a political nanosecond.

I recall these crucial differences between thin and strong democracy and rehearse the critiques of earlier theorists in order to remind us that some of what may appear to be the particular consequences of recent developments in ideology and political practice are actually fundamental issues for representative democracy as a form of government. The iron law of oligarchy, the bureaucratization of representation, the alienation from government of 'citizens' whose only task it is to vote, suggest longstanding problems of democracy that may be reinforced by recent developments but that need to be seen in historical perspective.

We may, as Michels suggested, be 'free' in a meaningful sense only once a year (or once every other year) on election day. For the rest, we may look and act as if we are living under what Thomas Jefferson called 'an elective aristocracy', a system in which we may choose those who govern us, but are otherwise passive subjects of those we choose. As participants in politics as a spectator sport, we are apt to retreat into private and personal lives to make friends and fortunes on our own, and to leave the governing to others. At best, we demand accountability and transparency, the latter in order to secure the former. The chief activities of citizens today would appear to be – no, not even voting – but watching and complaining. In this 'culture of complaint', to assume responsibility means to utter a grievance or blame someone else for deficits that clearly (since we do live in a democracy) issue from our own neglected responsibilities. The consequence is a pathology of disaffection that replaces politics with a debilitating form of 'blamitus'. Democracy is in disarray because ... someone else isn't doing his or her job. We exonerate ourselves.

When we talk about the role of governance in modern life, then, I think we have first to come to terms with the fact that we are rooted in a system of representation that has rescued democracy from its dependency both on small, rustic republicanism and (as the Federalist Papers had it) on those 'nurseries of discord' ancient republics inevitably manifested. This victory over time and scale was won, however, at the cost of real participation by citizens in government. Without representation, democracy probably would not have survived the coming of mass societies on a scale ancient theorists deemed incompatible with active citizenship. The question today, however, is whether democracy can survive the representative system that rescued it.

The debate over these questions was central to the confrontation between democrats and republicans at the American Constitutional Convention in Philadelphia in 1787. The founders were struggling to preserve principles of popular sovereignty under conditions of what Madison called the founding of a Republic of potentially continental extent. Canada must wrestle with similar challenges as a nation of continental compass trying to hold together French, English and native subcultures in a fashion that affords a singular citizenship and a meaningful democracy. In the new European Union, citizens must ask whether the form of diluted citizenship offered to them by a system more interested in euros than Europeans can really meet the requirement of engaged responsibility and civic virtue. If representation has been necessary to the formulas advanced in large nations like Canada and the USA, as well as in new transnational 'polities' like Europe, it has nonetheless forced a fundamental compromise with democracy and self-governance everywhere it has been introduced. We need, both as citizens and officeholders, to be aware of this fateful compromise.

Some believe that technology may offer a 'fix' for these problems. It may address the problems of scale virtually in a way political actuality never could, allowing representative democracy to adjust to demands for greater participation and citizen engagement. For while in the heyday of mass industrial society, in an urban world, under conditions of entrepreneurial capitalism, there seemed no alternative to representation, entrepreneurial capitalism has itself produced new technologies and a new information society that seem to reopen the door to some of the very direct democratic principles, the strong democratic principles, that mass society had rendered irrelevant. To what extent do new telecommunication technologies afford new opportunities for direct democracy? Do computers and the Internet provide tools that make possible a kind of direct engagement and ongoing civic activity among citizens that can flank mass society? Will technology, as I suggested fifteen years ago in *Strong Democracy*, promise a reversion to a virtual *polis* even in societies with hundreds of millions of citizens?

I will try to answer these questions towards the end of the larger discussion, but first I want to set the scene for those final remarks by looking directly at the challenges representative democracy faces. The irony of a postmodern economy that has both undermined the workings of representative democracy and simultaneously provided new means for reestablishing a virtual version of direct democracy and hence reopened the door to strong democratic principles can then be faced.

GLOBALIZATION

Technology has itself been implicated in and reinforced by the most powerful challenge democracy faces: the challenge of globalization. For at the very moment when technology is offering the nation state new forms of direct civic engagement, it is pushing the globalization of the economy in a manner that undermines the nation state and its governing democratic institutions. I have tried to examine the dynamics of globalization in *Jihad vs McWorld*, and I do not want to rehearse its arguments here. Yet we cannot go around the issue of globalization in evaluating democracy today. Nor will it suffice, as some critics have suggested, to trivialize our current era of internationalization by comparing it to what in some ways seems an analogous period before the First World War. It is certainly true that in the period at the end of the nineteenth century's age of empires, there was an internationalization of economics on a very large scale. If one measures international trade as a percentage of GNP, it turns out to have been between 10 and 12 per cent, little different from today.

There is a crucial difference today, however. For today trade is in information, in images, in ideas, in films and advertising and brand names and merchandising. It is in the very stuff of the international nexus, the bytes and bits that punch holes in national frontiers and unite the world. In the nineteenth century, trade was in durable goods, natural resources, the hard economy of the industrial/manufacturing world. Hard trade actually reinforced nationalism, gave national economies their power, and so helped create a world of nation states and nationalisms of the kind that both made autonomy and democracy possible –

and also led to that clash of nations that gave rise in time to two world wars. Where trade reinforced nationalism then, today it undermines it, eroding parochial borders of every kind and turning the global economy into an engine of transformation. It is not just percentages that tell the story, because perhaps 80 per cent of trade today remains in manufactured goods and raw materials. But the remaining 20 per cent representing the service and information economy dominates the character and impact of trade as a whole, and gives globalization its genuinely transnational character.

Globalization has a second feature that makes it unique today. It is almost exclusively economic (and socioeconomic and hence cultural) in character. We have, in fact, managed to globalize markets, globalize the economy, globalize corporations, globalize corporate and pop culture, without globalizing the democratic institutions that historically were the context for the evolution of free markets and the emergence of powerful corporations. We have created a radical asymmetry that the world has not seen before between anarchic international economic institutions and national civic and political institutions that can have little impact on them.

The history of capitalism and free markets has been one of synergy with democratic institutions. Free economies have grown up within, and have been fostered and contained and controlled by, democratic states. Democracy has been a precondition for free markets – not, as economists try to argue today, the other way round. One finds in the history of any national democracy a natural symmetry between the emergence of democratic institutions, representation and extended suffrage, and the development of entrepreneurial capitalism. As England's monarchy became first constitutional and then gave way to genuinely democratic elements, its economy moved from mercantalism to industrial capitalism and free trade. Only in the nineteenth century, well after the unwritten constitution had evolved in clearly democratic directions, did mass industrial capitalism and free trade become hallmarks of the British economy and the British Empire. The freedom of the market has helped sustain freedom in politics and freedom in the political domain has helped sustain the market and also helped to regulate and contain its irregularities, its contradictions, its tendencies towards self-destruction around monopoly, around the eradication of competition. On the global plane today, that symmetry has been destroyed because we have globalized the marketplace without globalizing democracy.

There are, of course, some transnational civic and governmental organizations, though most are either paralysed by national conflicts or by non-participation by principals (the United Nations) or have little power.

Which NGO can hold a candle to the powerful telecommunications MNCs? Is Civicus a match for Murdoch's News Corporation? Can the International Labor Organization (ILO) give Viacom/CBS or Disney/ABC a run for their money? Where nation states do try to use the political sovereignty collectively through common action to contain and regulate multinational corporations it turns out that their governments often seem more interested in protecting the autonomy and sovereignty of markets than insisting on their own public interests. Privatization inside national governments reinforces an outlaw globalism in markets by in effect giving markets and those who run them decisive control over national government policies. In the USA, the relationship is secured by the private funding of elections, which actually legitimates the control of the political sovereign by private interests. What results is a radical and dangerous asymmetry in power between an organized global economy and an anarchic global political climate. This asymmetry not only serves democracy badly, but serves the economy poorly as well.

For a picture of what the new global anarchy may look like if it is allowed to continue unabated and unregulated, one need travel only to Moscow or Smolensk. There free market institutions have been introduced in the absence of any genuine democratic regulation and control or the establishment of a foundation of civic institutions to secure citizenship and democracy. In these far reaches of the 'newly' free world, the result has been a kind of mafiacracy-cum-anarchy, a brutal social Darwinism sometimes called 'wild capitalism', which has not only been deeply destructive to emergent democracy but has also undone capitalism as well, leaving the economy in considerable chaos. My fear is that neither London nor Washington, neither Geneva nor Strasbourg, but Moscow will become the model for the global economy. Why? Because, as in Russia, the global marketplace is without centred democratic institutions to contain its anarchy and regulate its assault on competition. Moscow potentially still has governing institutions, which, if strengthened, might eventually bring capitalism under control. Undergirded with new civic institutions, Russia might tame its wild capitalism as the USA did after the Civil War had unleashed forces of monopoly that the administrations of Teddy Roosevelt and Woodrow Wilson (and in time Franklin Roosevelt) were left to bring under control. But in the international arena there is no such possibility because there are *no* viable governing institutions of any kind, or any apparent way of creating them or even thinking about them. At the very moment when we can strengthen representative institutions by reinjecting a degree of direct democracy in governance through the new technologies, we are destroying the national institutions, including the nation state itself, which have been the seed-bed for democratic institutions.

Economic globalization in the absence of civic and political global-ization has meant a globalization of our vices without a parallel globalization of virtues. As the prescient sociologist Manuel Castells has argued in his three-volume study of the future called *The Network Society*, we have globalized crime, globalized the rogue weapons trade, glob-alized terror and hate propaganda – sometimes using the Internet itself and the new technologies to spread ideologies hostile to technology and modernity. We have globalized drugs, pornography and the trade in women and children made possible by 'porn tourism'. The most egre-gious globalization has been the globalization of the exploitation and pornographic trade in children. Nowhere are children more abused now than in this international arena where there are no real regulations. Think of the abuse that comes from the utilization of child labour in unregu-lated developing economies trying to climb into competition by using underpaid children working in near slave condition; think of child pornography in countries like Thailand which advertise on the Internet and attract people from all over the world, inviting them to come and exploit and abuse virgins in a pornographic trade that goes untouched by democratic authority; think of the use of children as soldiers, 10- and 12-year-old kids with deadly automatic weapons, killing each other and their parents in Third World tribal wars.

Manuel Castells sums up the awful toll in terms that link the abuses directly with the new logic of economic globalization. He insists that the exploitation of children is not an *ad hoc* add-on, but an integral feature of the new global market. He describes the linkage between the exploitation of children and a world economy dominated by rogue forces rather than by law and democracy this way:

> There is a systematic link between the current, unchecked characteristics of informational capitalism and the destruction of lives in a large segment of the world's children. What is different is the disintegration of traditional societies through the world exposing children to the unprotected lands of mega-cities' slums. What is different is children in Pakistan weaving carpets for world-wide export via networks of suppliers to large department stores in affluent markets. What is new is mass global tourism organized around pedophilia. What is new is electronic child pornography on the Net, worldwide. What is new is the disintegration of patriarchalism without being replaced by systems of protection of children provided either by new families or the state. What is new is the weakening of

institutions of support for children's rights such as labor unions or the politics of social reform. (Castells, 1996–98, vol. III, p. 159)

Castells' frightening summary suggests how in just one domain of globalization – the abuse of children – the globalization of markets in the absence of globalization of democratic institutions is increasingly undermining the values and institutions of the family and faith we claim most to cherish.

PRIVATIZATION

Globalization does not occur in a vacuum, however. Its corrosive impact on democratic governance is being hastened by a cognate ideology of privatization that is prevalent both in the international scene and within the countries whose economies are being globalized. Privatization is an ideology that saps democracy by attacking public power, by arguing that markets can do everything government once did better than government, and with more freedom for citizens. Privatization within nation states opens the way for a deregulation of markets that in turn facilitates the globalization of the economy. It softens up citizens to accept the decline of political institutions and tries to persuade them that they will be better off that way – more 'free'. As an ideology, it insists that government is about illegitimate public power and calls for the substitution of private power, which is simply assumed, without any argument, to be legitimate.

In effect the public sector – governance itself – is under attack within the nation state, making an ungoverned globalism seem more desirable. It is important to note in this regard that privatization is not synonymous with decentralization. With decentralization, the public sector and its governing institutions transfer power down the governing hierarchy to provinces, to states, to cities, and to neighbourhoods, thereby empowering citizens to take greater public responsibility and become engaged in government on the local level. This is an instance of subsidiarity: power remains public but is shared. The principle is one of bottom-up power that remains public, not top-down power that becomes private. Privatization does not decentralize at all, however. It shifts power that is public, accountable but perhaps inefficient and bureaucratic to the private sector. It gives power away, often leaving it at the top of the hierarchical ladder, but now in powerful private hands beyond scrutiny. Citizens do not come closer to power: rather new, high-powered, hierarchical bureaucracies are empowered, which, however, are now private, non-transparent, and unaccountable. In place of what were, to be sure, large and rather bureaucratic but nevertheless semi-transparent and semi-accountable public institutions it offers private and entirely unaccountable institutions. Privatization may in some sense 'free' us from the bureaucracy of big government, but only by indenturing us to big business and private bureaucracy.

In a famous State of the Union Address, President Clinton announced the 'end of the era of big government', signalling the willingness of 'new Democrats' to be sceptical about traditional welfare state strategies. However, in pronouncing big government dead without commenting on big business, the President in effect proclaimed the defeat of government and the eclipse of the public sector. He was effectively yielding all centralized power to monopolistic corporations unlikely to be much less large than government, but guaranteed to be far less accountable. Such a one-sided announcement was a pact with the devil, because the effect of unilaterally 'ending' big government was not to make war on bureaucracy, but to make war on democracy. To be sure, big government in the era of the 'great society' and the unbounded welfare state had become bloated, bureaucratic, inefficient and dependency breeding. However, to redress these defects requires the reform of democracy not its elimination. Government belongs to its citizens and if it is removed rather than improved, the citizenry loses its only effective instrument for realizing its public interests.

There is another line of argument that affirms privatization as a reasonable strategy for democracy. It averts these problems by insisting that democracy is served by the private sector through what is sometimes called the consumer vote. After all, the argument goes, through the purchasing power of the yen, the dollar, the Canadian dollar and the Deutschmark, citizens are able to 'vote' as private persons, and have a powerful effect on national outcomes. Privatization does not eliminate politics; it only privatizes it and permits us to vote powerful dollars in the consumer marketplace rather than meaningless preferences in the voting booth. The market can be described as market democracy: a democracy of individuals who show their preferences and express their choices through their spending habits. Fashionable as this argument may be, it suffers from two fatal errors related to a misunderstanding of how democracy works and a failure to comprehend the meaning of the distinction between the public and private domains.

First, we need to recognize that how we spend our dollars is not always truly 'voluntary', since 'choice' is subject to marketing, merchandizing, advertising, and packaging – all of which (as the billions spent suggest) are intended to 'compel' and 'divert' choice to what producers want to sell. The 'free' consumer may not be the 'autonomous' chooser. The multibillion dollar annual advertising budget of the Fortune 500 is nothing if not an attempt to encroach on the autonomy of consumers and both influence preferences and 'force' choices. Merchandising and marketing have become to markets what propaganda was to authoritarian regimes. Recent efforts at the wholesale commercialization of education are obvious attempts at manipulating preferences and coercing choice. Student unions have become malls devoted to the pedagogy of brand loyalty; four-year-olds are now targets for the selling of brand identities on the Internet; school buses (in cities like Colorado Springs) have become acceptable advertising venues; what was once Chris Whittle's Channel One (now sold) for schools, now elicits time for hard advertising during history and social studies classes in return for the loan of hardware that many inner-city schools cannot otherwise afford. These strategies of persuasion and manipulation are not necessarily fatal. Human autonomy has survived far more grievous assaults, and I am no fan of 'false consciousness' arguments that deny ordinary people an intrinsic capacity to judge and an ability to resist those who would condition them. Yet consumer choice in an era of unbounded advertising and merchandizing where almost every domain has been both privatized and commercialized is surely something less than an exercise in unattenuated liberty.

The case against private liberty as a surrogate for public choice does not depend on the compromised character of consumer autonomy, however. The second and more important argument is that consumer choice, even if it is genuinely free, is always and necessarily private, and private personal choices – even when autonomous – cannot affect public outcomes. Democratic governance is about public choosing, about dealing with the social consequences of private choices and behaviour. What we do as citizens is precisely to deal with the public consequences of our private choices, to treat together with the social entailments of what we do alone. One may enjoy fast cars and – other things being equal – choose as a consumer to fuel one's roadster with efficient (but environmentally unsafe) leaded petrol and drive on roads with no speed limit. But other things are not equal. In buying a fast car as a private consumer, one is not wishing for highway casualties or dead forests. And it is as a citizen that one reckons the public costs of private decisions. Hence, as a citizen one may gladly veto one's own private preferences as a consumer, and vote for a reasonable speed limit and insist on unleaded fuel, and enact powerful sanctions against those who disobey the laws (including against oneself as a consumer and private driver). For as a citizen, one can assess the consequences of one's behaviour as a consumer. In Rousseau's language, through participation in the general will we can regulate our private wills. Like all thinking people, we can distinguish easily enough between the self as citizen and the self as consumer. And as citizens, we will voluntarily deal with the social consequences of the private choices we make (even if voluntarily) as consumers.

The marketplace offers us the opportunity to express our economic preferences, but we cannot make political or social decisions in this fashion. We need public institutions to react to the social and public consequences of a marketplace that is more expansive than ever before. The distinction here is between what J.S. Mill called self-regarding behaviour, where we have a right to personal autonomy and privacy, and other-regarding behaviour, which is subject to public legislation and control. Democracy is how we guarantee that legislating other-regarding behaviour will be fair and legitimate. We make such distinctions regularly within families: we understand that as a father or a mother we make choices that are not necessarily identical with what we might reach on our own. The same is true for the neighbourhood, for local government and eventually for a community of a whole nation.

Citizens are public choosers, and democracy is how we assure that public choosing is legitimate. These are the parameters for the creation of a democratic community and it is obvious that private consumer choice can never accommodate them. As citizens, we make 'us' or 'we' choices that sometimes force us to put aside our own 'me' preferences. To think one can replace citizens with consumers and then believe the result is still a democracy is, then, to make a deep category mistake. There are many things government cannot do very well but there are many others that *only* government can do, not because it does them well, or even 'better' than the market, but because they are public things ('*res publica*') that can only be done by public institutions.

Thirty years ago, many subscribed to the Great Society myth that government could do just about everything. Today that myth has been banished. But it has been replaced with the equally dangerous myth that government can do nothing and markets can do everything. This second myth is in some sense more insidious than the first, because it seems the natural consequence of rejecting the first. That is to say, if the first myth is false, then the second must be true!

COMMERCIALIZATION

Privatization brings with it a commercialization of much of what is privatized. One might expect that the transfer of governmental power to the private sector would include an empowerment of such civic associations as the neighbourhood, the church, the foundation and the family.

For in fact these domains remain public though they are non-governmental and are defined by liberty though they are not private. Yet on the whole they have not benefited at all from the privatization of power. Instead, with the economic domain's empowerment, civil society has actually seen its power diminished, subjected to the commercializing forces of a runaway economic sector that dominates every other domain. Privatization has in effect commercialized what used to be a pluralistic zone of many identities. Earlier in this chapter, I have already referenced to the 'selling' of students to corporations for the highest bid, which violates the spirit of liberal education and contradicts the principles of any autonomous pedagogy. Schools compelled by insufficient public funding (another consequence of privatization) are selling themselves and selling their students (access to their students) in return for small donations from the corporate sector. Universities are becoming tools of corporate research, with patents and research results being reserved for private profit. Can a democratic pedagogy content itself with creating little consumers in place of grown-up citizens?

Prisons are also being privatized, with one out of six prisoners in the USA now incarcerated in private, for-profit prisons. Under monarchy, the death penalty and the right to take away a man's freedom were inalienable marks of the king's sovereignty. The same ought to hold for a democracy. For the privatization of incarceration is incompatible with the very idea of popular sovereignty. We have also commercialized our transportation terminals (every airport, every train station, every international flight, is seen as an opportunity for shopping) and the Internet – that once fabled promise of a new frontier of democratic interactivity. It is possible today to have free phone service, free computers, free access to the net ... if one is willing to sell oneself to merchandisers and advertisers.

TECHNOLOGY AND DEMOCRACY

Here we return to the issue of technology with which we began. For it is technology that both holds out the promise of a transformative means for creating a more participatory and engaged democracy, and in practice has introduced still another privatized venue for commerce, shopping and private interest. The 1996 US Federal Communications Act, intended to update the 1934 Act that had made radio a public utility, actually had a deregulative impact on telecommunications. It left the telecommunications industry to market forces for their development, giving away the right to digitalize the broadcast spectra for nothing to those already in control of the airwaves – something Senator Robert Dole, then a candidate for the Presidency, called the 'giveaway of the century'.

The new communications legislation has recognized the reality of privatization and commercialization in the domain of telecommunications. The Internet seemed once to promise a possible redemocratization of the postmodern world: its innovative interactivity and point-to-point capacity seemed to have the potential to turn thin representative democracy back into strong (or at least a stronger) democracy. What started out as a military instrument in the 1960s had, by the early 1980s, become a new electronic frontier for anarchists and democrats – for people who thought its technical architecture made it an ideal means of democratic and civic communication. After all, it could eliminate the middleman, eliminate the editor, and eliminate the hierarchical boss, leaving people free to talk to one another directly. Yet today, nearly all of the traffic on the Internet is commercial, and one-quarter of that commercial traffic is in pornography. The German magazine *Focus* recently called sex the new 'engine' of the net. Dot-com (.com or eCommerce) has absolutely inundated and overcome dot-org (.org) and dot-edu (.edu), which were once imagined to be the domains that would define the Internet in its essential character.

We may still imagine that the Internet can be a bridge among NGOs and civic associations, that because every man and woman can put up his or her own web page, any one citizen on the net can be as powerful as any corporate mogul. Yet can a web page make John Doe the equal of Bill Gates or Michael Eisner? To think that technology can somehow remedy all the problems created by politics and economics in the pre-technological era is an illusion. President Clinton has worked hard to wire America's schools and libraries, as if a wired nation is the same thing as an educated nation. But literacy depends on what comes over the wires. If the wires are so many sewers for society's commercial and pornographic detritus, then schools are being wired into a national sewer system – just about the worst thing we can do to students in a nation where schools are already in trouble and literacy compromised. If the new wires pipe in new knowledge we benefit, but if they are tentacles of a commercial push technology octopus reaching out to capture students and turn them into consumers, education and citizenship may actually be harmed. Tech companies offering free Internet access in return for captive kid audiences for advertising, companies giving free software to schools that will wed those schools to one company's business, are serving only themselves in the name of serving education. Society should reject the deal. When governments pipe propaganda through their public communications, we call it totalitarianism. When corporations do the same thing, we call it market freedom. But is there really so obvious a difference?

New technology also promises new sources of information and hence putatively adds to the resources of knowledge available to educators. The promise of more or faster information and easier access to data is not the same thing as more knowledge, however. Unfiltered information and endless access to unedited data inundate users without offering the context and linkages that turn information into knowledge. We tend too often to use the language of 'information technology', 'information war', and 'information society', whereas what we seek as a democratic, civil society ought to be 'knowledge technology' and a 'knowledge society'. Information is not knowledge; nor, for that matter, is knowledge wisdom. One of the more troublesome features of the Internet is that it abounds in gossip, rumours, flaming, prejudice and lies. Little can be found on it that is useful in filtering, assessing or judging such information as it does provide. Knowledge and wisdom are products of how information is organized and dealt with and that depends on background skills that users must have before they go on line and which the technology itself cannot help engender.

Moreover, those uses of the Internet that are educational may be less significant than they seem as a consequence of what we may call the generational fallacy. By this I mean the fallacy of thinking that a later generation will mimic how an earlier generation utilizes a technology the earlier generation introduces. The founders and early users of information technology were themselves born and educated in an age of traditional libraries, books, magazines and newspapers. As children of a print culture who invented an image culture (movies, television and the net), we assume the new technology will be a surrogate print culture. And, indeed, we have used the Internet as a kind of souped-up telegraph – an electronic tablet for scrolling words. Educated in print, can we really anticipate how a generation brought up in images will eventually use a technology rooted in images? Knowing how to do research in libraries, we turn the net into a search engine for the kinds of research we know from our own experience. But young people without book and library experience may not be able to utilize the new technology for research at all. People who do not read at all will not become readers on the net. The new technology cannot create habits of reading or research, especially when its forte will, in its broad-bank incarnation, be pictures.

The consequence of the generational fallacy is that while the inventors of the new technology look forward to a medium that will look like an electronic Widener Library (Harvard University), the kids who inherit it expect it to be a medium more like MTV. With these issues in mind, it seems imprudent to think that technology alone is going to provide solutions to the problems of globalization, privatization and commercialization that confront democracy today; or that, because it has a potential to facilitate strong democracy, it will actually succeed in doing so.

In the end we return to the essence of the challenge of democracy: the issue of political will. Bruno Kreisky, the great statesman of postwar Austria, when asked what it would take to turn fascist war-time Austria into a working democracy, recommended *Mut zur Politik* – the courage to engage in politics. Political will depends, however, on political organization and political organization is itself a product of the very citizenship under threat today. To develop political will takes engaged citizens, engaged citizens require the foundation of a robust civil society and civil society depends on active citizens and an effective civil society. This is a perfect examplar of the so-called vicious circle. There is one useful feature of vicious circles, however: they can be broken anywhere. By a student protesting commercialization of schools; by a consumer unwilling to reduce her citizenship to shopping; by a citizen who insists that voting is only the first mark of an engaged democrat and stays involved when elections are over; by a policymaker willing to involve citizens in questions of governance. Once the circle is broken, and at whatever point, the circular logic of defeat unravels, and democracy becomes possible.

FURTHER READING

Arendt, Hannah (1965) *On Revolution* (New York: Viking Press). A comparison of the French and American revolutions that highlights the differences between political and socio-economic change.

Barber, Benjamin R. (1995) *Jihad vs. McWorld* (New York: Times Books). A portrait of a world at once coming together around the global economy and pop culture, and fracturing along tribal and ethnic lines – and why the contest between the two cripples democracy.

Barber, Benjamin R. (1984) *Strong Democracy* (Berkeley: University of California Press). A philosophical analysis and political defence of participatory democracy contrasted to traditional 'thin' or representative democracy.

Castells, Manuel (1996–98) *The Information Age* (Malden: Blackwell). A magisterial three-volume study of the impact of the new technologies on global societies.

Dahl, Robert (1956) *A Preface to Democratic Theory*. Dahl's classic introduction to varieties of democracy including his own version of 'polyarchy'.

Friedman, Thomas (2000) *The Lexus and the Olive Tree* (New York: Farrar, Straus, Giroux). A celebration of the triumph of capitalism over its tribal adversaries.

Fukuyama, Francis (1992) *The End of History and the Last Man* (New York: Free Press). A portrait of the triumph of global capitalism as the 'end of history'.

Huntington, Samuel, (1996) *The Clash of Civilizations and the Remaking of World Order* (New York: Simon & Schuster). A harsh portrait of a world at cultural war – a perfect and opposite companion to Friedman and Fukuyama.

Madison, James *et al.*, *The Federalist Papers*. First published 1787/1788. Many subsequent editions. American democracy justified in its classical liberal variation.

Michels, Robert (1999) *Political Parties*. Trans. by Eden and Cedar Paul (New Brunswick, NJ: Transaction). The early twentieth-century classic critique of representative government.

INDEX